# THE CASSELL
# CROSSWORD
# DICTIONARY

# THE CASSELL
# CROSSWORD
# DICTIONARY

**Betty Kirkpatrick**

CASSELL

This edition first published in the UK 1996 by
Cassell
Wellington House
125 Strand
London
WC2R 0BB

Distributed in the United States by
Sterling Publishing Co. Inc.
387 Park Avenue South
New York, NY 10016
USA

Distributed in Australia
by Capricorn Link (Australia) Pty Ltd
2/13 Carrington Road
Castle Hill
NSW 2154

British Library Cataloguing-in-Publication Data

A catalogue entry for this book is available from the British Library

ISBN 0–304–34785–X

Printed and bound in Great Britain by
The Bath Press, Avon

# Introduction

Crossword puzzles are a perennial favourite with a very large section of the population. This is testified to by the fact that so many newspapers, whether daily or weekly, include a crossword for their readers. Indeed it is quite likely that newspaper sales are boosted by the inclusion of crosswords, some regular purchasers never getting past the crossword section.

Some regular solvers develop great expertise and phenomenal degrees of speed in solving crossword clues, especially if they are able to get on the same wavelength as the regular compiler of the crossword. Such people often pride themselves not only on their success and speed but on the fact that they achieve success all by themselves, not asking anyone for help and not consulting a dictionary.

Even the elite among crossword solvers do not always stick to these rigorous standards, and many of them have been known to cast a sly look at a dictionary when they have one or two seemingly unsolvable clues and are running out of the timespan that they have set themselves. Of course they do not always admit to this unless you catch them in the act.

The vast majority of crossword puzzlers, however, are not super-solvers and have no particular wish to be. They are quite content to move at a leisurely pace and to seek help when the compiler succeeds in bamboozling them. This help can often come from dictionaries, long an essential part of the word-puzzler's library.

Dictionaries are, of course, not specially tailored towards the needs of word-puzzlers. They contain more information than the puzzler requires, and so it might take some time to locate the *mot juste*. Also, although it is an essential part of their charm, dictionaries always seem to divert you from your purpose when you turn to one for help with a crossword clue. In no time at all you find yourself absorbedly wandering from definition to definition, crossword clue unsolved, and probably work undone.

A more efficient book for your crossword-solving is Cassell's *Crossword Dictionary*, which has been specially designed for everyone involved in crossword puzzles. Not all of us feel that we must set ourselves strict personal deadlines when we are solving crossword puzzles, but we at least like to get today's solved before tomorrow's is published.

The method of arrangement of words in the *Crossword Dictionary* will undoubtedly save you time. The answers to crossword clues are all of a specified length, and all the words and phrases in the *Crossword Dictionary* are arranged in word lists according to length and then alphabetically within the relevant word list. Thus, if what you are looking for is an eight-letter word beginning with the letter B, you will be able to see a range of potential words at a glance. The *Crossword Dictionary* does not give you definitions, but you will be able to spot the combination of letters that your crossword is showing. You may know, for example, what the second and fifth letters are, and so on.

Containing more than 60,000 entries, Cassell's *Crossword Dictionary* consists of a comprehensive and varied list of words and phrases. This list contains not only everyday expressions but also old and obscure words that are of great value in word puzzles, such as 'qanat', 'zebu' and 'zho', and new and voguish terms, such as 'autocrime', 'living will', 'road rage' and 'spin doctor'.

A special feature of the word list is the inclusion of many idiomatic phrases. These include, for example, 'babe in arms', 'fill the bill', 'chance one's arm', 'dressed to kill', 'know the ropes', 'quick on the uptake', and 'walls have ears'.

This book is entitled Cassell's *Crossword Dictionary* and as such will prove to be a boon to everyone connected with crossword puzzles, whether you are a solver intent on pitting your wits against the wiles of the compiler, or whether you are a compiler seeking inspiration with which to baffle your solvers. It is, however, of value not only to crossword buffs but to any one who is a wordgame enthusiast. For example, Scrabble players will find it useful when trying to devise high-scoring words or when checking the existence of a word.

# Three-letter words

| A | ash | bin | cob | day | ebb |
|---|---|---|---|---|---|
| abb | ask | bit | COD | DDT | ECG |
| aby | asp | boa | cod | deb | ECT |
| ace | ass | bob | cog | den | écu |
| act | ate | bog | col | dew | EEC |
| add | auk | boo | con | dib | eel |
| ado | ave | bop | coo | did | e'en |
| aft | awe | bot | cop | die | e'er |
| aga | awl | bow | cor | dig | eff |
| age | awn | box | cos | dim | eft |
| ago | axe | boy | cot | din | egg |
| aha | aye | bud | cow | dip | ego |
| aid | | bug | cox | DNA | eke |
| ail | **B** | bum | coy | doc | elf |
| aim | baa | bun | coz | doe | elk |
| air | bad | bur | cry | dog | ell |
| ait | bag | bus | cub | dom. | elm |
| à la | bah! | but | cud | don | ems |
| a.k.a. | ban | buy | cue | dot | emu |
| alb | bap | bye | cum | dry | end |
| ale | bar | | cup | dub | ens |
| all | bat | **C** | cur | dud | eon |
| alp | bay | cab | cut | due | era |
| amp | BBC | cad | cwt | dug | ere |
| and | bed | cal. | | dun | erf |
| ant | bee | cam | **D** | duo | erg |
| any | beg | can | dab | dup. | erk |
| ape | bel | cap | dad | dux | ern |
| apt | ben | car | dag | dye | err |
| arc | bet | cat | dal | | ESP |
| are | bey | caw | dam | **E** | esp. |
| ark | bib | cay | dan | ear | eta |
| arm | bid | cep | dap | eat | etc. |
| art | big | chi | daw | eau | eve |

| | | | | | |
|---|---|---|---|---|---|
| ewe | fry | **H** | Hun | jot | lib |
| eye | fug | had | hut | joy | lid |
| | fun | hag | | jug | lie |
| | fur | hah! | **I** | jut | lip |
| **F** | | ham | Ibo | | lit |
| fad | | hap | ice | **K** | lob |
| fag | **G** | has | icy | kef | log |
| fah | gab | hat | ilk | keg | loo |
| fan | gad | haw | ill | ken | lop |
| far | gag | hay | I'll | key | lor |
| fat | gal | he'd | IMF | kHz | lot |
| fax | gam | he's | imp | kid | low |
| fay | gap | hem | Inc. | kif | lox |
| FBI | gar | hen | ink | kin | LSD |
| fed | gas | her | inn | kip | Ltd |
| fee | gat | hew | ion | kit | lug |
| fen | gay | hex | IOU | kob | lux |
| feu | gee | hey | IRA | k.o.'d | lye |
| few | gel | HGV | ire | kye | |
| fey | gem | hid | irk | kyu | **M** |
| fez | gen | hie | it's | | mac |
| fib | get | him | its | **L** | mad |
| fid | gie | hip | I've | lab | mam |
| fie | gig | his | ivy | lac | man |
| fig | gin | hit | | lad | map |
| fig. | gip | HIV | **J** | lag | mar |
| fin | GMT | hob | jab | lam | Mar. |
| fir | gnu | hod | jag | lap | mat |
| fit | gob | hoe | jah | law | maw |
| fix | god | hog | jam | lax | max. |
| flu | goo | Hon. | jar | lay | May |
| fly | got | hop | jaw | lea | may |
| fob | Gov. | hot | jay | led | men |
| foe | Goy | how | jet | lee | met |
| fog | GPO | hoy | Jew | leg | mew |
| fop | gum | hub | jib | lei | Mgr |
| for | gun | hue | jig | lek | mid |
| fox | gut | hug | jit | Leo | mil |
| foy | guy | huh! | job | let | mix |
| Fra | gym | hum | jog | ley | moa |
| fro | gyp | | | | |

| | | | | | |
|---|---|---|---|---|---|
| mob | nut | Pan | pug | rod | ski |
| mod | nye | pan | pun | roe | sky |
| mom | | pap | pup | rot | sly |
| moo | **O** | par | pus | row | Snr |
| mop | oaf | pas | put | rpm | sob |
| mow | oak | pat | PVC | rub | sod |
| mpg | oar | paw | pyx | rue | sog |
| mph | oat | pax | | rug | soh |
| Mrs | obi | pay | **Q** | rum | sol |
| mss | obs. | p.d.q. | QED | run | Sol |
| mud | och | pea | qua | rut | son |
| mug | odd | ped | | rye | sop |
| mum | ode | pee | **R** | | SOS |
| | o'er | peg | rad | **S** | sot |
| **N** | off | pen | RAF | sac | sou |
| nab | oft | pep | rag | sad | sow |
| nag | ohm | per | rah | s.a.e. | soy |
| nan | oho! | pet | raj | sag | spa |
| nap | oil | pew | ram | sal | spy |
| nay | old | phi | ran | sap | STD |
| NCO | one | pie | rap | sat | sty |
| neb | ope | pig | rat | saw | sub |
| ned | opt | pin | raw | sax | sue |
| née | ora | pip | ray | say | sum |
| net | orb | pit | red | sea | sun |
| new | orc | pix | ref | see | sup |
| nib | ore | plc | rep | set | |
| nil | öre | ply | ret | sew | **T** |
| nip | øre | PMT | rev | sex | tab |
| nit | our | pod | Rex | she | tad |
| nix | out | poi | rho | shy | tag |
| nob | ova | pop | rib | sib | tan |
| nod | owe | pot | rid | sic | Tao |
| nog | owl | POW | rig | sin | tap |
| Noh | own | pox | rim | sip | tar |
| nor | | ppm | RIP | sir | tau |
| not | **P** | pro | rip | sis | taw |
| now | pad | pry | RNA | sit | tax |
| nub | pah! | PTO | rob | six | tea |
| nun | pal | pub | roc | ska | ted · |

| | | | | | |
|---|---|---|---|---|---|
| tee | tow | use | vow | wig | ycp |
| ten | toy | ute | vox | win | yes |
| the | try | | VSO | wit | yet |
| tho' | tub | **V** | vug | woe | yew |
| thy | tug | vac | | wog | yid |
| tic | tum | van | **W** | wok | yin |
| tie | tun | vas | wad | won | yip |
| tin | tup | VAT | wag | woo | yob |
| tip | tut | vat | wan | wop | yon |
| 'tis | two | VCR | war | wot | you |
| tit | | VDU | was | wow | yrs |
| TNT | **U** | veg | wax | wry | |
| tod | UFO | vet | way | | **Z** |
| toe | ugh | vex | web | **Y** | zap |
| tog | ugh! | VHF | we'd | yah | zed |
| tom | UHT | via | wed | yak | zee |
| ton | una | vie | wee | yam | Zen |
| too | uni | vim | wen | yap | zho |
| top | ups | VIP | wet | yaw | zip |
| tor | urn | vis | who | yea | zit |
| tot | USA | viz | why | yen | zoo |

# Four-letter words

| | | | | |
|---|---|---|---|---|
| **A** | alar | aria | baba | baud |
| abbé | alas | arid | babe | bawd |
| abed | alee | aril | babu | bawl |
| abet | alga | arms | baby | bead |
| able | ally | army | bach | beak |
| ably | alms | arse | back | beam |
| abut | aloe | arty | bade | bean |
| ache | Alps | arum | bags | bear |
| acid | also | arvo | bail | beat |
| acme | alto | a.s.a.p | bait | beau |
| acne | alum | ashy | bake | beck |
| acre | amah | assn | bald | Beeb |
| adit | ambo | asst | bale | beef |
| adze | amen | atom | balk | been |
| aeon | amid | atop | ball | beep |
| aery | amir | attn | balm | beer |
| afar | ammo | aunt | band | beet |
| Afro | amok | aura | bane | bell |
| agar | amyl | auto | bang | belt |
| aged | anal | aver | bank | bend |
| agha | anew | avid | bans | bent |
| agin | anil | avow | barb | berg |
| agio | ankh | away | bard | berk |
| agog | anna | AWOL | barc | berm |
| ague | anon | awry | bark | best |
| ahem | ante | axel | barm | beta |
| ahoy | anus | axil | barn | bevy |
| aide | apex | axis | base | bias |
| AIDS | apse | axle | bash | bice |
| ain't | aqua | axon | bask | bide |
| airs | Arab | ayah | bass | bier |
| airy | arak | | bast | biff |
| ajar | arch | **B** | bate | bike |
| akin | area | Baal | bath | bile |

| | | | | |
|---|---|---|---|---|
| bilk | bolt | buck | cane | chug |
| bill | bomb | buff | cans | chum |
| bind | bond | buhl | cant | ciao |
| bine | bone | bulb | can't | cist |
| bing | bonk | bulk | cape | cite |
| biog. | bony | bull | capo | city |
| bird | boob | bump | card | clad |
| Biro® | book | bund | care | clam |
| birr | boom | bung | carl | clan |
| bise | boon | bunk | carp | clap |
| bisk | boor | bunt | cart | claw |
| bite | boot | buoy | case | clay |
| bitt | bora | burg | cash | clef |
| blab | bore | burk | cask | cleg |
| blae | born | burl | cast | clew |
| blag | bort | burn | caul | clip |
| blah | bosh | burp | cave | clod |
| bldg | bosk | burr | cavy | clog |
| bleb | boss | bury | cede | clot |
| bled | both | bush | ceil | cloy |
| blew | bott | busk | cell | club |
| blip | bout | buss | Celt | clue |
| blob | bowl | bust | celt | co-ed |
| bloc | bozo | busy | cent | co-op |
| blot | brad | butt | cere | coal |
| blow | brae | buzz | cert | coat |
| blub | brag | byre | cess | coax |
| blue | bran | byte | chap | coca |
| blur | brat | | char | cock |
| boar | bray | **C** | chat | coco |
| boat | bred | cadi | chef | coda |
| bode | brer | café | chew | code |
| body | brew | cage | chez | C of E |
| Boer | Brie | cake | chic | coif |
| bogy | brig | calf | chin | coil |
| boil | brim | calk | chip | coin |
| bola | brio | call | chit | coir |
| bold | Brit | calm | chop | Coke® |
| bole | brow | came | chow | coke |
| boll | bubo | camp | chub | cola |

| | | | | |
|---|---|---|---|---|
| cold | crib | Dane | deny | doit |
| cole | crit. | dang | derm | dojo |
| colt | crop | dank | desk | dole |
| coma | crow | dare | deva | doll |
| comb | crud | dark | dewy | dolt |
| come | crus | darn | dhak | dome |
| cone | crux | dart | dhal | done |
| conk | cube | dash | dhow | don't |
| cony | cues | data | dial | dook |
| cook | cuff | date | dibs | doom |
| cool | cull | daub | dice | door |
| coon | culm | dawn | dick | dope |
| coop | cult | days | dido | dopy |
| coot | cunt | daze | died | dorp |
| cope | curb | D-day | dies | dory |
| Copt | curd | dead | diet | dose |
| copy | cure | deaf | diff. | dosh |
| cord | curl | deal | dike | doss |
| core | curt | dean | dill | dost |
| corf | cusp | dear | dime | dote |
| cork | cuss | debt | dine | doth |
| corm | cute | deck | ding | dour |
| corn | cyan | deed | dint | dout |
| cosh | cyma | deem | dire | dove |
| cost | cyme | deep | dirk | dowl |
| cosy | cyst | deer | dirt | down |
| cote | czar | deft | disc | doxy |
| coup | | defy | dish | doze |
| cove | **D** | deil | disk | dozy |
| cowl | dace | dele | diss | drab |
| cows | Dada | delf | diva | drag |
| coxa | dado | deli | dive | dram |
| cozy | daff | dell | doab | drat |
| crab | daft | delt | doat | draw |
| crag | dago | deme | dock | dray |
| cram | dais | demi | dodo | dree |
| cran | dale | demo | doer | dreg |
| crap | dame | demy | does | drew |
| craw | damn | dene | doff | drey |
| crew | damp | dcnt | doge | drip |

| | | | | |
|---|---|---|---|---|
| drop | Edam | evil | feat | flat |
| drub | Edda | ewer | feed | flaw |
| drug | eddo | ewes | feel | flax |
| drum | eddy | exam | fees | flay |
| duad | Eden | exit | feet | flea |
| dual | edge | exon | fell | fled |
| duce | edgy | eyas | felt | flee |
| duck | edit | eyed | fend | flew |
| duct | eels | eyes | fern | flex |
| dude | efts | eyot | feta | flip |
| duel | egad! | eyra | fête | flit |
| duet | eggs | eyre | feud | floc |
| duke | Eire | | fiat | floe |
| dull | élan | **F** | fibs | flog |
| duly | else | face | fico | flop |
| dumb | emir | fact | fief | flow |
| dump | emit | fade | fife | flue |
| dune | ends | fail | figs | flux |
| dung | enol | fain | file | foal |
| dunk | enow | fair | fill | foam |
| dupe | ENSA | fake | film | foci |
| dusk | envy | fall | find | foes |
| dust | épée | fame | fine | fogy |
| duty | epha | fane | Finn | föhn |
| dyad | epic | fang | fino | foil |
| dyer | EPOS | fare | fire | foin |
| dyke | epos | farl | firm | fold |
| dyne | ergo | farm | firs | folk |
| | Erin | faro | fisc | fond |
| **E** | erne | fart | fish | font |
| each | Eros | fash | fist | food |
| earl | Erse | fast | fits | fool |
| earn | erst | fate | five | foot |
| ears | espy | faun | fizz | ford |
| ease | et al. | faux | flab | fore |
| east | etch | fawn | flag | fork |
| easy | Etna | fays | flak | form |
| ebon | étui | faze | flam | fort |
| echo | even | feal | flan | foss |
| ecru | ever | fear | flap | foul |

four
fowl
foxy
frap
Frau
fray
free
fret
frit
froe
frog
from
frow
fuck
fuel
full
fume
fumy
fund
funk
furl
fury
fuse
fuss
fuze
fuzz
fyke
fyrd

**G**
gaby
Gael
gaff
gaga
gage
Gaia
gain
gait
gala
gale

gall
game
gamp
gamy
gang
gaol
gape
garb
gash
gasp
gate
gaud
Gaul
gaun
gaup
gaur
gave
gawd
gawk
gaze
gean
gear
geek
geld
gene
gens
gent
geod.
geog.
germ
gest
geum
ghat
ghee
gibe
gift
gild
gill
gilt
gimp

ging
gink
gird
girl
girn
giro
girr
girt
gist
gîte
give
glad
glee
glen
gley
glia
glib
glim
glob
glow
glue
glum
glut
G-man
gnat
gnaw
goad
goal
goal
goat
gobo
goby
go-by
goer
gold
golf
gone
gong
good
goof

goon
goop
gore
gory
gosh!
Goth
gout
Govt
gowk
gown
grab
grad
gram
grav
gray
grew
grey
grid
grig
grim
grin
grip
grit
grog
grot
grow
grub
guck
guff
gulf
gull
gulp
gunk
guru
gush
gust
guts
gyal
gybe
gyre

gyro
gyve

**H**
haaf
hack
hade
hadj
haem
haft
ha-ha
haik
hail
hair
haji
hajj
hake
hale
half
hall
halm
halo
halt
hame
hand
hang
hank
hard
hare
hark
harm
harp
hart
hash
hask
hasp
hast
hate
hath
hats

| | | | | |
|---|---|---|---|---|
| haud | hilt | huge | inky | jive |
| hauf | hind | hula | inly | jobs |
| haul | hint | hulk | in re | jock |
| have | hire | hull | inst. | joey |
| hawk | hiss | hump | into | john |
| haze | hist | hung | iota | join |
| hazy | hive | hunk | iris | joke |
| head | hiya | hunt | iron | jolt |
| heal | hoar | hurl | ISBN | josh |
| heap | hoax | hurt | Isis | joss |
| hear | hobo | hush | isle | jouk |
| heat | hock | husk | isn't | Jove |
| Hebe | hold | hymn | itch | jowl |
| heck | hole | hype | item | jube |
| heed | holm | | it'll | judo |
| heel | holp | **I** | iwis | Judy |
| heft | holt | iamb | | juju |
| heir | holy | ibex | **J** | July |
| held | home | ibid. | jack | jump |
| hell | homo | ibis | jade | June |
| he'll | homy | iced | jail | junk |
| helm | hone | icon | Jain | Juno |
| help | hong | idea | jamb | jury |
| hemp | honk | idem | jape | just |
| hent | hood | ides | jarl | jute |
| herb | hoof | idle | jaws | |
| herd | hook | idly | jazz | **K** |
| here | hoop | idol | jean | kadi |
| hern | hoot | iffy | jeep | kail |
| hero | hope | ikan | jeer | kaka |
| Herr | hops | ikat | Jehu | kaki |
| hers | horn | ikon | jell | kale |
| hest | hose | ilex | jerk | Kali |
| hewn | host | ilia | jess | kali |
| hick | hour | imam | jest | kame |
| hide | hove | iman | jibe | kami |
| hi-fi | howl | impi | jiff | kart |
| high | hoya | Inca | jilt | kava |
| hike | hued | inch | jink | kcal |
| hill | huff | info | jinn | keck |

| | | | | |
|---|---|---|---|---|
| keef | knee | lamp | lich | lock |
| keek | knew | land | lick | loco |
| keel | knit | lane | lido | lode |
| keen | knob | lank | lied | loft |
| keep | knop | lard | lief | loge |
| kelp | knot | lark | lien | logo |
| kelt | know | lash | lies | loin |
| keno | knur | lass | lieu | loll |
| kent | koan | last | life | lone |
| képi | kohl | late | lift | long |
| kept | kola | lath | like | look |
| kerb | kolo | laud | Lilo® | loom |
| kerf | kook | lava | lilt | loon |
| kern | kora | lawn | lily | loop |
| keys | koto | laze | limb | loot |
| khan | kris | lazy | lime | lope |
| khat | kudu | lead | limn | lops |
| kibe | kula | leaf | limo | lord |
| kick | Kurd | leak | limp | lore |
| kief | kvas | leal | limy | lorn |
| kier | kyat | lean | line | lory |
| kill | kyle | leap | ling | lose |
| kiln | kype | lech | link | loss |
| kilo | | leek | linn | lost |
| kilt | **L** | leer | lino | lota |
| kina | lace | lees | lint | loth |
| kind | lack | left | lion | lots |
| kine | lacy | lend | lips | loud |
| king | lade | leno | lira | lour |
| kink | lady | lens | lire | lout |
| kino | laic | Lent | lisp | love |
| kirk | laid | lent | list | luau |
| kiss | lain | less | live | luce |
| kist | lair | lest | load | luck |
| kite | lake | let's | loaf | luff |
| kith | lakh | levy | loam | luge |
| kiwi | laky | lewd | loan | lull |
| knag | lama | liar | lobe | lulu |
| knap | lamb | Lias | loch | lump |
| knar | lame | lice | loci | Luna |

| | | | | |
|---|---|---|---|---|
| lune | mask | mild | moot | nape |
| lung | Mass | mile | mope | nard |
| lure | mass | milk | more | nary |
| lurk | mast | mill | MORI® | NATO |
| lush | mate | milt | morn | nave |
| lust | math | mime | mort | navy |
| lute | matt | mina | moss | Nazi |
| lynx | maud | mind | most | neap |
| lyre | maul | mine | mote | near |
| lyse | Maya | mini | moth | neat |
| | maya | mink | moue | neck |
| **M** | maze | mint | move | need |
| maam | mazy | minx | mown | neep |
| ma'am | mead | mire | moxa | ne'er |
| mace | meal | mirk | much | neon |
| Mach | mean | misc. | muck | nerd |
| mack | meat | miso | muff | nesh |
| made | Mede | miss | mule | ness |
| mage | meed | Miss | mull | nest |
| magi | meek | mist | mump | nett |
| maid | meet | mite | murk | névé |
| mail | melt | mitt | muse | news |
| maim | memo | moan | mush | newt |
| main | mend | moat | musk | next |
| make | menu | mock | muss | nice |
| male | meow | mode | must | nick |
| mall | mere | moil | mute | nigh |
| malm | mesa | moke | mutt | nine |
| malt | mesh | moki | muzz | nipa |
| mama | mess | moko | myna | nisi |
| mane | mete | mold | myth | nock |
| Manx | mewl | mole | myxo | node |
| many | mews | moll | | Noel |
| marc | mica | moly | **N** | noil |
| mare | mice | monk | naff | noir |
| mark | Midi | mono | Naga | noma |
| marl | midi | mood | naib | nome |
| Mars | mien | moon | naïf | none |
| mart | miff | Moor | nail | nook |
| mash | mike | moor | name | noon |

| | | | | |
|---|---|---|---|---|
| nope | olio | **P** | pear | pith |
| nork | olla | paca | peat | pity |
| norm | omen | pace | peck | pixy |
| Norn | omit | pack | peek | plan |
| nose | once | paco | peel | plat |
| nosh | oner | pact | peen | play |
| nosy | only | page | peep | pleb |
| note | onto | paid | peer | plié |
| noun | onus | pail | peke | plod |
| nous | onyx | pain | pelf | plop |
| nova | oops | pair | pelt | plot |
| nude | ooze | pale | pend | plow |
| nuke | oozy | Pali | pent | ploy |
| null | opah | pall | peon | plug |
| numb | opal | palm | peri | plum |
| nuts | open | palp | perk | plus |
| | opus | paly | perm | pock |
| **O** | oral | pane | pert | poco |
| oaks | orgy | pang | peso | poem |
| oaky | orle | pant | pest | poet |
| oars | orts | papa | phew! | poke |
| oary | oryx | para | phon | poky |
| oast | ossa | pard | pica | pole |
| oath | otic | pare | pice | poll |
| oats | otto | park | pick | polo |
| obey | ouch | parr | pied | pome |
| obit | ours | part | picr | pomp |
| oboe | oust | pass | pike | pond |
| obol | ouzo | past | pile | pone |
| odds | oval | pate | pill | pong |
| odea | oven | pâté | pimp | pony |
| ogam | over | path | pine | pooh! |
| ogee | ovum | patu | ping | pool |
| ogle | owed | paua | pink | poop |
| Ogpu | owns | pave | pint | poor |
| ogre | oxen | pawl | piny | pope |
| oily | Oxon. | pawn | pipe | pore |
| oink | oyer | peak | pipi | pork |
| okay | oyes! | peal | pish! | porn |
| okra | oyez! | pean | piss | port |

| | | | | |
|---|---|---|---|---|
| pose | **Q** | rath | rite | rung |
| posh | quad | rave | rive | runt |
| post | quag | raze | road | ruru |
| posy | quay | razz | roam | rusa |
| pour | quid | read | roan | ruse |
| pout | quin | real | roar | rush |
| pram | quip | ream | robe | rusk |
| pray | quit | reap | rock | rust |
| prep | quiz | rear | rode | ruth |
| prey | | rec'd | roil | ryot |
| prig | **R** | redo | role | |
| prim | race | reed | roll | **S** |
| proa | rack | reef | romp | sack |
| prod | racy | reek | rood | safe |
| prof | raff | reel | roof | saga |
| Prof. | raft | rein | rook | sage |
| prom | raga | rely | room | sago |
| prop | rage | rend | root | said |
| prow | ragi | rent | rope | sail |
| puce | raia | repp | ropy | sake |
| puck | raid | rest | rose | saki |
| puff | rail | rhea | rosy | sale |
| puke | rain | rice | rota | salt |
| pule | raja | rich | rote | same |
| pull | rake | rick | roué | samp |
| pulp | raki | ride | roup | sand |
| puma | rale | rife | rout | sane |
| pump | ramp | riff | roux | sang |
| pung | rand | rift | rove | sank |
| punk | rang | rile | RSVP | sans |
| punt | rani | rill | rube | sard |
| puny | rank | rime | ruby | sari |
| pupa | rant | rimy | ruck | sark |
| pure | rape | rind | rudd | sash |
| purl | rapt | ring | rude | sass |
| purr | rare | rink | ruff | sate |
| push | rase | riot | ruin | save |
| puss | rash | ripe | rule | sawn |
| putt | rasp | rise | rump | scab |
| pyre | rate | risk | rune | scad |

| scan | she's | skin | snip | spat |
|------|-------|------|------|------|
| scar | shea | skip | snob | spay |
| scat | shed | skit | snog | spec |
| Scot | shew | skol | snot | sped |
| scot | Shia | skua | snow | spew |
| scow | shim | slab | snub | spin |
| scud | shin | slag | snug | spit |
| scum | ship | slam | so-so | spiv |
| scut | shit | slap | soak | spot |
| seal | shod | slat | soap | spry |
| seam | shoe | Slav | soar | spud |
| sear | shoo | slaw | sock | spue |
| seat | shop | slay | soda | spun |
| sect | shot | sled | sofa | spur |
| seed | show | slew | soft | stab |
| seek | shun | slid | soho | stag |
| seel | shut | slim | soil | star |
| seem | sial | slip | sold | stay |
| seen | sice | slit | sole | stem |
| seep | sick | slob | soli | step |
| seer | side | sloe | solo | stet |
| self | sift | slog | soma | stew |
| scll | sigh | slop | some | stir |
| semi | sign | slot | sone | stoa |
| send | Sikh | slow | song | stop |
| sent | sild | slub | soon | stow |
| sept | silk | slue | soot | stub |
| sera | sill | slug | Sorb | stud |
| Serb | silo | slum | sorb | stun |
| sere | silt | slur | sore | stye |
| serf | sine | slut | sorn | such |
| seta | sing | smew | sort | suck |
| sewn | sink | smir | souk | sudd |
| sexy | sire | smit | soul | suds |
| shad | site | smog | soup | suet |
| shag | size | smug | sour | Suez |
| shah | sizy | smur | soya | suit |
| sham | skew | smut | Spam® | sulk |
| shaw | skid | snag | span | sumo |
| she'd | skim | snap | spar | sump |

| | | | | |
|---|---|---|---|---|
| sung | taps | thro' | tool | tune |
| sunk | tare | thru | toot | turd |
| sunn | tarn | thud | tope | turf |
| surd | taro | thug | topi | Turk |
| sure | tart | thus | tore | turn |
| surf | task | tick | torn | tush |
| swab | tass | tide | torr | tusk |
| swag | ta-ta | tidy | tort | tutu |
| swam | taut | tied | Tory | 'twas |
| swan | taxi | tier | tosh | twat |
| swap | teak | tiff | toss | twee |
| swat | teal | tike | tote | twig |
| sway | team | tile | tour | twin |
| swig | tear | till | tout | twit |
| swim | teat | tilt | town | tyke |
| swop | tech | time | trad | type |
| swot | teem | tine | tram | typo |
| swum | teen | ting | trap | tyre |
| sync | TEFL | tint | tray | tyro |
| | tell | tiny | tree | tzar |
| **T** | temp | tire | trek | |
| tabu | tend | tiro | tret | **U** |
| tace | tent | toad | trey | Ugli® |
| tack | term | toby | trig | ugly |
| taco | tern | toed | trim | ulan |
| tact | test | to-do | trio | ulna |
| tael | text | toft | trip | umbo |
| ta'en | Thai | tofu | trod | undo |
| tahr | than | toga | trot | unit |
| tail | that | toil | trow | unto |
| take | thaw | told | troy | upas |
| talc | thee | toll | true | upon |
| tale | them | tolu | tsar | Urdu |
| talk | then | tomb | tuba | urea |
| tall | thew | tome | tube | urge |
| tame | they | tone | tuck | uric |
| tamp | thin | tong | tufa | Ursa |
| tang | this | Tony | tuff | urus |
| tank | Thor | tony | tuft | used |
| tape | thou | took | tuna | user |

| | | | | |
|---|---|---|---|---|
| USSR | visé | watt | whit | word |
| uvea | viva | waul | whiz | wore |
| | Vlei | wave | who'd | work |
| **V** | void | wavy | who's | worm |
| vail | vole | waxy | whoa | worn |
| vain | *volk* | we'll | whom | wort |
| vair | volt | we're | whop | wove |
| vale | vote | we've | wick | wrap |
| vamp | vugg | weak | wide | wren |
| vane | vugh | weal | wife | writ |
| vang | | wean | wild | wych |
| vary | **W** | wear | wile | |
| vase | wack | weed | will | **X** |
| vast | wade | week | wilt | Xian |
| veal | wadi | ween | wily | Xmas |
| Veda | wady | weep | wimp | X-ray |
| veer | waft | weft | wind | xyst |
| vega | wage | weir | wine | |
| veil | waif | weld | wing | **Y** |
| vein | wail | well | wink | yack |
| Vela | wain | welt | wino | yaff |
| veld | wait | wend | winy | yain |
| vena | wake | went | wipe | yair |
| vend | wale | wept | wire | yank |
| vent | walk | were | wiry | yard |
| verb | wall | wert | wise | yare |
| vert | wand | west | wish | yarn |
| very | wane | wham | wisp | yawl |
| vest | wank | what | with | yawn |
| veto | want | whee | wive | yawp |
| vial | ward | when | woad | yaws |
| vice | ware | whet | woke | yean |
| vide | warm | whew | wold | year |
| view | warn | whey | wolf | yegg |
| vile | warp | Whig | womb | yeld |
| vina | wart | whim | won't | yelk |
| vine | wary | whin | wont | yell |
| viny | wash | whip | wood | yelp |
| viol | wasp | whir | woof | yeti |
| visa | wast | Whit | wool | yo-yo |

| | | | | |
|---|---|---|---|---|
| yoga | yowl | zarf | zeta | zone |
| yogi | yuan | zeal | Zeus | zool. |
| yoke | yuck | zebu | zimb | zoom |
| yolk | yule | zeds | zinc | zoon |
| yomp | yurt | zein | zing | zouk |
| yore | | Zend | Zion | Zulu |
| you'd | **Z** | zero | zoea | Zuñi |
| your | zany | zest | zoic | zyme |

# Five-letter words

| | | | | |
|---|---|---|---|---|
| **A** | act up | afire | alate | alter |
| abaca | acute | afoot | album | alula |
| abaci | adage | afore | alder | alway |
| aback | adapt | afrit | alert | amain |
| abaft | a-days | after | algae | amass |
| abare | addax | again | algal | amate |
| abase | added | agama | algid | amaze |
| abash | adder | agami | algin | amber |
| abate | addle | Agape | algor | ambit |
| abbey | add up | agape | algum | amble |
| abbot | adept | agate | alias | ambon |
| abeam | *à deux* | agave | alibi | ambry |
| abele | ad hoc | agent | alien | ameba |
| abhor | adieu | aggro | align | ameer |
| abide | ad lib | agile | alike | amend |
| abies | ad-lib | agism | alive | ament |
| abode | adman | agist | Allah | amice |
| A-bomb | admin | aglet | allay | amide |
| abort | admit | agley | alley | amine |
| about | admix | aglow | all in | amiss |
| above | adobe | agony | all-in | amity |
| abuse | adopt | agora | allod | ammon |
| abuzz | adore | agree | allot | among |
| abysm | adorn | agrin | allow | amort |
| abyss | adown | agued | alloy | amour |
| acerb | *ad rem* | ahead | almug | ample |
| ached | adsum | aheap | aloes | amply |
| achor | adult | aider | aloft | ampul |
| acorn | adust | aired | alone | amuck |
| acred | aegis | aisle | along | amuse |
| acrid | aerie | aitch | aloof | ancle |
| acted | Aesop | alack! | aloud | ancon |
| acton | aetat. | alarm | alpha | Andes |
| actor | affix | alary | altar | anear |

| | | | | |
|---|---|---|---|---|
| anele | April | ashen | avoid | b. and b. |
| anent | apron | ashes | await | bandy |
| angel | apses | Asian | awake | banjo |
| anger | apsis | aside | award | banks |
| angle | aptly | asked | aware | banns |
| Anglo | arack | asker | awash | Bantu |
| angor | arbor | askew | awful | barbs |
| angry | ardor | aspen | awned | bared |
| angst | areas | asper | awoke | barge |
| anile | areca | aspic | axial | baric |
| animé | arena | assai | axile | barky |
| anion | aren't | assay | axiom | barmy |
| anise | arête | asses | axled | baron |
| anker | argil | asset | azoic | *barre* |
| ankle | argol | aster | azote | basal |
| annex | argon | astir | Aztec | based |
| annoy | argot | ataxy | azure | bases |
| annul | argue | atilt | | basic |
| anode | Argus | atlas | **B** | basil |
| antic | Arian | atoll | Babel | basin |
| antre | Ariel | atone | baboo | basis |
| anura | ariel | atony | babul | bason |
| anvil | Aries | atrip | bacon | basse |
| Anzac | arise | attar | baddy | basso |
| aorta | armed | Attic | badge | *basta*! |
| apace | armor | attic | badly | baste |
| apart | aroma | audio | BAFTA | basti |
| apeak | arose | audit | bagel | batch |
| apery | Arran | auger | baggy | bated |
| aphid | arras | aught | bairn | bathe |
| aphis | array | augur | baize | batik |
| apian | arris | aulic | baked | baton |
| aping | arrow | aunty | baker | batte |
| apish | arsis | aural | balas | batty |
| apnea | arson | auric | baler | baulk |
| aport | Artex® | avail | balmy | bavin |
| appal | artel | avast | balsa | bawdy |
| apple | Aryan | avens | balti | bayed |
| apply | ascus | avert | banal | bayou |
| appui | asdic | avian | banco | bazar |

| | | | | |
|---|---|---|---|---|
| beach | berry | blare | bobby | bosom |
| beads | berth | blasé | Boche | bossy |
| beady | beryl | blast | bodle | bosun |
| be-all | beset | blaze | boffo | botch |
| beamy | besom | bleak | bogey | bothy |
| beano | besot | blear | boggy | bough |
| beard | betel | bleat | bogie | boule |
| beast | beton | bleed | bogle | boult |
| beaus | bevel | bleep | bogus | bound |
| beaut | bezel | blend | bohea | bourg |
| beaux | bhang | bless | boiar | bourn |
| bebop | Bible | blest | bolar | bouse |
| bedad! | biddy | blimp | bolas | bouts |
| bedel | bidet | blind | bolus | bowed |
| bedew | bifid | blini | bombe | bowel |
| bedim | bight | blink | bonce | bower |
| beech | bigly | bliss | boned | bowse |
| beefy | bigot | blite | bongo | boxen |
| beery | bijou | blitz | bonne | boxer |
| befie | biker | bloat | bonny | boyar |
| befit | bilbo | blobs | bonus | brace |
| befog | bilge | block | bonze | brach |
| began | billy | bloke | booby | bract |
| beget | bimbo | blond | books | braid |
| begin | binge | blood | boose | brail |
| begot | bingo | bloom | boost | brain |
| begum | biped | blown | boosy | brake |
| begun | bipod | blows | booth | braky |
| beige | birch | blowy | boots | brand |
| being | birth | blues | booty | brank |
| belay | bison | bluey | booze | brant |
| belch | bitch | bluff | boozy | brash |
| belie | biter | blunt | borax | brass |
| belle | bitty | blurb | bored | brave |
| belly | black | blurs | borer | bravo |
| below | blade | blurt | boric | brawl |
| bench | blain | blush | borne | brawn |
| benne | blame | board | boron | braxy |
| beret | bland | boart | bortz | braze |
| berme | blank | boast | bosky | bread |

| | | | | |
|---|---|---|---|---|
| break | buffo | **C** | carat | chalk |
| bream | buffy | caaba | cards | champ |
| breed | buggy | cabal | cared | chank |
| brent | bugle | cabas | carer | chant |
| breve | build | cabby | caret | chaos |
| briar | built | caber | carex | chape |
| bribe | bulge | cabin | cargo | chaps |
| brick | bulgy | cable | Carib | chapt |
| bride | bulky | cabob | carle | chard |
| brief | bulla | cacao | carob | chare |
| brier | bully | cache | carol | charm |
| brill | bulse | cacti | carom | charr |
| brine | bumpy | caddy | carry | chart |
| bring | bunch | cadet | carse | chary |
| brink | bunny | cadge | carte | chase |
| briny | buret | cadre | carus | chasm |
| brise | burgh | caeca | carve | chaya |
| brisk | burin | cagey | caste | cheap |
| brize | burke | cairn | catch | cheat |
| broad | burly | Cajun | cater | check |
| broch | burnt | calid | cates | cheek |
| brock | burro | calif | catty | cheep |
| broil | burry | calix | caulk | cheer |
| broke | bursa | calla | cause | chela |
| brome | burse | calve | cavie | chert |
| brood | burst | calyx | cavil | chess |
| brook | busby | camel | cavin | chest |
| broom | buses | cameo | CD-ROM | chevy |
| brose | bushy | canal | cease | chewy |
| broth | bussu | candy | cecum | Chian |
| brown | butch | canna | cedar | chica |
| Bruin | butte | canny | 'cello | chich |
| bruit | butty | canoe | cense | chick |
| brume | buxom | canon | cento | chico |
| brunt | buyer | canto | ceorl | chide |
| brush | bwana | canty | chaco | chief |
| brute | by-end | caper | chafe | child |
| bucko | bylaw | capon | chaff | chili |
| buddy | byssi | capot | chain | chill |
| budge | byway | carap | chair | chimb |

| | | | | |
|---|---|---|---|---|
| chime | cirri | clown | cooky | crack |
| chimp | cisco | clubs | cooly | craft |
| China | civet | cluck | coomb | crake |
| china | civic | clump | co-opt | cramp |
| chine | civil | clung | copal | crane |
| chink | civvy | clunk | coped | crank |
| chino | clack | coach | cop it | crape |
| chirk | claim | coact | copra | craps |
| chirm | clamp | coaly | copse | crash |
| chirp | clang | coast | copsy | crass |
| chirr | clank | coati | coral | crate |
| chive | clary | coble | cords | crave |
| chivy | clash | cobra | corgi | crawl |
| chock | clasp | cocci | corky | craze |
| chode | class | cocky | corny | crazy |
| choir | clave | cocoa | corps | creak |
| choke | clean | codex | corse | cream |
| choky | clear | coign | corvy | credo |
| chomp | cleat | colic | cosec | creed |
| chops | cleek | colly | cosen | creek |
| chord | cleft | colon | costa | creel |
| chore | clepe | color | cotta | creep |
| chose | clerk | colza | couch | crème |
| chuck | click | combo | cough | crepe |
| chuff | cliff | comer | could | crêpe |
| chump | climb | comet | count | crept |
| chunk | clime | comfy | coupe | cress |
| churl | cling | comic | coupé | crest |
| churn | clink | comma | court | crick |
| churr | cloak | compo | coved | cried |
| chuse | clock | conch | coven | crier |
| chute | cloff | condo | cover | crime |
| chyle | cloke | coney | covet | crimp |
| chyme | clomb | conga | covey | crisp |
| cibol | clone | congé | covin | croak |
| cider | close | conic | cower | Croat |
| cigar | cloth | conin | cowry | crock |
| cilia | cloud | *conte* | coyly | croft |
| cinch | clout | cooee | coypu | crone |
| circa | clove | cooey | cozen | crony |

| | | | | |
|---|---|---|---|---|
| crook | cusec | debut | diced | dodgy |
| croon | cushy | decad | dicer | dogal |
| crore | cutch | decaf | dicey | doggo |
| cross | cutie | decay | dicky | doggy |
| croup | cutin | decor | dicta | dogma |
| crowd | cutis | decoy | didn't | doily |
| crown | cut up | decry | didst | doing |
| crude | cut-up | dedal | dight | Dolby |
| cruel | cycad | defer | digit | dolce |
| cruet | cycle | de-ice | digyn | dolly |
| crumb | cyder | deify | diked | domed |
| crump | cymar | deign | dildo | donee |
| cruse | cynic | deism | dilly | donna |
| crush | Czech | deist | dimly | donor |
| crust | | deity | dinar | donut |
| crwth | **D** | dekko | diner | dooly |
| cryer | dacha | delay | dingo | dopey |
| crypt | daddy | Delft | dingy | Doric |
| CS gas | daily | delta | dinky | dorse |
| cubeb | dairy | delve | diode | dotal |
| cubic | daisy | demit | dippy | doter |
| cubit | dally | demob | dipso | dotty |
| cuddy | daman | demon | dirge | doubt |
| cuish | damar | Demos | dirty | douce |
| culch | dance | demos | disci | dough |
| cully | D and C | demur | disco | douse |
| cumin | dandy | denim | dishy | dowdy |
| cupel | daric | dense | ditch | dowel |
| Cupid | dated | depot | ditto | dower |
| curdy | datum | depth | ditty | dowle |
| curer | dauby | derby | divan | downy |
| curet | daunt | derma | diver | dowry |
| curia | davit | deter | divot | dowse |
| curie | dazed | deuce | divvy | doyen |
| curio | dealt | devil | Dixie | dozen |
| curly | deary | dhobi | dixie | dozer |
| curry | death | dhole | dizen | draff |
| curse | debar | dhoti | dizzy | draft |
| curst | debit | Diana | docks | drail |
| curve | debug | diary | dodge | drain |

| | | | | |
|---|---|---|---|---|
| drake | ducat | educe | enema | ethos |
| drama | duchy | educt | enemy | ethyl |
| drank | ducky | eerie | enjoy | étude |
| drape | dulia | egest | ennui | etwee |
| drave | dully | egger | enrol | evade |
| drawl | dulse | egret | ensky | evens |
| drawn | dummy | eider | ensue | event |
| dread | dumpy | eight | enter | evert |
| dream | dunce | eikon | entry | every |
| drear | duper | eject | enure | evict |
| dregs | duple | eland | envoy | evoke |
| dress | durra | elate | Eolic | exact |
| drest | durst | elbow | eosin | exalt |
| dried | dusky | elder | epact | excel |
| drier | dusty | elect | ephah | exeat |
| drift | Dutch | elegy | ephod | exert |
| drill | duvet | elemi | ephor | exile |
| drily | dwale | elfin | epoch | exist |
| drink | dwarf | elide | epode | expel |
| drive | dwell | elite | epoxy | extol |
| droit | dying | elmen | equal | extra |
| droll | | eloge | equip | exude |
| drone | **E** | elogy | erase | exult |
| drool | eager | elope | Erato | eyrie |
| droop | eagle | elude | erect | |
| drops | eagre | elvan | ergot | **F** |
| dross | eared | elver | erica | fable |
| drove | early | elves | erode | faced |
| drown | earth | embay | erose | facer |
| druid | easel | embed | erred | facet |
| drunk | eater | ember | error | facia |
| drupe | eaves | emend | eruct | faddy |
| Druse | eblis | emery | erupt | fadge |
| druse | ebony | emmet | eskar | faery |
| Druze | éclat | emote | esker | faint |
| dryad | edema | empty | essay | fairy |
| dryer | edged | enact | ester | faith |
| dryly | edict | ender | estop | fakir |
| dry up | edify | endow | ether | false |
| ducal | edile | endue | ethic | famed |

| | | | | |
|---|---|---|---|---|
| fancy | fibre | flame | flush | freed |
| fanny | fiche | flamy | flute | freer |
| farad | fichu | flank | fluty | fresh |
| farce | field | flare | flyby | friar |
| farcy | fiend | flash | flyer | fried |
| fatal | fiery | flask | flyte | frier |
| fated | fifer | flawy | foamy | frill |
| Fates | fifth | flaxy | focal | frisk |
| fatly | fifty | fleam | focus | frith |
| fatty | fight | fleck | foehn | fritt |
| fatwa | filar | fleer | fogey | frizz |
| faugh | filch | fleet | foggy | frock |
| fault | filer | flesh | foist | frond |
| fauna | filet | flews | folio | frons |
| favus | filly | flick | folly | front |
| feast | filmy | flier | foots | frore |
| feaze | filth | flies | footy | frost |
| fecal | final | fling | foray | froth |
| feces | finch | flint | force | frown |
| feign | finer | flirt | fordo | froze |
| feint | finis | flite | forge | fruit |
| felly | finny | float | forgo | frump |
| felon | fiord | flock | forky | frush |
| femur | firer | flong | forme | fryer |
| fence | firry | flood | forte | f-stop |
| fenny | first | floor | forth | fucus |
| feoff | firth | flora | forty | fudge |
| feral | fishy | flory | forum | fudge! |
| ferny | fisty | floss | fossa | fugal |
| ferry | fitch | flour | fosse | fugue |
| fesse | fitly | flout | found | fully |
| fetal | fiver | flown | fount | fumid |
| fetch | fives | fluff | foyer | fungi |
| feted | fixed | fluid | frail | funky |
| fetid | fixer | fluke | frame | funny |
| fetor | fjord | fluky | franc | furor |
| fetus | flail | flume | Frank | furry |
| fetwa | flair | flung | frank | furze |
| fever | flake | flunk | fraud | furzy |
| fewer | flaky | fluor | freak | fusee |

| | | | | |
|---|---|---|---|---|
| fusel | gazer | glass | gorge | grind |
| fusil | gecko | glave | gorse | gripe |
| fussy | geese | glaze | gorsy | grist |
| fusty | gelid | gleam | Gouda | grits |
| futon | gemma | glean | gouge | groan |
| fuzee | gemmy | glebe | gourd | groat |
| fuzzy | gemot | gleby | gouty | groin |
| f-word | genet | glede | gowan | groom |
| | genie | gleed | graal | grope |
| **G** | genii | gleet | grace | gross |
| gabby | genre | glide | grade | group |
| gabel | genus | glint | graff | grout |
| gable | geode | glitz | graft | grove |
| gaffe | gesso | gloat | grail | growl |
| gaige | get at | globe | grain | grown |
| gaily | get on | gloom | graip | gruel |
| galea | get up | glory | grama | gruff |
| galop | get-up | gloss | grand | grume |
| gamey | ghaut | glove | grant | grump |
| gamic | Ghazi | gloze | grape | grunt |
| gamin | ghost | gluey | graph | G-suit |
| gamma | ghoul | glume | grapy | guaco |
| gamut | giant | glyph | grasp | guano |
| ganja | giber | gnarl | grass | guard |
| gaper | gibus | gnash | grate | guava |
| garth | giddy | gnome | grave | Guelf |
| gassy | gigot | godly | gravy | guess |
| gated | gigue | go far | graze | guest |
| gaudy | gills | gofer | great | guide |
| gauge | gilly | go for | grebe | guild |
| gault | gipsy | going | greed | guile |
| gaunt | girth | golly | Greek | guilt |
| gauss | given | gonad | green | guise |
| gauze | giver | goner | greet | gular |
| gauzy | glacé | goods | grice | gulch |
| gavel | glade | goody | gride | gules |
| gawky | glady | gooey | grief | gully |
| gayal | glair | go off | grill | gumbo |
| gayly | gland | goofy | grime | gumma |
| gazel | glare | goose | grimy | gummy |

| | | | | |
|---|---|---|---|---|
| gunny | harry | heron | hoppy | hydro |
| guppy | harsh | herse | horal | hyena |
| gushy | harum | hertz | horde | Hymen |
| gusto | hasn't | het up | horny | hymen |
| gusty | haste | hewer | horse | hyoid |
| gutsy | hasty | hexad | horsy | hyrax |
| gutta | hatch | hider | horus | hyson |
| Gypsy | hater | hilar | Hosea | |
| gyral | haugh | hilly | hotel | **I** |
| gyrus | haulm | hilum | hough | iambi |
| | haunt | himbo | hound | ichor |
| **H** | Hausa | Hindi | houri | icily |
| habit | haven | Hindu | house | icing |
| Hades | haver | hinge | hovel | ictus |
| hadji | havoc | hinny | hover | ideal |
| hadn't | hawse | hippo | howdy | idiom |
| hafiz | hazel | hippy | howel | idiot |
| haiku | H-bomb | hired | hubba | idler |
| haily | heady | hirer | hubby | idola |
| hairy | heald | hitch | huffy | idyll |
| hajji | heard | hives | hulky | igloo |
| hakim | heart | hoard | hullo! | ihram |
| halal | heath | hoary | hully | ileac |
| hallo! | heave | hobby | human | ileal |
| halma | heavy | hocus | humid | ileum |
| halos | hedge | hodge | humor | iliac |
| halve | hefty | hoist | humph! | ilium |
| hamal | heigh! | holey | humpy | image |
| hammy | heist | holla! | humus | imago |
| hanch | helix | hollo! | hunch | imaum |
| handy | hello! | holly | hunks | imbed |
| hanky | helot | homer | hurly | imbue |
| Hansa | helve | homey | hurry | impel |
| Hanse | hemal | honey | hurst | imply |
| haply | he-man | honky | husky | inane |
| happy | he-men | honor | hussy | inapt |
| hards | hence | hooch | hutch | incur |
| hardy | henna | hooey | huzza! | incus |
| harem | henry | hoofs | hyads | index |
| harpy | herby | hooky | hydra | India |

| | | | | |
|---|---|---|---|---|
| Indic | **J** | jowly | khadi | kylie |
| indie | jabot | Judas | khaki | Kyrie |
| indue | jaded | judge | kiang | |
| inept | jaggy | juice | kibla | **L** |
| inert | jalap | juicy | kiddy | label |
| infer | jalop | julep | kinky | labia |
| infix | Japan | jumbo | kiosk | labor |
| in for | japan | jumpy | kitty | laden |
| ingle | jasey | junky | kloof | ladle |
| ingot | jaunt | junta | knack | lagan |
| inkle | jawed | jural | knarl | lager |
| in-law | jazzy | jurat | knave | laird |
| inlay | jehad | juror | knead | laity |
| inlet | jello | jutty | kneed | lamed |
| inner | jelly | | kneel | lamia |
| input | jemmy | **K** | knell | lance |
| inset | jenny | kaaba | knelt | lande |
| inter | jerid | Kafir | knife | lanky |
| in tow | jerky | kaiak | knock | lapel |
| intro | Jesse | kalif | knoll | lapse |
| Inuit | Jesus | kapok | knout | larch |
| inure | jetty | kappa | known | lardy |
| inurn | jewel | kaput | knubs | lares |
| Invar | Jewry | karat | knurl | large |
| iodic | jiffy | Karen | knurr | largo |
| Ionic | jigot | karma | koala | larum |
| ionic | jihad | karob | Kodak | larva |
| irade | jingo | karoo | kooky | laser |
| irate | jinks | kauri | kopek | lasso |
| Irish | jinni | kayak | kopje | latch |
| irons | joint | kazoo | Koran | later |
| irony | joist | kebab | kraal | latex |
| Islam | joker | kedge | krait | lathe |
| islet | jokey | keeve | krill | lathi |
| issue | jolly | kelpy | krona | lathy |
| istle | Jonah | Kendo | krone | Latin |
| itchy | jorum | kerne | kudos | laugh |
| ivied | joual | ketch | Kufic | laura |
| ivory | joule | kevel | kulak | laver |
| ixtle | joust | keyed | kvass | lawny |

| | | | | |
|---|---|---|---|---|
| laxly | Lewis | loach | lucid | major |
| layer | lexis | loamy | lucky | maker |
| lazar | liana | loath | lucre | malar |
| leach | liane | lobar | luffa | Malay |
| leady | libel | lobby | lumen | malic |
| leafy | liber | lobed | lumpy | mamba |
| leaky | Libra | local | lunar | mamma |
| leant | liche | locum | lunch | mammy |
| learn | licit | locus | lunge | maned |
| lease | liege | lodge | lungi | manes |
| leash | lieve | loess | lupus | mange |
| least | lifer | lofty | lurch | mango |
| leave | ligan | logan | lurgg | mangy |
| leavy | light | logic | lurgy | mania |
| leben | liken | logos | lurid | manic |
| ledge | lilac | lolly | lusty | manis |
| ledgy | limbo | loner | luvvy | manky |
| leech | limen | longe | *lycée* | manly |
| leery | limey | looby | Lycra® | manna |
| lefty | limit | loofa | lying | manor |
| legal | linen | loony | lymph | manse |
| leggy | liner | loopy | lynch | manta |
| leg it | lingo | loose | lyric | manus |
| legit. | links | loris | lysin | Maori |
| leman | lipid | lorry | lysis | maple |
| lemma | lisle | losel | Lysol® | March |
| lemon | lisse | loser | | march |
| lemur | lists | lotah | **M** | marge |
| lento | liter | lotto | macaw | marly |
| leper | lithe | lotus | macer | marry |
| lepto- | litho | lough | macle | marsh |
| letch | litre | louis | madam | Masai |
| Lethe | lived | loury | madly | mason |
| let up | liven | louse | madre | massy |
| let-up | liver | lousy | Mafia | match |
| levee | lives | lover | magic | mater |
| level | livid | lowed | magma | matey |
| lever | livre | lower | magus | maths |
| levin | llama | lowly | Mahdi | matin |
| Levis® | llano | loyal | maize | matte |

| | | | | |
|---|---|---|---|---|
| matty | mezzo | molar | mower | nadir |
| maund | miaul | moldy | Mr Big | nagor |
| mauve | micra | molto | mucky | naiad |
| mavis | micro | momma | mucus | naïve |
| maxim | middy | mommy | muddy | naked |
| maybe | midge | monad | mudir | namer |
| mayn't | midst | *monde* | mufti | nance |
| mayor | miffy | money | muggy | nancy |
| mazer | might | monte | mujik | nandu |
| mealy | milch | month | mulch | nanny |
| means | milky | mooch | mulct | nappy |
| meant | mimic | moody | mulla | nasal |
| meany | mince | moony | mulsh | nasty |
| mease | miner | moose | mummy | natal |
| meaty | mingy | moped | mumps | natch |
| Mecca | minim | moper | munch | nates |
| medal | minor | moral | mungo | natty |
| media | minus | morel | mural | naval |
| medic | mirth | mores | Murex | navel |
| Médoc | misdo | moron | murky | navew |
| mêlée | miser | Morse | muser | navvy |
| melic | misty | Mosel | muses | nawab |
| melon | miter | mosey | mushy | neath |
| menad | mitre | mossy | music | needs |
| mercy | mixed | motel | musky | needy |
| merge | mixen | motet | musth | neese |
| merit | mixer | mothy | musty | Negro |
| merle | mix up | motif | mutch | negus |
| merry | mix-up | motor | Muzak® | neigh |
| meshy | mizen | motto | mużzy | nerve |
| mesne | Mlles | mould | myall | nervy |
| meson | mocha | moult | myope | netty |
| messy | modal | mound | myops | never |
| metal | model | mount | myopy | nevus |
| meter | modem | mourn | myrrh | newel |
| meths | modus | mouse | | newly |
| Métis | mogul | mousy | **N** | nexus |
| metol | mohur | mouth | nabob | niche |
| metre | moiré | mover | nacho | nidor |
| metro | moist | movie | nacre | nidus |

| | | | | |
|---|---|---|---|---|
| niece | noted | ogler | Oscar | pager |
| nifty | novel | oiled | osier | pains |
| night | noway! | oiler | otary | paint |
| nihil | noyau | okapi | other | palea |
| nimby | nudge | olden | otter | pally |
| ninny | nurse | oleic | ought | palmy |
| ninon | nutty | olein | Ouija® | palpi |
| ninth | nylon | olive | ounce | palsy |
| Niobe | nymph | -ology | ousel | panda |
| nippy | | omber | outdo | paned |
| Nisan | **O** | ombre | outer | panel |
| niton | oaken | omega | outgo | panic |
| nitre | oakum | on ice | outré | panne |
| nitry | oared | onion | ouzel | pansy |
| nival | oases | onset | ovary | panto |
| nizam | oasis | on tap | ovate | pants |
| nobby | oaten | oomph | overt | papal |
| noble | oaths | oozed | ovine | papaw |
| nobly | obeah | op. cit. | ovoid | paper |
| nodal | obese | opera | ovolo | pappy |
| noddy | occur | opine | ovule | parch |
| nodus | ocean | opium | owing | pared |
| nohow | ocher | optic | owlet | parer |
| noils | ochre | orach | owner | parka |
| noise | ochry | orang | oxbow | parry |
| noisy | ocker | orate | oxeye | parse |
| no joy | ocrea | orbed | Oxfam | party |
| nomad | octad | orbit | oxide | pasha |
| nonce | octal | orcin | oxlip | passé |
| nones | octet | order | ozone | pasta |
| nonet | oddly | oread | | paste |
| noone | odeon | organ | **P** | pasty |
| noose | odeum | oriel | paced | patch |
| nopal | odium | Orion | pacer | pated |
| noria | odour | Orlon® | pacha | paten |
| Norse | offal | orlop | paddy | paths |
| north | offer | ormer | padre | patin |
| nosed | often | ornis | paean | patio |
| nosey | ogham | orpin | paeon | patsy |
| notch | ogive | orris | pagan | patty |

| | | | | |
|---|---|---|---|---|
| pause | phial | pithy | polka | prize |
| pavan | phlox | pivot | polyp | probe |
| paver | phone | pixel | poppy | proem |
| pavid | phony | pixie | porch | prone |
| pawed | photo | pizza | porer | prong |
| pawky | phyla | place | pores | proof |
| payee | piano | plack | porgy | prose |
| payer | picot | plaid | porky | prosy |
| peace | picra | plain | porno | proud |
| peach | picul | plait | porte | prove |
| peaky | piece | plane | poser | prowl |
| pearl | piend | plank | posit | proxy |
| pease | pietà | plant | posse | prude |
| peaty | piety | plash | potto | prune |
| pecan | piggy | plasm | potty | pryer |
| pedal | pig it | plate | pouch | psalm |
| peeve | pigmy | plaza | poult | pshaw |
| pekoe | piked | plead | pound | psoas |
| penal | pilaf | pleat | power | psora |
| pence | pilau | plica | prang | pubes |
| penis | pilaw | plonk | prank | pubic |
| penna | pilch | pluck | prase | pubis |
| penny | piles | plumb | prate | pudgy |
| peony | pilot | plume | prawn | puffy |
| peppy | pinch | plump | preen | pukka |
| perch | piney | plumy | press | pulpy |
| perdu | pinky | plunk | price | pulse |
| peril | pinna | plush | prick | punch |
| perky | pinny | Pluto | pride | Punic |
| perry | pinto | plyer | prier | punka |
| perse | pin-up | poach | prima | punty |
| pesky | pious | pocky | prime | pupae |
| petal | pipal | podgy | primo | pupal |
| peter | piped | poesy | primp | pupil |
| petit | piper | point | prink | puppy |
| petto | pipit | poise | print | puree |
| petty | pique | poker | prior | purge |
| pewit | piqué | pokey | prise | Purim |
| pharo | piste | polar | prism | purse |
| phase | pitch | polio | privy | pursy |

| | | | | |
|---|---|---|---|---|
| pushy | quite | ratch | refix | rinse |
| pussy | quits | rated | regal | Rioja |
| putid | quoin | ratel | reify | ripen |
| putto | quoit | rater | reign | risen |
| putty | Quorn® | rathe | reins | riser |
| pygmy | quota | ratio | relax | risky |
| pylon | quote | rat on | relay | ritzy |
| Pyrex® | quoth | ratty | relet | rival |
| pyxis | | raved | relic | rivel |
| | **R** | ravel | relit | river |
| **Q** | rabbi | raven | remit | rivet |
| qanat | rabid | raver | remix | riyal |
| quack | raced | ravin | renal | roach |
| quaff | racer | rawly | renew | roast |
| quail | radar | rayed | rente | robin |
| quake | radii | rayon | repay | robot |
| quaky | radio | razor | repel | rocky |
| qualm | radix | reach | reply | rodeo |
| quant | radon | react | rerun | Roger |
| quark | raged | ready | reset | roger |
| quart | rainy | realm | resin | rogue |
| quash | raise | rearm | retch | Roman |
| quasi | Rajah | reast | retro- | Romeo |
| quean | raked | reave | revel | rondo |
| queen | rakee | rebec | revet | rooky |
| queer | raker | rebel | revue | roomy |
| quell | rally | rebus | rheum | roost |
| quern | Rambo | rebut | rhino | rooty |
| query | ramee | recap | rhomb | roper |
| quest | ramie | recto | rhumb | rorid |
| queue | ranch | recur | rhyme | rosin |
| quick | R and R | redan | riant | rotor |
| quiet | randy | redly | rider | rouge |
| quiff | ranee | reedy | ridge | rough |
| quill | range | reefy | ridgy | round |
| quilt | rangy | reeky | rifle | rouse |
| quint | raphe | reest | right | roust |
| quire | rapid | reeve | rigid | route |
| quirk | raspy | refer | rigor | rover |
| quirt | Rasta | refit | riled | rowan |

| | | | | |
|---|---|---|---|---|
| rowdy | saker | sauté | scope | sepal |
| rowel | sakia | saved | score | sepia |
| rower | sakai | saver | scorn | sepic |
| royal | salad | savin | Scots | sepoy |
| rub in | salep | savor | scour | septa |
| ruble | sales | savoy | scout | serac |
| ruche | Salic | savvy | scowl | serai |
| ruddy | Salix | sawer | scrag | serge |
| rugae | *salle* | Saxon | scram | Sergt |
| rugby | sally | sayer | scrap | serif |
| ruler | salmi | sayid | scree | serin |
| rumba | salon | say-so | screw | serum |
| rumen | salop | scala | scrim | serve |
| rummy | salsa | scald | scrip | servo |
| rumor | salse | scale | scrub | setae |
| runic | salts | scall | scrum | seton |
| run-in | salty | scalp | scuba | set to |
| runny | salve | scaly | scudi | set-to |
| run up | salvo | scamp | scudo | set up |
| run-up | samba | scant | scuff | set-up |
| rupee | sambo | scape | sculk | seven |
| rural | samey | scare | scull | sever |
| rushy | sandy | scarf | scurf | sewer |
| rusty | Santa | scarp | scute | scxed |
| rutty | sapan | scart | seals | sexes |
| | sapid | scary | seamy | shack |
| **S** | sapor | scatt | sebum | shade |
| sabin | sappy | scaup | sedan | shady |
| sable | saree | scaur | Seder | shaft |
| sabot | sarge | scena | sedge | shake |
| sabra | sasin | scene | sedgy | shako |
| sabre | sassy | scent | seedy | shaky |
| sacra | Satan | schmo | seems | shale |
| *sacré* | satay | sci fi | seine | shall |
| sadhu | satin | scion | seize | shalm |
| sadly | satyr | scoff | semen | shalt |
| sahib | sauce | scold | senna | shaly |
| saiga | saucy | scone | señor | shame |
| saint | sauna | scoop | sense | shank |
| sajou | saury | scoot | senza | shan't |

| | | | | |
|---|---|---|---|---|
| shape | shook | siren | slice | snarl |
| shard | shoon | sisal | slick | snary |
| share | shoot | sissy | slide | sneak |
| shark | shore | sitar | slier | sneer |
| sharp | shorl | sit in | slime | snick |
| shave | shorn | sit-in | slimy | snide |
| shawl | short | sit up | sling | sniff |
| shawm | shout | sit-up | slink | snipe |
| sheaf | shove | sixer | sloop | snood |
| sheal | shown | sixth | slope | snook |
| shear | showy | sixty | slosh | snoop |
| sheen | shred | sized | sloth | snoot |
| sheep | shrew | skate | slump | snore |
| sheer | shrub | skeet | slung | snort |
| sheet | shrug | skein | slunk | snout |
| sheik | shuck | skied | slurp | snowy |
| shelf | shunt | skiff | slush | snuck |
| shell | shush | skill | smack | snuff |
| she'll | shyly | skimp | small | soapy |
| sherd | sibyl | skink | smalt | sober |
| shewn | sicko | skint | smart | socks |
| Shiah | sided | skirl | smash | socle |
| shied | sider | skirt | smear | soddy |
| shier | sides | skive | smell | Sodom |
| shift | sidle | skoal | smelt | sofas |
| shily | siege | skulk | smile | softa |
| shine | sieve | skull | smirk | softy |
| shiny | sight | skunk | smite | soggy |
| ships | sigma | slack | smith | solan |
| shire | silex | slain | smock | solar |
| shirk | silky | slake | smoke | soles |
| shirr | silly | slang | smoky | sol-fa |
| shirt | silty | slant | smolt | solid |
| shite | silva | slash | smote | Solon |
| shive | since | slate | snack | solos |
| shoal | sinew | slave | snafu | solus |
| shock | singe | sleek | snail | solve |
| shoer | sinks | sleep | snake | sonar |
| shoes | sinus | sleet | snaky | sonde |
| shone | Sioux | slept | snare | songs |

| | | | | |
|---|---|---|---|---|
| sonic | spick | sputa | stele | stria |
| sonny | spicy | squab | steps | strip |
| sooth | spied | squad | stere | strop |
| sooty | spiel | squat | stern | strow |
| soppy | spies | squaw | stich | strum |
| sorry | spike | squib | stick | strut |
| sorts | spiky | squid | sties | stubs |
| sorus | spile | stack | stiff | stuck |
| sough | spill | stade | stile | study |
| souls | spilt | staff | still | stuff |
| sound | spine | stage | stilt | stump |
| souse | spiny | stagy | sting | stung |
| south | spire | staid | stink | stunk |
| sowar | spirt | stain | stint | stunt |
| sower | spiry | stair | stipe | stupa |
| space | spite | stake | stoat | stupe |
| spacy | splay | stale | stock | style |
| spade | split | stalk | Stoic | suave |
| Spain | spode | stall | stoke | sucks |
| spait | spoil | stamp | stole | sucre |
| spake | spoke | stand | stoma | suede |
| spank | spoof | stank | stomp | suety |
| spare | spook | stare | stone | sugar |
| spark | spool | stark | stony | suint |
| spasm | spoon | stars | stood | suite |
| spate | spoor | start | stook | sulci |
| spats | spore | stash | stool | sulks |
| spawl | sport | state | stoop | sulky |
| spawn | spots | stave | store | sully |
| speak | spout | stays | stork | sumac |
| spear | sprat | stead | storm | Sunna |
| speck | spray | steak | story | Sunni |
| specs | spree | steal | stoup | sunny |
| speed | sprig | steam | stout | super |
| spell | sprit | steed | stove | surah |
| spelt | spume | steel | strap | sural |
| spend | spumy | steep | straw | surfy |
| spent | spunk | steer | stray | surge |
| sperm | spurn | stein | strep | surgy |
| spice | spurt | stela | strew | surly |

| | | | | |
|---|---|---|---|---|
| sushi | syrup | targe | tenor | thowl |
| swain | sythe | tarot | tense | three |
| swami | | tarry | tenth | threw |
| swamp | **T** | tarsi | tepee | thrid |
| swang | tabby | tasks | tepid | throb |
| swank | tabes | tasse | terce | throe |
| sward | tabid | taste | terms | throw |
| sware | table | tasty | terra | thrum |
| swarm | taboo | tatty | terry | thumb |
| swart | tabor | taunt | terse | thump |
| swash | tacet | taupe | tesla | thyme |
| swath | tache | tawer | Tessa | thymy |
| swear | tacit | tawny | testy | tiara |
| sweat | tacks | tawse | thane | tibia |
| Swede | tacky | taxed | thank | ticks |
| swede | tafia | taxer | thaws | tidal |
| sweep | taiga | taxis | theca | tie-in |
| sweet | tails | taxon | theft | tiers |
| swell | taint | tazza | thegn | tie-up |
| swept | taken | T-cell | their | tiger |
| swift | taker | teach | theme | tight |
| swill | takes | tears | there | tigon |
| swine | tales | tease | therm | tilde |
| swing | tally | techy | these | tiled |
| swink | talon | teddy | theta | tiler |
| swipe | talus | teens | thews | tiles |
| swirl | tamed | teeny | they'd | tilth |
| swish | tamer | teeth | thick | timed |
| Swiss | Tamil | teind | thief | timer |
| swoon | tamis | telex | thigh | times |
| swoop | tammy | telic | thill | timid |
| sword | tango | telly | thine | tinct |
| swore | tanka | tempi | thing | tinea |
| sworn | tanks | tempo | think | tined |
| swung | tansy | tempt | third | tinge |
| sylph | taper | temse | thole | tinny |
| sylva | tapir | tench | thong | tipsy |
| synch | tapis | tends | thorn | tired |
| synod | tardy | tenet | thorp | tires |
| synth | tares | tenon | those | tiros |

| | | | | |
|---|---|---|---|---|
| tisan | torsk | trick | turfs | umbel |
| Tisri | torso | tried | turfy | umber |
| titan | torte | trier | Turki | umbra |
| titer | torus | trike | turns | umiak |
| tithe | total | trill | turps | unapt |
| title | totem | trine | tusks | unban |
| titre | touch | tripe | tusky | unbar |
| tizzy | tough | trite | tutor | unbid |
| toady | touse | troll | tutti | uncap |
| toast | towed | tromp | twain | uncle |
| today | towel | troop | twang | uncut |
| toddy | tower | trope | twank | under |
| toffy | towny | troth | tweak | undue |
| toils | toxic | trout | tweed | unfit |
| toise | toxin | trove | 'tween | unfix |
| Tokay | toyer | truce | tweet | unhat |
| token | trace | truck | 'twere | unify |
| tolls | track | trull | twerp | union |
| toman | tract | truly | twice | unite |
| tommy | trade | trump | twill | units |
| tonal | trail | trunk | 'twill | unity |
| toned | train | truss | twine | unman |
| toner | trait | trust | twins | unmew |
| tonga | tramp | truth | twirl | unpeg |
| tongs | trape | try on | twirp | unpen |
| tonic | traps | try-on | twist | unpin |
| tonka | trash | tryst | 'twixt | unsay |
| tonne | trass | tubby | typic | unset |
| tools | trave | tuber | tyros | unsex |
| tooth | trawl | Tudor | | untie |
| topaz | tread | tufts | **U** | until |
| topee | treat | tulip | U-boat | unwed |
| toper | trend | tulle | udder | up-end |
| topic | tress | tumid | uh-huh | upper |
| topsy | trews | tummy | Uhlan | upset |
| toque | triad | tumor | ukase | up top |
| torah | trial | tuned | ulcer | urate |
| torch | Trias | tuner | ulema | urban |
| torii | tribe | tunic | ulnar | urges |
| torsi | trice | tunny | ultra | urine |

| | | | | |
|---|---|---|---|---|
| usage | verse | voice | washy | whine |
| usher | verso | voile | wasn't | whirl |
| usual | verst | volar | waste | whirr |
| usurp | vertu | volta | watch | whisk |
| usury | verve | vomer | water | whist |
| utter | Vesta | vomit | waved | white |
| U-turn | vesta | voter | waver | whizz |
| uvula | vetch | vouch | waves | whole |
| | vexed | vowel | waxed | who'll |
| **V** | vexer | vulva | waxen | whoop |
| vagal | viand | vying | weald | whore |
| vague | vibes | | weary | whorl |
| vagus | vicar | **W** | weave | whort |
| valet | video | wacke | webby | whose |
| valid | views | wacky | weber | whoso |
| valor | viewy | waddy | wedge | widen |
| valse | vigil | wader | weeds | widow |
| value | vigor | wafer | weedy | width |
| valve | villa | wafts | weeny | wield |
| vapid | villi | wager | weepy | Wigan |
| vapor | vinic | wages | weigh | wight |
| varec | vinyl | wag it | weird | wilco |
| varix | viola | wagon | welch | wiles |
| varus | viper | wails | Welsh | willy |
| vasty | viral | waist | welsh | wince |
| vatic | vireo | waits | wench | winch |
| vault | Virgo | waive | whack | windy |
| vaunt | virtu | waked | whale | wings |
| Vedic | virus | waken | whang | winze |
| veery | visit | waker | wharf | wiped |
| vegan | visor | wakes | wheal | wiper |
| veiny | vista | walla | wheat | wired |
| velar | vital | wally | wheel | wiser |
| veldt | vitta | waltz | whelk | wispy |
| velum | vivid | wanly | whelm | witan |
| venal | vixen | wares | whelp | witch |
| venom | vizor | warms | where | withe |
| venue | vocal | warns | which | withy |
| Venus | vodka | warps | whiff | witty |
| verge | vogue | warty | while | wives |

| wizen | would | **X** | yeast | **Z** |
|-------|-------|-------|-------|-------|
| wodge | wound | x-axis | yerba | zabra |
| woman | woven | xebec | yield | zambo |
| women | wrack | xenon | yobbo | zamia |
| wonky | wrapt | Xerox® | yodel | zappy |
| woods | wrath | xylem | yodle | zebec |
| woody | wreak |  | yogin | zebra |
| wooer | wreck | **Y** | yogis | zibet |
| wootz | wrest | yacca | yoick | zilch |
| woozy | wrier | yacht | yokel | zinco |
| wordy | wring | Yager | you'll | zincy |
| works | wrist | yahoo | young | zippy |
| world | write | yamen | you're | zloty |
| worms | wrong | yamph | yours | zombi |
| wormy | wrote | yapok | youth | zonal |
| worry | wroth | yauld | you've | zoned |
| worse | wrung | y-axis | yucca | zooid |
| worst | wryly | yearn | yucky | zoril |
| worth | wurst | years | yummy | zymic |

# Six-letter words

**A**
abacus
abaser
abated
abater
abatis
abbacy
abbess
abbeys
abduce
abduct
abject
abjure
ablate
ablaut
ablaze
abloom
aboard
abound
abrade
abroad
abrupt
abseil
absent
absorb
absurd
abulia
abuser
acacia
acajou
acarid
acarus
accede
accent

accept
access
accord
accost
accrue
accuse
acedia
acetic
Achean
achene
aching
acidic
acquit
across
acting
action
active
actual
acuity
acumen
adagio
Adamic
addict
adduce
adduct
adhere
adieus
adieux
adipic
adjoin
adjure
adjust
admass
admire

adnate
adnoun
Adonis
adorer
adrift
adroit
adsorb
advene
advent
adverb
advert
advice
advise
adytum
adzuki
aedile
Aeolic
aerate
aerial
aerify
aerobe
aerose
affair
affect
affeer
affirm
afflux
afford
affray
affuse
Afghan
afield
aflame
afloat

afraid
afreet
afresh
agamic
agaric
ageism
agency
agenda
age-old
aghast
agnail
agnate
agoing
agonic
agouti
agouty
aguish
aiglet
aigret
ailing
air-bag
air-bed
airbus
air-gas
air-gun
airily
airing
airman
air sac
airway
aisled
akimbo
alalia
alarum

albata
albedo
albeit
albino
Albion
albite
albugo
alcade
alcaic
alcove
aldern
aldine
alegar
alexia
alexin
algine
algous
alight
aliped
alkali
allege
allele
all for
allied
allies
all one
all out
all-out
all set
allude
allure
almond
almost
alpaca

| | | | | |
|---|---|---|---|---|
| alpine | Andean | apathy | argala | ashore |
| Altaic | anemia | apeman | argali | ashram |
| althea | anemic | apepsy | argent | askant |
| aludel | anergy | *aperçu* | Argive | aslant |
| alumna | angary | apexes | argosy | asleep |
| alumni | angina | aphony | arguer | aslope |
| alveus | angled | aphtha | argufy | aspect |
| alvine | angler | apiary | argute | aspick |
| always | angora | apical | aright | aspire |
| amadou | animal | apices | arioso | assail |
| amatol | animus | apiece | arista | assent |
| amazon | ankled | aplomb | armada | assert |
| ambari | anklet | apnoea | armful | assess |
| ambary | annals | apodal | armlet | assets |
| ambler | anneal | apogee | armory | assign |
| ambles | annexe | *à point* | armour | assist |
| ambush | annual | Apollo | armpit | assize |
| *amende* | anoint | appall | arnica | assoil |
| amends | anonym | appeal | aroint! | assort |
| amenta | anorak | appear | around | assume |
| amerce | ansate | append | arouse | assure |
| amidst | answer | appose | aroynt! | astern |
| amnion | ant-cow | approx. | arrack | asthma |
| amoeba | ante up | aptote | arrant | astony |
| amoral | anthem | Arabic | arrear | astral |
| amorce | anther | arable | arrect | astray |
| amoret | antiar | arbour | arrest | astrut |
| amount | antler | arcade | arride | astute |
| ampere | Antlia | Arcady | arrive | aswarm |
| ampule | antrum | arcane | arroba | asylum |
| amulet | any day | arched | arrowy | ataxia |
| amuser | anyhow | archer | arroyo | ataxic |
| amylic | anyone | archil | artery | at hand |
| anabas | anyway | archly | artful | atomic |
| analog | aorist | archon | artist | atonal |
| ananas | aortal | Arctic | ascend | atoned |
| anarch | aortic | arctic | ascent | atonic |
| anbury | aoudad | ardent | ashame | atrial |
| anchor | Apache | ardour | ashlar | at risk |
| ancone | apache | areola | ashler | atrium |

| | | | | |
|---|---|---|---|---|
| attach | avoset | balata | barony | beaked |
| attack | avouch | baldly | barque | beaker |
| attain | avowal | baleen | barred | bearer |
| attend | avower | Balkan | barrel | bear on |
| attest | awaken | ballad | barren | bear up |
| attire | awakes | ballet | barrow | beaten |
| attorn | aweary | ballot | Barsac | beater |
| attune | aweigh | balsam | barter | beat in |
| aubade | awhile | bamboo | baryon | beat it |
| auburn | awning | banana | baryta | beat up |
| audile | axilla | banded | basalt | beauty |
| *au fait* | ayeaye | bandit | basely | beaver |
| *au fond* | azalea | bandog | bashaw | becalm |
| Augean | azotic | banger | basify | became |
| augite | | bangle | basket | becket |
| augury | **B** | bang on | basnet | beckon |
| August | babble | banian | Basque | become |
| august | babies | banish | basque | bedaub |
| *au lait* | babish | banker | basset | bedbug |
| auntie | babism | banner | bateau | bedeck |
| au pair | baboon | bantam | bather | bedell |
| aurate | backer | banter | bathos | bedlam |
| Auriga | back up | banyan | batist | bed-pan |
| aurist | back-up | banzai | batlet | bed-rid |
| aurora | baddie | baobab | batman | bedrop |
| aurous | bad egg | barbed | batoon | bed-sit |
| auspex | badger | barbel | batten | beechy |
| Aussie | baffle | barber | batter | beef up |
| author | bagful | barbet | battle | beeper |
| autism | bagman | Barbie® | battue | beetle |
| autumn | bagmen | barbie | bauble | beeves |
| *avanti* | bagnio | bardic | bawble | beezer |
| avatar | bag-wig | barège | bawdry | befall |
| avaunt | bailee | barely | bayard | befell |
| avenge | bailer | bargee | bay-rum | befool |
| avenue | bailey | barite | bazaar | before |
| averse | bailie | barium | beacon | befoul |
| aviary | Bairam | barker | beaded | beggar |
| aviate | bakery | barley | beadle | begird |
| avocet | baking | barman | beagle | begone! |

| | | | | |
|---|---|---|---|---|
| behalf | bestir | billet | blouse | boodle |
| behave | bestow | billon | blower | boogie |
| behead | bestud | billow | blowsy | boo-hoo |
| beheld | betake | Bimana | blow up | bookie |
| behest | bethel | binary | blow-up | boomer |
| behind | betide | binate | blowze | booted |
| behold | bêtise | binder | blowzy | bootee |
| behoof | betony | bionic | bluing | Boötes |
| behove | betook | biopsy | bluish | borage |
| Beiram | betray | biotic | blunge | borate |
| belace | better | biotin | B-movie | border |
| belate | bettor | birdie | boater | boreal |
| belaud | be up to | bireme | bobbin | boreas |
| beldam | bewail | bisect | bobble | boring |
| belfry | beware | bishop | bobcat | borrow |
| Belial | beweep | bisque | bob-wig | borsch |
| belief | bewray | bisson | bodega | borzoi |
| belike | beyond | bister | bodice | bosket |
| belled | bezant | bistre | bodied | botany |
| bellow | bezoar | bistro | bodily | botchy |
| belong | biased | biting | bodkin | botfly |
| belted | biascs | bitter | boffin | bother |
| beluga | biaxal | bladed | boggle | bothie |
| bemire | bibber | blamer | boiler | bo-tree |
| bemoan | biceps | blanch | bolary | bottle |
| bemuse | bicker | blazer | boldly | bottom |
| bender | bicorn | blazon | bolero | bouclé |
| benign | bidder | bleach | bolide | bought |
| benumb | bidery | bleary | bolshy | bougie |
| benzol | biffin | blench | bolter | boules |
| berate | bifold | blende | bomber | boulle |
| Berber | biform | blenny | bonbon | bounce |
| bereft | bigamy | blight | bonded | bouncy |
| Berlin | big cat | blinis | bonder | bounty |
| berlin | biggin | blithe | bonito | bourne |
| bertha | big top | blonde | *bon mot* | bourse |
| beseem | big-wig | bloody | bonnet | bovine |
| beside | bijoux | bloomy | bonnic | bowery |
| besmut | bikini | blotch | bonsai | bowing |
| bespot | billed | blotto | *bon ton* | bowler |

| | | | | |
|---|---|---|---|---|
| bowman | bricky | buffer | bushel | cactus |
| bowmen | bridal | buffet | busily | caddie |
| bow out | bridge | bugger | busing | caddis |
| bow-saw | bridle | bugler | busker | cadent |
| bow-tie | briery | bulbed | buskin | cadger |
| bow-wow | bright | bulbel | bussed | caecal |
| bowyer | briony | bulbil | buster | caecum |
| box-car | Briton | bulbul | bustle | Caesar |
| boxing | broach | bulimy | bust up | Caffre |
| boyish | brogan | bullet | bust-up | caftan |
| bracer | brogue | bumbag | butane | cahier |
| Brahma | broken | bumble | butler | caiman |
| brains | broker | bum boy | butter | caïque |
| brainy | bromic | bummer | button | cairus |
| braise | bronco | bumper | buy-out | cajole |
| braize | bronze | bunchy | buzzer | calash |
| branch | brooch | bundle | by-blow | calcar |
| brandy | broody | bungle | bye-bye | calces |
| branks | broomy | bunion | byelaw | calcic |
| branny | browse | bunker | bygone | calefy |
| brassy | bruise | bunkum | by-lane | calico |
| bravos | brumal | bunyip | byline | caliph |
| brawny | brunch | bunyon | byname | calker |
| brayer | brunet | burble | bypass | calkin |
| brazen | brushy | burbot | bypath | callan |
| Brazil | brutal | burden | by-play | caller |
| brazil | bryony | bureau | byroad | callet |
| breach | bubble | burgee | byssus | callow |
| breast | bubbly | burger | by-view | call up |
| breath | buboes | burgle | byword | call-up |
| breech | buccal | burgoo | | callus |
| breeks | bucker | burial | C | calmer |
| breeze | bucket | buried | cabala | calmly |
| breezy | buckie | burlap | cabbie | calory |
| Breton | buckra | burner | cabman | calpac |
| brevet | Buddha | burnet | cabmen | calque |
| brewer | buddle | burrow | cachet | calves |
| briary | budget | bursar | cachou | camber |
| briber | budgie | burton | cackle | camera |
| bribes | budlet | bushed | cacoon | camion |

| | | | | |
|---|---|---|---|---|
| camise | capric | castor | celled | chaser |
| camlet | captor | casual | Celtic | chasse |
| camper | carack | catchy | cement | chaste |
| campus | carafe | catena | censer | chatty |
| Canaan | carbon | catgut | censor | cheeky |
| canapé | carboy | Cathay | census | cheers |
| canard | carder | cation | cental | cheery |
| canary | careen | catkin | center | cheese |
| cancan | career | cat-lap | centos | cheesy |
| cancel | caress | cat-nap | centre | chelae |
| Cancer | caries | cat-nip | cerate | chemic |
| cancer | carina | catsup | cereal | cheque |
| candid | caring | cattle | cereus | cherry |
| candle | carman | caucus | ceriph | cherty |
| cangue | carmen | caudal | cerise | cherub |
| canine | carnal | caudex | cerite | chesty |
| caning | carnet | caudle | cerium | chetah |
| canker | carpal | caught | certes | chevet |
| canned | carpel | cauker | ceruse | chevin |
| cannel | carpet | caulis | cervix | chiasm |
| cannie | carpus | causal | cesium | chicha |
| cannon | carrel | causer | cestus | chi-chi |
| cannot | carrot | causey | cesura | chicle |
| canopy | cartel | cautel | chabuk | chigoe |
| Cantab. | carter | cavass | cha-cha | chigre |
| canter | carton | caveat | chacma | childe |
| canthi | carvel | cavern | chafer | chilli |
| cantle | carver | caviar | chaffy | chilly |
| canton | casaba | caving | chaise | chinch |
| cantor | casbah | cavity | chalet | chined |
| cantos | casein | cavort | chalky | chinky |
| Canuck | casern | cawass | chammy | chintz |
| Canute | cashew | cayman | chance | chippy |
| canvas | casing | cayuse | chancy | chirpy |
| canyon | casino | cedarn | change | chisel |
| capful | casket | cedria | chanty | chitin |
| capias | casque | Ceefax® | chapel | chiton |
| caplin | cassia | celery | chappy | chives |
| capote | caster | celiac | charge | chivvy |
| capped | castle | cellar | charry | choice |

| | | | | |
|---|---|---|---|---|
| choker | cirque | closer | cogent | comply |
| choler | cirrus | closet | cognac | Comsat® |
| choose | cistus | clothe | coheir | concha |
| choosy | cither | clotty | cohere | concur |
| chopin | citify | cloudy | cohort | condom |
| choppy | citric | clough | coifed | condor |
| choral | citron | cloven | coiled | confab |
| chorea | citrus | clover | coiner | confer |
| choree | civics | clumpy | coin-op | congee |
| choric | civism | clumsy | coitus | conger |
| chorus | clammy | clutch | coldly | congou |
| chosen | clamor | coaita | coleus | conics |
| chough | claque | coarse | collar | conine |
| chouse | claret | coatee | collet | conium |
| chowry | classy | coaxal | collie | conker |
| chrism | clause | coaxer | collop | conman |
| Christ | clawed | cobalt | colony | conoid |
| chrome | clayey | cobber | colour | consul |
| chromo | cleans | cobble | colter | contra |
| chubby | cleave | cobnut | column | convex |
| chuffy | clench | coburg | colure | convey |
| chukka | clergy | cobweb | comate | convoy |
| chummy | cleric | cocain | combat | cooker |
| chunky | clever | coccus | combed | cookie |
| church | cliché | coccyx | comber | cooler |
| cicada | client | cocker | comedo | coolie |
| cicala | cliffy | cocket | comedy | cool it |
| cicely | climax | cockle | comely | coolly |
| cicone | clinch | cocoon | come on | cooper |
| cicuta | clingy | codded | come-on | cootie |
| cierge | clinic | coddle | comfit | copeck |
| cilery | clip-on | codger | comfry | copier |
| cilice | clique | codify | coming | coping |
| cinder | cloaca | codlin | comity | cop out |
| cinema | cloche | coerce | commie | cop-out |
| cinque | cloddy | coeval | commit | copper |
| cipher | cloggy | coffee | commix | 'copter |
| cippus | clonic | coffer | common | Coptic |
| circle | clonus | coffin | comose | copula |
| circus | closed | coffle | compel | copyer |

| | | | | |
|---|---|---|---|---|
| coquet | coupon | crewel | culmen | cutlet |
| corban | course | crinal | cultch | cut off |
| corbel | cousin | cringe | cultus | cut-off |
| corbie | covert | crinum | culver | cut out |
| corcle | coving | crises | cumber | cut-out |
| corded | coward | crisis | cummin | cutter |
| cordon | cowboy | crispy | cumuli | cuttle |
| corium | cowpat | critic | cuneal | cyanic |
| corked | cowpox | croaky | cupful | cyclic |
| corker | cowrie | crocus | cupola | Cyclop |
| cormel | coyote | croppy | cupric | cygnet |
| cornea | crabby | crosse | cupula | cymbal |
| corned | cradle | crotch | cupule | cymose |
| cornel | crafty | croton | curacy | cymous |
| corner | craggy | crouch | curare | Cymric |
| cornet | crambo | cruces | curari | cypher |
| corona | cranky | cruise | curate | Cyprus |
| corpse | cranny | cruive | curdle | cystic |
| corpus | crappy | crumby | curfew | |
| corral | cratch | crummy | curios | **D** |
| corrie | crater | crunch | curium | dabber |
| corset | cravat | crural | curled | dabble |
| Cortes | craven | cruset | curler | *da capo* |
| cortex | crayon | crusts | curlew | dacoit |
| corvée | creaky | crusty | cursed | dactyl |
| corymb | creamy | crutch | curser | daedal |
| coryza | crease | crying | cursor | daemon |
| cosher | create | cubage | curtal | dagger |
| cosine | crèche | cubism | curtly | daggle |
| cosmic | credit | cuboid | curtsy | dagoba |
| cosmos | creeky | cuckoo | curule | dahlia |
| cosset | creepy | cuddle | curved | daimio |
| costly | creese | cuddly | curvet | dainty |
| cottar | cremor | cudgel | cuscus | dakoit |
| cotter | creole | cuisse | cushat | damage |
| cotton | cresol | cuiter | cuspid | damask |
| cougar | cressy | culdee | cussed | dammar |
| coulee | cresta | culler | custom | dammer |
| county | Cretan | cullet | custos | damned |
| couple | cretin | cullis | cutler | dampen |

| | | | | |
|---|---|---|---|---|
| damper | debase | deific | derail | dibble |
| damsel | debate | *déjà vu* | deride | dicast |
| damson | debile | deject | derive | dicing |
| dancer | déblai | de jure | dermal | dicker |
| dander | debris | delate | dermic | dickey |
| dandle | debtor | delete | dermis | dictum |
| danger | debunk | Delian | dervis | diddle |
| dangle | decade | delict | descry | diesel |
| Danish | decamp | delude | desert | diesis |
| daphne | decant | deluge | design | dieter |
| dapper | decare | de luxe | desire | differ |
| dapple | deceit | delver | desist | digest |
| Dardan | decent | demain | desman | digger |
| daring | decern | demand | despot | diglot |
| darken | decide | demark | des res | dik-dik |
| darkle | decker | demean | detach | dilate |
| darkly | deckle | dement | detail | dilute |
| darnel | decoct | demise | detain | dimity |
| darner | decode | *démodé* | detect | dimmer |
| darter | decree | demote | detent | dimple |
| dartre | deduce | demure | detest | dimply |
| Darwin | deduct | denary | detour | dimwit |
| dasher | deepen | dengue | *de trop* | dingey |
| dative | deeply | denial | deuced | dinghy |
| datura | deface | denier | devest | dingle |
| dauber | defame | denote | device | dinkum |
| dawdle | defeat | dental | devise | dinner |
| day-bed | defect | dentil | devoid | diodon |
| day-fly | defend | dentin | devoir | diplex |
| dazzle | defier | denude | devote | diploe |
| deacon | defile | deodar | devour | dipnoi |
| deaden | define | depart | devout | dipole |
| deadly | deform | depend | dewlap | dipper |
| deafen | defray | depict | dexter | direct |
| deafly | defuse | deploy | dharma | dirndl |
| dealer | defyer | depone | dhurra | disarm |
| dearie | *dégagé* | deport | diadem | disbar |
| dearly | degree | depose | diaper | disbud |
| dearth | dehorn | depute | diatom | discal |
| debark | dehort | deputy | dibber | discus |

| | | | | |
|---|---|---|---|---|
| diseur | domain | dredge | dumdum | effect |
| dishes | domino | dreggy | dunder | effete |
| dismal | donate | drench | dunlin | effigy |
| dismay | donjon | dressy | dunner | efflux |
| disown | donkey | drifty | dupery | effort |
| dispel | doodad | drivel | duplex | effuse |
| distal | doodah | driven | durbar | efreet |
| distil | doodle | driver | duress | EFTPOS |
| disuse | doomed | drogue | durian | egence |
| dither | Dorian | drongo | during | egesta |
| ditone | dormer | droopy | durion | egg-cup |
| divers | dorsal | drop in | duster | eggery |
| divert | dosage | drop-in | dyeing | eggler |
| divest | dossal | dropsy | dynamo | egg-nog |
| divide | dossel | drosky | dynast | egoism |
| divine | dossil | drossy | dysury | egoist |
| diving | dotage | drouth | | egress |
| djerid | dotard | drover | **E** | eighth |
| docent | do time | drowse | eaglet | eighty |
| docile | doting | drowsy | earing | either |
| docker | dotted | drudge | earthy | ejecta |
| docket | dottle | dry ice | earwax | elapse |
| doctor | double | dry-rot | earwig | elated |
| dodder | doubly | dry-run | easily | elater |
| dodger | douche | dubbin | Easter | elchee |
| do down | doughy | ducker | easter | eldest |
| doesn't | dowlas | duckie | eatage | elects |
| dogate | downer | dudeen | eating | elench |
| dog-day | doyley | duello | écarté | eleven |
| dogged | drachm | duenna | echoes | elfish |
| dogger | draffy | duetto | echoic | elicit |
| dog-leg | drafty | duffel | eclair | Elijah |
| doings | dragée | duffer | ectype | Elisha |
| dolent | dragon | duffle | eczema | elixir |
| dollar | draper | duff up | eddish | Elohim |
| dollop | drawee | dugong | Edenic | eltchi |
| dolman | drawer | dug-out | edging | elvish |
| dolmen | dreamt | duiker | edible | elytra |
| dolmen | dreamy | dulcet | editor | embalm |
| dolour | dreary | dumbly | efface | embank |

| | | | | |
|---|---|---|---|---|
| embark | enmesh | equity | Euclid | extasy |
| emblem | enmity | eraser | eulogy | extend |
| embody | ennage | erbium | eunuch | extent |
| emboss | ennead | Erebus | eureka | extern |
| embrue | ennuyé | ere now | Europe | extine |
| embryo | enough | eringo | eutaxy | extoll |
| emerge | enrage | ermine | evenly | extort |
| emetic | enrich | erotic | evicts | extras |
| *émeute* | enrobe | errand | evince | *ex-voto* |
| émigré | *en rôle* | errant | evolve | eyeful |
| empale | enroll | errata | exarch | eyelet |
| empery | ensign | ersatz | exceed | eyelid |
| empire | ensile | eryngo | except | |
| employ | ensure | escape | excern | **F** |
| enable | entail | escarp | excess | Fabian |
| enamel | entice | eschar | excise | fabled |
| enamor | entire | eschew | excite | fabric |
| *en bloc* | entity | escort | excuse | façade |
| encage | entomb | escrow | excuss | facial |
| encamp | entrap | escudo | exempt | facies |
| encase | entrée | Eskimo | exeunt | facile |
| encave | envier | espial | exhale | facing |
| encore | enwrap | espied | exhort | factor |
| encyst | enzyme | espier | exhume | facula |
| endear | Eocene | esprit | Exocet® | fading |
| ending | Eolian | Essene | exodus | faecal |
| endive | eonian | estate | exogen | faeces |
| endure | eonism | esteem | exotic | faerie |
| energy | eosine | estray | expand | fag-end |
| enface | Eozoic | estrum | expect | faggot |
| enfold | eparch | estrus | expend | faille |
| engage | epaule | etcher | expert | fairly |
| engine | ephebe | ethane | expire | fakeer |
| engird | epizoa | ethene | expiry | falcon |
| engore | epodic | ethics | export | fal-lal |
| engulf | eponym | ethnic | expose | fallen |
| enigma | epopee | etymic | exposé | fallow |
| enjoin | equate | etymon | expugn | falter |
| enlace | equine | etypic | exsert | family |
| enlist | Equity | euchre | extant | famine |

| | | | | |
|---|---|---|---|---|
| famish | feller | fierce | flagon | fluted |
| famous | felloe | fiesta | flambé | fluter |
| fanged | fellow | figure | flamen | flying |
| fanner | felony | filial | flange | fo'c'sle |
| fan-tan | female | filing | flashy | fodder |
| fantom | fenced | filler | flatly | foeman |
| fardel | fencer | fillet | flaunt | foemen |
| farina | fender | fillip | flavin | foetal |
| farmer | Fenian | filose | flavor | foetid |
| far-off | fennec | filter | flaxen | foetus |
| far-out | fennel | filthy | flayer | fogeys |
| farrow | feodal | finale | flèche | fogies |
| fasces | ferial | finder | fledge | foible |
| fascia | ferine | finely | fleece | foiler |
| fasten | ferity | finery | fleecy | foison |
| faster | ferret | finger | flench | folder |
| fastly | ferric | finial | flense | foliar |
| fat cat | ferula | fining | fleshy | folksy |
| father | ferule | finish | fleury | follow |
| fathom | fervid | finite | flexor | foment |
| fatten | fervor | finned | flight | fondle |
| fatwah | fescue | finner | flimsy | fondly |
| faucal | festal | fin-ray | flinch | fondue |
| fauces | fester | fiorin | flinty | fontal |
| faucet | fetial | firing | flitch | foodie |
| faulty | fetich | firkin | flocky | footed |
| faunal | fetish | firman | floozy | footer |
| favose | fetter | firmly | floppy | footie |
| favour | fettle | fiscal | floral | footle |
| fawner | feudal | fisher | floret | foozle |
| fealty | fiacre | fishes | florid | forage |
| fecula | fiancé | fistic | florin | forbad |
| fecund | fiasco | fitful | flossy | forbid |
| fedora | fibber | fitter | floury | forcat |
| feeble | fibril | fixity | flower | forced |
| feebly | fibrin | fizgig | fluent | forcer |
| feeder | fibula | fizzle | fluffy | forego |
| feeler | fickle | flabby | flukey | forest |
| feline | fiddle | flacon | flunky | forger |
| fellah | fidget | flaggy | flurry | forget |

| | | | | |
|---|---|---|---|---|
| forgot | fringy | fustet | gamete | gazebo |
| forked | frisky | fustic | gamine | gazing |
| formal | frivol | futile | gaming | gazump |
| format | frizzy | future | gammer | geezer |
| former | froggy | fylfot | gammon | geisha |
| formic | frolic | | gander | Gemini |
| formol | frosty | **G** | ganger | gemmae |
| fornix | frothy | gabble | gangly | gemote |
| forted | frouzy | gabbro | gangue | gender |
| fossae | frowst | gabies | gannet | genera |
| fossil | frowsy | gabion | ganoid | Geneva |
| foster | frowzy | gables | gantry | genial |
| fother | frozen | gablet | gaoler | genius |
| fought | frugal | gadder | garage | gentes |
| foully | fruity | gadfly | garble | gentle |
| fourth | frusta | gadget | *garçon* | gently |
| fowler | frying | gadoid | garden | gentry |
| fox-bat | fucoid | Gaelic | garget | gerbil |
| foxery | fuddle | gaffer | gargle | gerent |
| fracas | *Führer* | gaggle | garish | German |
| fraise | fulcra | gaiety | garlic | german |
| framer | fulfil | gainer | garner | germen |
| frappé | fulgid | gainly | garnet | gerund |
| frater | fuller | 'gainst | garret | gestic |
| frazil | fulmar | gaited | garrot | get off |
| freely | fumble | gaiter | garter | getter |
| freeze | fundus | galago | gasbag | gewgaw |
| French | fun fur | galaxy | Gascon | geyser |
| frenzy | fungal | galena | gasify | gharri |
| fresco | fungus | galiot | gas-jet | gharry |
| fretty | funnel | galley | gasket | ghetto |
| friary | fun run | Gallic | gasman | giaour |
| Friday | furfur | gallon | gastar | gibber |
| fridge | Furies | gallop | gâteau | gibbet |
| friend | furore | galore | gather | gibbon |
| frieze | furred | galosh | gauche | gib-cat |
| fright | furrow | gambir | gaucho | giblet |
| frigid | fusile | gambit | gauger | gifted |
| frijol | fusion | gamble | gavial | giggle |
| fringe | fusted | gambol | gayety | giglet |

giglot
gigolo
gilder
gillie
gimbal
gimlet
ginger
gingko
ginkgo
girder
girdle
girlie
glacis
gladly
glairy
glaive
glamor
glance
glassy
glazer
gleamy
glibly
glider
glioma
glitch
global
globin
gloomy
Gloria
glossa
glossy
gloved
glover
glowed
glower
glozer
glumly
gluten
glycol
gnarly

gnawer
gneiss
gnomic
gnomon
gnosis
goalie
goatee
gobbet
gobble
gobies
goblet
goblin
go bust
go-cart
go down
godson
godwit
goffer
goggle
goitre
go-kart
golden
golfer
golosh
gomuti
gone on
goodly
gopher
gorget
Gorgon
go slow
go-slow
gospel
gossip
Gothic
gotten
gouger
govern
go west
Graces

gradin
grainy
graith
grakle
gramme
grange
granny
grassy
grater
gratis
gravel
graven
graver
graves
gravid
grazer
grease
greasy
greave
greedy
greeny
greyly
grieve
grille
grilse
grimly
gringo
grippe
grisly
grison
gritty
grivet
groats
grocer
groggy
groove
groovy
groped
grotto
grouch

ground
grouse
grovel
grower
growth
groyne
grubby
grudge
grugru
grumpy
grunge
Gueber
Guebre
Guelph
guffaw
guggle
guidon
guilty
guimpe
guinea
guiser
guitar
gulden
gullet
gumlac
gun-dog
gunman
gunnel
gunner
gun-shy
gun-wad
gurgle
gurnet
gusher
gusset
guttae
gutted
gutter
guttle
guzzle

gymnic
gypsum
gyrate
gyrose

**H**

habile
hackee
hacker
hack it
hackle
hadgee
hadith
haemal
hagbut
hagged
haggis
haggle
hairdo
haired
halide
hallal
*Hallel*
halloa!
halloh!
halloo!
hallow
hallux
halter
halves
hamate
Hamite
hamlet
hammal
hammer
hamose
hamous
hamper
handed
handle

| | | | | |
|---|---|---|---|---|
| hangar | healer | heriot | holily | hot air |
| hanger | health | hermit | holism | hot-air |
| hang up | heaper | hernia | holloa! | hotbed |
| hang-up | hearse | heroes | hollow | hotdog |
| hanker | hearth | heroic | holpen | hotpot |
| hankie | hearty | heroin | homage | houdah |
| hansom | heated | herpes | hombre | houmus |
| happen | heater | hetman | homely | hourly |
| haptic | heathy | heyday | homily | housel |
| harass | heaven | hiatus | homing | houses |
| harden | heaver | hibrid | hominy | howdah |
| hardly | Hebrew | hiccup | honcho | howler |
| hard-on | Hecate | hickup | honest | howlet |
| hard-up | heckle | hidden | honied | hoyden |
| harken | hectic | hiding | honour | hubbub |
| harlot | hector | hiemal | hooded | hubcap |
| harper | heddle | higgle | hoodoo | hubris |
| harp on | hedger | higher | hoofed | huckle |
| harrow | heehaw | highly | hoof it | huddle |
| hartal | heeler | high-up | hookah | hugely |
| hasten | Hegira | hijack | hooked | humane |
| hatbox | heifer | hilted | hooker | humble |
| hatred | height | hinder | hooper | humbly |
| hatted | Hejira | Hindoo | hoop-la | humbug |
| hatter | helium | hip-hop | hoopoe | humeri |
| hauler | helmed | hipped | hoopoo | hummer |
| haunch | helmet | hippie | hoorah! | hummus |
| Havana | helper | hispid | hooray! | humour |
| haven't | hemmer | hither | hooves | humous |
| have on | hempen | hit man | hopper | humped |
| having | heptad | hitter | hopple | hunger |
| havock | herald | hoarse | horary | hungry |
| haw-haw | herbal | hobble | horned | hunker |
| hawker | hereat | hob-nob | horner | hunter |
| hawser | hereby | hockey | hornet | hurdle |
| hay-box | herein | hodman | horrid | hurler |
| hazard | hereof | hoiden | horror | hurley |
| headed | hereon | holder | horsey | hurrah! |
| header | heresy | hold up | hosier | hurtle |
| head-on | hereto | hold-up | hostel | husked |

| | | | | |
|---|---|---|---|---|
| hussar | imbrue | indigo | inrush | iodise |
| hussif | immesh | indite | insane | iodism |
| hustle | immune | indium | insect | iodize |
| huzzah! | immure | indoor | insert | iolite |
| Hyades | impact | induce | inside | Ionian |
| hyaena | impair | induct | insist | ionise |
| hybrid | impala | indult | *in situ* | ionize |
| hydric | impale | infamy | insole | ipecac |
| hyemal | impark | infant | inspan | ireful |
| hyetal | impart | infect | instal | irenic |
| Hygeia | impawn | infelt | instep | iridal |
| hymnal | impede | infest | instil | irides |
| hymnic | impend | infirm | insult | iridic |
| hyphen | impish | inflow | insure | irised |
| hyssop | implex | influx | intact | irises |
| | import | infold | intake | iritis |
| **I** | impose | inform | intend | ironer |
| iambic | impost | infula | intent | ironic |
| iambus | impugn | infuse | interj. | irrupt |
| iatric | impure | ingest | intern | Isabel |
| ibises | impute | ingulf | in time | island |
| ice age | inarch | inhale | intone | isobar |
| icebox | in a rut | in hand | *in toto* | isogon |
| ice-cap | inborn | inhere | in-tray | isohel |
| ice-saw | inbred | in hock | intuit | isomer |
| icicle | incage | inhume | inulin | isopod |
| ID card | incase | inject | invade | issued |
| ideate | incept | injure | invent | italic |
| idiocy | incest | injury | invert | itself |
| idolon | incise | inking | invest | |
| idolum | incite | ink-sac | invite | **J** |
| ignite | income | inlaid | in vivo | jabber |
| ignore | incubi | inland | invoke | jabiru |
| iguana | incult | inmate | inwall | jacana |
| illude | incuse | inmesh | inward | jackal |
| illume | indeed | inmost | in with | jacket |
| ill-use | indent | innate | inworn | jadish |
| imaret | Indian | inning | inwrap | jagged |
| imbibe | indict | Innuit | iodide | jaguar |
| imbody | indign | inroad | iodine | jailer |

| | | | | |
|---|---|---|---|---|
| jailor | jocose | kabuki | kiblah | kumiss |
| jalopy | jocund | Kabyle | kibosh | kümmel |
| jangle | jogger | Kaffir | kicker | kung fu |
| jargon | joggle | kaftan | kiddie | kvetch |
| jarool | joiner | Kaiser | kidnap | |
| jarrah | jojoba | kakapo | kidney | **L** |
| jasmin | Joseph | kalian | killer | laager |
| jasper | jostle | kalmia | kilted | labial |
| jaunty | jotter | Kalmuk | kilter | labile |
| Jaycee | jounce | Kalmyk | kimono | labium |
| jeerer | jovial | kalong | kincob | labour |
| jejune | Jovian | kalpak | kindle | labret |
| jennet | joyful | kamala | kindly | labrum |
| jerbil | joyous | kamsin | kingly | laches |
| jerboa | jubate | kaolin | kipper | lacing |
| jereed | Judaic | karate | kirsch | lacker |
| jerked | judder | karroo | kirtle | lackey |
| jerkin | Judean | kavass | kismet | lacmus |
| jersey | jugate | kawass | kisser | lactic |
| jessed | juggle | keblah | kit-cat | lacuna |
| jester | juicer | kecksy | kitsch | ladder |
| Jesuit | jujube | keddah | kitten | laddie |
| jet-lag | Julian | keeled | kittle | la-de-da |
| jetsam | jumble | keenly | klaxon | la-di-da |
| jet-set | jumper | keeper | knaggy | ladies |
| jetsom | jungle | kelpie | knight | lading |
| jewels | jungly | kelson | knives | lagoon |
| Jewess | junior | Keltic | knobby | lagune |
| Jewish | *Junker* | kelvin | knotty | laical |
| jigger | junker | kennel | knower | lambda |
| jiggle | junket | kermes | kobold | lamely |
| jigsaw | junkie | kermis | koodoo | lament |
| jingal | juries | kernel | kookie | lamina |
| jingle | jurist | kersey | kopeck | Lammas |
| jingly | justle | ketone | Korean | lampas |
| jinnee | justly | kettle | kosher | lanate |
| jitter | just so | keypad | kosmos | lancer |
| jobber | | khalif | kowtow | lancet |
| job lot | **K** | kibble | kraken | landau |
| jockey | kabala | kibitz | Kronia | landed |

| | | | | |
|---|---|---|---|---|
| lander | layman | *l'envoi* | lilies | lizard |
| langur | laymen | *l'envoy* | limbed | llanos |
| lankly | lay off | leonid | limber | Lloyd's |
| lanner | lay-off | lepton | limner | loaded |
| lap-dog | layout | lesion | limous | loader |
| lapper | lazily | lessee | limpet | loadsa |
| lappet | lazuli | lessen | limpid | loafer |
| lapsed | leaded | lesser | linage | loathe |
| lapsus | leaden | lesson | linden | loaves |
| lap-top | leader | lessor | lineal | lobate |
| larder | leafed | lethal | linear | lobule |
| largen | league | letter | line-up | locale |
| lariat | leanly | Levant | lingam | locate |
| larvae | lean on | levant | linger | locker |
| larval | lean-to | levier | linhay | locket |
| larynx | leaper | levies | lining | lock up |
| lascar | leased | Levite | link up | lock-up |
| lasher | leaved | levity | link-up | locule |
| lassie | leaven | lewdly | linnet | loculi |
| lastly | leaves | liable | lintel | locust |
| lateen | lecher | liaise | lionet | lodger |
| lately | lector | libido | liplet | loggat |
| latent | ledger | Libyan | lipoid | loggia |
| latest | leeway | lichee | lipped | loggie |
| lathen | legacy | lichen | liquid | log-hut |
| lather | legate | lictor | liquor | log-jam |
| Latino | legato | lidded | lisper | loiter |
| latish | leg-bye | lie low | lissom | lollop |
| latria | legend | lierne | listed | loment |
| latten | legged | lifter | listen | lonely |
| latter | legion | ligate | litany | loofah |
| launch | legist | ligger | litchi | looker |
| laurel | legume | lights | lithia | look in |
| lavabo | lender | lignin | lithic | look up |
| lavish | length | lignum | litmus | looney |
| lawful | lenity | ligula | litter | looper |
| lawyer | lenses | ligule | little | loosen |
| laxity | lenten | ligure | lively | lopper |
| laying | lentil | likely | livery | loquat |
| lay low | lentor | liking | living | lorate |

| | | | | |
|---|---|---|---|---|
| lorcha | lustra | make do | manual | mastic |
| lordly | lustre | make it | manure | matins |
| lorica | Lutine | make up | maraca | matrix |
| loring | lutist | make-up | maraud | matron |
| lorrie | luxate | making | marble | matted |
| losing | luxury | Makkah | marbly | matter |
| lost on | Lyceum | malady | marcel | mature |
| lotion | lychee | malaga | marcid | maugre |
| louche | Lydian | malice | margay | maxima |
| louden | lyrate | malign | margin | maxixe |
| loudly | lyrist | mallee | Marian | May-bug |
| lounge | lysine | mallet | marina | May Day |
| louver | | mallow | marine | Mayday |
| louvre | **M** | maltha | marish | May-dew |
| lovage | macaco | mammae | marked | mayfly |
| lovely | mackle | mammal | markee | mayhap |
| loving | macron | mammee | marker | mayhem |
| lowboy | macula | mam- | market | Maying |
| lowery | macule | mon | mark up | mazard |
| lowest | madame | manage | mark-up | mazier |
| low-fat | madcap | mañana | marlin | mazily |
| lowing | madden | Manchu | marmot | mazuma |
| low-key | madder | *manège* | maroon | meadow |
| lubber | madman | manful | marque | meagre |
| lucent | madmen | manger | marrow | meanie |
| lucern | madras | mangle | marshy | meanly |
| lugger | maduro | maniac | marten | measly |
| lumbar | maenad | Manila | martin | meatus |
| lumber | maggot | manioc | martyr | meddle |
| lumpen | magian | manito | marvel | medial |
| lumper | magilp | manitu | mascle | median |
| lump it | magnet | manned | mascot | Medica |
| lunacy | magnum | manner | masher | Medici |
| lunate | magpie | manqué | mashie | medick |
| lunged | maguey | mantel | masked | medico |
| lunula | Magyar | mantic | masker | medium |
| lunule | mahout | mantis | masque | medlar |
| lupine | maiden | mantle | massif | medley |
| lurdan | maigre | mantra | masted | medusa |
| lurker | mainly | mantua | master | meekly |

| | | | | |
|---|---|---|---|---|
| meetly | metric | minuet | molten | motive |
| megass | mettle | minute | moment | motley |
| megilp | miasma | miosis | Monday | motmot |
| megohm | mickle | mirage | moneys | motory |
| megrim | micron | mirror | monger | mottle |
| mellay | midair | misery | Mongol | mottos |
| melley | midday | misfit | monied | moujik |
| mellow | midden | mishap | monies | mouldy |
| melody | middle | Mishna | monism | moulin |
| melter | midget | mislay | monist | Mounty |
| melton | mid-leg | missal | monkey | mouser |
| member | midrib | missee | monody | mousey |
| memoir | midway | missis | moorva | mousse |
| memory | mighty | missus | mopish | mouths |
| menace | mikado | mister | moppet | moving |
| *ménage* | milady | misuse | morale | mowing |
| mender | milage | mitral | morass | mozzie |
| menhir | milden | mitred | morbid | mucker |
| menial | mildew | mitten | moreen | muck in |
| menses | mildly | mizzen | morgue | mucose |
| mental | milieu | mizzle | Morian | mucous |
| mentor | milker | mob-cap | morion | muddle |
| mercer | milled | mobile | morish | muesli |
| merely | miller | mob law | Mormon | muffin |
| merger | millet | mocker | mornay | muffle |
| merino | milord | mock-up | morose | muftee |
| Merlin | milter | modern | morris | muggar |
| merlin | mimosa | modest | morrow | muggee |
| merlon | minced | modify | morsel | mugger |
| merman | minded | modish | mortal | muggur |
| mesail | minder | module | mortar | mulish |
| mesial | mingle | moggie | morula | Mullah |
| Messrs | minify | moghul | Mosaic | mullen |
| mestee | minima | mohair | mosaic | muller |
| metage | mining | Mohawk | Moslem | mullet |
| meteor | minion | moiety | mosque | mumble |
| method | minish | molder | mostly | mummer |
| methyl | minium | molest | mother | mumper |
| métier | minnow | Mollah | motile | murder |
| metope | minter | Moloch | motion | murine |

| | | | | |
|---|---|---|---|---|
| murmur | naiant | Nemean | nipple | nudism |
| murphy | nailer | nephew | nitric | nudist |
| murrey | namely | Nereid | nitwit | nudity |
| Muscat | nandou | nereis | nobble | nugget |
| muscat | nankin | neroli | nobody | nullah |
| muscle | napalm | nerved | noddle | number |
| museum | napery | nestle | nod off | nuncio |
| musing | napkin | Nestor | nodose | nursed |
| musket | napper | nether | nodule | nutant |
| musk-ox | nardoo | netted | noetic | nutmeg |
| Muslim | narial | nettle | noggin | nutria |
| muslin | narine | neural | no joke | nutter |
| mussel | narrow | neuron | nomade | nuzzle |
| mustee | narwal | neuter | nonage | nylgau |
| muster | nasute | New Age | nonego | nympho |
| mutant | natant | Newark | noodle | |
| mutate | nation | newish | Nordic | **O** |
| mutely | native | New Man | normal | oafish |
| mutiny | natron | newton | Norman | obelus |
| mutism | natter | nibble | nosing | obeyer |
| mutter | nature | nicely | notary | object |
| mutton | naught | Nicene | notice | oblate |
| mutual | nausea | nicety | notify | oblige |
| mutule | nautch | niched | notion | oblong |
| muzhik | neaped | nickel | nougat | oboist |
| muzzle | nearby | nicker | nought | obolus |
| myopia | nearly | nidify | nounal | obsess |
| myosis | neaten | nid-nod | novena | obtain |
| myotic | neatly | niello | novice | obtect |
| myriad | nebula | niggle | noways | obtest |
| myrica | necked | nighty | nowise | obtund |
| myrtle | nectar | nilgai | noyade | obtuse |
| myself | needed | nilgau | nozzle | obvert |
| mystic | needle | nimble | nuance | occult |
| mythic | needly | nimbly | nubbin | occupy |
| | needn't | nimbus | nubile | ocelli |
| **N** | negate | Nimrod | nuchal | ocelot |
| naevus | nekton | ninety | nuclei | ochrea |
| nagana | nelson | niobic | nudely | o'clock |
| Nagari | nem. con. | nipper | nudged | octane |

octant
octave
octavo
octroi
ocular
oddity
odds-on
odious
oedema
oeuvre
off day
offend
office
offing
offish
off-key
off-set
of note
ogdoad
ogress
oidium
oilbag
oilcan
oilery
oil-gas
oilman
oil rig
Old Boy
old boy
old hat
oldish
old man
oleate
olefin
omasum
omelet
omened
*omertà*
onager
on edge

one-off
one-way
on-line
onrush
on time
onward
oodles
ooidal
oolite
oology
oolong
oomiak
oompah
opaque
opened
opener
openly
ophite
opiate
oppose
oppugn
optics
option
orache
oracle
orally
orange
orator
orchid
orchil
orchis
ordain
ordeal
orders
ordure
orgasm
orgeat
orgies
Orient
orient

origin
oriole
orison
ormolu
ornate
ornery
oroide
orphan
Orphic
orpine
orrery
osiery
osmium
osmose
osmund
ospray
osprey
ossein
ossify
osteal
ostler
oswald
otalgy
otiose
otitis
ouster
outbid
outcry
outfit
outfox
outgun
outing
outlaw
outlay
outlet
output
outrun
outsat
outset
outsit

outvie
outwit
ovally
overdo
ovisac
owlery
owlish
oxalic
oxalis
ox-eyed
ox-gall
ox-gang
ox-horn
ox-tail
oxygen
oxymel
oyster

**P**
pacify
packer
packet
padder
paddle
paella
pagoda
paigle
pained
pakeha
pakora
palace
palate
paleae
palely
paling
palish
pallah
pallet
pallia
pallid

pallor
palmar
palmed
palmer
palpus
palter
paltry
pampas
pamper
panada
panama
panary
pander
pandit
pantry
panzer
papacy
papaya
papery
papist
pappus
papula
papule
papyri
parade
paramo
parang
paraph
parcel
pardon
parent
parget
pariah
Parian
paring
parish
parity
parley
parody
parole

| | | | | |
|---|---|---|---|---|
| parrot | peahen | penult | phylum | pinked |
| parsec | peaked | penury | physic | pinkie |
| Parsee | peanut | people | phyton | pinnae |
| parson | pearly | peplum | piaffe | pintle |
| partan | pebble | peplus | pianos | piping |
| partly | pebbly | pepper | piazza | pipkin |
| parvis | pecker | pepsin | pickax | pippin |
| pascal | pecten | peptic | picked | piquet |
| passée | pectic | perdue | picker | piracy |
| passer | pectin | period | picket | pirate |
| passim | pedalo | perish | pickle | Pisces |
| pass up | pedant | permit | pick-up | pistil |
| pastel | pedate | perron | picnic | pistol |
| pastil | peddle | person | picric | piston |
| pastor | pedlar | pertly | piddle | pitchy |
| pastry | pedler | peruke | pidgin | pitier |
| patchy | peeler | peruse | piecer | pitman |
| patent | peeper | pesade | pierce | pitmen |
| patera | peepul | peseta | piffle | pitsaw |
| pathos | peeved | pester | pigeon | pitted |
| patina | peewit | pestle | piggin | placer |
| patois | pegged | petard | piglet | placid |
| patrol | peg out | petite | pignut | plagal |
| patron | peg-top | petrel | pig out | plague |
| patten | pelage | petrol | pigsty | plaguy |
| patter | pellet | pewter | pilaff | plaice |
| paunch | pelmet | pharos | pile-up | plaint |
| pauper | pelota | phases | pileus | planar |
| pavage | peltry | phasis | pilfer | planet |
| pavane | pelvic | phenol | piling | plaque |
| paving | pelvis | phenyl | pillar | plashy |
| pavise | pencil | phlegm | pillau | plasma |
| pawner | penile | phloem | pillow | platan |
| pawpaw | penman | phobia | pilose | plated |
| paxwax | penmen | pholas | pilule | platen |
| payday | penner | phoney | pimple | plater |
| paynim | pennon | phonic | pimply | player |
| payola | pen pal | photic | pineal | play up |
| pay-out | pentad | phrase | pinery | pleach |
| peachy | pent-up | phreak | pinion | please |

| | | | | |
|---|---|---|---|---|
| pledge | polype | potent | prolix | punter |
| Pleiad | polypi | pother | prolog | pupate |
| plenty | pomace | potion | prompt | puppet |
| plenum | pomade | potted | pronto | purana |
| pleura | pommel | potter | propel | purdah |
| plexor | Pomona | pottle | proper | purely |
| plexus | pompom | pounce | proser | purfle |
| pliant | pompon | pouter | pro tem | purger |
| pliers | poncho | powder | proton | purify |
| plight | ponder | powwow | proven | purine |
| plinth | pongee | praise | prover | purism |
| plough | ponies | prance | pruner | purist |
| plover | poodle | prater | prying | purity |
| plucky | poonac | praxis | pseudo | purlin |
| plumed | pooped | prayer | psyche | purple |
| plummy | poorly | preach | ptosis | purser |
| plumpy | pop art | précis | public | pursue |
| plunge | popery | prefab | pucker | purvey |
| plural | pop-gun | prefer | puddle | pusher |
| poachy | popish | prefix | puddly | putlog |
| pocket | poplar | prepay | pueblo | putrid |
| podded | poplin | preset | puffer | putsch |
| podium | poppet | presto | puffin | puttee |
| poetic | porgie | pretor | pug-dog | putter |
| poetry | porism | pretty | puisne | puzzle |
| pogrom | porker | pre-war | puling | pyemia |
| poiser | porous | prey on | pulkha | pygarg |
| poison | portal | priced | pullet | pyrope |
| polder | porter | pricey | pulley | python |
| police | portly | priest | pulpit | pyuria |
| policy | poseur | primal | pulque | |
| Polish | posset | primer | pulsar | **Q** |
| polish | possum | primly | pumice | quagga |
| polite | postal | primus | pummel | quaggy |
| polity | poster | prince | pumper | quahog |
| pollan | potale | priory | punchy | quaint |
| polled | potash | prison | pundit | Quaker |
| pollen | potato | privet | punish | quango |
| pollex | pot-boy | profit | punkah | quanta |
| polony | poteen | proleg | punner | quarry |

quarte
quarto
quartz
quasar
quaver
queasy
quench
quiche
quince
quinoa
quinsy
quirky
quitch
quiver
quorum
quoter
quotha!
qwerty

**R**
rabbet
rabbin
rabbis
rabbit
rabble
rabies
raceme
rachis
racial
racily
racing
racism
racker
racket
racoon
raddle
radial
radian
radish
radium

radius
radome
radula
raffia
raffle
rafter
ragbag
ragged
raggee
raging
Raglan
ragman
ragout
raider
railer
raiser
raisin
raking
rakish
ramble
ramify
ram-jet
rammer
ramose
ramous
ramrod
ramson
rancho
rancid
rancor
random
ranger
rankle
rankly
ransom
ranter
rapids
rapier
rapine
rapist

rappee
rappel
rapper
raptor
rarefy
rarely
raring
rarity
rascal
rasher
rashly
rasper
raster
rasure
ratbag
rather
ratify
rating
ration
ratios
ratite
ratlin
ratoon
rat-pit
rat-run
rattan
ratten
ratter
rattle
ravage
rave-up
ravine
raving
ravish
rawish
razzia
reader
really
realty
reaper

reason
reaver
rebate
rebeck
rebuff
rebuke
recall
recant
recast
recede
recent
recess
recipe
recite
reckon
recoil
record
recoup
rectal
rector
rectum
rectus
redact
red-cap
redden
reddle
redeem
red-eye
red fox
red-hot
redout
redraw
reduce
re-echo
reechy
reeded
reefer
refill
refine
reflex

reflux
refold
reform
reform
refuel
refuge
refund
refuse
refute
regain
regale
regard
regent
reggae
regime
regina
region
regius
reglet
regnal
regret
rehash
rehear
reject
rejoin
relate
relent
relict
relief
relier
relish
relive
relume
remain
remake
remand
remark
remedy
remind
remiss

| | | | | |
|---|---|---|---|---|
| remora | retail | ribose | roller | rugged |
| remote | retain | riches | roll on | rugger |
| remove | retake | richly | roll-on | rugose |
| rename | retard | rictus | Romaic | rugous |
| renard | retina | ridden | Romany | ruiner |
| render | retire | riddle | Romish | ruling |
| renege | retort | riding | rondel | rumble |
| rennet | return | rifely | ronion | rummer |
| renown | retuse | riffle | roofer | rumour |
| rental | revamp | rifler | rookie | rumple |
| renter | reveal | rigger | rooted | rumpus |
| reopen | revels | rigour | rope in | runlet |
| repaid | reverb | rillet | ropery | runnel |
| repair | revere | rimple | ropily | runner |
| repand | revers | ringed | rosary | runnet |
| repass | revert | ringer | rosery | run-off |
| repast | revery | rinser | rosiny | runrig |
| repeal | review | rioter | roster | runway |
| repeat | revile | ripely | rostra | rupiah |
| repent | revise | rip-off | rotary | rushes |
| repine | revive | ripost | rotate | russet |
| report | revoke | ripple | rot-gut | rustic |
| repose | revolt | riprap | rotten | rustle |
| repute | reward | rip-saw | rotund | |
| resale | rewind | rising | rouble | **S** |
| rescue | rewire | risker | rubber | Sabine |
| reseat | reword | risqué | rubble | sachem |
| resect | rework | ritual | rubied | sachet |
| resent | Rexine® | rivage | rubies | sacker |
| reship | rhesus | rivery | rubigo | sacque |
| reside | rheumy | roadie | rubine | sacral |
| resign | rhinal | roamer | rubric | sacred |
| resile | rhymer | roarer | rudder | sacrum |
| resiny | rhythm | robber | ruddle | sadden |
| resist | rialto | robust | ruddoc | saddhu |
| resorb | riancy | rochet | rudely | saddle |
| resort | ribald | rocker | rueful | sadism |
| result | riband | rocket | ruffle | safari |
| resume | ribbed | rococo | rufous | safely |
| resumé | ribbon | rodent | rugate | safety |

| | | | | |
|---|---|---|---|---|
| sagely | sanity | scarfs | scummy | seeing |
| saggar | sanjak | scarry | scurfy | seeker |
| sagger | sannah | scathe | scurry | seemer |
| sailer | sannup | scatty | scurvy | seemly |
| sailor | santon | scenic | scutch | see red |
| sakieh | sapper | schema | scutum | see-saw |
| salaam | sarong | scheme | scuzzy | seethe |
| salami | sashay | schism | scythe | seggar |
| salary | sasine | schist | sea-cat | seiche |
| salify | sateen | schizo | sea-cow | seiner |
| salina | satiny | schlep | sea-dog | seizer |
| saline | satire | school | sea-ear | seizin |
| saliva | satori | schuss | sea-eel | sejant |
| sallet | satrap | scilla | sea-egg | seldom |
| sallow | Saturn | sclera | sea-fir | select |
| salmis | saucer | sconce | sea-fox | seller |
| salmon | savage | scorch | sea-god | selves |
| saloon | savant | scorer | sealer | Semite |
| saloop | savate | scoria | seaman | semola |
| salter | savine | Scotch | seamen | sempre |
| saltly | saving | scotch | seamer | Semtex® |
| Saluki | savory | scoter | sea-mew | senary |
| salute | savour | scotia | séance | senate |
| salver | saw-fly | Scouse | searce | sendal |
| salvia | sawpit | scrape | search | sender |
| salvor | saw-set | scrawl | seared | send up |
| samara | sawyer | screak | season | send-up |
| Samian | Saxony | scream | seated | Seneca |
| samite | saying | screed | sea-way | senega |
| samlet | sayyid | screen | secant | senile |
| Samoan | 'sblood | screes | secede | senior |
| samosa | scabby | screwy | secern | sennit |
| sampan | scalar | scribe | second | señora |
| sample | scaled | scrimp | secret | sensor |
| sancta | scaler | script | sector | sentry |
| sandal | scampi | Script. | secund | sepsis |
| sander | scanty | scroll | secure | septet |
| sandix | scapus | scruff | sedate | septic |
| sandyx | scarab | scrump | seduce | septum |
| sanies | scarce | sculpt | seeded | sequar |

| | | | | |
|---|---|---|---|---|
| sequel | shanty | shower | simmer | ski tow |
| sequin | shaper | shrank | simony | skiver |
| seraph | sharer | shrewd | simoom | skivvy |
| serene | shaven | shriek | simoon | slabby |
| serial | shaver | shrift | simous | slaggy |
| series | sheafy | shrike | simper | slalom |
| seriph | shears | shrill | simple | slangy |
| sermon | sheath | shrimp | simply | slap-up |
| seroon | sheave | shrine | Sinaic | slated |
| serous | sheeny | shrink | sin bin | slater |
| serval | sheers | shrive | sinewy | slaver |
| server | sheikh | shroud | sinful | Slavic |
| sesame | sheila | shrove | singer | slayer |
| sestet | shekel | shrunk | single | sleave |
| set off | shelfy | shtoom | singly | sleaze |
| set-off | shelly | shucks | sinker | sleazy |
| setose | shelty | shufti | sinner | sledge |
| settee | shelve | shufty | sinter | sleeky |
| setter | shelvy | sicken | Siouan | sleepy |
| settle | Sherpa | sickie | siphon | sleety |
| severe | sherry | sickle | sippet | sleeve |
| Sèvres | shewed | sickly | sirdar | sleigh |
| sewage | shield | siding | Sirius | sleuth |
| sewing | shiest | sienna | sirrah | slicer |
| sewn-up | shifty | sierra | sirree | slider |
| sexism | Shiite | siesta | siskin | sliest |
| sexist | shimmy | sifter | sister | slight |
| sextet | shiner | signal | sitcom | slinky |
| sexton | Shinto | signer | sit out | slip-on |
| sexual | shinty | signet | sitter | slippy |
| shabby | shirty | signor | size up | slip up |
| shadow | shiver | silage | sizing | sliver |
| shaggy | shoaly | silent | sizzle | slogan |
| shaken | shoddy | silica | skater | sloppy |
| shaker | shogun | silken | skerry | slouch |
| shaman | shoo-in | silure | sketch | slough |
| shammy | shoppy | silvan | skewer | Slovak |
| shamoy | shored | silver | skibob | sloven |
| shandy | should | simian | skimpy | slowly |
| shanny | shovel | simile | skinny | sludge |

| | | | | |
|---|---|---|---|---|
| sludgy | soaker | souled | spoken | stadia |
| sluice | socage | source | sponge | staffs |
| sluicy | soccer | sourly | spongy | stager |
| slurry | social | soviet | spoony | staith |
| slushy | socket | sovran | sporan | stalag |
| smarmy | sodden | sowans | sporty | stalky |
| smegma | sodium | sowens | spot-on | stamen |
| smilax | sodomy | spaced | spotty | stance |
| smiler | soever | spacey | spouse | stanch |
| smirch | soffit | spadix | sprain | stanza |
| smiter | soften | sparry | sprang | stapes |
| smithy | softly | sparse | sprawl | staple |
| smoker | soigné | Sparta | spread | starch |
| smooch | soirée | spathe | sprier | stared |
| smooth | solace | spavin | spring | starer |
| smudge | solder | specie | sprint | starry |
| smudgy | sold on | speech | sprite | starve |
| smugly | solely | speedy | sprout | stated |
| smutch | solemn | spence | spruce | States |
| smutty | soleus | sphere | sprung | states |
| snaggy | solidi | sphery | spunge | static |
| snappy | so long | sphinx | spunky | stator |
| snarer | solute | spider | spurge | statue |
| snatch | solver | spiffy | spurge | status |
| snazzy | Somali | spigot | sputum | staves |
| sneaky | somber | spilth | squall | stayer |
| sneeze | sombre | spinal | squama | steady |
| sniffy | somite | spined | square | steamy |
| snitch | sonant | spinel | squash | steely |
| snivel | sonata | spinet | squawk | steeve |
| snobby | sonnet | spinny | squeak | stelae |
| Sno-Cat® | soothe | spiral | squeal | stench |
| snooty | sorbet | spired | squill | step in |
| snooze | sordid | spirit | squint | steppe |
| snorer | sorely | splash | squire | step up |
| snotty | sorrel | spleen | squirm | step-up |
| snouty | sorrow | splice | squirt | stereo |
| snuffy | sorter | spline | squish | steric |
| snugly | sortie | splint | stable | sterol |
| soaked | sought | spoilt | stably | sticky |
| | | | stacte | |

stifle
stigma
stilly
stingo
stingy
stinko
stipes
stitch
stithy
stiver
stocks
stocky
stodge
stodgy
stoker
stolen
stolid
stolon
stoned
stoner
stones
stoney
stooge
storax
storer
storey
stormy
strafe
strain
strait
strake
strand
strass
strata
strath
strawy
streak
stream
street
stress

striae
strict
stride
strife
strike
Strine
string
stripe
strive
strobe
strode
stroke
stroll
strong
strove
struck
struma
strung
stubby
stucco
studio
stuffy
stumpy
stupid
stupor
sturdy
stylar
stylet
stylus
stymie
suable
subdue
sublet
submit
suborn
subtle
subtly
suburb
subway
sucker

suckle
sudden
suffer
suffix
sugary
suitor
sulcus
sulfur
sullen
sultan
sultry
sumach
summer
summit
summon
sun-bow
sundae
sunder
sundew
sundry
sunken
sunlit
sunset
suntan
superb
supine
supper
supple
supply
surely
surety
surtax
survey
sutile
sutler
suttee
suture
svelte
swampy

swardy
swarth
swathe
sweaty
sweepy
swerve
swinge
swipes
switch
swivel
sylvan
symbol
syndic
syntax
syphon
Syriac
Syrian
syrinx
syrupy
system
syzygy

**T**
tabard
tablet
tabour
tabret
tabula
tackle
tactic
taenia
tag-end
tag-rag
tahini
tailed
tailor
taipan
take in
taking
talcky

talent
talion
talker
talkie
tallow
Talmud
tamale
tamely
tamine
taminy
tamper
tampon
tam-tam
tan-bed
tandem
tangle
tangly
tanist
tanked
tanker
tanner
tannic
tannin
tan-pit
tanrec
tan-vat
Taoism
tappet
target
Targum
tariff
Tarmac®
tarpan
tarpon
tarsal
tarsia
tarsus
tartan
tartar
tarter

| | | | | |
|---|---|---|---|---|
| tartly | temper | thenar | thwack | tinner |
| tasker | temple | thence | thwart | tin-pot |
| tassel | tenant | theory | thymol | tinsel |
| taster | tender | theses | thymus | tip-cat |
| tatami | tendon | thesis | thyrse | tip off |
| tatter | tenner | Thetis | thyrsi | tip-off |
| tattle | tennis | thewed | tibial | tippet |
| tattoo | ten-pin | they'll | ticker | tipple |
| taught | tenrec | they're | ticket | tiptoe |
| Taurus | tenson | they've | tickle | tip-top |
| tauten | tensor | thieve | tickly | tirade |
| tautog | tented | thinly | tidbit | tiring |
| tavern | tenter | thirst | tiddly | tissue |
| tawdry | tenure | thirty | tidily | tis-was |
| tawery | tenuto | thorax | tied up | titbit |
| tax cut | tepefy | thorny | tie-dye | tither |
| t-cloth | teraph | thoron | tie-pin | titled |
| tea-bag | tercel | thorpe | tierce | titter |
| tea-cup | tercet | though | tie-rod | tittle |
| teapot | teredo | thowel | tie-wig | tiz-woz |
| teapoy | terete | thrall | tiffin | tmesis |
| tearer | tergal | thrash | tights | to a man |
| teasel | termly | thread | tiglon | tocsin |
| teaser | terror | threat | tilery | toddle |
| tea-set | tester | three-D | tiling | toe-cap |
| teated | testes | threne | tiller | toe-rag |
| tea-urn | testis | thresh | tilter | toffee |
| teazel | tetchy | thrice | timber | toggle |
| teazle | tether | thrift | timbre | toiler |
| tedder | tetrad | thrill | timely | toilet |
| Te Deum | tetter | thrips | timing | toller |
| tedium | Teuton | thrive | timist | tomato |
| teemer | thaler | throat | timous | tomaun |
| teepee | thanks | throes | tinder | tombac |
| teeter | thatch | throne | tinges | tomboy |
| teethe | thecal | throng | tingle | tom-cat |
| Teflon® | theine | throve | tin god | tom-tit |
| teledu | theirs | thrown | tinker | tom-tom |
| teller | theism | thrush | tinkle | tongue |
| telson | theist | thrust | tinman | tonite |

| | | | | |
|---|---|---|---|---|
| tonsil | trance | trophi | turkey | ulster |
| tonsor | trapan | trophy | turner | ultima |
| too bad | trapes | tropic | turnip | ultimo |
| tooter | trashy | trough | turn on | umbles |
| toothy | trauma | troupe | turn-on | umlaut |
| top dog | travel | trover | turn-up | umpire |
| top-hat | treaty | trowel | turret | unable |
| topper | treble | truant | turtle | unbend |
| topple | trebly | trudge | turves | unbias |
| torero | tremor | truism | Tuscan | unbind |
| Tories | trench | trumps | tusked | unbolt |
| toroid | trendy | trusty | tusker | unborn |
| torpid | trepan | trying | tussle | uncase |
| torpor | tressy | tryout | tut-tut | uncial |
| torque | triage | tsetse | tuxedo | uncoil |
| torrid | tribal | T-shirt | tuyère | uncord |
| tosser | tricky | tubful | twelve | uncork |
| toss up | trifid | tubing | twenty | uncurl |
| toss-up | trifle | tubule | twiggy | undies |
| tother | trigon | tucker | twilit | undine |
| totter | trilby | tucket | twinge | undoer |
| toucan | trimly | tuffet | twisty | undone |
| touché | trinal | tufted | twitch | unduly |
| touchy | triode | tugger | two-bit | uneasy |
| toupee | triple | tulwar | two-ply | uneven |
| toupet | triply | tumble | 'twould | unfair |
| tousle | tripod | tumefy | two-way | unfelt |
| touter | tripos | tumour | tycoon | unfold |
| towage | Triton | tumult | tympan | unfree |
| toward | triton | tundra | typhus | unfurl |
| towery | triune | tune up | typify | ungird |
| townie | trivet | tune-up | typist | unglue |
| toxoid | trivia | tuning | tyrant | ungual |
| toy-boy | trocar | tunnel | Tyrian | unhand |
| toyman | troche | turban | | unholy |
| tracer | trogon | turbid | **U** | unhood |
| traces | troika | turbot | ubiety | unhook |
| trader | Trojan | tureen | uglily | unhung |
| trades | trolly | turfen | ullage | unhurt |
| tragic | troops | turgid | Ulster | uniped |

| | | | | |
|---|---|---|---|---|
| unique | unship | uprush | valuer | vermin |
| unisex | unshod | upshot | valuta | vernal |
| unison | unsold | upside | valvar | versed |
| united | unstop | upsoar | valved | versus |
| uniter | unsung | uptake | vamose | vertex |
| unjust | untidy | upturn | vamper | vervet |
| unkind | untold | upward | vandal | vesica |
| unknit | untrod | upwind | vanish | vesper |
| unlace | untrue | uranic | vanity | vessel |
| unlade | untune | Uranus | vapour | vestal |
| unlaid | unused | urbane | varied | vested |
| unless | unveil | urchin | varlet | vestry |
| unlike | unwary | ureter | vassal | vetchy |
| unlink | unwell | uretic | vastly | viable |
| unload | unwept | urgent | vatful | vibrio |
| unlock | unwind | urinal | vector | victim |
| unmake | unwise | ursine | veiled | victor |
| unmask | unworn | usable | veined | vicuña |
| unmeet | unwrap | usance | Velcro® | vid-kid |
| unmixt | unyoke | useful | vellum | vielle |
| unmoor | upbear | usurer | veloce | viewer |
| unpack | upbeat | uterus | velour | vigour |
| unpaid | upbind | utmost | velure | viking |
| unpick | upcast | utopia | velvet | vilely |
| unread | upcoil | uvular | vendee | vilify |
| unreal | upcurl | | vender | villus |
| unrest | update | **V** | vendor | vinery |
| unripe | uphill | vacant | vendue | vinose |
| unrobe | uphold | vacate | veneer | vinous |
| unroll | upkeep | vacuum | venery | violas |
| unroof | upland | vagary | venial | violet |
| unroot | uplift | vagina | Venite | violin |
| unruly | up-line | vainly | venose | virago |
| unsafe | upmost | valgus | venous | virgin |
| unsaid | uppish | valine | venter | virile |
| unseal | uppity | valise | verbal | virose |
| unseat | uprear | vallar | verger | virtue |
| unseen | uprise | valley | verify | visage |
| unsent | uproar | valour | verily | visard |
| unshed | uproot | valued | verity | viscid |

| | | | | |
|---|---|---|---|---|
| viscum | walker | wax-end | whinge | winkle |
| viscus | walk-in | waylay | whinny | winner |
| vision | walk it | way-out | whisky | winnow |
| visual | walk on | weaken | whiten | winsey |
| vitals | walk-on | weakly | whites | winter |
| vitric | wallah | wealth | whitey | wintry |
| vittae | walled | weapon | wholly | wiring |
| vivace | waller | wearer | whoops! | wisdom |
| vivify | wallet | weasel | whoosh | wisely |
| vizard | wallop | weaver | whydah | wisher |
| vizier | wallow | weazen | wicked | withal |
| voiced | walnut | webbed | wicker | wither |
| voided | walrus | web-eye | wicket | within |
| voider | wampum | wedded | widdle | witted |
| volant | wander | weeder | widely | witter |
| volley | wangle | weekly | widget | wivern |
| volume | wanion | weeper | wieldy | wizard |
| volute | wanker | weepie | wifely | wobble |
| volvox | wanted | weever | wigeon | woeful |
| voodoo | wanter | weevil | wigged | wolves |
| vortex | wanton | wee-wee | wiggle | wombat |
| votary | wapiti | weight | wigwam | wonder |
| votive | warble | weirdo | wilder | wonted |
| vox pop | war-cry | welder | wildly | wooded |
| voyage | warden | welkin | wilful | wooden |
| voycur | warder | welter | wilily | woofer |
| Vulcan | warily | weren't | willow | wooing |
| vulgar | warmer | wether | wimble | woolly |
| | warmly | wet rot | wimple | woopie |
| **W** | warmth | whaler | wincer | worker |
| wabble | warm-up | wharfs | wincey | wormed |
| waddle | warner | wheeze | winded | worrit |
| wadmal | warped | wheezy | winder | worsen |
| waffle | warper | whence | window | worthy |
| wafter | warren | wherry | wind up | wowser |
| waggle | washer | wheyey | wind-up | wraith |
| waggon | wasted | whilom | winery | wrap up |
| wainer | waster | whilst | winged | wrasse |
| waiter | watery | whimsy | wing it | wreath |
| waiver | wattle | whiner | winker | wrench |

wrests

wretch

wriest

wright

writer

writhe

wrongs

wyvern

**X**

xenian

xyloid

xylose

xyster

xystos

xystus

**Y**

yabber

Yahveh

Yahweh

yammer

Yankee

yapock

Yardie

yarrow

yatter

yaupon

yclept

yearly

yeasty

yellow

yeoman

yeomen

yes-man

yes-men

yester

yields

yippee

yogurt

yoicks!

yonder

yttria

yttric

yum-yum

yuppie

**Z**

zaccho

zaffre

zander

zantha

zapper

zareba

zariba

zealot

zebeck

zechin

zenana

zenith

zephyr

zereba

zeugma

zigzag

zillah

Zimmer®

zincky

zinnia

zipper

zircon

zither

zodiac

zombie

zonary

zonate

zonked

zonule

Zouave

zounds!

zygoma

zygote

# Seven-letter words

**A**
Aaronic
abaddon
abalone
abandon
abashed
abattis
abaxial
abdomen
abetter
abiding
abietic
abigail
ability
ableism
ableist
abluent
abolish
aboulia
abreact
abreast
abridge
abroach
abscess
abscind
abscond
absence
absinth
absolve
abstain
abusive
abuttal
abutter
abysmal

abyssal
academy
Acadian
acaudal
accidie
acclaim
accompt
account
accrete
accurse
accurst
accused
accuser
acerbic
acerose
acerous
acetate
acetify
acetone
acetose
acetous
achaean
Achates
achieve
acicula
acidify
acidity
acolyte
aconite
acorned
acquire
acreage
acrobat
acrogen

acronym
acrylic
actable
actinia
actinic
actress
actuary
actuate
aculeus
acutely
adagial
adamant
Adamite
adapter
adaptor
adaxial
addable
addible
address
adducer
adenoid
adenoma
adherer
adhibit
adipose
adjourn
adjudge
adjunct
adjurer
admiral
admirer
adopter
adrenal
adulate

advance
adverse
advised
adviser
Aeolian
aeonian
aerator
aerobic
aerosol
affable
affably
affiche
affixal
afflict
affront
African
against
agatine
agatise
agatize
ageless
age-long
agendum
aggress
agilely
agility
agitate
agitato
agnomen
agnosia
agonise
agonist
agonize
agraffe

aground

aidless

aileron

ailment

aimless

air base

air cell

aircrew

air-drop

air-head

airless

air-lift

air-line

air-lock

airmail

air-miss

air-play

airport

air-pump

air raid

airship

air-sick

air side

air-time

ajutage

alameda

alamode

*à la mode*

albumen

alcaide

alcalde

alcazar

alchemy

alcohol

alcoran

*al dente*

alecost

alembic

alewife

alfalfa

algebra

alienee

alienor

aliform

aliment

alimony

aliquot

alkanet

alkoran

all ears

allegro

allergy

all-hail

all over

all-over

allowed

all-star

all-time

all told

almanac

almoner

almonry

aloetic

already

alright

also-ran

althaea

althorn

alumina

alumnus

alunite

amalgam

amateur

amative

amatory

amazing

ambatch

ambient

amboina

amboyna

ambroid

ambs-ace

amender

amenity

amentia

amentum

Amerind

ames-ace

amiable

amiably

amianth

ammeter

ammonal

ammonia

amnesia

amnesty

amongst

amorino

amorist

amoroso

amorous

amphora

amplify

ampoule

ampulla

amusing

amusive

amylase

amylene

amyloid

anaemia

anaemic

anagoge

anagogy

anagram

analect

analogy

analyse

analyst

analyze

anapest

anarchy

anatomy

anberry

anchovy

ancient

andante

andiron

android

anemone

aneroid

angelic

angelus

Angevin

angioma

anglify

angling

angrily

anguine

anguish

angular

aniline

animate

animato

animism

animist

aniseed

annates

annatto

annelid

annotto

annuent

annuity

annular

annulet

annulus

anodyne

anomaly

anorexy

anosmia

another
antacid
ant-bear
ant-bird
antenna
ant-hill
anthine
anthrax
antigen
antilog
antique
ant-lion
antonym
anurous
anxiety
anxious
anybody
anymore
anywise
apagoge
apanage
apatite
apepsia
aphagia
aphasia
aphemia
aphesis
aphetic
aphonia
aphthae
apishly
apocope
apogamy
apology
apostil
apostle
apparel
appease
applaud
applied

appoint
apprise
apprize
approve
appulse
apraxia
apricot
a priori
apropos
apsidal
apteral
apteryx
aptness
aquatic
aqueous
Arabian
arachis
Aramaic
Aramean
araneid
arbiter
arblast
arbutus
arcaded
Arcadia
arcanum
archaic
archery
archive
archway
arcuate
ardency
arduous
areolar
argyria
aridity
arietta
armhole
armiger
armilla

Armoric
armoury
arnotto
arousal
arraign
arrange
arrears
arrival
arsenal
arsenic
Art Deco
article
artisan
artiste
artless
aruspex
ascetic
ascites
ascribe
asepsis
asexual
ashamed
ashtray
Asiatic
asinine
askance
asocial
asperse
asphalt
aspirer
aspirin
asquint
assagai
assault
assayer
assegai
asshole
assizer
assuage
assumer

assured
assurer
at stake
astatic
asteria
astound
astrict
astride
asunder
ataraxy
atavism
atelier
at heart
atheism
atheist
atheous
athirst
athlete
athwart
atomise
atomism
atomist
atomize
atropal
atrophy
atropin
attaché
attaint
attempt
attract
auberge
auction
audible
audibly
auditor
augitic
augment
augural
aurated
aureate

aurelia
aureola
aureole
auricle
aurochs
auroral
auspice
austere
austral
autarky
autocar
Autocue®
automat
autopsy
avarice
avenger
average
averter
aviator
avidity
avocado
awarder
awesome
awfully
awkward
awnless
axially
axillar
axolotl
Azilian
azimuth
azotise
azotize
azurite
azygous

**B**
Baalism
Baalite
babbler

babyish
babyism
baby-sit
baccate
bacchic
back-end
backing
backlog
back-pay
bad debt
baddish
badness
baffler
bagasse
baggage
bagging
bag lady
bagpipe
bailiff
bail out
baklava
balance
balanus
balcony
balding
baldric
baleful
ballade
ballast
ball boy
balloon
balls-up
baloney
bambino
bandage
bandana
bandbox
bandeau
bandlet
bandora

bandore
bandrol
band-saw
baneful
banking
banksia
bannock
banquet
banshee
banting
baptise
baptism
Baptist
baptize
barbate
barbell
barbule
bar code
bargain
barilla
bar-iron
bark-bed
barking
barmaid
barm pot
barn-owl
baronet
baroque
barrack
barrage
barrier
barring
bar-shot
barwood
barytes
barytic
bascule
baseman
bashful
basilar

basinet
bassist
bassoon
bastard
bastion
bath-tub
batiste
batsman
battery
battish
bauxite
bay-leaf
bayonet
bay-salt
baywood
bazooka
beached
beading
beaming
beanbag
bearded
bear hug
bearing
bearish
beastly
beatify
beating
beauish
bebeeru
be big of
because
becharm
becloud
bedding
bedegar
bedevil
bedight
bedizen
Bedouin
bed-post

| | | | |
|---|---|---|---|
| bedrock | benison | big game | bivalve |
| bedroom | benthos | biggish | bivouac |
| bedside | benzene | big guns | bizarre |
| bed-sore | benzine | big-head | blabber |
| bed-tick | benzoin | big-horn | blacken |
| beechen | bequest | big name | blackly |
| beef-tea | bereave | bigness | bladder |
| beehive | berried | bigoted | blanket |
| beeline | berserk | bigotry | blankly |
| bee-moth | beshrew | big shot | blarney |
| beestie | beshrew | big time | blasted |
| beeswax | besides | biliary | blaster |
| beggary | besiege | bilious | blatant |
| Beghard | besmear | billing | blather |
| begonia | bespeak | billion | bleakly |
| begorra! | bespoke | billman | bleater |
| begrime | bestead | billowy | bleeder |
| beguile | bestial | bilobed | blemish |
| beguine | best man | biltong | blender |
| behoove | bestrew | binacle | blesbok |
| bejewel | beta ray | bindery | blessed |
| belated | bethink | binding | blether |
| Belgian | betimes | binocle | blewits |
| believe | betoken | biogeny | blinded |
| bell-boy | betroth | biology | blinder |
| bell-hop | between | bionics | blindly |
| bellied | betwixt | biotaxy | blinker |
| belljar | bevvied | biplane | blister |
| bellman | bewitch | bipolar | bloated |
| bellmen | bezetta | birchen | bloater |
| bellows | bezique | biretta | blooded |
| beloved | biaxial | biryani | bloomer |
| Beltane | bibasic | biscuit | blooper |
| belting | bibelot | bismuth | blossom |
| bemused | bicycle | bistort | blotchy |
| bencher | bidding | bit-part | blotter |
| beneath | bifilar | bit-rate | bloused |
| benefit | bifocal | bittern | blow-dry |
| Bengali | big bang | bitters | blow-fly |
| benight | big deal | bitumen | blow-job |

| | | | |
|---|---|---|---|
| blow-out | book-end | boyhood | brevity |
| blowzed | bookish | brabble | brewage |
| blubber | booklet | bracing | brewery |
| Blucher | bookman | bracken | brewing |
| blue-cap | bookmen | bracket | bribery |
| blue-gum | boorish | bradawl | bricole |
| blueing | booster | bragget | bridoon |
| blunder | bootleg | Brahman | briefly |
| bluntly | boracic | Brahmin | brigade |
| blusher | bordure | braided | brigand |
| bluster | boredom | Braille | brigate |
| boarded | bornite | brained | brimful |
| boarder | borough | bramble | brimmer |
| boarish | borscht | brambly | brinded |
| boaster | boscage | branchy | brindle |
| boat-fly | boskage | branded | bringer |
| boating | bosquet | brander | brinish |
| boatman | botanic | brangle | brioche |
| boatmen | botargo | bran-new | briquet |
| bob-sled | botcher | brasier | brisket |
| bobstay | bottine | brassie | briskly |
| bob-tail | boudoir | brattle | bristle |
| bodeful | bouilli | bravado | bristly |
| body-bag | boulder | bravely | British |
| boggler | bouncer | bravery | Brit pop |
| boiling | bounced | bravura | brittle |
| boletus | bounden | brawler | britzka |
| bollard | bounder | brazier | broaden |
| boloney | bouquet | breaded | broadly |
| bolshie | bourbon | breadth | brocade |
| bolster | bourdon | breaker | brocage |
| bombard | bourrée | break in | brocard |
| bombast | bow-hand | break-in | brocket |
| bonanza | bow-head | break up | broider |
| bondage | bowline | break-up | broiler |
| bondman | bowling | breathe | brokage |
| bone-ash | bowshot | breathy | broking |
| bone-bed | box-tree | breccia | bromate |
| bone-dry | boxwood | breeder | bromide |
| bonfire | boycott | brevier | bromine |

bronchi
bronzed
brothel
brother
brought
Brownie
brownie
bruiser
brush up
brush-up
brusque
brutify
brutish
bryozoa
buck-eye
buckish
buckler
buckram
bucolic
budding
buffalo
buffoon
bug-bear
buggery
bugloss
builder
built-in
built-up
bulbous
bulimia
bullace
bullate
bulldog
bullion
bullock
bulrush
bulwark
bumboat
bumpkin
bungler

bunk bed
bunting
buoyage
buoyant
burdock
burette
burgage
burgeon
burgess
burghal
burgher
burglar
Burmese
burning
burnish
burnous
burn out
burrito
bursary
burthen
bush-cat
bushing
bushman
bushmen
bussing
bustard
bustier
bustler
busy bee
butcher
buttery
buttock
butyric
buxomly
buzzard
buzz-saw
by and by
bygones
byssine
by the by

**C**
cabaret
cabbage
cabbala
cabined
cabinet
cable TV
caboose
cachexy
cacique
cackler
cacodyl
cacolet
cadaver
caddice
cadence
cadenza
Cadmean
cadmium
caesium
caesura
cahoots
caisson
caitiff
cajoler
cajuput
calamus
calando
calcify
calcine
calcite
calcium
caldera
caldron
calèche
calends
calibre
calices
calipee
caliper

caliver
callant
call-box
call-boy
calling
callous
calomel
caloric
calorie
calotte
caloyer
calpack
caltrap
caltrop
calumba
calumet
calumny
Calvary
calycle
calypso
camaieu
cambist
cambium
cambric
camelry
Camorra
camphor
campion
camwood
canakin
canasta
candela
candent
candida
candied
candour
canella
cannery
cannula
canonry

cantata
canteen
canthus
canting
cantlet
cantrip
canvass
canzona
canzone
capable
capably
cap-à-pie
capelin
caperer
capital
Capitol
caporal
caprice
caprine
caproic
capsize
capstan
capsule
captain
caption
captive
capture
capuche
caracal
caracol
caramel
caravan
caravel
caraway
carbide
carbine
carcake
carcase
carcass
cardiac

cardoon
careful
car hire
caribou
cariole
carious
carline
carling
Carlist
carlock
carmine
carnage
carnify
caroche
carolus
carotid
carouse
car-park
carping
car port
carrack
carrier
carrion
carroty
car-sick
cartage
cartoon
cart-way
carving
cascade
cascara
case-law
caseous
caserne
cashier
cassaba
cassada
cassata
cassava
cassock

casting
castled
castlet
cast off
cast-off
casuist
Catalan
catalpa
catarrh
catawba
cat-bird
cat-boat
catcall
catcher
catch it
catchup
catch up
catechu
cateran
caterer
cat-fish
cat-head
cathode
cathood
cat-like
catling
catmint
Cat scan
Cat's eye®
cat's-eye
cat's paw
cattery
cat-walk
caudate
cauline
caustic
cautery
caution
cavalry
caveman

caveson
cavetto
caviare
cayenne
cazique
cedilla
cedrate
ceiling
celadon
celesta
celeste
cellist
Cellnet®
cellule
Celsius
Celtist
censure
centage
centaur
centavo
centime
centner
central
centric
century
ceramic
cereous
certain
certify
cerumen
cervine
cession
cesspit
cestoid
cetacea
chablis
chabouk
chaffer
chagrin
Chaldee

chalice
challis
chamade
chamber
chamfer
chamois
champac
chancel
chancre
changer
channel
chanson
chanter
chantey
chantry
chaotic
chapati
chapeau
chaplet
chapman
chapmen
chapped
chapter
charade
charger
charily
chariot
charism
charity
charmed
charmer
charnel
charpai
charpie
charpoy
charqui
charter
chasmed
chassis
chasten

chateau
chattel
chatter
cheapen
cheaply
cheater
checker
check up
check-up
Cheddar
cheerer
cheetah
chemise
chemist
chequer
cherish
cheroot
chervil
chesnut
chessel
chested
cheviot
chevron
Chianti
chiasma
chibouk
chicane
Chicano
chicken
chicory
chiefly
chiffon
chignon
chiliad
chimera
chimere
chimney
Chinese
chinned
Chinook

chintzy
chinwag
chipper
chirper
chirrup
chisleu
chlamys
chloral
chloric
cholera
chooser
chopine
chopper
chorale
chorion
chorist
chorizo
choroid
chortle
chowder
chrisom
chromic
chronic
chuckle
chukker
chunder
Chunnel
chunter
chutney
chutzpa
chylify
chylous
chymify
chymous
ciliary
Cimbric
cimeter
cindery
cineast
cipolin

Circean
circled
circler
circlet
circuit
cirrose
cirrous
cissoid
cistern
citable
citadel
cithara
cithern
citizen
citrate
citrine
cittern
civilly
clachan
clacker
clamant
clamber
clamour
clanger
clangor
clap-net
clapper
clarify
clarion
clarity
clarkia
clasper
classic
clastic
clatter
clavate
clavier
clay-pit
cleaner
cleanly

cleanse
clearer
clearly
cleaver
clement
clerisy
clerkly
clicker
climate
climber
clinger
clinker
clipper
clivers
cloacal
clobber
closely
close-up
closing
closure
clothes
clouded
clouted
clovery
cloying
club-law
clumber
clupeid
cluster
clutter
clypeal
clypeus
clyster
coagent
coal-bed
coal-gas
coalman
coalmen
coal-oil
coal-pit

coal-tar
coaming
coarsen
coaster
coating
coaxial
cobbler
cocaine
cochlea
cockade
cockney
cockpit
cock-shy
coconut
cocotte
coctile
coction
codeine
codicil
codilla
codling
coehorn
coeliac
coequal
coexist
cogency
cognate
cognise
cognize
cohabit
cohibit
coinage
coition
cojuror
cola-nut
coldish
cold war
colibri
colicky
colitis

collage
collate
collect
colleen
college
collide
collier
colloid
collude
colobus
cologne
colonel
colored
coloury
coltish
combine
combing
combust
come out
comfort
comfrcy
comical
comique
comitia
command
commend
comment
commode
commons
commove
commune
commute
compact
company
compare
compart
compass
compeer
compend
compere

compete
compile
complex
complin
complot
comport
compose
compost
compote
compute
comrade
conacre
con brio
concave
conceal
concede
conceit
concept
concern
concert
concisc
concoct
concord
concuss
condemn
condign
condole
condone
conduce
conduct
conduit
condyle
confect
confess
confest
confide
confine
confirm
conflux
conform

| | | | |
|---|---|---|---|
| confuse | cookery | Cossack | cow-fish |
| confute | cookout | costard | cowgirl |
| congeal | coolant | costate | cowhage |
| congest | coolish | costive | cow-heel |
| conical | copaiba | costrel | cowherd |
| conifer | copilot | costume | cowhide |
| conjoin | copious | coterie | cowitch |
| conjure | coppery | cothurn | cowlick |
| conjury | coppice | cotidal | cowling |
| con moto | copyist | cottage | cow-poke |
| connate | coquito | cottier | cow-pony |
| connect | coracle | cottony | cowslip |
| conning | corbeil | couchée | cow-tree |
| connive | corcule | coucher | coxcomb |
| connote | cordage | cougher | coyness |
| conquer | cordate | couldn't | cozener |
| consent | cordial | couloir | crabbed |
| consign | cordite | coulomb | cracked |
| consist | corkage | coulter | cracker |
| console | corkleg | council | crackle |
| consols | corn-cob | counsel | cragged |
| consort | cornice | counter | crammer |
| consult | Cornish | country | cramped |
| consume | cornute | coupler | crampon |
| contact | corolla | couplet | cranage |
| contain | coronal | coupure | cranial |
| contemn | coroner | courage | cranium |
| contend | coronet | courier | crankle |
| content | corpora | courser | crannog |
| contest | correct | courter | craunch |
| context | corrode | courtly | craving |
| contort | corrupt | couture | crawler |
| contour | corsage | couvade | crazily |
| control | corsair | coverer | creamer |
| contuse | corslet | cover up | creatin |
| convene | corsned | cover-up | creator |
| convent | cortege | coveter | credent |
| convert | corvine | cow-bane | credits |
| convict | cosaque | cow-bird | creeper |
| convoke | cosmism | cow-calf | cremate |

cremona
crenate
creosol
cresset
crested
crevice
crew cut
cribble
cricket
cricoid
crimper
crimple
crimson
cringer
cringle
crinite
crinkle
crinoid
cripple
crisper
crispin
crisply
critter
crizzle
croaker
crochet
crocket
crofter
crooked
cropper
croquet
crosier
crossed
crossly
croûton
crowbar
crowded
crowned
crozier
crucial

crucify
crudely
crudity
cruelly
cruelty
cruiser
cruisie
crumble
crumbly
crumpet
crumple
crunchy
crupper
crusade
crusado
crusher
crybaby
cryogen
cryptal
cryptic
crystal
cry wolf
ctenoid
cubhood
cubical
cubicle
cubital
cuckold
cudbear
cudweed
cue ball
cuirass
cuisine
cullion
culprit
culture
culvert
cumshaw
cumulus
cuneate

cunning
cupping
cuprite
cuprous
curable
curaçao
curator
curbing
curcuma
curette
curious
curling
currant
current
currier
currish
cursing
cursive
cursory
curstly
curtail
curtain
curtsey
curvity
cushion
custard
custody
cut-away
cut-back
cut dead
cuticle
cutlass
cutlery
cutting
cutwork
cyanate
cyanean
cyanide
cyclist
cycloid

cyclone
Cyclops
cynical
cypress
Cyprian
Cypriot
cystoid
czardas
czarina

**D**
dabbler
dab hand
dacoity
dahbiah
daisied
dakoity
dallier
damnify
damning
dampish
dandify
Danelaw
dangler
*danseur*
dappled
darkish
darling
darning
dashing
dashpot
dastard
dasyure
daunter
dauphin
dawdler
dawning
day-book
day-long
days-man

| | | | |
|---|---|---|---|
| day-star | decuple | demerit | despond |
| daytime | deedful | demesne | dessert |
| day-work | deep-fry | demigod | destine |
| dazzler | deep-sea | demi-rep | destiny |
| dead-end | defacer | demonic | destroy |
| dead-eye | de facto | demotic | détente |
| deadpan | defamer | denizen | deterge |
| dead set | default | densely | detinue |
| dealing | defence | density | detract |
| deanery | defiant | dentate | detrain |
| deathly | deficit | dentine | detrude |
| debacle | defiler | dentist | deutzia |
| debased | defined | dentoid | devalue |
| debaser | definer | denture | develop |
| debater | deflate | deodand | deviant |
| debauch | deflect | deplane | deviate |
| debouch | deforce | deplete | devilry |
| debrief | defraud | deplore | devious |
| decadal | defrock | deplume | devisee |
| decagon | defrost | deposer | deviser |
| decanal | defunct | deposit | devisor |
| decapod | de-gauss | deprave | devoirs |
| decease | degrade | dcpress | devolve |
| deceive | dehisce | deprive | devoted |
| decency | deicide | derange | devotee |
| decibel | deictic | derider | dew-claw |
| decided | deiform | deriver | dew-drop |
| decider | deistic | dermoid | dew-fall |
| decidua | dejecta | derrick | dextral |
| decimal | delaine | dervish | dextrin |
| declaim | delayer | descant | diabase |
| declare | delight | descend | diagram |
| decline | delimit | descent | dialect |
| decoder | deliver | deserve | dialist |
| decorum | delouse | desirer | dialyse |
| decreer | Delphic | desmoid | diamond |
| decreet | deltaic | despair | diapasm |
| decrial | deltoid | despise | diarchy |
| decrier | deluder | despite | diarian |
| decuman | demerge | despoil | diarist |

| | | | |
|---|---|---|---|
| dibasic | direful | distent | done for |
| dibbler | dirt-bed | distich | donnish |
| dice-box | dirtily | distill | do or die |
| dickens | disable | distort | doorman |
| dictate | disavow | disturb | doormen |
| diction | disband | disyoke | doormat |
| Didache | discage | ditcher | doorway |
| die hard | discard | dittany | do out of |
| die-hard | discern | diurnal | do proud |
| dietary | discoid | diverge | dormant |
| dieting | discord | diverse | dossier |
| dietist | discous | divider | dottrel |
| difform | discuss | diviner | doublet |
| diffuse | disdain | divisor | doubter |
| digamma | disease | divorce | douceur |
| digging | disgust | divorcé | doughty |
| digital | dishing | divulge | dove-cot |
| dignify | disjoin | dizzily | dovelet |
| dignity | dislike | djereed | dowager |
| digraph | dislink | dockage | dowered |
| digress | dismask | doeskin | drabble |
| dilater | dismast | dog-cart | drachma |
| dilator | dismiss | dog-days | draftee |
| dilemma | disobey | dog-fish | draggle |
| diluent | dispark | doggish | dragman |
| dimeter | dispart | doggone | dragmen |
| dimmish | display | dog-hole | drag-net |
| dimness | dispone | dog-rose | dragoon |
| dimpled | disport | dog's-ear | drainer |
| dimyary | dispose | dog-sick | drapery |
| dinette | dispute | dog-skin | drapier |
| diocese | disrobe | dog-trot | drastic |
| dioptre | disroot | dogwood | dratted |
| diorama | disrupt | dolabra | draught |
| diorite | dissect | doleful | drawing |
| dioxide | dissent | dolphin | drayage |
| diploma | distaff | doltish | drayman |
| diplopy | distain | domical | draymen |
| dipolar | distant | domicil | dreamer |
| diptych | distend | dominie | dredger |

dresser
dribble
driblet
drifter
drinker
drip-dry
drive-in
drizzle
drizzly
dromond
dronish
droplet
drop off
dropout
drop out
dropper
droshky
drought
drouthy
drugget
druidic
drummer
drum out
drunken
dry dock
dryness
dry-salt
dry-shod
dualism
dualist
duality
dubbing
dubiety
dubious
ducally
duchess
ductile
dudgeon
dukedom
dulcify

dullard
dullish
dulness
dumpish
duncery
dungeon
dunnage
dunnish
dunnite
dupable
durable
durably
duramen
durance
durmast
duskily
duskish
dustbin
dustman
dustmen
duteous
dutiful
duumvir
dweller
dwindle
dyarchy
dye-wood
dyingly
dynamic
dynasty
dyslogy
dyspnea
dysuria
dysuric

**E**

eagerly
eanling
earache
ear-drop

ear-drum
ear-hole
earldom
earless
ear-mark
earnest
earning
ear-pick
ear-plug
earring
earshot
earthen
earthly
easeful
eastern
easting
eatable
eat crow
ebb-tide
ebonise
ebonite
ebonize
ebriety
ecbatic
ecbolic
ecdysis
echelon
echidna
echinus
eclipse
eclogue
ecology
economy
Ecstasy
ecstasy
ectopia
ectopic
ectozoa
ectypal
edacity

edictal
edifice
edition
educate
eel-buck
eel-pout
effable
Effendi
effulge
egg-bird
egg-flip
egg-head
egotise
egotism
egotist
egotize
ego trip
eidolon
ejector
elastic
elation
elderly
eldrich
elector
electro
elegant
elegiac
elegise
elegist
elegize
element
elevate
elf-bolt
elfland
elf-lock
elision
elitism
elixate
ellagic
ellipse

| | | | |
|---|---|---|---|
| elogium | emulous | ensnare | epizoan |
| Elohist | enactor | en suite | epizoon |
| elusion | enamour | entasis | epochal |
| elusive | enchain | entente | epsilon |
| elusory | enchant | enteric | equable |
| Elysian | enchase | enthral | equably |
| Elysium | enclasp | enthuse | equally |
| elytron | enclave | enticer | equator |
| elytrum | enclose | entitle | equerry |
| emanant | encrust | entomic | equinox |
| emanate | endemic | entonic | erasion |
| embargo | endless | entrail | erasure |
| embassy | endlong | entrain | erecter |
| emblaze | endogen | entrant | erectly |
| embolus | endorse | entreat | erector |
| embosom | endower | entropy | ere long |
| embowel | endways | entrust | eremite |
| embower | endwise | entwine | ergoted |
| embrace | energic | entwist | eristic |
| embroil | enfeoff | E-number | ermined |
| embrown | enforce | envelop | erosion |
| embryos | engaged | envenom | erotica |
| emerald | English | envious | erotism |
| emerods | engorge | environ | erratic |
| emersed | engraft | epacrid | erratum |
| eminent | engrail | eparchy | erudite |
| emirate | engrain | epaulet | escapee |
| emotion | engrave | epergne | escheat |
| emotive | engross | epicarp | esparto |
| empanel | enhance | epicene | espouse |
| empathy | enjoyer | epicure | esquire |
| emperor | enlarge | epiderm | essence |
| empiric | enliven | epidote | esthete |
| emplane | en masse | epigene | estival |
| empower | ennoble | epigram | estuary |
| empress | enounce | episode | étagère |
| emprise | enquire | epistle | etching |
| emptier | enquiry | epitaph | eternal |
| empyema | en route | epithet | etesian |
| emulate | enslave | epitome | ethical |

| | | | |
|---|---|---|---|
| ethmoid | exscind | falbala | fateful |
| euphony | externe | falcate | fathead |
| evacuee | extinct | fallacy | fatidic |
| evangel | extract | fall guy | fatigue |
| evasion | extreme | fall-out | fatling |
| evening | extrude | falsely | fatness |
| evident | exudate | falsify | fattism |
| evil eye | exuviae | falsism | fattist |
| ewe lamb | exuvial | falsity | fatuity |
| exactly | eyeball | famulus | fatuous |
| examine | eyebrow | fanatic | faunist |
| example | eyelash | fan-belt | faux pas |
| exarchy | eyeless | fancied | fearful |
| excerpt | eyeshot | fancier | feaster |
| excited | eyesore | fancies | feather |
| exclaim | eye-spot | fan club | feature |
| exclave | eye-wash | fanfare | febrile |
| exclude | | fan-palm | fedayee |
| excreta | **F** | fantail | federal |
| excrete | fabliau | fantasm | feeding |
| execute | faceted | fantast | feeling |
| exergue | faction | fantasy | feigned |
| exhaust | factoid | fanzine | feigner |
| exhibit | factory | faradic | felsite |
| exigent | factual | faraway | felspar |
| exoderm | facular | farceur | felting |
| exogamy | faculty | farcing | felucca |
| exotica | faddish | fardage | fencing |
| expanse | faddist | farming | feodary |
| exparte | fadedly | farmost | feoffee |
| expense | faecula | farness | feoffer |
| expiate | faience | farrago | feoffor |
| explain | failing | farrier | ferment |
| explode | failure | farther | fermion |
| exploit | faintly | fascine | fermium |
| explore | fair do's | fascism | fernery |
| exposed | fairily | fascist | fern-owl |
| expound | fairing | fashion | ferrate |
| express | fairish | fast day | ferrous |
| expunge | fairway | fatally | ferrule |

fertile
fervent
fervour
festive
festoon
fetlock
feudary
feudist
fewness
fiancée
fiascos
fibrine
fibroid
fibroin
fibroma
fibrous
fibster
fictile
fiction
fictive
fiddler
fidgety
fielder
fierily
fifteen
fifthly
fighter
figment
figural
figured
filbert
filcher
filemot
filiate
filibeg
filical
filings
filling
Filofax®
finable

finagle
finally
finance
fin-back
finding
finesse
finical
finicky
finikin
finless
Finnish
firearm
firebox
fire-bug
fire-dog
fired up
firefly
fireman
firemen
fire-new
fire-pan
fire-pot
firstly
fishery
fishily
fishing
fishnet
fissile
fission
fissure
fistula
fitchet
fitchew
fitment
fitness
fitting
fixable
fixated
fixedly
fixings

fixture
flaccid
flag day
flambée
flaming
flaneur
flanker
flannel
flapper
flare up
flare-up
flaring
flasket
flat-cap
flatten
flatter
flattie
flaunty
flavine
flavour
fleapit
fleeced
fleecer
fleerer
fleetly
Fleming
Flemish
fleshed
flesher
fleshly
fleuret
flexile
flexion
flexure
flicker
flighty
flipper
flitter
flivver
floater

floccus
flogger
floorer
floosie
floozie
florist
flotage
flotsam
flounce
flouter
flowage
flowery
flowing
fluency
flummox
flunkey
fluoric
fluorin
fluster
flutina
fluting
flutist
flutter
fluvial
fluxion
fly-away
fly-blow
fly-leaf
fly-over
fly-past
fly-trap
f-number
foggage
foggily
fog-horn
fogyism
folacin
folding
foliage
foliate

| | | | |
|---|---|---|---|
| foliole | for good | freshen | fulmine |
| foliose | forlorn | fresher | fulness |
| fondant | formate | freshet | fulsome |
| foolery | Formica® | freshly | fulvous |
| foolish | formula | fretful | fumbler |
| footage | forsake | fretsaw | fumette |
| footing | for show | fretted | funeral |
| footman | fortify | friable | fungoid |
| footmen | fortlet | fribble | fungous |
| foot-pad | Fortran | friezed | funicle |
| foot-rot | fortune | frigate | funnily |
| footsie | forward | fringed | furbish |
| footway | forwent | Frisbee® | furcate |
| fopling | fossick | Frisian | furcula |
| foppery | foulard | frisket | furioso |
| foppish | foumart | frisson | furious |
| forager | founder | frit-fly | furlong |
| foramen | foundry | fritter | furmety |
| forayer | fourgon | frizzle | furnace |
| forbade | foveate | frizzly | furnish |
| forbear | fox-hole | frocked | furrier |
| forbore | foxtail | frogged | furring |
| forceps | fox-trot | frogman | furrowy |
| forcing | fragile | frogmen | further |
| forearm | frailty | frontal | furtive |
| foreign | frame-up | fronted | fuscous |
| foreleg | framing | frounce | fusible |
| foreman | frankly | froward | fussily |
| foremen | frantic | frowsty | fustian |
| forerun | fraught | fruiter | futharc |
| foresee | frazzle | frustum | futhark |
| foretop | freckle | fuchsia | futhorc |
| forever | freckly | fuchsin | futhork |
| forfeit | freebie | fuddler | futtock |
| forfend | freedom | *Fuehrer* | |
| forgave | freeman | fueller | **G** |
| forgery | freemen | fuguist | gabbler |
| forging | freesia | fulcrum | gabelle |
| forgive | freezer | fulgent | gadroon |
| forgoer | freight | fulling | gadwall |

| | | | |
|---|---|---|---|
| gahnite | gaseity | geology | glebous |
| gainful | gaseous | georgic | gleeful |
| gaining | gastric | germane | gleeman |
| gainsay | gateman | gestalt | gleemen |
| galanga | gateway | Gestapo | gliding |
| Galatea | gaudery | gestate | glimmer |
| galatea | gaudily | gesture | glimpse |
| galeate | gauffer | getaway | glisten |
| Galenic | Gaulish | ghastly | glister |
| Galilee | gauntly | gherkin | glitter |
| galipot | gavotte | ghillie | globate |
| gallant | gayness | ghostly | globoid |
| galleon | gazelle | giantly | globose |
| gallery | gazette | giantry | globous |
| Gallice | gear-box | gibbose | globule |
| galling | gearing | gibbous | glorify |
| galliot | Gehenna | giblets | glosser |
| gallium | gelatin | giddily | glossic |
| gall-nut | gelding | giggler | glottal |
| galloon | gelidly | gilding | glottic |
| gallows | gemmate | gimbals | glottis |
| galumph | gemmule | gimblet | glowing |
| gambado | gemsbok | gimmick | glucina |
| gambier | general | gingham | glucose |
| gambler | generic | ginseng | gluteal |
| gamboge | genesis | gipsies | gluteus |
| gambrel | genetic | giraffe | glutton |
| gangway | genette | girasol | glyphic |
| gantlet | Genevan | girlish | glyptic |
| garbage | genipap | girosol | gnarled |
| garbler | genital | gittern | gnathal |
| garboil | genitor | gizzard | gnathic |
| gardant | genteel | glacial | gnocchi |
| garfish | gentian | glacier | gnostic |
| garland | gentile | gladden | go-ahead |
| garment | genuine | glamour | goatish |
| garnish | genuses | glaring | gobbler |
| garotte | geodesy | glazier | goddess |
| garpike | geogeny | glazing | Godhead |
| garrote | geogony | gleaner | Godhood |

| | | | |
|---|---|---|---|
| godless | grained | griddle | guarded |
| godlike | grainer | griffin | gubbins |
| godlily | gramary | griffon | gudgeon |
| godsend | grammar | grimace | guerdon |
| godship | grampus | grimily | guesser |
| go Dutch | granary | grinder | guilder |
| godward | grandam | griping | guildry |
| goitred | grandee | gripper | guipure |
| golfing | grandly | griskin | gumboil |
| goliard | grandma | grisled | gum-boot |
| gondola | grandpa | gristle | gumming |
| gonidia | granger | gristly | gummous |
| goodbye | granite | grizzle | gum-tree |
| good job | grannie | grizzly | gunboat |
| goodman | grantee | grocery | gun-fire |
| goolies | granter | grockle | gunnery |
| goosery | grantor | grogram | gunshot |
| Gordian | granule | grogran | gunwale |
| gorilla | grapery | groined | gurnard |
| gormand | graphic | grommet | gushing |
| goshawk | grapnel | grooved | gutless |
| go short | grapple | grossly | guttate |
| gosling | grasper | grottos | guttler |
| go spare | gratify | grouchy | guzzler |
| gossipy | grating | grouper | gymnast |
| go to pot | gravely | groupie | |
| gouache | gravity | growler | **H** |
| goujons | grazier | grown-up | habitat |
| goulash | grazing | grubber | habited |
| gourami | greaser | grudger | habitué |
| gourmet | greatly | gruffly | hachure |
| goutily | greaves | grumble | hackbut |
| grabber | Grecian | grummet | hacking |
| grabble | Grecise | grumous | hackler |
| gracile | Grecism | grunter | hackles |
| grackle | Grecize | Gruyère | hackney |
| gradate | gremlin | gryphon | hack-saw |
| gradine | grenade | G-string | haddock |
| gradual | greyish | guanaco | hafnium |
| grafter | grey lag | guanine | haggard |

| | | | |
|---|---|---|---|
| haggish | happily | heading | hepatic |
| haggler | harbour | headman | herbage |
| hair-cut | hardily | headmen | herbist |
| hair-net | hardish | head-set | herbose |
| hair-pin | hard-pan | headway | herbous |
| *Halacha* | hare-lip | healing | herdman |
| *Halakah* | haricot | healthy | heretic |
| halberd | harmful | hearing | heritor |
| halbert | harmony | hearken | hernial |
| halcyon | harness | hearsay | heroine |
| halfway | harpist | hearted | heroise |
| half-wit | harpoon | hearten | heroism |
| halibut | harrier | heathen | heroize |
| halidom | harshly | heather | heronry |
| halogen | harvest | heating | herring |
| halyard | has-been | heavily | herself |
| Hamburg | hashish | Hebraic | Hessian |
| Hamitic | hassock | heckler | hetaera |
| hammaum | hastate | hectare | hetaira |
| hammock | hastily | hedging | hexagon |
| hamster | hatable | hedonic | hexapla |
| hamulus | hat-band | heedful | hexapod |
| hanaper | hatchel | heel-tap | hickory |
| handbag | hatcher | heinous | hidalgo |
| handful | hatchet | heirdom | hideous |
| handily | hateful | heiress | higgler |
| handler | hauberk | helical | high-boy |
| hand-out | haughty | helices | high-hat |
| hand-saw | haulage | helipad | highway |
| handsel | haulier | Hellene | hilding |
| hand-set | haunted | hellish | hillock |
| hands-on | haunter | helotry | hill-top |
| hang-dog | hautboy | helpful | himself |
| hanging | hauteur | helping | hippish |
| hangman | have a go | hem-line | hircine |
| hangmen | hawking | hemlock | hire car |
| hang-out | haycock | hen-bane | hirsute |
| Hansard | hayrick | hennery | history |
| hapless | haywire | henotic | hit list |
| haploid | headily | henpeck | Hittite |

| | | | |
|---|---|---|---|
| hoarder | hot seat | **I** | immerge |
| hobnail | hotshot | iambise | immerse |
| hog-fish | Hotspur | iambize | immoral |
| hoggish | houmous | Iberian | impanel |
| hogwash | housing | iceberg | impasse |
| hold-all | howbeit | ice-fall | impaste |
| holding | however | ice-floe | impasto |
| holibut | howling | ice-foot | impeach |
| holiday | hueless | ice-pack | imperil |
| holland | huffish | ice-pick | impetus |
| holmium | hulking | ichnite | impiety |
| holster | humanly | iciness | impinge |
| Homburg | humdrum | icterus | impious |
| Homeric | humeral | ideally | implant |
| home run | humerus | identic | implead |
| hominid | humidly | idiotcy | implode |
| homonym | humidor | idiotic | implore |
| honesty | hummock | idolise | impound |
| honeyed | humoral | idolize | impress |
| hoodlum | hundred | idyllic | imprest |
| hopeful | hunting | igneous | imprint |
| hoplite | hurling | ignoble | improve |
| horizon | hurried | ignobly | impulse |
| hormone | hurtful | ikebana | imputer |
| hornist | husband | illapse | in a hole |
| hornlet | huskily | ill-bred | inanity |
| horrent | Hussite | illegal | in a spot |
| horrify | huswife | illicit | inboard |
| hosanna | hyaline | illness | inbreak |
| hose-man | hyalite | ill will | inbreed |
| hosiery | hyaloid | ill wind | inbuilt |
| hospice | hydatid | imagery | incense |
| hostage | hydrant | imagine | incisor |
| hostess | hydrate | imagist | incivil |
| hostile | hydride | imamate | incline |
| hostler | hydrous | imbiber | inclose |
| hot-foot | hygeian | imbosom | include |
| hot-head | hygiene | imitant | incomer |
| hot line | hymnody | imitate | incrust |
| hotness | hyped up | immense | incubus |

| | | | |
|---|---|---|---|
| incurve | in-group | intense | **J** |
| in-depth | inhabit | interim | jacamar |
| indexer | inhaler | interne | jacinth |
| indexes | inherit | intrant | jackass |
| indices | inhibit | introit | jackdaw |
| indicia | in-house | intrude | jackpot |
| indigen | inhuman | intrust | jacksie |
| inditer | initial | intwine | jack-tar |
| indoors | injurer | intwist | Jacobin |
| indorse | inkhorn | *in utero* | Jacobus |
| indraft | inkling | inutile | jaconet |
| inducer | inkwell | *in vacuo* | Jacuzzi® |
| indulge | inlayer | invader | jadeite |
| indulin | in limbo | invalid | jaggary |
| indusia | innards | inveigh | jaggery |
| in Dutch | innerve | inverse | jaghire |
| indwell | innings | inviter | Jainism |
| ineptly | in posse | in vitro | jam tart |
| inertia | inquest | invoice | janitor |
| inertly | inquire | involve | January |
| incxact | inquiry | inwards | jargoon |
| infancy | inshore | inweave | jasminc |
| infanta | insider | Iranian | jaspery |
| infante | insight | iricism | javelin |
| infeoff | insipid | iridian | jaw-bone |
| inferno | insnare | iridium | jay-walk |
| infidel | insofar | irksome | jealous |
| infield | inspect | Iron Age | Jehovah |
| inflame | inspire | ironing | jejunum |
| inflate | install | ischium | jellies |
| inflect | instant | isohyet | jemadar |
| inflict | instate | isolate | jemidar |
| infulae | instead | isonomy | jeopard |
| ingénue | instill | isotope | jetties |
| ingesta | in store | isotron | jeweler |
| ingoing | in style | isthmus | jewelry |
| ingraft | insular | Italian | Jezebel |
| ingrain | insulin | itemise | jim-jams |
| ingrate | insurer | itemize | jittery |
| ingress | integer | iterate | jobbery |

jobless
jocular
Joe Soap
jog-trot
John Doe
joinder
joinery
joining
jointed
jointer
jointly
jollify
jollily
jollity
jonquil
jotting
journal
journey
jouster
Joycean
joyless
joyride
jubilee
Judaise
Judaism
Judaize
Judases
jugated
juggins
juggler
jugular
jujitsu
juke-box
jumbuck
jump jet
juniper
junkman
Jupiter
juridic
juryman

jurymen
jussive
justice
justify

**K**
kabaddi
kabbala
kaddish
kainite
kalends
Kalmuck
kamseen
Kantian
karakul
karaoke
karting
katydid
keelson
keeping
keep mum
kenosis
keramic
keratin
kerbing
kestrel
ketchup
keyhole
keynote
khaddar
khaliff
khamsin
khanate
Khedive
kibbitz
kibbutz
kick ass
kick off
kick-off
kidskin

killick
killing
kill-joy
killock
kiloton
kindred
kinetic
king-cup
kingdom
kinglet
king-pin
kinless
kinship
kinsman
kinsmen
kirtled
kitchen
kithara
knacker
knagged
knarled
knarred
knavery
knavish
knee-cap
kneeler
knees-up
knitter
knobbed
knocker
knotted
know-all
know-how
knowing
knuckle
Kohinor
kolkhoz
koumiss
Kremlin
kreuzer

Krishna
krypton
krytron
kumquat
Kurdish
kursaal
kyanise
kyanize

**L**
labarum
labiate
labored
laborer
laconic
lacquer
lactate
lacteal
lactine
lactone
lactose
lacunae
lacunar
ladanum
la-di-dah
ladybug
Lady Day
laggard
lagging
laicise
laicize
lakelet
lamaism
lamaist
lambada
lambast
lambent
lambert
lambkin
lamella

| | | | |
|---|---|---|---|
| laminae | lazaret | leprous | lineate |
| laminar | leading | lesbian | lingual |
| lampion | leafage | letdown | lingula |
| lampoon | leaflet | let drop | linkage |
| lamprey | leagued | Lethean | link-boy |
| landing | leaguer | let slip | link-man |
| Landtag | leakage | lettuce | Linnean |
| land-tax | leaning | leucoma | linocut |
| languid | learned | levator | linsang |
| languor | learner | levelly | linseed |
| laniard | leasing | leveret | lioness |
| laniary | leather | Levitic | lionise |
| lanolin | lechery | lexical | lionism |
| lantern | lectern | lexicon | lionize |
| lanyard | lection | ley-line | lip-read |
| lapilli | lecture | liaison | lip-sync |
| lapwing | leeward | Liassic | liquate |
| larceny | leftist | liberal | liquefy |
| largely | legally | liberty | liqueur |
| largess | legatee | library | lissome |
| largish | legging | librate | listing |
| lasagna | leghorn | licence | literal |
| lasagne | legible | license | lithium |
| lashing | legibly | licitly | lithoid |
| lasting | legitim | licking | litotes |
| latchet | legless | lidless | lituate |
| latency | leg room | lift-off | liturgy |
| lateral | legwork | lighten | livable |
| lathing | leister | lighter | livered |
| latrine | leisure | lightly | loading |
| lattice | lemming | lignify | loather |
| laugher | lengthy | lignine | loathly |
| launder | lenient | lignite | lobated |
| laundry | lentigo | ligroin | lobelet |
| lawless | lentoid | likable | lobelia |
| lawsuit | leonine | limbate | lobiped |
| laxness | leopard | limited | lobster |
| layette | leotard | limiter | lobular |
| lay odds | leprose | limpkin | lobworm |
| layover | leprosy | lineage | locally |

| | | | |
|---|---|---|---|
| lockage | lucarne | macaque | mamelon |
| lockjaw | lucency | machete | mamilla |
| lock-out | lucerne | machine | mammary |
| locular | lucidly | macramé | mammock |
| loculus | Lucifer | maculae | mammoth |
| lodging | luckily | madding | manacle |
| loftily | luckout | Madeira | manager |
| log-book | luggage | madness | manakin |
| logging | lug-sail | Madonna | manatee |
| logical | lugworm | madwort | manchet |
| logwood | lullaby | maestro | mandate |
| Lollard | lumbago | mae west | mandrel |
| Lombard | lumping | Mafioso | mandril |
| longbow | lumpish | magenta | mangler |
| longing | lump sum | maggoty | manhole |
| longish | lunated | magical | manhood |
| lookout | lunatic | magnate | man-hour |
| look-see | lunette | magneto | manhunt |
| loosely | lunular | magnify | Manihot |
| lopping | lunulet | Mahatma | manikin |
| lorgnon | lupulin | mahjong | manilla |
| lose out | lurcher | mailman | maniple |
| lottery | lurdane | mailmen | manitou |
| lounger | lustful | maintop | mankind |
| loutish | lustily | majesty | manlike |
| lovable | lustral | make hay | man-made |
| low-born | lustrum | make way | mannish |
| low-bred | luteous | Malacca | mannite |
| lowbrow | lychnis | malaise | mansard |
| low-down | lycopod | malaria | mansion |
| lowland | lyddite | Malayan | mantlet |
| low life | lying-in | malefic | manumit |
| Low Mass | lyingly | malison | marabou |
| lowness | lyncean | mallard | marbled |
| low-rise | lyrated | malleus | marbler |
| low-tech | lyrical | malmsey | marcher |
| low tide | | Maltese | maremma |
| loyally | **M** | malting | marimba |
| loyalty | macabre | maltman | mariner |
| lozenge | macadam | maltose | marital |

| | | | |
|---|---|---|---|
| marking | maxilla | menthol | milling |
| marline | maximal | mention | million |
| marling | maximum | mercery | milreis |
| marplot | maxwell | mercies | mimesis |
| marquee | mayoral | mercury | mimetic |
| marquis | maypole | mermaid | mimicry |
| married | maziest | merrily | minaret |
| marrowy | mazurka | mersion | mincing |
| Marsala | mazzard | meseems | mindful |
| marshal | meadowy | mesquit | mind-set |
| martial | mealies | message | mineral |
| Martian | meander | Messiah | miniate |
| Martini® | meaning | mestizo | minibar |
| martlet | measled | metayer | minibus |
| martyry | measles | methane | minicab |
| Marxian | measure | metrics | minicar |
| Marxism | Mechlin | mettled | minikin |
| mascara | meconic | miasmal | minimal |
| masonic | medalet | microbe | minimum |
| masonry | meddler | microhm | miniver |
| masquer | mediant | midland | minster |
| massage | mediate | Mid-lent | mintage |
| masseur | medical | mid-life | minuend |
| massive | medigap | midmost | Miocene |
| mastaba | mediums | midnoon | miracle |
| mastery | medulla | midrash | mirific |
| mastiff | medusae | midriff | miscall |
| mastoid | meeting | midship | misdate |
| matador | megasse | midwife | misdeed |
| matelot | megaton | mightn't | misdeem |
| matinal | meiosis | migrant | misdoer |
| matinée | mélange | migrate | miserly |
| matrass | melanic | mileage | misfire |
| mattery | melanin | milfoil | misgave |
| matting | melilot | miliary | misgive |
| mattock | melodic | militia | Mishnah |
| maudlin | melting | milkman | mislead |
| maunder | memento | milkmen | mislike |
| mawkish | mending | milk-run | misname |
| mawworm | menisci | milksop | misread |

misrule
missile
missing
mission
missive
mistake
mistily
mistime
mitosis
mixable
mixedly
mixed-up
mixture
Moabite
mobbish
mobster
mockery
modally
modesty
modicum
modiste
modular
modulus
mofette
Mohican
moidore
moisten
molding
mollify
mollusc
mollusk
momenta
monadic
monarch
monergy
moneyed
moneyer
mongrel
moniker
monitor

monkeys
monkish
monocle
monodic
monogyn
monsoon
monster
montage
montane
montero
monthly
moonish
moonlit
moorage
moor-hen
mooring
Moorish
moraine
morally
morassy
morceau
mordant
mordent
moreish
morello
Moresco
Morisco
morning
morocco
morphia
morrice
mortice
mortify
mortise
moselle
mothery
mottled
mottoes
mouflon
mouillé

moulder
mounted
Mountie
mourner
mousaka
mousing
mouthed
mouther
movable
movably
mowburn
Mr Clean
Mr Right
mucific
muddily
mudlark
muezzin
muffled
muffler
muggins
muggish
mug-shot
mugwort
mugwump
mulatto
mullein
mullion
mullock
multure
mumbler
mummery
mummify
mumpish
muncher
mundane
muntjac
muntjak
muraena
muriate
murices

murkily
murrain
murrine
murther
muscled
muscoid
Muscovy
musette
musical
musk-rat
mustang
mustard
mustily
mutable
mutably
myalgia
myalism
mycelia
mycosis
myeloid
Mylodon
mynheer
myology
myosote
myotomy
myrrhic
mystery
mystify

N
nacelle
naïvely
naïveté
naivety
nakedly
namable
nankeen
naphtha
napless
nardine

narrate
narthex
narwhal
nasally
nascent
nastily
nattily
natural
naughty
navvies
nebulae
nebular
necklet
neck-tie
nectary
needful
needily
neglect
negress
Negrilo
Negrito
negroes
Negroid
neither
nelumbo
nemesis
nemoral
neology
Neozoic
Neptune
nervate
nervous
nervure
nest-egg
netsuke
netting
network
neuroma
neurone
neutral

neutron
new-born
New Deal
new moon
newness
newsboy
newsman
newsmen
new town
nibbler
niblick
nictate
niggard
niggler
nightie
nightly
Nilotic
ninthly
niobium
nippers
Nirvana
nitrate
nitride
nitrify
nitrite
nitrous
niveous
Noachic
noctule
nocturn
nocuous
nodated
nodding
nodical
nodular
no end of
no-fault
nogging
noisily
noisome

nomadic
nomarch
nombril
nominal
nominee
nonagon
nonplus
non-stop
nonsuch
non-suit
noology
noonday
nooning
nose-bag
nosegay
nose-job
nostril
nostrum
no sweat!
notable
notably
not half
nothing
notions
not much
nourish
novella
novelty
nowhere
noxious
nuclear
nucleus
nullify
nullity
numbles
numeral
numeric
nummary
nunnery
nunnish

nuptial
nursery
nursing
nurture
nutcase
nutting
nymphet

**O**

oakling
oarlock
oarsman
oarsmen
oatcake
oatmeal
obconic
obelise
obelisk
obelize
obesity
obliged
obligee
obliger
obligor
oblique
obloquy
obovate
obscene
obscure
observe
obtrude
obverse
obviate
obvious
ocarina
occiput
occlude
oceanic
Oceanid
ocellus

| | | | |
|---|---|---|---|
| octagon | olivary | opsonin | ossicle |
| octavos | olivine | optical | ossific |
| octette | Olympic | optimal | ossuary |
| October | omental | optimum | osteoma |
| octopod | omentum | opulent | ostiary |
| octopus | omicron | opuntia | ostiole |
| octuple | ominous | opuscle | ostitis |
| oculate | omnibus | oration | ostrich |
| oculist | onanism | oratory | otalgia |
| odalisk | onanist | orbital | otarian |
| oddball | oneness | orcgeny | otocyst |
| oddment | onerary | orchard | otolite |
| oddness | onerous | orcinol | otolith |
| odorous | oneself | ordered | otology |
| Odyssey | one-time | orderer | ottoman |
| oersted | one-up on | orderly | ourself |
| oestrus | ongoing | ordinal | outback |
| of a kind | onicolo | oregano | outcast |
| off-beam | onshore | organdy | outcome |
| offbeat | on the go | organic | out-crop |
| offence | onwards | organon | outdare |
| offerer | oolitic | organum | outdoor |
| off-hand | oosperm | orifice | outface |
| officer | ootheca | origami | outfall |
| off-line | opacity | Orleans | outflow |
| off-load | opacous | orogeny | outgrew |
| offside | opaline | orology | outgrow |
| ogreish | opalise | orotund | outlast |
| oilcake | opalize | Orphean | outlier |
| oil-palm | open air | orphrey | outline |
| oilskin | opening | ortolan | outlive |
| oil-well | operant | osculum | outlook |
| old gold | operate | osiered | outmost |
| old hand | operose | Osmanli | out of it |
| old lady | opinion | osmosis | outport |
| old maid | opossum | osmotic | outpost |
| oldness | oppidan | osmunda | outpour |
| Old Nick | opposed | osseine | outrage |
| old-time | opposer | osselet | outrank |
| olitory | oppress | osseous | outride |

outroom
outrush
outsail
outside
outsize
outspan
outstay
out-talk
outvote
outwalk
outward
outwear
outwork
ovarial
ovarian
ovation
overact
overall
overarm
overawe
overbid
overdue
overeat
overjoy
overlap
overlay
overlie
overman
overpay
overran
overrun
oversaw
oversea
oversee
overset
oversew
overtax
overtly
overtop
oviduct

oviform
ovoidal
ovulate
own-goal
oxalate
oxidate
oxidise
oxidize
Oxonian
oxytone
ozonise
ozonize

**P**
pabular
pabulum
pacable
pachisi
pacific
package
pack-ice
packing
paction
pactive
padding
paddler
paddock
padella
padlock
padrone
pageant
page boy
paginal
Pahlavi
pailful
painful
painter
paisley
pajamas
paktong

paladin
palatal
palaver
paletot
palette
palfrey
pallial
pallium
palmary
palmate
palmist
palmyra
palpate
paludal
pampean
pampero
panacea
panache
pancake
Pandean
pandect
pandore
panicle
pannier
panoply
pansies
panther
panties
pantile
pantler
papally
papilla
papoose
paprika
Pap test
papulae
papular
papyrus
parable
paradox

paragon
parapet
parasol
parboil
pareira
paresis
paretic
parfait
parlour
parlous
parodic
parolee
paronym
parotid
parquet
parsley
parsnip
partake
partial
parties
parting
partitc
partlet
partner
partook
parvenu
parvise
paschal
pasquil
pasquin
passage
passant
pass for
passing
passion
passive
pass out
passout
pastern
pastime

| | | | |
|---|---|---|---|
| pasture | pelagic | perfidy | phantom |
| patcher | pelecan | perform | Pharaoh |
| patch up | pelican | perfume | pharynx |
| patella | pelisse | perfuse | phellem |
| paterae | peloria | pergola | philtre |
| pathway | peloric | perhaps | phloeum |
| patient | peltate | periapt | Phoebus |
| patrial | pemican | peridot | phoenix |
| patriot | penally | perigee | phonate |
| patrist | penalty | periwig | phone-in |
| pattern | penance | perjure | phonics |
| patties | Penates | perjury | phrasal |
| paucity | pendant | Permian | phrenic |
| Pauline | pendent | permute | physics |
| paunchy | pendent | perpend | phytoid |
| paviour | pending | perplex | pianino |
| payable | penfold | Persian | pianist |
| pay-dirt | penguin | persist | piastre |
| payload | pen-name | persona | pibroch |
| payment | pennant | pertain | picador |
| pay-roll | pennies | perturb | piccolo |
| peacock | pensile | pertuse | piceous |
| peafowl | pension | perusal | pickaxe |
| pearled | pensive | peruser | picking |
| peasant | pentice | pervade | pickled |
| peascod | peonage | pervert | picotee |
| pebbled | peonism | pessary | picture |
| peccant | peppery | petiole | piddock |
| peccary | pep pill | petrify | piebald |
| peccavi | pepsine | Petrine | pierage |
| peckish | pep-talk | petrous | piercer |
| pectose | peptone | pettily | pierrot |
| peddler | percale | pettish | Pietism |
| pedicab | per cent | petunia | Pietist |
| pedicel | percept | pewtery | piggery |
| pedlary | percher | Pfennig | piggish |
| pedlery | percuss | phaeton | pigment |
| peerage | per diem | phalanx | pigskin |
| peeress | perdure | phallic | pigtail |
| peevish | perfect | phallus | pikeman |

| | | | |
|---|---|---|---|
| pileate | pitcher | pleaser | poitrel |
| pilgrim | piteous | pledgee | polacca |
| pillage | pitfall | pledger | Polaris |
| pill-box | pithily | pledget | poleaxe |
| pillion | pitiful | plenary | polecat |
| pillock | pivotal | plenish | polemic |
| pillory | pivoted | plessor | polenta |
| pillowy | placard | pleurae | politic |
| pilular | placate | pleural | pollack |
| pimento | placebo | pliable | pollard |
| pimpled | placket | pliably | pollock |
| pin-case | placoid | pliancy | poll-tax |
| pincers | plafond | plicate | pollute |
| pinched | plaguer | plodder | polygon |
| pincher | plaguey | plonker | polygyn |
| pinetum | plaided | plotter | polymer |
| pinfold | plainly | plucker | polypod |
| pin-hole | plaited | plugger | polypus |
| pink-eye | plaiter | plumage | Polyzoa |
| pinnace | planish | plumber | pomatum |
| pinnate | planner | plumbic | pompano |
| pinners | plantar | plumery | pompion |
| pinnula | planter | plummet | pompous |
| pinnule | plasmic | plumose | poniard |
| pinocle | plaster | plumous | pontage |
| pintail | plastic | plumper | pontiff |
| pioneer | platane | plumule | pontoon |
| piously | plateau | plunder | poofter |
| pipette | platina | plunger | popcorn |
| piquant | plating | pluvial | popedom |
| piragua | platoon | plywood | pop-eyed |
| piranha | platter | poacher | poppied |
| piratic | plaudit | pochard | popular |
| pirogue | play-act | podagra | porcine |
| piscina | playboy | poetess | porifer |
| piscine | playful | poetics | porrigo |
| pismire | playlet | poetise | portage |
| piss off | playpen | poetize | portend |
| pistole | pleader | pointed | portent |
| pit-a-pat | pleased | pointer | portico |

| | | | |
|---|---|---|---|
| portion | predial | primate | propose |
| portray | predict | primely | pro rata |
| possess | predoom | priming | prosaic |
| postage | pre-empt | primula | prosody |
| post-boy | preface | printer | prosper |
| postern | prefect | prithee | protean |
| post-fix | prelacy | privacy | protect |
| postman | prelate | private | protégé |
| postmen | prelect | privily | proteid |
| posture | prelims | privity | protein |
| potable | prelude | probang | protend |
| potably | premier | probate | protest |
| potassa | premise | probity | protist |
| potency | premiss | problem | proudly |
| pothole | premium | proceed | proverb |
| pot-shot | prepaid | process | provide |
| pottage | prepare | proctor | proviso |
| pottery | prepuce | procure | provoke |
| pouched | prequel | prodigy | provost |
| poultry | presage | produce | prowess |
| pounced | present | product | prowler |
| poundal | preside | profane | proximo |
| pounder | presser | profess | prudent |
| poverty | press-up | proffer | prudery |
| powdery | presume | profile | prudish |
| praetor | pretend | profuse | prurigo |
| prairie | pretext | progeny | psalter |
| praiser | pretzel | program | psychic |
| praline | prevail | project | ptarmic |
| prancer | prevent | prolate | ptomain |
| prating | preview | pro-life | ptomaic |
| prattle | previse | prolong | ptyalin |
| pravity | pricker | promise | puberty |
| praying | pricket | promote | publish |
| preachy | prickle | pronate | puckery |
| prebend | prickly | pronely | puckish |
| precede | pridian | pronged | pudding |
| precept | primacy | pronoun | puddler |
| precise | primage | propane | pudency |
| predate | primary | prophet | pudenda |

puerile
puffery
pug-nose
pulleys
Pullman
pulsate
pumpion
pumpkin
puncher
pungent
punning
punster
puppies
purfled
purging
puritan
purlieu
purline
purloin
purples
purport
purpose
purpura
pursuer
pursuit
purview
pushing
push off
pustule
put it on
putrefy
puttock
put upon
puzzler
pyaemia
pyaemic
pygmean
pygmies
pyjamas
pyloric

pylorus
pyramid
pyretic
pyrexia
pyrites
pyritic
pyrosis
Pyrrhic
Pythian

**Q**

quadrat
quaffer
qualify
quality
quantum
quarrel
quartan
quarter
quartet
quartic
quartzy
quassia
quayage
queenly
queerly
queller
queries
querist
quester
questor
quetzal
quibble
quicken
quickie
quickly
quids in
quieten
quietly
quietus

quilled
quinary
quinate
quinine
quintal
quintan
quintet
quitter
qui vive
quondam

**R**

rabidly
raccoon
racquet
radiant
radiate
radical
radices
radicle
raffish
raggedy
rag-time
ragwort
railing
railway
raiment
rainbow
Ramadan
rambler
Ramboid
ramekin
rammish
rampage
rampant
rampart
rampion
ram-raid
ramsons
rancher

rancour
ranking
ransack
rapidly
rapport
rapture
rarebit
rare gas
rasbora
Rasores
ratable
ratably
ratafia
ratchet
ratline
rat race
ratteen
rattler
rattoon
raucous
raunchy
ravager
ravelin
ravioli
raw deal
rawhide
rawness
rayless
reacher
reactor
readily
reading
readmit
read-out
reagent
realgar
realign
realise
realism
realist

| | | | |
|---|---|---|---|
| reality | redound | regular | reposer |
| realize | redpoll | regulus | reposit |
| realtor | redraft | re-inter | repress |
| reannex | redress | reissue | reprint |
| reargue | redskin | rejoice | reprise |
| rebirth | red-tail | rejudge | reproof |
| rebound | red-tape | relapse | reprove |
| rebuild | reducer | related | reptant |
| rebuker | red wine | relater | reptile |
| receipt | redwing | relator | repulse |
| receive | redwood | release | reputed |
| recency | re-enter | reliant | request |
| recense | re-entry | relieve | requiem |
| recital | referee | relievo | require |
| reciter | refined | relight | requite |
| reclaim | refiner | remarry | reredos |
| recline | reflect | remnant | rescind |
| recluse | reforge | remodel | rescuer |
| recount | refound | remorse | reserve |
| recover | refract | remould | reshape |
| re-cover | refrain | remount | residue |
| recruit | refresh | removal | resieze |
| rectify | refugee | removed | resolve |
| rectory | refusal | remover | resound |
| rectrix | refuser | renewal | respect |
| recurve | refuter | renewer | respell |
| recycle | regaler | rent boy | respire |
| red-back | regalia | *rentier* | respite |
| red book | regally | renuent | respond |
| red card | regatta | repaint | restart |
| red cent | regency | repiner | restate |
| red-coat | regimen | replace | restful |
| red deer | regnant | replant | restiff |
| reddish | regorge | replete | restive |
| red flag | regrant | replevy | restore |
| redhead | regrate | replica | retable |
| red lead | regreen | replier | rethink |
| redneck | regreet | repo man | retiary |
| redness | regress | repo men | reticle |
| redoubt | regroup | reposal | retinal |

retinue
retiral
retired
retouch
retrace
retract
retreat
retrial
retsina
reunion
reunite
revelry
revenge
revenue
reverer
reverie
reverse
reviler
revisal
reviser
revisit
revival
reviver
revolve
rewrite
reynard
rhachis
Rhenish
rhenium
rhizoid
rhizoma
rhizome
rhodium
rhombic
rhombus
rhubarb
ribbing
ribcage
rickets
rickety

ricksha
ricotta
ride out
rifling
rigging
righter
rightly
right on
rigidly
rilievo
rimless
ringent
ringlet
Riot Act
riotous
rip-cord
riposte
riptide
risible
risibly
risotto
rissole
rivalry
riveted
riveter
riviera
rivulet
road hog
roadman
road map
roadway
roaring
roaster
robbery
rockery
roebuck
roe-deer
roguery
roguish
roister

rollbar
rollick
rolling
rollmop
rollock
romance
Romanic
romaunt
rompers
rompish
rondeau
röntgen
roofing
rookery
roomful
roomily
rooster
rootlet
root out
rorqual
roseate
roseola
rosette
rosolio
rostral
rostrum
rotator
rotifer
rotunda
roughen
roughly
roulade
rouleau
rounded
roundel
rounder
roundly
round up
round-up
rousing

routine
row-boat
rowlock
royally
royalty
rubbing
rubbish
rubella
rubeola
rubific
rucking
ruction
ruddily
ruddock
ruffian
ruffled
ruffler
ruinate
ruinous
rulable
rummage
run-away
run-down
run high
running
run riot
run wild
rupture
rurally
Russian
rustily
rustler
ruthful
ruttish

S
Sabaoth
Sabbath
saccate
saccule

| | | | |
|---|---|---|---|
| sackage | sand-box | savoury | sciatic |
| sackbut | sandman | saw-bill | science |
| sacking | sand-pit | saw-buck | scissel |
| sacring | sangria | sawdust | scissor |
| sacrist | sanicle | saw-fish | scoffer |
| saddler | sanious | sawmill | scolder |
| sadness | sapajou | sawn-off | scollop |
| safe sex | saphead | saxhorn | scooper |
| saffian | sapient | scabbed | scooter |
| saffron | sapless | scabies | scoriae |
| saguaro | sapling | scabrid | scorify |
| sailing | sapphic | scaldic | scorner |
| sainted | Saracen | scalene | Scorpio |
| saintly | sarcasm | scalled | scotoma |
| salable | sarcode | scallop | Scottie |
| salchow | sarcoid | scalpel | scourer |
| salicin | sarcoma | scamper | scourge |
| salient | sarcous | scandal | scraggy |
| Salique | sardine | scanner | scraper |
| sallies | sardius | scantly | scrappy |
| salmiac | sashimi | scapula | scratch |
| salsify | satanic | scarfed | scrawny |
| saltant | satchel | scarify | screech |
| saltern | satiate | scarlet | screwed |
| saltier | satiety | scarped | screwer |
| saltire | satinet | scarper | screw up |
| saltish | satiric | scarves | scribal |
| salt-pan | satisfy | scatter | scriber |
| saluter | satrapy | scenery | Scrooge |
| salvage | satsuma | scented | scrotal |
| samisen | satyric | sceptic | scrotum |
| samovar | saucily | sceptre | scrubby |
| Samoyed | saunter | schemer | scruffy |
| sampler | saurian | scherzo | scrunch |
| samurai | sauroid | schlepp | scruple |
| sanable | sausage | schmalz | scudder |
| sanctum | savable | schmuck | scuffle |
| Sanctus | savanna | schnaps | sculler |
| sand-bag | saveloy | scholar | sculpin |
| sand-bar | saviour | scholia | scumbag |

| | | | |
|---|---|---|---|
| scumble | securer | servant | sharply |
| scummer | sedilia | service | shaster |
| scunner | seducer | servile | shastra |
| scupper | seedbed | serving | shatter |
| scutage | seedily | sessile | Shavian |
| scutate | see life | session | shaving |
| scuttle | seeming | set-back | shearer |
| scythed | seepage | set-line | sheathe |
| sea-bass | segment | setting | sheathy |
| sea-cock | seismal | settled | sheaves |
| seafood | seismic | settler | shebang |
| seagull | seizure | seventh | shebeen |
| sea-kale | sejeant | seventy | shedder |
| sea-lane | selenic | several | shellac |
| sealant | selfish | sexless | shelled |
| sea-legs | sell off | sex shop | shelter |
| sea-lily | sell out | sextain | sheltie |
| sealing | selvage | sextant | shelves |
| sea-lion | sematic | shackle | sherbet |
| sea-mile | seminal | shadily | sheriff |
| sea-pink | seminar | shading | shifter |
| sea-port | Semitic | shadoof | shimmer |
| sea-sick | senator | shadowy | shindig |
| seaside | senatus | shafted | shiness |
| seating | send off | shakers | shingle |
| sea-wall | send-off | shake-up | shingly |
| seaward | sensory | shallop | shining |
| seaweed | sensual | shallot | shipper |
| sebacic | sequela | shallow | shippon |
| seceder | sequent | shamble | shirker |
| seclude | sequoia | shammer | shivery |
| secrecy | seraphs | shampoo | shocker |
| secrete | Serbian | shandry | shodden |
| sectary | seredom | shanked | shooter |
| sectile | seriate | shapely | shopman |
| section | serious | shape up | shopper |
| sectism | serpent | shape-up | shorten |
| sectist | serpigo | sharded | shortly |
| sective | serrate | sharpen | shotgun |
| secular | serried | sharper | shot-put |

| | | | |
|---|---|---|---|
| shotten | signore | skeptic | slavery |
| shouter | silence | sketchy | slavish |
| show biz | silicic | skid row | sleekly |
| showery | silicle | skiffle | sleeper |
| showily | silicon | ski-jump | sleeved |
| showing | silimar | skilful | sleight |
| showman | siliqua | ski-lift | slender |
| showmen | silique | skilled | slicker |
| show off | silk hat | skillet | sliding |
| show-off | Sillery | skimmed | slimmer |
| shreddy | sillily | skimmer | sliness |
| shrilly | Silurus | Skimmia | slinger |
| shrivel | silvern | skinful | slipper |
| shrubby | silvery | skinned | slipway |
| shudder | similar | skinner | slither |
| shuffle | simious | ski-pole | slitter |
| shunter | simitar | skipper | slobber |
| shut-eye | sincere | skirret | sloe gin |
| shutter | *sine die* | skitter | sloshed |
| shuttle | sinewed | skulker | sloughy |
| shyness | singing | sky-blue | Slovene |
| shyster | singlet | sky-high | slubber |
| siamang | sinking | skyjack | slumber |
| Siamese | sinless | skylark | slyness |
| sibling | sinople | sky-line | smacker |
| siccate | sinuate | skyward | smarten |
| siccity | sinuous | slabber | smartly |
| sick-bay | siquare | slacken | smashed |
| sick-bed | Sirenia | slacker | smasher |
| sickish | sirloin | slackly | smash-up |
| sick pay | sirname | slag off | smatter |
| sidecar | sirocco | slammer | smeller |
| sideway | sistrum | slander | smelter |
| siemens | sitting | slangam | smidgen |
| sighted | situate | slanted | smidgin |
| sightly | sixfold | slantly | smiling |
| sigmoid | six-pack | slashed | smitten |
| signify | sixteen | slasher | smokily |
| signior | sixthly | slating | smoking |
| signora | sizable | slatted | smoothy |

| | | | |
|---|---|---|---|
| smother | solidus | spanner | spindly |
| smuggle | soliped | sparely | spinner |
| snaffle | soloist | sparing | spinney |
| snakish | soluble | sparkle | spin off |
| snapper | solvent | sparrer | spinose |
| snarler | somatic | sparrow | spinous |
| snarl-up | someday | Spartan | spiraea |
| sneaker | somehow | spastic | spirant |
| sneerer | someone | spathal | spitter |
| snicker | some way | spathed | spittle |
| sniffle | sonance | spathic | splashy |
| snifter | sondage | spatial | spleeny |
| snigger | sonless | spatter | splenic |
| snipper | sonship | spattle | splodge |
| snippet | soother | spatula | splotch |
| snooker | sophism | spawner | splurge |
| snorkel | sophist | speaker | spoiler |
| snorter | sopping | special | spondee |
| snouted | soprani | species | sponger |
| snowcap | soprano | specify | sponson |
| snowish | sorcery | speckle | sponsor |
| snowman | sordino | spectra | sporran |
| snuffer | sorghum | spectre | sporule |
| snuff it | sororal | specula | spotted |
| snuffle | sorosis | speller | spotter |
| snuggle | sorrily | spelter | spousal |
| soakage | sottish | spencer | spouter |
| soaking | soufflé | spender | sprayey |
| so and so | soulful | spheral | spriggy |
| soapbox | soundly | spheric | spright |
| soberly | soupçon | spicate | springe |
| society | sourish | spicery | springy |
| sockeye | soutane | spicily | spurner |
| sofa bed | sozzled | spicula | spurred |
| softish | spacial | spicule | sputnik |
| soignée | spangle | spidery | sputter |
| sojourn | spangly | spiller | squabby |
| soldier | spaniel | spinach | squalid |
| solicit | Spanish | spinage | squally |
| solidly | spanker | spindle | squalor |

| | | | |
|---|---|---|---|
| squamae | startle | stick-up | stringy |
| squashy | stately | stiffen | striped |
| squeeze | statics | stiffly | striver |
| squelch | station | stigmas | stroker |
| squiffy | statism | stiller | strophe |
| squinch | statist | stilted | stroppy |
| stabber | statued | Stilton | strudel |
| stabile | stature | stimuli | strumae |
| stabler | statute | stinker | stubbed |
| stacked | staunch | stinter | stubble |
| staddle | stealer | stipend | stubbly |
| stadium | stealth | stipple | stuck on |
| stagger | steamer | stipule | stuck-up |
| staging | stearic | stir-fry | studded |
| staidly | stearin | stirrer | student |
| stainer | steepen | stirrup | studied |
| stalked | steeper | stoical | studier |
| stalker | steeple | stomach | studies |
| stamina | steeply | stomata | stuffer |
| stammer | steerer | stonily | stumble |
| stamper | stellar | stooped | stumper |
| stand by | stencil | stopgap | stun gun |
| stand-by | Sten gun | stopper | stunner |
| stander | stepper | stopple | stunted |
| stand in | stepson | storage | stupefy |
| stand-in | sterile | storied | stutter |
| stand up | sterlet | stories | Stygian |
| stand-up | sternal | stoutly | stylise |
| staniel | sterned | stowage | stylish |
| stannic | sternly | strange | stylist |
| stanzas | sternum | stratum | stylite |
| stapler | steroid | stratus | stylize |
| starchy | stetson | strayer | styloid |
| stardom | steward | streaky | styptic |
| staring | sthenic | streamy | suasion |
| starkly | stibial | stretch | suasive |
| starlet | stichic | strewth | suavely |
| starlit | stick by | striate | suavity |
| starred | sticker | strigil | subacid |
| starter | stickle | striker | subaqua |

subdean
subdual
subduce
subduct
subdued
subduer
suberic
subhead
subject
subjoin
sublime
sub rosa
subside
subsidy
subsist
subsoil
subsume
subtend
subtile
subvene
subvert
succeed
success
succory
succour
succuba
succumb
sucking
sucrose
suction
suffice
suffuse
suggest
suicide
sulcate
sulfate
sulkily
sullens
sulphur
sultana

sumless
summary
summons
sumpter
sunbeam
sunburn
sundial
sundown
sunfish
sunlamp
sunless
sunrise
sunroof
sunspot
suntrap
sunward
support
suppose
supreme
supremo
surbase
surcoat
surface
surfeit
surfing
surgeon
surgery
surlily
surloin
surmise
surname
surpass
surplus
surreal
surtout
survive
suspect
suspend
sustain
sutlery

sutural
sutured
swabber
swaddle
swagger
Swahili
swallow
swarthy
swear by
swearer
sweater
Swedish
sweeper
sweeten
sweetie
sweetly
swelter
sweltry
swiftly
swiller
swimmer
swindle
swingle
swinish
switzer
swollen
sycosis
syenite
syllabi
sylphid
symptom
synapse
syncope
synergy
synesis
synodal
synodic
synonym
synovia
syringa

syringe
systole

**T**

tabaret
Tabasco®
tabbies
tabetic
tabinet
tableau
tabloid
taborer
taboret
tabulae
tabular
tachism
tachyon
tacitly
tactics
tactile
taction
tactual
tadpole
taffeta
taffety
tail-end
take off
take-off
take-out
talcose
talcous
taliped
talipes
talipot
talking
tallage
tallboy
tallier
tallies
tallith

| | | | |
|---|---|---|---|
| tallowy | teach-in | termini | thermal |
| tally-ho | tea-cosy | termite | thermic |
| tamable | tearful | ternary | Thermos® |
| tamarin | tear gas | ternate | theurgy |
| tambour | tearing | ternery | thiamin |
| tampion | tea-room | terpene | thicken |
| tanager | tea rose | terrace | thicket |
| tanbark | tea-shop | terrain | thickly |
| tangent | teasing | terrene | thieves |
| tanghin | techily | terrier | thiller |
| tangram | technic | terrify | thimble |
| tankage | tedious | terrine | thinker |
| tankard | teeming | tersely | think up |
| tank top | tegular | tertian | thinner |
| tanling | tektite | tessera | thirdly |
| tannage | telamon | testacy | thirsty |
| tannery | telecom | testate | thistle |
| tanning | telling | test ban | thistly |
| tantara | tempera | test-bed | thither |
| tantivy | tempest | testify | thorium |
| tantrum | templar | tetanic | thought |
| tapioca | templet | tetanus | thready |
| tapping | tempter | textile | three Rs |
| tap-room | tempura | textual | thrifty |
| tapster | tenable | texture | thriver |
| tarbush | tenably | thalami | throaty |
| tardily | tenancy | thallus | through |
| tarnish | tendril | thanage | thrower |
| tartish | tenfold | theatre | throw in |
| tastily | tenioid | theorbo | throw up |
| tatting | tenpins | theorem | thrummy |
| tattler | tensely | the pits | thuggee |
| taunter | tensile | therapy | thulium |
| taurine | tension | thereat | thumbed |
| taverna | tensity | thereby | thummim |
| taxable | tenthly | therein | thumper |
| tax-free | tenuity | thereof | thunder |
| taxi-cab | tenuous | thereon | thyroid |
| taxiway | tequila | thereto | thyrsus |
| teacher | terbium | thermae | thyself |

| | | | |
|---|---|---|---|
| tiaraed | toaster | tornado | traffic |
| ticking | tobacco | torpedo | tragedy |
| tickler | toby-jug | torpefy | trailer |
| tide-rip | toccata | torrefy | trained |
| tidings | toddler | torrent | trainee |
| tie down | toehold | torsion | trainer |
| tie-line | toenail | tortile | traipse |
| tiercel | togated | tortive | traitor |
| tiffany | toilful | torture | trammel |
| tighten | tollage | Toryism | tramper |
| tightly | toll-man | tostado | trample |
| tigress | toluene | totally | tramway |
| tigrine | tombola | tote-bag | tranche |
| tigrish | tom-fool | totemic | trannie |
| tillage | tompion | tottery | transit |
| timbale | tone arm | touched | transom |
| timbrel | tone pad | toucher | trapeze |
| time lag | tongued | toughen | trapper |
| timeous | tonight | toughly | travail |
| time off | tonnage | touraco | trawler |
| time out | tonsile | tourism | treacle |
| time was | tonsure | tourist | treader |
| timidly | tontine | tournay | treadle |
| timpani | tooling | tourney | treason |
| tindery | toothed | towards | treater |
| tinfoil | top-coat | towered | treddle |
| tinning | top gear | tow-line | trefoil |
| tinting | topiary | tow-path | trekker |
| tinware | topical | tow-rope | Trekkie |
| tippler | top-knot | toxemia | trellis |
| tipsily | topless | toxical | tremble |
| tipster | topmast | toyshop | tremolo |
| titanic | topmost | tracery | trenail |
| tithing | topping | trachea | trental |
| titlark | topsail | tracing | trepang |
| titling | top-side | tracker | tressed |
| titmice | top-soil | tractor | trestle |
| titrate | topspin | trade-in | triable |
| titular | torment | trading | triadic |
| toadies | tormina | traduce | tribune |

| | | | |
|---|---|---|---|
| tribute | trooper | tunnies | typeset |
| triceps | trophic | turbine | typhoid |
| tricker | tropism | turgent | typhoon |
| trickle | tropist | Turkish | typhous |
| tricksy | trotter | turkois | typical |
| tricorn | trouble | turmoil | tyranny |
| trident | trounce | turnery | tzarina |
| trifler | trouper | turning | |
| triform | truancy | turnkey | **U** |
| trigamy | trucker | turn off | ufology |
| trigger | truckle | turn-off | ukelele |
| trigram | truffle | turn out | ukulele |
| trilith | trumpet | turn-out | ulcered |
| trilogy | trundle | turnsol | ululate |
| trimmer | trunked | tussock | umbilic |
| tringle | trussed | tutelar | umbrage |
| trinity | trustee | twaddle | umpteen |
| trinket | truster | twaddly | unacted |
| triolet | tryable | twangle | unaided |
| tripang | try it on | twattle | unarmed |
| tripart | trypsin | tweeter | unasked |
| tripery | tsarina | twelfth | unaware |
| triplet | T-square | twibill | unblest |
| tripoli | tsunami | twiddle | unbosom |
| tripper | tubbing | twin bed | unbound |
| trireme | tubbish | twining | unbowed |
| trisect | tubular | twinkle | unbrace |
| trishaw | Tuesday | twinned | unburnt |
| trismus | tugboat | twin set | uncanny |
| tritely | tuition | twin-tub | uncared |
| tritium | tumbler | twister | unchain |
| triumph | tumbrel | twitter | uncivil |
| trivial | tumbril | twofold | unclasp |
| trochal | tumidly | twosome | unclean |
| trochar | tumular | two-step | uncloak |
| trochee | tumulus | two-time | unclose |
| trodden | tunable | two-tone | uncouth |
| troller | tunably | tympana | uncover |
| trolley | tuneful | tympani | uncrown |
| trollop | tunnage | tympany | unction |

| | | | |
|---|---|---|---|
| undated | unmoved | upstage | vaginal |
| underdo | unnamed | upstart | vagrant |
| undergo | unnerve | upstate | vaguely |
| undoing | unnoted | upsurge | valance |
| undress | unowned | upswing | valence |
| undying | unpaved | upthrow | valency |
| unearth | unquiet | uptight | valiant |
| unequal | unquote | upwards | validly |
| unfitly | unravel | uraemia | vallary |
| unfrock | unready | uranium | vallate |
| unglove | unscrew | urethra | valleys |
| ungodly | unshorn | urgency | valonia |
| ungreen | unsized | urinary | valuate |
| unguent | unsling | urinate | valvate |
| unhandy | unsound | Urodela | valvule |
| unhappy | unspent | urodele | vamoose |
| unhardy | unswept | urology | vampire |
| unheard | unsworn | useless | vanilla |
| unhinge | untamed | usually | vantage |
| unhitch | untaxed | usurper | vanward |
| unhoped | unteach | utensil | vapidly |
| unhorse | untried | uterine | vapoury |
| unhouse | untruly | utilise | variant |
| unicorn | untruth | utility | varices |
| unideal | untwine | utilize | variety |
| uniform | untwist | Utopian | variola |
| unitary | unusual | utricle | variole |
| unities | unwaged | utterer | various |
| unitise | unweave | utterly | varmint |
| unitive | unwooed | uxorial | varnish |
| unitize | unwrung | | varsity |
| unkempt | upbraid | **V** | vascula |
| unknown | upbreak | vacancy | vatical |
| unlatch | upfront | vacator | Vatican |
| unlearn | upgrade | vaccine | vaulted |
| unleash | upheave | vacuity | vaulter |
| unloose | upraise | vacuole | vaunter |
| unlucky | upright | vacuous | vavasor |
| unmanly | uprouse | vacuums | Vedanta |
| unmixed | upsilon | vaginae | vedette |

| | | | |
|---|---|---|---|
| veering | veteran | visiere | waggish |
| vegetal | vexilla | visiter | wagoner |
| vehicle | viaduct | visitor | wagtail |
| veining | vibrant | visored | wailing |
| veinlet | vibrate | vitally | waiting |
| velamen | vibrato | vitamin | wakeful |
| velaria | vibrios | vitiate | wakener |
| velites | viceroy | vitrify | walking |
| velours | vicinal | vitriol | Walkman® |
| velouté | vicious | vivaria | walk out |
| velvety | victory | vividly | walkout |
| venatic | victual | vivific | walkway |
| vendace | vicugna | vixenly | wallaby |
| venison | vidette | vocable | wall-eye |
| ventage | vidimus | vocably | walling |
| ventail | viduity | vocalic | Walloon |
| ventral | village | vocally | waltzer |
| venture | villain | Volapük | wanna-be |
| veranda | villein | volcano | wanness |
| verbena | villose | volleys | wannish |
| verbify | villous | voltage | wanting |
| verbose | vincula | voltaic | warbler |
| verdant | vinegar | voluble | warfare |
| verdict | vintage | volubly | war-game |
| verdure | vintner | volumed | warhead |
| verismo | violate | voluted | warlike |
| vermeil | violent | voucher | warlock |
| vernier | violist | voyager | warlord |
| Veronal® | violone | Vulgate | warning |
| verruca | virelay | vulpine | war-path |
| versant | virgate | vulture | warrant |
| versify | virgule | | warring |
| version | virtual | **W** | warrior |
| vertigo | visaged | wadding | warship |
| vervain | vis à vis | waddler | wart-hog |
| vesical | viscera | waddles | wartime |
| vesicle | viscose | wadmoll | washing |
| vespine | viscous | waftage | wash-out |
| vestige | visible | wagerer | wash-tub |
| vesture | visibly | waggery | waspish |

| | | | |
|---|---|---|---|
| wassail | well man | whistle | winsome |
| wastage | well-off | whither | wintery |
| wasting | wencher | whiting | wire-tap |
| wastrel | wergild | whitish | wise guy |
| watcher | werwolf | whitlow | wishful |
| watered | western | Whitsun | wistful |
| wattage | westing | whittle | wistiti |
| wattled | wetness | whiz-kid | withers |
| wavelet | wet suit | whoever | withies |
| waverer | wettish | whoopee | without |
| waxwork | whaling | whopper | witless |
| way-bill | wharves | whorish | witling |
| wayside | whatnot | whorled | witness |
| wayward | whatsit | who's who | wittily |
| way-worn | wheaten | widgeon | wizened |
| wealden | wheedle | widower | wobbler |
| wealthy | wheeled | wielder | wolfish |
| wearily | wheeler | wiggery | wolfkin |
| wearing | wheelie | wigging | wolfram |
| weasand | whene'er | wigless | womanly |
| weather | whereas | wildcat | woodcut |
| weaving | whereat | wilding | woodman |
| weazand | whereby | wildish | woodmen |
| webbing | where'er | wild oat | woollen |
| Web site | wherein | wileful | woorali |
| webster | whereof | willful | wordily |
| wedding | whereon | willies | wording |
| wedlock | whereto | willing | work-box |
| weekday | whether | willowy | workday |
| weekend | whetter | wimpish | working |
| weeping | whiffle | wimpish | workman |
| weevily | whimper | windage | workmen |
| weigher | whimsey | windbag | work out |
| weigh-in | whipper | winding | work-out |
| weighty | whippet | windrow | work-shy |
| weigh up | whip-saw | wine bar | work-top |
| weirdie | whirler | wine-box | worldly |
| welcome | whisker | winglet | worn-out |
| welfare | whiskey | wing-nut | worrier |
| wellies | whisper | winning | worship |

worsted
would-be
wouldn't
wounder
wourali
wrangle
wrapper
wreathe
wreathy
wrecked
wrecker
wrester
wrestle
wriggle
wringer
wrinkle
wrinkly
write-up
writing
written
wronger
wrongly
wrought

wry-neck
wryness
WYSIWYG

**X**

xanthic
xanthin
xerasia
xerosis
xerotes
x-height
xiphoid

**Y**

yachter
yardage
yard-arm
yard-man
yashmac
yashmak
yatagan
yawning
yclyped

yelling
yestern
Y-fronts
Yiddish
yielder
yoghurt
yolk-sac
Yorkist
youngly
younker
yttrium
Yule log
yuppify

**Z**

Zairean
Zairese
zanyism
zealous
zebrine
zedoary
zemstvo
zeolite

zetetic
zillion
zincoid
zincous
Zionism
ZIP Code
zithern
zomboid
zonated
zonular
zonulet
zoogamy
zoogeny
zoogony
zoolite
zoology
zoonomy
zootomy
zorille
zymogen
zymosis
zymotic
zymurgy

# Eight-letter words

**A**
aardvark
aardwolf
abattoir
abbatial
abdicant
abdicate
abducent
abductor
abelmosk
aberrant
abetment
abeyance
abhorrer
*ab initio*
abjectly
ablation
ablative
ablepsia
ablution
abnegate
abnormal
abomasum
abomasus
abortion
abortive
abradant
abrasion
abrasive
abrogate
abruptly
abscissa
absentee
absently

absinthe
absolute
absolver
absonant
absterge
abstract
abstruse
absurdly
abundant
abutment
academic
acanthus
acaridan
acarpous
acaudate
acauline
acaulose
acaulous
Accadian
accentor
accepter
acceptor
accident
accolade
accoutre
accredit
accresce
accuracy
accurate
accursed
accustom
acentric
acerbity
acervate

acescent
achiever
acicular
acid drop
acidific
acidosis
acid rain
acid test
acierage
acierate
aconitic
aconitum
acosmism
acoustic
acquaint
acquirer
acreable
acre-dale
acridity
acrimony
acrolith
acromion
acrostic
actinism
actinium
actinoid
activate
actively
activist
activity
act of God
act of war
actually
aculeate

adamitic
Adam's ale
addendum
addition
additive
adducent
adductor
adenitis
adenoids
adequacy
adequate
adherent
adhesion
adhesive
adiantum
adjacent
adjuster
adjutant
adjuvant
admonish
adoption
adoptive
adorable
adorably
adroitly
adscript
adulator
adultery
adumbral
advanced
advancer
advisory
advocaat
advocacy

| | | | |
|---|---|---|---|
| advocate | agrestic | aldermen | allodium |
| advowson | agrimony | aleatory | allogamy |
| adynamia | agronomy | aleberry | allopath |
| aeration | ague-cake | ale-house | allottee |
| aerially | aigrette | alfresco | alloyage |
| aeriform | aiguille | algaroba | all right |
| aerobics | airborne | Algerian | all-round |
| aerobium | air-brake | Algerine | allspice |
| aerocyst | air-brick | algerine | all there |
| aerofoil | air-brush | algidity | alluring |
| aerogram | air-cover | algology | allusion |
| aerolite | aircraft | algorism | allusive |
| aerology | air-drain | alguazil | alluvial |
| aeronaut | Airedale | alienage | alluvion |
| aerostat | airfield | alienate | alluvium |
| aesthete | airforce | alienism | almagest |
| aestival | airiness | alienist | almanack |
| affected | airliner | aliquant | almighty |
| afferent | air-plant | alizarin | alms-deed |
| affiance | air-shaft | alkahest | alopecia |
| affinity | airspace | alkalify | alphabet |
| affirmer | air speed | alkaline | alpha-ray |
| afflatus | air-strip | alkalise | alpigene |
| affluent | air-tight | alkalize | alpinist |
| afforest | air-to-air | alkaloid | Alsatian |
| affright | air-valve | alkarsin | alterant |
| affusion | Akkadian | all along | alter ego |
| after-wit | à la carte | all at sea | although |
| agalloch | alacrity | all clear | altitude |
| agar-agar | alarm-gun | allegory | alto clef |
| agastric | alarming | alleluia | altruism |
| agenesis | alarmism | allergen | aluminum |
| aggrieve | alarmist | alley cat | alum root |
| agiotage | albacore | all-fours | alveolar |
| agitated | albinism | all hours | alveolus |
| agitator | alburnum | alliance | amadavat |
| agnostic | alcahest | all in all | amaranth |
| Agnus Dei | alchemic | all my eye | amazedly |
| agraphia | aldehyde | allocate | amberoid |
| agrarian | alderman | allodial | ambiance |

| | | | |
|---|---|---|---|
| ambience | anasarca | antibody | appetize |
| ambition | anathema | antidote | applause |
| amblygon | ancestor | anti-hero | apple-pie |
| ambrosia | ancestry | antilogy | appliqué |
| ambulant | anchoret | antimask | apposite |
| ambulate | andesite | antimere | appraise |
| amenable | andirons | antimony | approach |
| amenably | androgen | antinomy | approval |
| American | anecdote | antiphon | approver |
| amethyst | aneurism | antipode | après-ski |
| amicable | aneurysm | antipope | apterous |
| amicably | Angeleno | antitype | aptitude |
| ammoniac | angelica | antlered | apyretic |
| ammonite | Anglican | anything | aqualung |
| ammonium | angstrom | anywhere | aquarium |
| amoebean | angulate | aoristic | Aquarius |
| amoretti | aniconic | aperient | aquatics |
| amoretto | animated | aperitif | aquatint |
| amortise | animater | aperture | aqueduct |
| amortize | animator | aphelion | aquiform |
| amperage | anisette | aphorism | aquiline |
| Amphibia | ankylose | aphorist | arachnid |
| amphipod | annalist | apiarian | arbalest |
| amphoral | annotate | apiarist | arbalist |
| amputate | announce | aplastic | arboreal |
| anabasis | annually | apodosis | arborist |
| anabatic | annulata | apologia | Arcadian |
| anableps | annulate | apologue | Archaean |
| anaconda | annulose | apophyge | archaise |
| an Adonis | anointer | apoplexy | archaism |
| anaerobe | anorexia | apostasy | archaize |
| anaglyph | anserine | apostate | archduke |
| analects | anserous | apothegm | archives |
| analogue | answerer | appanage | archness |
| analyser | ant-eater | apparent | arch-wise |
| analysis | antecede | appellee | arc-light |
| analytic | antedate | appendix | Arcturus |
| anapaest | antelope | appetent | ardently |
| anaphora | anterior | appetise | argental |
| anarchic | anteroom | appetite | argonaut |

arguable
arguably
argument
Arianism
aristate
armament
armature
armchair
Armenian
Arminian
armorial
armoured
armourer
arms race
army-list
aromatic
arpeggio
arquebus
arranger
arrestee
arrester
arrestor
arrogant
arrogate
arsenate
arsenous
artefact
arterial
Artesian
artfully
articled
artifact
artifice
artistic
artistry
asbestos
ascender
ascidian
ascidium
asperity

asphodel
asphyxia
aspirant
aspirate
aspiring
assailer
assassin
assaying
assemble
assembly
assertor
assessor
assignat
assignee
assigner
assignor
assonant
assorted
assuager
assuming
Assyrian
astatine
asterisk
asternal
asteroid
asthenia
asthenic
astonish
astragal
astutely
at a pinch
at a price
ataraxia
atheling
Atheneum
Athenian
atheroma
athletic
atlantes
Atlantic

atmology
atomiser
atomizer
atonable
at random
atrocity
atropine
attached
attacker
attemper
attender
attester
attestor
Atticism
Attic wit
attitude
attorney
atypical
aubretia
audacity
audience
audition
auditory
au gratin
Augustan
augustly
*au revoir*
auricula
auriform
Austrian
autarchy
autobahn
autocrat
auto-da-fé
autogamy
autogeny
autogiro
autogyro
automate
autonomy

autotype
autumnal
avadavat
Ave Maria
averment
aversion
aviation
avifauna
avionics
avoucher
avowable
avowedly
avulsion
a-weather
axillary
axle-tree

**B**

babirusa
baby boom
babyhood
baby wipe
baccarat
bacchant
bachelor
bacillar
bacillus
backache
backbite
backbone
back-chat
back-comb
back-date
back-door
back down
backdrop
backfall
back-fire
backhand
backlash

backlist
backmost
back pack
back-rest
backside
back spin
back-stay
backward
backwash
back yard
Baconian
bacteria
baculine
bad blood
badigeon
badinage
badly off
bad-mouth
bagpiper
bailable
bailment
bailsman
Bakelite®
balancer
baldness
balefire
ball-cock
ballista
ballonet
ballyhoo
ballyrag
balmoral
balsamic
baluster
banality
banausic
bandanna
bandelet
banderol
band-fish

bandsman
banged up
banisher
banister
bankable
bank-bill
bankbook
bank-note
bank-rate
bankrupt
bannered
banneret
bannerol
banterer
bantling
baptiser
baptizer
barathea
barbaric
barbecue
barberry
barbette
barbican
barbital
bardling
bareback
barefoot
bareness
bargeman
baritone
barnacle
barnyard
barogram
baronage
baroness
baronial
barouche
barracan
barracks
barranca

barranco
barrater
barrator
barratry
barterer
bartizan
barytone
basaltic
basanite
bascinet
baseball
base-born
baseless
base-line
basement
baseness
base rate
basicity
basidium
basilary
basilica
basilisk
bass clef
bassinet
bass-viol
bastardy
Batavian
bat-horse
bath robe
bathroom
battle-ax
bayadère
bayberry
bdellium
beaconed
bead-roll
beadsman
beam-ends
beamless
beam-tree

bean-king
bean-tree
bearable
bearably
bear's ear
bearskin
bearward
beatific
beat to it
beautify
beavered
béchamel
bechance
becoming
bedabble
bedeguar
bedesman
bedmaker
bed-plate
bedstead
bedstraw
bee-bread
beechnut
bee-eater
beefcake
beef-wood
beeswing
beetling
beetroot
befriend
befuddle
begetter
beggarly
beginner
begotten
begrudge
beguiler
behemoth
beholden
beholder

| | | | |
|---|---|---|---|
| belabour | bewilder | bird-lime | blinkard |
| believer | bezonian | birdseed | blissful |
| belittle | biannual | bird's-eye | blistery |
| bell-bird | biathlon | birthday | blithely |
| bell-buoy | biblical | bisector | blizzard |
| bell-pull | bibulous | biserial | blockade |
| bell push | biconvex | bisexual | blockage |
| bell-rope | bicuspid | bistoury | blockish |
| bellyful | biddable | biting in | block-tin |
| below par | biennial | bitingly | bloodily |
| Bel paese | bifacial | bitterly | blood-red |
| bemoaner | bifocals | bivalent | bloomers |
| bendable | bigamist | biweekly | bloomery |
| benedick | Big Apple | black art | blooming |
| benedict | big-mouth | black box | blossomy |
| benefice | big noise | black cap | blow-hard |
| benignly | bignonia | black eye | blow-hole |
| bentwood | big of you | blackfly | blow-lamp |
| bequeath | Big Smoke | black ice | blow over |
| berceuse | big stick | blacking | blow-pipe |
| bergamot | bijugate | blackish | bludgeon |
| bergmehl | bilander | blackleg | blue baby |
| beriberi | bilberry | black-out | bluebell |
| berthage | bill-fold | Black Rod | bluebird |
| besieger | bill-hook | black tie | Blue book |
| besmirch | billyboy | bladdery | blue chip |
| besotted | billy-can | blamable | blueness |
| besought | bilobate | blamably | bluenose |
| bespread | bimanous | blameful | bluntish |
| besprent | bimensal | blandish | blushing |
| bestiary | binaural | blastema | boarding |
| bestowal | bind-weed | blast-off | boastful |
| bestower | binnacle | blastula | boat-bill |
| bestride | binomial | blazoner | boat-hook |
| beta wave | biologic | blazonry | bobbinet |
| betel-nut | biometry | bleacher | bobby pin |
| betrayal | bioplasm | bleeding | bobolink |
| betrayer | biparous | blessing | bock beer |
| beverage | biramous | blindage | bodement |
| bewailer | bird-call | blinding | bodiless |

| | | | |
|---|---|---|---|
| bodywork | bordello | brandied | britzska |
| Boeotian | borderer | brandish | broacher |
| bogeyman | borecole | brand-new | brocaded |
| boggling | borrower | brasilin | broccoli |
| Bohemian | botanise | brassard | brochure |
| boldness | botanist | brassart | brokenly |
| bollocks | botanize | brassica | bronchia |
| bolt-head | botchery | bratpack | bronchus |
| bolt-hole | botherer | brattice | bronzite |
| bolt-rope | botryoid | brawling | brooklet |
| bomb site | bottomed | brazenly | brougham |
| bombycid | bottomry | brazilin | brouhaha |
| bona fide | botulism | breadnut | browbeat |
| bondmaid | bouffant | breakage | browning |
| bondsman | bouillon | break out | brownish |
| bone-dust | bouncing | break-out | brunette |
| bonehead | boundary | breasted | brush-off |
| bone idle | bourgeon | breather | brutally |
| bone-lace | boutique | breeched | bryology |
| bone-meal | bouzouki | breeches | bryozoan |
| bonhomie | bowmaker | breeding | bryozoon |
| boniface | bow-sprit | brethren | buckaroo |
| bonneted | boxmaker | breviary | buckbean |
| bonspiel | box-pleat | breviate | buckshee |
| bontebok | boyishly | breviped | buckshot |
| boobyish | Boy Scout | brewster | buck-skin |
| book-case | bracelet | bribable | Buddhism |
| book-club | brachial | brickbat | Buddhist |
| book-mark | brackish | brick-red | buddleia |
| book-oath | bradypod | brick-tea | bughouse |
| bookworm | braggart | bridging | building |
| boom town | Brahmani | brighten | bulkhead |
| boot camp | braiding | brightly | bull bars |
| boot-jack | brainish | brimless | bull-calf |
| bootlace | brain-pan | brimming | bulldoze |
| bootless | brakeman | brindled | bulletin |
| boot-tree | brakemen | brine-pan | bull-frog |
| borachio | brake-van | brine-pit | bull-head |
| boracite | branched | brisling | bull-ring |
| Bordeaux | branchia | bristled | bull's-eye |

bullshit
bull-whip
bully boy
bullyrag
bulrushy
bum's rush
bum steer
buncombe
bungalow
bung-hole
bungling
buntline
buoyancy
burganet
burgeois
burglary
burgonet
burgrave
Burgundy
burletta
burnable
burnouse
burrower
bush-baby
bush fire
business
buskined
bust a gut
busybody
butchery
butter up
buttress
butyrate
buzzword
by chance
by-corner
by rights
bystreet
by the bye
by the way

**C**
caballer
cabin-boy
cable-car
cabochon
caboodle
cabriole
cachalot
cachepot
cachexia
cachucha
cacology
cadaster
cadastre
caducean
caduceus
caducity
caducous
caesural
*café noir*
caffeine
cageling
cajolery
cake-walk
calabash
calamary
calamine
calamint
calamite
calamity
calciner
calcspar
calc-tuff
calcular
calculus
calendar
calender
calf-love
calfskin
califate

calipash
calipers
calisaya
call-bird
call-girl
calliope
calliper
call-loan
call-note
call sign
calmness
calotype
calthrop
calvados
calycine
calyptra
Cambrian
cameleer
cameleon
cameline
camellia
camisade
camisole
camomile
campaign
camp-fire
camphene
camphine
camp-site
camshaft
Canadian
canaille
canalise
canalize
canaster
cancelli
cancroid
candidly
cane-mill
canister

cannabin
cannabis
cannibal
cannikin
cannonry
canoeist
canoness
canonise
canonist
canonize
canon law
canoodle
canopied
canorous
canticle
cantonal
canzonet
capacity
Capetian
cap it all
capitate
caponise
caponize
capriole
capsicum
capsizal
capsular
captious
Capuchin
capuchin
capybara
carabine
caracara
caracole
carageen
carapace
carbolic
carbonic
carburet
carcajou

carcanet
cardamom
cardamon
cardamum
card-case
card file
cardigan
cardinal
carditis
carefree
careless
care-worn
caricado
carillon
carinate
carnally
carnauba
carnival
Carolean
Caroline
carousal
carousel
carouser
car phone
carriage
carriole
carry-all
carrycot
carry-out
cartload
cartouch
carucate
caruncle
caryatid
Casanova
cascabel
casemate
casement
case shot
casework

caseworm
cash-book
cash crop
cash flow
cashmere
casimere
cassette
castanet
castaway
cast-down
cast-iron
castling
castrate
castrato
casually
casualty
catacomb
catalyse
catalyst
catalyze
catamite
catapult
cataract
catch-all
catch-fly
catching
category
catenary
catenate
cateress
cathedra
catheter
Catholic
catholic
cat-house
Catonian
cat's-tail
caudated
caudicle
cauldron

caulicle
causable
causally
causerie
causeway
cautious
cavalier
cavatina
cave-bear
cave-fish
caverned
cavesson
cavicorn
caviller
celeriac
celerity
celibacy
celibate
cellarer
cellaret
cellular
cemetery
cenobite
cenotaph
Cenozoic
centaury
centiare
centoist
centrist
centroid
centuple
cephalic
ceramics
ceramist
cerastes
ceratose
Cerberus
cerebral
cerebrin
cerebrum

cerement
ceremony
cerulean
cerulein
cerusite
cervical
Cesarean
Cesarian
cesspool
cetacean
cetology
chaconne
chain-saw
chairman
chairmen
chaldaic
Chaldean
chaldron
chamfron
champion
chance it
chancery
chandler
chantage
chaology
chapatti
chapbook
chaperon
chapiter
chaplain
charcoal
charisma
charlock
charming
Chartism
chartist
chasseur
chastely
chastise
chastity

| | | | |
|---|---|---|---|
| chasuble | chivalry | circular | clemency |
| chat show | chloasma | cirriped | clencher |
| chauffer | chlorate | cirrouse | clerical |
| cheatery | chloride | ciselure | clerihew |
| cheating | chlorine | citation | cleverly |
| check-out | chlorite | citatory | clew-line |
| cheerful | choicely | civet-cat | cliental |
| cheerily | choirboy | civilian | climatic |
| cheering | choleric | civilise | climbing |
| chemical | chopping | civilist | clincher |
| chenille | chop suey | civility | clinical |
| cherubic | choragus | civilize | clippers |
| chessman | chorally | civil war | clipping |
| chessmen | chow mein | claimant | cliquish |
| chestnut | chrismal | clambake | cliquism |
| chewed up | christen | clangour | clitoris |
| chiasmus | chromate | clannish | cloak-bag |
| chicaner | chromite | clanship | cloddish |
| chick-pea | chromium | clansman | clod-poll |
| chiefdom | chthonic | clansmen | cloister |
| chiefery | chuffily | claptrap | clothier |
| chiefess | churlish | claqueur | clothing |
| childbed | chutzpah | clarence | cloudily |
| childing | ciborium | clarinet | cloudlet |
| childish | cicatrix | classics | clownish |
| children | cicerone | classify | clubable |
| chiliasm | ciderage | classism | clubbist |
| chilling | ciderish | classist | club-foot |
| chill out | ciderist | clavecin | club-haul |
| chilopod | ci-devant | clavicle | club-moss |
| chimaera | ciliated | claw back | club-room |
| chimeric | cimolite | clay-cold | clueless |
| China ink | cinchona | claymore | clumsily |
| chinless | cincture | clean-cut | clypeate |
| chipmunk | cineaste | cleanser | coach-box |
| chipping | Cinerama® | clear-cut | coach dog |
| chip-shot | cinerary | clearing | coachman |
| chiragra | cingulum | cleavage | coachmen |
| chit-chat | cinnabar | cleavers | coaction |
| chitlins | cinnamon | clematis | coactive |

| | | | |
|---|---|---|---|
| coagency | coincide | commence | confused |
| coagulum | coin it in | commerce | congener |
| coalesce | colander | commoner | conglobe |
| coal-fish | cold-call | commonly | congress |
| coal-mine | cold feet | communal | conicity |
| coarsely | coldness | commuter | conidium |
| coasting | cold sore | compiler | coniform |
| co-author | cole-seed | complain | conjoint |
| cobaltic | coleslaw | complect | conjugal |
| cobwebby | colewort | complete | conjunct |
| Coca-Cola® | coliseum | complice | conjurer |
| cocculus | collagen | complier | conjuror |
| cockaded | collapse | compline | conniver |
| cockatoo | collared | composed | conquest |
| Cockayne | colleret | composer | conserve |
| cock-boat | collator | compound | consider |
| cock-crow | colliery | compress | consoler |
| cockerel | colloquy | comprise | consommé |
| cock-eyed | colonial | computer | conspire |
| cockloft | colonise | con amore | constant |
| cocksure | colonist | conation | construe |
| cocktail | colonize | conative | consular |
| code name | colophon | conceder | consumer |
| code word | colorant | conceive | consumpt |
| codifier | colossal | concerto | contango |
| cod-piece | colossus | conchoid | contempt |
| coercion | colotomy | conclave | continue |
| coercive | coloured | conclude | contract |
| coextend | columnar | concrete | contrary |
| coffered | columned | condense | contrast |
| cogently | colza-oil | conferee | con trick |
| cogitate | comatose | conferva | contrite |
| cognomen | combined | confetti | contrive |
| cog-wheel | combiner | confined | convener |
| coherent | come-back | conflate | converge |
| cohesion | comedian | conflict | converse |
| cohesive | come-down | confocal | convexly |
| cohobate | cometary | confound | conveyal |
| coiffeur | comitial | confrère | conveyer |
| coiffure | commando | confront | conveyor |

convince
convolve
convulse
cony-wool
cookbook
coolness
copperas
copulate
copybook
copy-edit
copyhold
coq au vin
coquetry
coquette
coracoid
coral rag
cordless
cordovan
corduroy
cordwain
coregent
coreless
cormogen
corncrib
corneous
cornered
cornetcy
corn-flag
corn-husk
corniche
corn laws
corn-mill
corn-pipe
corn-pone
corn-rent
corn-rose
cornuted
coronach
coronary
coronoid

corporal
corridor
corrival
corselet
cortical
corundum
corvette
corybant
coryphee
cosecant
cosenage
cosmetic
cosmical
cost-free
costless
costmary
costumed
costumer
co-surety
cot death
cotenant
cotquean
cottager
cotyloid
couchant
couching
coulisse
coumarin
countess
coupling
coursing
court-day
courtesy
courtier
couscous
cousinly
covenant
coverage
cover-all
covering

coverlet
coverlid
covertly
covetous
covinous
cowardly
cow-berry
co-worker
coxalgia
coxswain
cozenage
crab-tree
crab-wood
crackers
cracking
cracknel
crackpot
cradling
craftily
cragsman
cragsmen
cranefly
crankily
crankpin
crannied
crawfish
crayfish
creamery
creasote
creatine
creation
creative
creature
credence
credible
credibly
creditor
cremator
crenated
crenelle

creosote
crescent
cresting
cretonne
creutzer
crevasse
crew neck
cribbage
cribrate
crimeful
criminal
crimping
crispate
cristate
critical
critique
croaking
Croatian
crockery
cromlech
cromorne
crop-full
crop-sick
cross-bar
cross-bow
crosscut
cross-eye
crossing
crosslet
cross-tie
cross-way
crotched
crotchet
croupier
crowfoot
crowning
crownlet
crown saw
cruciate
crucible

crucifer
crucifix
crude oil
crudités
crumpled
crusader
crush-hat
crushing
crustily
crutched
cryolite
cryonics
cubature
cube root
cubiform
Cub Scout
cucumber
cucurbit
cufflink
cul de sac
culinary
culottes
culpable
culpably
cultrate
cultural
cultured
culverin
Cumbrian
cumbrous
cumulate
cupboard
cupidity
cupreous
curarine
curarise
curarize
curassow
curative
curatrix

curbable
curb-roof
curculio
cureless
curlicue
currency
curricle
cursedly
cursores
curtness
cushiony
cuspidal
cuspidor
customer
cut a dash
cut-glass
cut-grass
cut it out
cut no ice
cut-price
cutpurse
cutwater
cyanamid
cyanogen
cyanosis
cyclamen
cyclical
cyclonic
Cyclopes
cyclopic
cylinder
cynanche
cynicism
cynosure
cyprinid
Cyrenaic
Cyrillic
cystitis
cytogeny
cytology

czarevna
czaritza

**D**
dab-chick
dacryoma
dactylic
daffodil
dahabeah
daintily
daiquiri
dairying
dairy-man
dairy-men
dalesman
dalesmen
dalmatic
dal segno
damassin
damnable
damnably
dampness
dandruff
dandyish
dandyism
Danegeld
Danelagh
*danseuse*
daringly
darkling
darkness
dark ride
dark room
darksome
dastardy
data-bank
data-base
dateless
date-line
date-palm

date rape
date-tree
daturine
daughter
dauphine
Davy lamp
dawn raid
daybreak
day by day
daydream
daylight
day to day
dazzling
dead-beat
dead-born
dead duck
dead-fall
deadhead
dead heat
deadline
deadlock
dead loss
dead meat
deadness
dead-well
dead-wood
deadwork
deaf-mute
deafness
dealfish
dealings
deanship
dearness
death-bed
deathful
death row
death tax
debasing
debility
debonair

| | | | |
|---|---|---|---|
| debutant | definite | demonist | desolate |
| decadent | deflower | demonise | despatch |
| decagram | defluent | demonize | despiser |
| decanter | deforest | demurely | despotic |
| deceased | deformed | demurrer | destruct |
| deceiver | deformer | denarius | detached |
| December | defrayal | denature | detailed |
| decemvir | deftness | dendrite | detailer |
| decently | degraded | dendroid | detainee |
| decimate | dejected | deniable | detainer |
| decipher | *déjeuner* | denounce | detector |
| decision | delation | denticle | detester |
| decisive | delegate | departed | dethrone |
| deckhand | deletion | depender | detonate |
| deckload | delicacy | depilate | detonise |
| declared | delicate | deplorer | detonize |
| declarer | delirium | deponent | detoxify |
| declassé | delivery | deportee | detrital |
| declinal | Delphian | depraved | detritus |
| decolour | delusion | depraver | deucedly |
| decorate | delusive | deprived | deuteron |
| decorous | delusory | depriver | devilish |
| decrease | demagogy | depurate | Devonian |
| decrepit | demander | deputise | devotion |
| decretal | demarche | deputize | devoutly |
| decurion | demeanor | deranged | dewberry |
| dedicate | demented | derelict | dewiness |
| deedless | dementia | derision | dewpoint |
| deemster | demersal | derisive | dewy-eyed |
| deep-laid | demijohn | derisory | dextrine |
| deepness | demilune | dermatic | dextrose |
| deer-hair | demi-tint | derogate | dextrous |
| defecate | demi-tone | describe | diabetes |
| defendee | demiurge | descrier | diabetic |
| defender | demivolt | deselect | diabolic |
| deferent | demi-wolf | deserter | diaconal |
| deferred | democrat | deserved | diadelph |
| deferrer | demolish | deserver | diademed |
| defiance | demoniac | designer | diaglyph |
| defilade | demonism | desirous | diagnose |

diagonal
diagraph
diallage
dialling
dialogue
dialyser
dialysis
dialyzer
diamanté
diameter
diameter
dianthus
diapason
Diaspora
diastase
diastema
diastole
diatomic
diatonic
diatribe
diazepam
dicentra
dichroic
dickhead
diclinic
dicrotic
dictator
didactic
didapper
didymium
didymous
diecious
dieresis
dietetic
diffract
diffuser
digamist
digester
diggable
digitate

digitise
digitize
digynian
digynous
dihedral
dihedron
dilation
dilative
dilatory
diligent
dilution
diluvial
diluvian
diluvion
diluvium
dimerous
diminish
ding-dong
Dinornis
dinosaur
diocesan
dioecian
diopside
dioptase
dioptric
dioramic
diplomat
diplopia
dipstick
dipteral
dipteran
directly
director
disabled
disabuse
disagree
disallow
disannex
disannul
disarray

disaster
disburse
disciple
disclaim
disclose
discount
discover
discreet
discrete
discrown
diseased
disendow
disgorge
disgrace
disguise
dishevel
dishorse
disinter
disjoint
disjunct
dislodge
disloyal
dismally
dismount
disorder
dispatch
dispeace
dispense
disperse
dispirit
displace
disposal
disposed
disproof
disprove
disquiet
disseise
disseize
dissever
dissolve

dissuade
distally
distance
distaste
distinct
distract
distrain
distrait
distress
district
distrust
disunion
disunite
disusage
ditheism
ditheist
diuretic
divalent
dividend
dividivi
dividual
divinely
divinity
division
divisive
divorcee
divorcer
docility
docimasy
dockyard
doctoral
doctrine
document
doddered
dog-cheap
dog-eared
dog-fight
doggedly
doggerel
dog-grass

doggy bag
dog-house
dog-Latin
dogmatic
do-gooder
dogsbody
dog-sleep
dog's life
dogtooth
dog-watch
doldrums
dolerite
dolomite
doloroso
dolorous
domainal
domesday
domestic
domicile
dominant
dominate
domineer
dominion
dominoes
donation
donative
doomsday
doomsman
doorbell
doorjamb
door-nail
door-post
doorstep
doorstop
dormancy
dormouse
dotation
dotingly
dotterel
doubling

doubloon
doubtful
dough-boy
dough-nut
dove-cote
dovetail
downbeat
downcast
downcome
downfall
downhill
downland
downless
down line
download
downlong
downpour
downside
downsize
downtown
downturn
downward
downwind
doxology
dracaena
draconic
dragoman
dragonet
drainage
dramatic
draughts
draughty
drawable
drawback
draw-well
dreadful
dreamily
drearily
dressage
dressing

driftage
drift-net
drift-way
drilling
dripping
driveway
drollery
drop-kick
dropping
dropsied
dropwort
droughty
drowsily
drubbing
drudgery
druggist
druidism
drum-head
drunkard
drupelet
dry-clean
dry-nurse
dry-point
dubitate
ducatoon
duck-bill
duckling
duckmeat
duck soup
duck-weed
duelling
duellist
dulcimer
dullness
dumb-bell
dumbness
dumfound
dumpling
dumpster
dungaree

dung-fork
dungheap
dunghill
duodenum
duologue
duration
dust-ball
dust-bowl
dust-cart
dust-coat
dutiable
duty-free
dwarfish
dwelling
dye-house
dye-stuff
dyeworks
dynamics
dynamise
dynamism
dynamite
dynamize
dynastic
dysgenic
dyslexia
dyspnoea

**E**

eagle-owl
earnings
earphone
earpiece
ear shell
earthing
earthish
earth-nut
earth-pig
easement
easiness
easterly

eastward
easy meat
eau de vie
eburnean
eburnine
ecaudate
echinate
echinite
echinold
eclectic
ecliptic
eco-label
economic
ecostate
écraseur
ecstatic
ectoderm
ecumenic
edacious
edentata
Edentate
edge-bone
edgeless
edge-tool
edgeways
edgewise
edifying
editress
educable
educator
educible
eel-spear
eeriness
effecter
effector
efferent
efficacy
effluent
effusion
effusive

egestion
egg-plant
eggshell
egg-slice
egg-spoon
egoistic
Egyptian
eight-day
eighteen
eighthly
ejection
elapsion
elatedly
Eldorado
El Dorado
eldritch
election
elective
electric
electron
electrum
elegance
elegancy
elegiast
elegious
elenchus
elephant
elevated
elevator
eleventh
elf-arrow
eligible
eligibly
ellipsis
elliptic
elongate
eloquent
eludible
clvishly
emaciate

embalmer
embattle
embezzle
embitter
emblazon
embolden
embolite
embolism
embracer
emergent
emeritus
emersion
emigrant
emigrate
eminence
eminency
emissary
emission
emissive
emissory
Emmental
empannel
emphasis
emphatic
employee
employer
empoison
emporium
empurple
empyreal
empyrean
emulator
emulgent
emulsify
emulsion
emulsive
enactive
enallage
enceinte
enchoric

encircle
enclitic
encomium
encrinal
encrinic
encroach
encumber
encyclic
endamage
endanger
endeavor
endermic
endocarp
endoderm
endogamy
endorser
end-paper
enduring
energise
energize
enervate
enfeeble
enfilade
enforest
engaging
engender
engineer
engorged
engraver
enhancer
enkindle
enlarged
enlarger
enneagon
enormity
enormous
enquirer
enroller
ensample
ensconce

| | | | |
|---|---|---|---|
| ensemble | epic poet | eructate | ethology |
| enshrine | epicycle | eruption | ethylene |
| enshroud | epidemic | eruptive | etiolate |
| ensiform | epidural | erythema | etiology |
| ensilage | epigeous | escalade | Etruscan |
| enslaver | epigraph | escalate | eucalypt |
| enswathe | epilepsy | escallop | eugenics |
| entailer | epilogic | escalope | eulogise |
| entangle | epilogue | escapade | eulogist |
| entellus | epinasty | escapism | eulogium |
| enthrone | Epiphany | escapist | eulogize |
| enticing | epiphyte | escargot | euonymus |
| entirely | epiploic | eschalot | eupepsia |
| entirety | epiploon | esculent | eupeptic |
| entoderm | episodic | esoteric | euphonic |
| entomoid | episperm | espalier | euphoria |
| entozoal | epistler | especial | euphrasy |
| entozoan | epistyle | espousal | euphuism |
| entozoic | eponymic | espouser | euphuist |
| entozoon | epulotic | espresso | Eurasian |
| entr'acte | equalise | essayist | Eurocrat |
| entrails | equality | estancia | European |
| entrance | equalize | estimate | europium |
| entreaty | equation | estoppel | evacuant |
| entrench | equipage | estovers | evacuate |
| entrepot | equitant | estrange | evadable |
| entresol | equivoke | esurient | cvaluate |
| enuresis | eradiate | etcctcra | evanesce |
| envelope | Erastian | eternise | evection |
| enviable | erectile | eternity | evenness |
| enviably | erection | eternize | evensong |
| environs | erective | etheling | eventful |
| envisage | eremitic | ethereal | eventide |
| enzootic | erethism | etherify | eventual |
| eolipile | ergotine | etherise | evermore |
| eolipyle | ergotism | etherism | eversion |
| ephemera | erotetic | etherize | everyday |
| Ephesian | erotical | ethicist | everyone |
| epiblast | errantry | Ethiopic | eviction |
| epicalyx | errorist | ethnical | evidence |

evil-doer
evilness
evulsion
exacting
exaction
examinee
examiner
excavate
exchange
excision
excitant
exciting
excursus
execrate
executes
executor
exegesis
exegetic
exemplar
exequial
exercise
exertion
ex gratia
exhalant
exhalent
exhorter
exigence
exigency
exigible
exiguity
exiguous
existent
ex libris
exocrine
exorable
exorcise
exorcism
exorcist
exorcize
exordial

exordium
exosmose
exoteric
expecter
expedite
expeller
expertly
expiable
expiator
explicit
explorer
exponent
exporter
exposure
exserted
extender
extensor
exterior
external
extoller
extrados
extrorse
exultant
exuviate
eye-glass
eye-liner
eye-piece
eye-print
eyesight
eye-teeth
eye-tooth
eye-water

F
fabulist
fabulous
face-ache
face-card
faceless
face-lift

facetiae
face-time
faceting
facially
facility
factious
factotum
fadeless
fadingly
Faeroese
fail-safe
faineant
fainting
fair game
fairness
fair play
faithful
falcated
falchion
falconer
falconet
falconry
falderal
fallible
fallibly
fall-trap
falsetto
fameless
familiar
famously
fanciful
fancy-man
fandango
fanfaron
fanlight
fantasia
faradise
faradize
farceuse
farcical

farewell
far-flung
farinose
farmable
farm-hand
farmyard
farouche
farriery
farthest
farthing
fasciate
fascicle
fashious
fastback
fastener
fast-food
fast lane
fastness
fatalism
fatalist
fatality
fatherly
fattener
faubourg
faultily
fauteuil
favonian
favoured
favourer
fearless
fearsome
feasible
feasibly
feathery
featured
February
feckless
feculent
federate
feedback

| | | | |
|---|---|---|---|
| feed-pipe | fiendish | finisher | flashily |
| feed-pump | fiercely | finitely | flashing |
| feldspar | fife-rail | finitude | flat fish |
| felicity | fiftieth | fireball | flatfoot |
| fellatio | fighting | fire-clay | flat-iron |
| fellness | figuline | firedamp | flatland |
| felo-de-se | figurant | fire-lock | flatling |
| felstone | figurate | fire-plug | flatlong |
| feme sole | figurine | fire-ship | flatness |
| feminine | figuring | fireside | flat spin |
| feminise | filagree | fire-trap | flattery |
| feminism | filament | firewood | flatting |
| feminize | filatory | firework | flatways |
| fencible | filature | firmness | flatworm |
| feracity | file-fish | first aid | flaunter |
| feretory | filester | fish-cake | flautist |
| fern-seed | filially | fish-hook | flawless |
| ferocity | filicoid | fish meal | flax-seed |
| ferreous | filiform | fish-pond | flea-bane |
| ferreter | filigree | fish-wife | flea-bite |
| ferriage | Filipino | fissiped | fletcher |
| ferryman | filister | fistular | flection |
| fervency | fillibeg | fitfully | fleeting |
| fervidly | film buff | fivefold | flesh-pot |
| festally | film card | fixation | flexible |
| festival | film noir | fixative | flexibly |
| fetation | film star | flabbily | flextime |
| fetching | filthily | flabella | flcxuose |
| feticide | filtrate | flagella | flexuous |
| feudally | finalise | flagging | flimflam |
| feverfew | finalist | flagpole | flinders |
| feverish | finality | flagrant | flip-flop |
| feverous | finalize | flagship | flippant |
| fibrilla | fineable | flake out | flipside |
| fibrosis | fine arts | flambeau | floatage |
| fiddling | fine-draw | flamenco | floating |
| fidelity | fineness | flamingo | floccose |
| fiducial | fine-spun | flanerie | floccule |
| field-day | fine-tune | flapjack | flogging |
| field-gun | fingered | flash gun | flooding |

| | | | |
|---|---|---|---|
| floorage | fontanel | forelock | fosterer |
| flooring | foodless | foremast | foulness |
| florally | foolscap | foremost | foul play |
| floridly | football | forenoon | fountain |
| floscule | footfall | forensic | fourfold |
| flotilla | foot-gear | forepart | foursome |
| flounder | foothill | forepeak | fourteen |
| flourish | foothold | foreplay | fourthly |
| flowered | footling | foresaid | foxglove |
| floweret | footmark | foresail | foxhound |
| fluently | footnote | foreshow | fraction |
| fluidity | footpath | foreside | fracture |
| flummery | footslog | foreskin | fragment |
| fluoride | footsore | forestal | fragrant |
| fluorine | footstep | forestay | francium |
| fluorite | footwear | forester | frankish |
| fluxible | footwork | forestry | franklin |
| fly a kite | foramina | foretell | fraudful |
| fly-paper | for a song | foretime | Fräulein |
| focalise | forborne | foreward | freakish |
| focalize | forcedly | forewarn | freckled |
| fog-bound | forceful | forewent | freeborn |
| fogeyism | forcible | forewind | freedman |
| foldaway | forcibly | foreword | freedmen |
| folderol | forclose | forgeman | free fall |
| foldless | fordable | for keeps | free hand |
| foliated | forebear | for kicks | free-hand |
| folkland | forebode | formalin | freehold |
| folk-lore | forecast | formally | free kick |
| folk-song | foredeck | formerly | freeload |
| folk-tale | foredeem | formless | free love |
| follicle | foredoom | formulae | freeness |
| follower | forefend | forsaker | free port |
| follow on | forefoot | forsooth | free will |
| follow-on | foregoer | forswear | freezing |
| follow up | foregone | fortieth | frenetic |
| follow-up | forehand | fortress | frenzied |
| fomenter | forehead | fortuity | frequent |
| fondling | foreknow | forwards | frescoed |
| fondness | foreland | forzando | frescoes |

| | | | |
|---|---|---|---|
| freshman | fugacity | **G** | garrison |
| freshmen | fugitive | gadabout | garrotte |
| fretwork | fugleman | gadgetry | gasalier |
| Freudian | fulcrate | Gadhelic | gaselier |
| fribbler | fulcrums | gainless | gaslight |
| fricando | fulgency | gain time | gasogene |
| friction | full back | galactic | gasolene |
| friendly | full face | galangal | gasolier |
| frighten | full moon | galavant | gasoline |
| frigidly | fullness | galbanum | gastrula |
| frilling | full stop | galeated | gas-works |
| frippery | full time | Galilean | gatefold |
| frisette | fulminic | galleass | gate-post |
| friskily | fumarole | galliard | gatherer |
| frizette | fumeless | Gallican | Gaullism |
| frog-fish | fumigate | gallipot | Gaullist |
| frolicky | fumitory | galloper | gauntlet |
| from A to Z | function | Galloway | gavelman |
| fromenty | fundable | galvanic | gazogene |
| from hell | funereal | game-cock | gazpacho |
| frontage | fungible | gameness | gelatine |
| frontier | funguses | gamesome | gelation |
| frontlet | furbelow | gamester | gelidity |
| frostily | furcated | gang-bang | geminate |
| frosting | furfural | gangland | geminous |
| frothily | furlough | gangliac | gemmeous |
| frou-frou | furmenty | gangling | gcmstone |
| fructify | furriery | ganglion | gendarme |
| fructose | furthest | gangrene | generant |
| frugally | furuncle | gangster | generate |
| fruitage | fusarole | ganister | generous |
| fruitery | fuselage | gantlope | genetics |
| fruitful | fusel oil | gaolbird | Genevese |
| fruit gum | fusiform | garboard | genially |
| fruition | fusileer | gardener | genitals |
| frumenty | fusilier | gardenia | genitive |
| frumpish | futilely | gargoyle | geniuses |
| frustule | futility | garishly | genocide |
| frustums | futurism | garlicky | gentrify |
| fuchsine | futurity | garotter | geodesic |

geodetic
geognosy
geomancy
geometer
geometry
geophagy
geoponic
Georgian
geranium
gerbille
Germanic
germ-cell
Germinal
gestural
get a grip
get a life
get off on
ghoulies
ghoulish
giantess
gibingly
gigantic
giggling
gimcrack
gingerly
gingival
girasole
girlhood
give away
give-away
glabrous
glaciate
gladiate
gladioli
gladness
glad rags
gladsome
glanders
glandule
glareous

glasnost
glassful
glassily
glaucoma
glaucous
gleaning
gleesome
glibness
glissade
gloaming
globated
globular
globulet
globulin
gloomily
gloriole
glorious
glossary
glossily
glow-worm
gloxinia
glucinum
glumness
gluttony
glycerin
glycerol
glycogen
glyptics
gnarring
gnatling
gnomical
gnomonic
goatfish
goatherd
goatskin
godchild
God speed
godwards
go easy on
go-getter

goings-on
goitrous
gold card
goldfish
gold leaf
gold-mine
gold rush
golf-ball
golf club
Golgotha
golliwog
gollywog
go native
gonfalon
gonfanon
gonidium
goodness
good turn
goodwill
go places
gorgeous
gossamer
gossiper
gossipry
go steady
go to seed
go to town
gourmand
goutweed
governor
gownsman
Graafian
graceful
gracious
gradient
graduate
Graecism
graffiti
graffito
graining

gralloch
gramarye
gramercy
granddad
grandeur
grand mal
grandson
granitic
granular
graphics
graphite
grasping
grateful
gratuity
gravamen
gravelly
grayling
greasily
great tit
Great War
greedily
greenery
greenfly
greening
greenish
green tea
greeting
grewsome
grey area
greyness
gridiron
gridlock
grievous
grillade
grillage
grimness
grinding
griseous
grisette
grizzled

groining
gromwell
grosbeak
groschen
grottoes
grouping
growling
grudging
gruesome
grumbler
grumpily
grumpish
grunting
guaiacum
guaranty
guardian
guerilla
Guernsey
guidable
guidance
guileful
guiltily
gulf-weed
gullible
gumption
gum-resin
gun-metal
gunpoint
gunsmith
gun-stock
gurgoyle
guttated
guttural
gymkhana
gymnasia
gymnotus
gynander
gynarchy
gypseous
gyration

gyratory
gyroidal
gyrostat

# H
Habakkuk
habitant
habitual
habitude
hacienda
haematic
haematin
Haggadah
Hail Mary
hairgrip
hairless
hairline
halation
haleness
half-back
half-cock
half-hour
half-life
half-mast
half-moon
half-note
half term
half-time
half-tone
halliard
hallmark
hamiform
hammerer
handbill
handbook
hand-cart
handcuff
hand down
handfast
handgrip

handicap
handless
hand-line
hand-made
handmaid
handrail
handsome
handy-man
handy-men
hang-bird
hanger-on
hang-nail
hangover
hapteron
hara-kiri
harangue
hardback
hard cash
hard copy
hard-core
hard disk
hardened
hard-line
hardness
hard sell
hardship
hard-tack
hardware
hardwood
hare-bell
hari-kari
harlotry
harmless
harmonic
harridan
haruspex
hastener
hatchery
hatchway
hatmaker

hat trick
haunting
hautbois
havildar
Hawaiian
hawfinch
hawk-eyed
hawk-weed
hawthorn
hay-fever
hay-maker
hay-stack
hazelnut
haziness
headache
headachy
headband
head-gear
headhunt
headlamp
headland
headless
headline
headlong
headmost
head-rest
head-room
headship
headsman
headwind
headword
headwork
healable
heartily
heat-wave
heavenly
hebdomad
hebetate
hebetude
hebraise

Hebraism
Hebraist
hebraize
hecatomb
hedgehog
hedgerow
hedonism
hedonist
heedless
heel-ball
Hegelian
hegemony
heighten
heirloom
heirship
heliacal
helicoid
heliport
hell-bent
Hellenic
helmeted
helminth
helmsman
helmsmen
helotism
helpless
helpmate
helpmeet
Helvetia
Helvetic
hematite
hematoid
hemipter
henchman
henchmen
henequen
hen-night
hen-party
hepatite
hepatize

heptagon
heraldic
heraldry
herbaria
herdsman
herdsmen
heredity
hereunto
hereupon
herewith
heritage
hermetic
hernshaw
herpetic
Hesiodic
hesitant
hesitate
Hesperus
hexagram
hiatuses
hibernal
hibiscus
hiccough
*hic jacet*
hiddenly
hidrosis
hidrotic
hierarch
hieratic
highball
high-born
highbrow
higher-up
high-five
highjack
high jump
highland
high life
High Mass
highness

high-rise
high road
high seas
high spot
hightail
high tide
high time
high wire
hilarity
himation
hinderer
hindmost
Hinduism
hired man
hireling
Hispanic
historic
hitherto
hit it off
hoarding
hoarsely
hock-shop
Hogmanay
hogshead
holdfast
hold good
holiness
hollands
hollowly
hologram
Holy Land
Holy Week
home-born
home-felt
home help
homeland
homeless
home loan
home-made
Home Rule

homesick
homespun
homeward
homework
homicide
homilies
homilist
hominoid
homodont
homology
homonymy
homopter
homotype
honestly
honey-bee
honey-dew
honorary
honourer
hoodwink
hook-worm
hooligan
hoosegow
hopeless
hopped-up
Horatian
horn-beak
hornbeam
hornbill
hornbook
horn in on
hornpipe
hornwork
horologe
horology
horrible
horribly
horridly
horrific
horse box
horseman

horsemen
hose-pipe
hospital
hostelry
hotchpot
hotelier
hot flush
hothouse
hot plate
hot water
house-boy
house-fly
houseman
how-d'ye-do
howitzer
huckster
hugeness
Huguenot
hula-hula
humanely
humanise
humanism
humanist
humanity
humanize
humanoid
humbling
humidify
humidity
humility
humorist
humorous
humpback
hungerer
hung-over
hungrily
hung up on
huntress
huntsman
huntsmen

hurtless
hush-hush
hustings
hyacinth
hydrogen
hydromel
hydropic
Hydrozoa
hygienic
hymeneal
hymenean
hymenium
hymn-book
hyoscine
hypnosis
hypnotic
hypogeal
hypogean
hypogene
hysteria
hysteric

**I**
iambuses
iatrical
ice-blink
ice-bound
ice-cream
ice-dance
ice-field
ice-plant
ice-skate
ichorous
ichthyic
idealess
idealise
idealism
idealist
ideality
idealize

ideation
*idée fixe*
identify
identity
ideogram
ideology
idiot box
idiotism
idleness
idocrase
idolater
idolatry
idoliser
idolizer
ignition
ignominy
ignorant
illation
illative
ill-fated
ill-timed
ill-treat
illumine
ill usage
illusion
illusive
illusory
imbecile
imbolden
imbution
imitable
imitancy
imitator
immanent
immature
imminent
immingle
immobile
immodest
immolate

immortal
immunise
immunity
immunize
impacted
impanate
imparity
imperial
imperium
impetigo
implicit
impolicy
impolite
importer
imposing
imposter
impostor
impotent
imprimis
imprison
improper
improver
impudent
impugner
impunity
impurely
impurity
impurple
inaction
inactive
inasmuch
in camera
inceptor
inchmeal
inchoate
incident
incision
incisive
incisory
incisure

| | | | |
|---|---|---|---|
| inclined | inflatus | insolent | intruder |
| in clover | inflexed | insomnia | intubate |
| incoming | influent | insomuch | inundate |
| increase | informal | inspired | invasion |
| incubate | informer | inspirer | invasive |
| indagate | info-tech | inspirit | inveigle |
| indebted | infra dig | instance | inventor |
| indecent | infra-red | instinct | inverted |
| indented | infringe | instruct | investor |
| indevout | infusion | insulate | in view of |
| India ink | infusive | intaglio | inviting |
| India-man | infusory | integral | invocate |
| indicant | ingrowth | intended | involute |
| indicate | inguinal | intently | inwardly |
| indigene | inhalant | interact | iodoform |
| indigent | inherent | intercom | irefully |
| indirect | inhesion | interest | irenical |
| indocile | inhumane | interior | iriditis |
| indolent | inimical | intermit | irisated |
| inductor | iniquity | intermix | iriscope |
| induline | initiate | internal | Irishism |
| indurate | injector | internee | ironbark |
| indusial | inkiness | Internet | ironclad |
| indusium | inkmaker | Interpol | iron-grey |
| industry | inkstand | interval | iron hand |
| inedible | inlander | in the air | ironical |
| inedited | inlaying | in the bag | iron lung |
| inequity | innately | in the can | Ironside |
| inertial | innocent | in the raw | ironware |
| inexpert | innovate | in the red | iron-wood |
| infamous | innuendo | *intifada* | ironwork |
| infantry | inquirer | intimacy | irrigate |
| infecund | insanely | intimate | irrision |
| inferior | insanity | intonate | irritant |
| infernal | inscribe | intrados | irritate |
| infilter | insecure | intrench | Isabella |
| infinite | inserted | intrepid | isagogic |
| infinity | inshrine | intrigue | ischuria |
| infirmly | insignia | intromit | Islamise |
| inflated | insolate | introrse | Islamite |

Islamize
islander
isocheim
isocryme
isogonic
isolated
isomeric
isotherm
issuable
issuance
Isthmian
iterance

**J**
jackaroo
jack-boot
jackeroo
jacketed
jack it in
Jacobean
Jacobite
jacquard
jagghery
jail bait
jail-bird
jalousie
jamboree
Japanese
japanner
Japhetic
japonica
jaundice
jauntily
Javanese
jealousy
Jehovist
jejunely
jeopardy
jeremiad
Jeremiah

jeroboam
jerry can
Jesuitic
Jesuitry
jet pilot
jettison
jeweller
jew's harp
jingoism
jocosely
jocosity
jocundly
jodhpurs
John Dory
jointure
jokingly
jolt-head
jovially
joyfully
joyously
joy-rider
joy-stick
jubilant
jubilate
Judaical
judgment
judicial
jugglery
julienne
jumbo jet
jump-lead
jump-suit
jump to it
junction
juncture
junk bond
junk food
junk mail
Jurassic
juristic

justness
juvenile

**K**
kailyard
kaimakan
kakemono
kalendar
kaleyard
kamikaze
kangaroo
kedgeree
keelhaul
keenness
keep it up
keep on at
keep pace
keepsake
keep time
keratose
kerchief
kernelly
kerosene
kerosine
keyboard
keystone
kibitzer
kick-back
kickshaw
kill time
kilobyte
kilogram
kilowatt
kindling
kindness
kinetics
king-like
kingling
kingship
king-size

kinkajou
kinsfolk
klystron
knapsack
knapweed
knee-deep
knee-jerk
knickers
knightly
knitting
knitwear
knocking
knock out
knockout
knot-hole
knotless
knotting
knowable
koh-i-noor
kohlrabi
kola nut
kolinsky
kreutzer
kromesky
kryolite

**L**
labellum
labially
laboured
labourer
laburnum
lacerate
laconism
lacrimal
lacrosse
lacrymal
lacunose
ladybird
ladyhood

| | | | |
|---|---|---|---|
| ladylike | lankness | laxative | leniency |
| lady-love | lanneret | layabout | lenitive |
| Lady Muck | lanoline | lay an egg | leporine |
| ladyship | lanthorn | lay waste | let alone |
| laically | lapelled | laziness | lethargy |
| laid-back | lapidary | lazulite | lettered |
| lamasery | lapidate | lead-free | leucosis |
| lambaste | lapidify | leadless | levanter |
| lambdoid | lappeted | leadsman | leveller |
| lamb-like | lapsable | lead time | leverage |
| lambling | larboard | lead up to | leviable |
| lambskin | larcener | leafless | levigate |
| lame duck | larkspur | leanness | levirate |
| lamellae | larrigan | leap-frog | levitate |
| lamellar | larrikin | leap year | levulose |
| lameness | larynges | learning | lewdness |
| lamented | last word | leathern | lewisite |
| laminary | latchkey | leathery | lewisson |
| laminate | lateness | leavings | libation |
| lamp-post | latently | lecithin | libatory |
| lancelet | Latinate | lecturer | libeller |
| lanceted | Latinise | left hand | liberate |
| landfall | Latinism | left-over | libretto |
| landfill | Latinist | leftward | licensee |
| landgirl | Latinity | left-wing | licenser |
| landlady | Latinize | legal aid | lichened |
| landless | latitude | legalese | lichenic |
| landlord | latterly | legalise | lich-gate |
| landmark | laudable | legalism | licorice |
| landmass | laudably | legality | lie doggo |
| land-mine | laudanum | legalize | liegeman |
| landslip | laughter | legatine | lientery |
| landsman | laureate | legation | life-belt |
| landsmen | lavation | leggings | lifeboat |
| landward | lavatory | leisured | lifebuoy |
| *Landwehr* | lavender | lemonade | lifeless |
| langlauf | lavishly | lemurine | lifelike |
| lang syne | lawfully | lemuroid | lifeline |
| language | lawgiver | lengthen | lifelong |
| languish | law-maker | lenience | life-peer |

| | | | |
|---|---|---|---|
| life raft | listener | logician | louis d'or |
| life-size | listeria | logistic | love-bird |
| lifetime | listless | logogram | loveless |
| ligament | literacy | logotype | love-lock |
| ligation | literary | loiterer | lovelorn |
| ligature | literate | Lollardy | love nest |
| lighting | literati | lollipop | lovesick |
| light pen | litharge | lomentum | lovingly |
| ligneous | litigant | lonesome | lowering |
| lignitic | litigate | lone wolf | low-keyed |
| ligulate | littoral | longboat | low water |
| likeable | liturgic | longeron | loyalist |
| likeness | liveable | longeval | lubberly |
| likewise | live a lie | longhand | lucernal |
| Lima bean | live it up | longhorn | lucidity |
| lime-kiln | livelily | long-jump | luckless |
| limerick | livelong | long shot | lucky dip |
| limitary | liveried | long-side | luculent |
| limonite | liverish | longsome | lukewarm |
| linchpin | live wire | long-term | lumberer |
| lincture | lividity | longueur | luminary |
| lineally | lixivial | long wave | luminous |
| linearly | lixivium | longways | lumpfish |
| lineated | loadstar | longwise | lunation |
| linesman | loanable | looker-on | lunchbox |
| lingerer | loathful | look in on | luncheon |
| lingerie | loathing | look up to | lungfish |
| linguine | lobbyist | loophole | lungwort |
| linguini | loblolly | lop-eared | lunulate |
| linguist | lobotomy | lop-sided | lupiform |
| liniment | localise | *loquitur* | lupuline |
| Linnaean | localism | lordling | lupulite |
| linoleum | locality | Lord Muck | luscious |
| Linotype® | localize | lordosis | lustrate |
| linstock | location | Lord's day | lustrine |
| lipogram | locative | lordship | lustring |
| lipoidal | loculate | loricate | lustrous |
| lipstick | locution | lorikeet | lustrums |
| lip-synch | lodestar | Lothario | lutanist |
| liquidly | lodgment | loudness | lutenist |

lutetium
Lutheran
luxation
lych-gate
lycopode
lymphoid
lymphoma
lynx-eyed
lyre-bird
lyricism
lyricist

**M**
macaroni
macaroon
maccaboy
macerate
machismo
mackerel
mackinaw
macropod
macrural
macruran
maculate
madhouse
madrigal
madwoman
maestoso
magazine
magdalen
magician
magnesia
magnetic
magneton
magnific
magnolia
maharaja
maharani
mahjongg
mahogany

maidenly
maieutic
mainland
main line
mainline
mainmast
mainsail
mainstay
maintain
majestic
majolica
majorate
majority
make good
make it up
make over
make up to
Malagasy
malamute
malapert
malarial
malarian
*mal de mer*
malemute
malignly
malinger
malodour
malstick
maltreat
maltster
malt-worm
Mameluke
Mammalia
mammifer
mammilla
manciple
mandamus
mandarin
mandible
mandolin

mandrake
mandrill
man-eater
maneless
maneuver
manfully
mangabey
manganic
mangonel
mangrove
maniacal
Manichee
manicure
manifest
manifold
maniform
mannered
mannerly
mannikin
man of war
manorial
manpower
mansuete
manta ray
mantelet
mantilla
mantissa
man to man
manually
manurial
marabout
marasmus
marathon
marauder
maravedi
marbling
margaric
marginal
margined
margrave

marigold
marinade
maritime
marjoram
markedly
marksman
marksmen
mark time
marmoset
Maronite
marquess
marquise
marriage
marrying
martagon
martinet
marzipan
massacre
masseter
masseuse
mastabah
mast cell
masterly
masthead
masticot
mastitis
mastless
mastodon
matchbox
mateless
matelote
material
materiel
maternal
matrices
matronal
matronly
mattress
maturate
maturely

| | | | |
|---|---|---|---|
| maturity | megavolt | mesozoic | milkweed |
| maverick | megawatt | mesquite | milkwort |
| maxillae | Meiocene | messmate | Milky Way |
| maxillar | melamine | messuage | millgirl |
| maximise | melanism | mestizos | milleped |
| maximist | melanite | metalise | millhand |
| maximize | melanoma | metalize | milliard |
| May-apple | melasses | metalled | milliner |
| mayoress | melinite | metallic | milliped |
| mazarine | melodeon | metamere | millpond |
| Mazdaism | melodics | metaphor | mill-race |
| maziness | melodise | metazoan | Miltonic |
| mazourka | melodist | meteoric | mimicker |
| meagrely | melodize | metewand | minatory |
| meanness | meltdown | meteyard | mindless |
| meantime | membered | methinks | mind's eye |
| measured | membrane | methodic | minimise |
| measurer | memorial | methylic | minimize |
| meat-ball | memorise | metonymy | minimums |
| meathead | memorize | metrical | minister |
| meat-loaf | memsahib | meunière | minstrel |
| mechanic | menhaden | mezereon | ministry |
| meconium | meninges | miasmata | Minorist |
| medalist | meniscus | microbic | Minorite |
| medallic | menology | microbus | minority |
| meddling | menstrua | microdot | Minotaur |
| mediator | mentagra | microzoa | minstrel |
| Medicare | mentally | middling | minutely |
| medicate | mephitic | midnight | minutiae |
| medicine | mephitis | midships | miriness |
| medieval | merchant | mightily | mirthful |
| mediocre | merciful | migraine | misapply |
| meditate | mercuric | milch-cow | miscarry |
| medullar | meridian | mildness | mischief |
| meekness | meringue | Milesian | miscible |
| meetness | merosome | miliaria | miscount |
| megabyte | mesdames | militant | misdoubt |
| megalith | mesmeric | military | miserere |
| mcgapode | mesocarp | militate | misguide |
| megastar | mesoderm | milkmaid | mishmash |

| | | | |
|---|---|---|---|
| misjudge | moisture | monsieur | motivate |
| misnomer | molasses | monticle | motivity |
| misogamy | molecule | monument | *mot juste* |
| misogymy | molehill | moonbeam | motor-bus |
| misogyny | moleskin | mooncalf | motor-car |
| misplace | molossus | moonless | motorial |
| misprint | molybdic | moonsail | motorise |
| misprise | momently | moonshee | motorist |
| misprize | momentum | moonwort | motorize |
| misquote | monachal | moor-cock | motorman |
| misshape | monadism | moor-fowl | motorway |
| misspeak | monander | moorland | moufflon |
| misspell | monandry | mootable | moulding |
| misspend | monarchy | moquette | mountain |
| misspent | monastic | moralise | mounting |
| misstate | monetary | moralism | mournful |
| mistaken | monetise | moralist | mourning |
| mistitle | monetize | morality | moussaka |
| mistreat | mongeese | moralize | mouthful |
| mistress | mongoose | Moravian | moveable |
| mistrust | monicker | morbidly | moveless |
| mitigant | monistic | morbific | movement |
| mitigate | monition | morceaux | movingly |
| mittimus | monitory | moreover | muchness |
| mixed bag | monitrix | moresque | muciform |
| mnemonic | monkfish | moribund | mucilage |
| mobilise | monkhood | morosely | muckworm |
| mobility | monocarp | morpheme | mucosity |
| mobilize | monocrat | Morpheus | mudguard |
| moccasin | monodist | morphine | mug's game |
| modality | monogamy | mortally | mulberry |
| modeller | monogram | mortgage | muleteer |
| moderate | monolith | mortmain | mulishly |
| moderato | monomial | mortuary | multeity |
| modestly | monopoly | Mosaical | multifid |
| modifier | monorail | mosquito | multiped |
| modiolus | monotone | mossback | multiple |
| modishly | monotony | mothball | multiply |
| modulate | monotype | motherly | mumbling |
| moffette | monoxide | motility | mungoose |

| | | | |
|---|---|---|---|
| muniment | N | Nazirite | new blood |
| munition | nacreous | Nearctic | new broom |
| muralist | nail-file | Near East | new-comer |
| murderer | nainsook | near-miss | newlywed |
| muriatic | naissant | nearness | newscast |
| muricate | nameable | neat-herd | newshawk |
| muriform | nameless | neatness | newsreel |
| murmurer | namesake | nebulise | newsroom |
| murrhine | nan bread | nebulize | New World |
| muscadel | nancy boy | nebulose | niceness |
| muscatel | napiform | nebulous | nickelic |
| muscular | napoleon | necklace | nicknack |
| mushroom | narceine | neckline | nickname |
| musician | narcosis | necropsy | nicotian |
| musingly | narcotic | necrosed | nicotine |
| musk-duck | narghile | necrosis | Niflheim |
| musketry | nargileh | nectared | niggling |
| muslinet | narrator | needfire | nightcap |
| musquash | narrowly | needless | night-jar |
| musquito | nasalise | negation | night-owl |
| mustache | nasalize | negative | nihilism |
| mutation | nascency | negligée | nihilist |
| mutchkin | nasicorm | Negrillo | nihility |
| muteness | nasiform | nematode | ninefold |
| mutilate | natation | nematoid | nine-pins |
| mutineer | natatory | neologic | nineteen |
| mutinous | national | neophyte | ninjutsu |
| mutterer | natively | neoplasm | nitrogen |
| mutually | nativism | neoteric | Noachian |
| mycelium | nativity | Nepalese | nobelium |
| mycetoma | naumachy | nepenthe | nobility |
| mycology | nauseate | nephrite | nobleman |
| myelitis | nauseous | nepotism | noblemen |
| mynabird | nautical | nepotist | noblesse |
| myosotis | nautilus | nerve-gas | nocturne |
| myriapod | navigate | nestling | nodosity |
| Myrmidon | navy blue | neuritis | nodulose |
| mystical | Nazarean | neurosis | nodulous |
| mythical | Nazarene | neurotic | noetical |
| myxedema | Nazarite | neutrino | no-go area |

noisette
nomadism
nomarchy
nominate
nomology
nonesuch
nonevent
non-juror
nonmetal
non-moral
non-party
nonsense
non-stick
non-toxic
non-union
noontide
noontime
normally
Norseman
Norsemen
northern
northing
nose-band
nose-dive
noseless
nosology
*nota bene*
notandum
notarial
notation
notching
notebook
noteless
notional
notornis
noumenon
Novatian
novelise
novelist
novelize

November
novercal
nowadays
no wonder
nubecula
nuciform
nucleate
nucleoli
nudeness
nugatory
nuisance
numberer
numbness
numerary
numerate
numerous
nummular
numskull
nuptials
nursling
nutation
nut-brown
nut-hatch
nutrient
nutshell
nymphean

**O**
oak-apple
obduracy
obdurate
obedient
obituary
objector
oblation
obligant
obligate
obligato
obliging
oblivion

obscurer
observer
obsidian
obsolete
obstacle
obstruct
obtainer
obtruder
obturate
obtusely
obvolute
occasion
occident
occulted
occultly
occupant
occupier
ocellate
ochreous
octopede
octoroon
ocularly
oculated
odiously
odometer
odontoid
oeillade
oenology
offender
offering
official
off-piste
off-print
offshoot
off-shore
off-stage
off-white
ofttimes
ohmmeter
oilcloth

oil-field
oiliness
oil slick
ointment
Old Glory
old guard
Old Style
old-timer
old trout
old woman
Old World
oleander
oleaster
olibanum
oligarch
olive oil
Olympiad
Olympian
omelette
omission
omissive
omniform
omnivore
omohyoid
omoplate
omphalic
omphalos
once-over
oncology
oncoming
oncotomy
one-horse
one-liner
one-sided
one-track
onlooker
on pain of
on record
on the air
on the dot

| | | | |
|---|---|---|---|
| on the job | ordinand | outflank | overdose |
| on the run | ordinant | outgoing | overdraw |
| on the way | ordinary | outhouse | overflow |
| ontogeny | ordinate | outlawry | overgrow |
| ontology | ordnance | outlying | overhand |
| oogamous | ordurous | outmatch | overhang |
| oologist | organdie | outmoded | overhaul |
| opaquely | organise | outpoint | overhead |
| open book | organism | outrance | overhear |
| open-eyed | organist | outreach | overheat |
| openness | organize | outrider | overhung |
| open-work | orichalc | outright | overkill |
| operable | oriental | outshine | overland |
| opera-hat | original | outsider | overleaf |
| operatic | orinasal | outskirt | overleap |
| operator | ornament | outsmart | overlive |
| operetta | ornately | outspeak | overload |
| ophidian | ornithic | outstare | overlong |
| opinicus | orpiment | outstrip | overlook |
| opopanax | orthodox | outswear | overlord |
| oppilate | orthoepy | outvalue | overmuch |
| opponent | orthogon | outwards | overnice |
| opposite | oscitant | outwatch | overpass |
| optative | osculant | outweigh | overplay |
| optician | osculate | ovaritis | overplus |
| optimise | osnaburg | oven-bird | overrate |
| optimism | osteitis | ovenware | override |
| optimist | otiosity | overalls | overripe |
| optimize | otoscope | overarch | overrule |
| optional | ouistiti | overbear | overseas |
| opulence | outargue | overbold | overseer |
| opuscule | outboard | overbook | oversell |
| oracular | outbrave | overbrim | overshoe |
| oragious | outbreak | overcall | oversize |
| orangery | outburst | overcame | oversman |
| oratorio | outcaste | overcast | overstay |
| orbitary | outclass | overcoat | overstep |
| Orcadian | outdated | overcome | overtake |
| orchella | outdoors | overcrop | overtask |
| ordainer | outfield | overdare | overtime |

overtone
overtook
overture
overturn
overview
overween
overwind
overwise
overwork
overworn
oviposit
own-brand
Oxbridge
oxidiser
oxidizer
ox-tongue
oxymoron

**P**
pacifier
pacifism
pacifist
pack it in
padishah
paduasoy
paganise
paganish
paganism
paganize
paginate
painless
painting
palatial
palatine
paleface
paleness
palestra
palimony
palinode
palisade

palliate
pall-mall
palmated
palmette
palmetto
palmiped
palmitic
palomino
palpable
palpably
palstaff
palstave
palterer
paludine
paludism
paludose
pamperer
pamphlet
pancreas
pandanus
pandemic
pangolin
panicled
pannikin
panorama
Pan-pipes
pantheon
papalise
papalist
papalize
papering
papillae
papistic
papistry
Pap smear
papulose
papulous
parabola
paradigm
paradise

paraffin
paragoge
paragram
parakeet
parallax
parallel
paralyse
paralyze
paramere
paramour
paranoia
paranoid
parasang
parasite
paravane
parcener
pardoner
parental
parergon
pargeter
parhelia
parhelic
parietal
Parisian
parlance
Parmesan
parodist
paronymy
paroxysm
partaker
parterre
Parthian
partible
particle
partisan
partizan
part-song
part-time
pashalic
passable

passably
pass away
pass-book
passer-by
Passeres
passible
Passover
passport
password
pastiche
pastille
pastoral
pastrami
patagium
patchery
patentee
patently
patentor
paternal
pathetic
pathless
pathogen
patience
patulous
pauldron
pavement
pavilion
pavonine
pawnshop
pay a call
pay-phone
peaceful
pea-green
pearl ash
pearmain
peccable
peccancy
pectinal
pectoral
peculate

peculiar
pedagogy
pedantic
pedantry
pederast
pedestal
pedicure
pediform
pedigree
pedimane
pediment
pedology
peduncle
peekaboo
peep-hole
peep-show
peerless
peignoir
Pekinese
pelagian
Pelasgic
pelerine
pellagra
pellicle
pell-mell
pellucid
peltated
pemmican
penalise
penalize
penchant
pendency
pendulum
penitent
penknife
penmaker
penology
penstock
pentacle
pentagon

pentagyn
penuchle
penumbra
peperine
peperino
per annum
perceive
perfecto
perforce
perfumer
periagua
perianth
pericarp
periderm
perigean
perilous
perineal
perineum
periodic
periplus
perjurer
permeate
peroneal
perorate
peroxide
perruque
personal
perspire
persuade
pertness
pertused
Peruvian
perverse
pervious
pesterer
petaline
petaloid
petiolar
petioled
petition

petit mal
petitory
petrific
petronel
petrosal
pettifog
petulant
petuntse
pewterer
phalange
phallism
phantasm
phantasy
Pharisee
pharmacy
pheasant
philibeg
philomel
pholades
phone-box
phonetic
phorminx
phormium
phosgene
phrasing
phthisic
phthisis
phylarch
phyletic
phyllode
phylloid
Physalia
physalis
physical
physique
piacular
pia mater
pianette
piassava
picaroon

picayune
piciform
pickerel
pickings
pick-lock
pick-me-up
piddling
piercing
pigeonry
pilaster
pilchard
pileated
pilewort
pilferer
piliform
pillager
pillared
pillowed
pill-worm
pilotage
pimiento
pinafore
pinaster
pince-nez
Pindaric
Ping-pong®
pin-money
pinnacle
pinnated
pinniped
pinochle
pinpoint
pin-prick
pin-wheel
pipe-clay
pipe-line
piquancy
piscator
pisiform
pisolite

pithless
pitiable
pitiably
pitiless
pittance
pityroid
pizzeria
placable
placeman
place-mat
placenta
placidly
plagiary
plaguily
planchet
plangent
planking
plankton
planless
plantain
plantlet
plastery
plastron
plateaus
plateaux
platelet
platform
platinum
Platonic
platonic
platting
platypus
plausive
play back
playback
play ball
play-bill
play down
playgoer
playmate

playtime
pleading
pleasant
pleasing
pleasure
plebeian
plectrum
Pleiades
plein air
pleonasm
plethora
pleurisy
pliantly
plicated
plighter
Pliocene
plodding
plougher
pluckily
plumbago
plumbean
plumbery
plumbing
plumbism
plum-cake
plum-duff
plumelet
plumiped
plurally
plutonic
pluvious
podagral
podagric
podalgia
poetical
poignant
poisoner
polarise
polarity
polarize

Polaroid®
polemics
policies
polished
polisher
politely
politico
politics
polka-dot
polliwog
pollster
pollywog
polonium
poltroon
polygamy
polyglot
polygram
polygyny
polymath
polypary
polypite
polypody
polypous
Polyzoon
pomander
pomology
pontifex
pony-tail
pony-trek
pooh-pooh
poorness
popinjay
popishly
poppadum
populace
populate
populism
populist
populous
poriform

poristic
porky pie
porosity
porously
porphyry
porpoise
porridge
portable
portfire
porthole
porticos
portière
portrait
portress
port-vent
port wine
position
positive
positron
posology
possible
possibly
post-bill
postcard
postcode
post-date
post-free
post-horn
postiche
postlude
postmark
post-obit
post-paid
postpone
post-town
posturer
potassic
potation
potatoes
potatory

| | | | |
|---|---|---|---|
| potbelly | pressing | proemial | provable |
| potently | pressman | profaner | provably |
| pot-house | pressmen | pro forma | provided |
| potmaker | pressure | profound | provider |
| pot-roast | prestige | progress | province |
| potshard | pretence | prohibit | proximal |
| potsherd | pretense | prolapse | prudence |
| pouldron | preterit | prolific | pruinose |
| poultice | prettify | prologue | prunella |
| poundage | prettily | promisee | prurient |
| powdered | previous | promiser | pruritus |
| powerful | priapism | promisor | Prussian |
| practice | price war | promoter | psalmist |
| practise | pricking | prompter | psalmody |
| prandial | prideful | promptly | psaltery |
| prankish | prie-Dieu | pronator | psychist |
| prattler | priestly | propense | pteropod |
| preacher | priggish | properly | ptomaine |
| preamble | primeval | property | ptyalism |
| precinct | primness | prophecy | publican |
| precious | primrose | prophesy | publicly |
| preclude | princely | proplasm | puddling |
| predator | princess | propolis | pudendum |
| predella | printing | proposal | puffball |
| pre-exist | print-out | proposer | pugilism |
| pregnant | priorate | propound | pugilist |
| prejudge | prioress | propylon | puissant |
| prelatic | priories | prorogue | pulingly |
| première | priority | prosaism | pullover |
| premolar | prismoid | prosaist | pulmonic |
| premorse | prisoner | prosodic | pump-room |
| prenatal | pristine | prospect | puncheon |
| prentice | probable | prostate | punctate |
| prepared | probably | prostyle | punctual |
| preparer | proceeds | protasis | puncture |
| prepense | proclaim | proteose | pungency |
| prescind | procurer | protocol | puniness |
| presence | procuror | Protozoa | punisher |
| preserve | prodigal | protract | punitive |
| presidio | producer | protrude | punitory |

punk rock
puparial
pupilage
pupilary
puppetry
puppyish
purblind
purchase
pureness
purifier
purplish
purseful
purse-net
purslane
pursuant
purulent
purveyor
pushover
pussycat
pustular
putative
put right
put-up job
puzzling
pyogenic
pyriform
pyrology
pyroxene
pythonic
pyxidium

**Q**
quackery
quadrant
quadrate
quadriga
quadroon
quaestor
quagmire
quaintly

qualmish
quandary
quandong
quantify
quantity
quarrier
quartern
quarters
quartile
quatrain
queasily
queerish
quencher
quenelle
quercine
question
quibbler
quick one
quickset
quiddity
quidnunc
quietism
quietist
quietude
quilling
quilting
quincunx
quintain
quirkish
quisling
quit-rent
quivered
quixotic
quixotry
quiz show
quotable
quotient

**R**
rabbinic

racemose
rachitic
rachitis
raciness
rack-rent
radially
radiance
radiator
radicate
raggedly
ragstone
rail-head
raillery
railroad
rain band
raincoat
raindrop
rainfall
rainless
rainy day
raisable
raisonné
rake-hell
rakishly
rambling
rambutan
rampancy
ranchero
rancidly
rankness
ransomer
rapacity
rape-cake
rapidity
rap music
Raptores
raptured
rara avis
rareness
rascally

rashness
rasorial
rat-arsed
rational
ratsbane
rattling
ravenous
ravingly
ravisher
reabsorb
reaction
reactive
readable
readably
read-only
readjust
reaffirm
realiser
realizer
realness
real-time
reappear
rear-lamp
rearmost
rearward
reasoned
reasoner
reassert
reassign
reassume
reassure
reattach
rebuttal
rebutter
recanter
receding
received
receiver
recently
recessed

| | | | |
|---|---|---|---|
| recharge | refinery | relieved | reporter |
| reckless | reflexed | reliever | repoussé |
| reckoner | reflexly | religion | reprieve |
| recommit | refluent | relisten | reprisal |
| reconvey | reforest | relocate | reproach |
| recorder | reformed | remanent | reproval |
| recourse | reformer | remarker | reprover |
| recovery | refunder | remarque | Reptilia |
| recreant | regality | remaster | republic |
| recreate | regarder | remedial | requital |
| recusant | regather | remember | requiter |
| redactor | regicide | reminder | re-reward |
| redargue | regiment | remissly | rescript |
| redbrick | regional | remittal | research |
| red cedar | register | remittee | resemble |
| Red Cross | registry | remitter | resenter |
| red dwarf | regrater | remotely | reserved |
| red earth | regrowth | renderer | reserver |
| redeemer | regulate | rendible | resetter |
| redeploy | rehearse | renegade | resident |
| red giant | rehoboam | reniform | residual |
| redirect | reimport | renneted | residuum |
| red light | reimpose | renounce | resigned |
| red ochre | reindeer | renovate | resigner |
| redolent | reinless | renowned | resinous |
| redouble | reinsert | rentable | resister |
| red route | reinsure | reoccupy | resistor |
| redshank | reinvest | reordain | resolute |
| redstart | rejecter | repairer | resolved |
| reed-band | rejoicer | repartee | resolver |
| reed-bird | rekindle | repealer | resonant |
| reed-mace | relation | repeated | resorter |
| reed-pipe | relative | repeater | resource |
| reef-knot | relaxant | repeller | response |
| re-engage | releaser | repenter | rest-home |
| re-enlist | relegate | repeople | restless |
| re-export | relevant | reperuse | restorer |
| refasten | reliable | repetend | restrain |
| referral | reliably | rephrase | restrict |
| referrer | reliance | replevin | rest room |

| | | | |
|---|---|---|---|
| resupine | rhizogen | roadshow | rosarian |
| retailer | rhizopod | roadside | rosemary |
| retainer | rhomboid | roadster | rose-pink |
| retarded | rhonchus | road test | rosewood |
| retarder | rhythmic | roadwork | rosiness |
| reticent | ribaldry | roborant | rosoglio |
| reticule | ribosome | robotics | rostella |
| retiform | rice-bird | roburite | rostrate |
| retiring | richness | rock-cork | rotation |
| retrench | rickrack | rocketry | rotative |
| retrieve | rickshaw | rock-rose | rotatory |
| retroact | ricochet | rock-ruby | rotiform |
| retrorse | riddance | rock-salt | rottenly |
| Retrovir® | ridicule | rock-soap | roughage |
| returner | riesling | rock wool | rough-cut |
| reusable | rifeness | rock-work | roulette |
| revealer | riffraff | Rodentia | round-arm |
| réveillé | rifle-man | roentgen | rowdyism |
| reveller | rifle-men | role-play | royalism |
| revenger | rigadoon | roll-call | royalist |
| reverend | right arm | roly-poly | rubicund |
| reverent | rightful | romancer | rubidium |
| reversal | rightist | Romanise | rub off on |
| reviewal | right off | Romanish | rubrical |
| reviewer | rigidity | Romanism | rucksack |
| revision | rigorous | Romanist | rudeness |
| revivify | ring-bolt | Romanize | rudiment |
| revolter | ring-bone | romantic | ruefully |
| revolute | ring-dove | romp home | ruffling |
| revolver | ringhals | rood-beam | ruggedly |
| rewarder | ring true | rood-loft | rugmaker |
| rewriter | ringworm | roofless | rugosity |
| rhapsode | riparial | roof rack | ruinable |
| rhapsody | ripeness | roof-tree | ruleless |
| rheology | ritually | room mate | ruminant |
| rheostat | river-bed | root beer | ruminate |
| rheotome | riverine | root-crop | rummager |
| rhetoric | riveting | rootedly | rum-shrub |
| rhinitis | road-book | rope-walk | runagate |
| rhizanth | road rage | ropiness | runner-up |

runology
ruralise
ruralism
ruralize
rush hour
rutabaga
ruthless
rye bread
rye-grass

**S**
sabbatic
sabotage
saboteur
sabulous
saccular
sack-race
sacredly
sacristy
saddlery
Sadducee
safeness
safe seat
sagacity
sagamore
sage-cock
sageness
sailboat
sail-fish
sailless
sail-loft
sainfoin
salad bar
salad oil
salaried
salaries
saleable
saleably
saleroom
salesman

salesmen
sales tax
salicine
Salic law
salience
salivant
salivate
salmonet
salt-bush
salt-junk
saltless
salt-lick
salt-mine
saltness
salt-work
salt-wort
salutary
salvable
samarium
samaroid
sameness
samizdat
samphire
sampling
sanative
sanatory
sanctify
sanction
sanctity
sand-bank
sand-bath
sand-flea
sand-hill
sandiver
sand-mole
sand-trap
sandwich
saneness
sangaree
Sangreal

sanguine
sanitary
sanitise
sanitize
sanserif
Sanskrit
sap-green
sapidity
sapience
saponify
sapphire
saraband
sarcenet
sardonic
sardonyx
Sargasso
sarmenta
sarsenet
sash-cord
Satanism
satiable
satiably
satirise
satirist
satirize
saturate
Saturday
sauce-box
saucepan
savagely
savagery
savagism
savannah
savingly
Savoyard
saw-bones
sawed-off
saw-horse
saxatile
saxe-blue

Saxonism
Saxonist
scabbard
scabious
scabrous
scaffold
scalable
scalawag
scallion
scammony
scampish
scandent
scandium
scansion
scantily
scaphoid
scapular
scarcely
scarcity
scathing
scavenge
scenario
scenical
scentful
sceptred
schedule
scheming
schemist
Schiedam
schizoid
schmaltz
schnapps
scholium
schooner
sciatica
scilicet
scimitar
sciolism
sciolist
scioptic

scirrhus
scissile
scission
scissors
sciurine
scleroma
sclerous
scolding
scoop-net
scorcher
scornful
scorpion
scot-free
Scotsman
Scottice
Scottify
Scottish
scourger
scouting
scowling
Scrabble®
scrabble
scrag end
scragged
scraggly
scramble
scrannel
scraping
scratchy
scrawler
screamer
screechy
screw-eye
screw key
screwtop
scribble
scrofula
scrolled
scrounge
scrubber

scrub-oak
scrupler
scrutiny
scuffler
scullery
scullion
sculptor
scurrile
scurvily
scutcher
scutella
Scythian
sea-acorn
sea-board
sea-borne
sea-bream
sea-coast
sea-devil
sea-eagle
seafarer
sea-fight
sea front
sea-going
sea-grape
sea-grass
sea-green
sea-holly
sea-horse
sea-lemon
sea-level
sea-louse
sealskin
seamless
sea-mouse
seamster
sea-onion
sea-otter
sea-plane
searcher
sea-rover

seascape
Sea Scout
seashell
sea-shore
sea-snail
sea-snake
seasonal
seasoner
seat-belt
sea-trout
sea-wrack
secluded
seconder
secondly
secretly
sectoral
securely
security
sedately
sedation
sedative
sederunt
sediment
sedition
sedulity
sedulous
seed-cake
seed-corn
seedless
seedling
seedsman
seership
see stars
seigneur
seignior
seignory
seizable
selector
selenite
selenium

self-help
selfless
self-love
self-made
self-pity
self-rule
selfsame
self-sown
self-will
selvedge
semantic
semester
semidome
semimute
seminary
Semitism
semitone
semolina
sempster
senility
señorita
sensible
sensibly
sensific
sensuous
sentence
sentient
sentinel
sentries
sepaline
sepaloid
sepalous
separate
Sephardi
septette
sequelae
sequence
seraglio
seraphic
seraphim

| | | | |
|---|---|---|---|
| serenade | shanties | shooting | sidestep |
| serenely | shantung | shopgirl | sidewalk |
| serenity | shapable | shopping | sidewall |
| sergeant | sharp-cut | shoptalk | sideward |
| serially | sharp-set | shop-worn | sideways |
| seriatim | shattery | shortage | side-wind |
| serjeant | shealing | shortcut | sidewise |
| serology | shearing | short rib | sigmatic |
| serosity | sheathed | shot-belt | signable |
| serrated | sheep-dip | shoulder | signally |
| servitor | sheepdog | shouldn't | signeted |
| sesamoid | sheepish | shoveler | signpost |
| sesterce | sheep-run | showcase | silencer |
| sestette | sheeting | showdown | silently |
| set about | sheiling | showgirl | silicate |
| setiform | shelduck | showroom | silicify |
| set-piece | shellack | shrapnel | silicium |
| set-screw | shelving | shrewdly | silicone |
| settle up | Shemitic | shrewish | silicula |
| settling | shepherd | shrieval | silicule |
| severely | shigella | shrimper | siliquae |
| severity | shilling | shrunken | silk-mill |
| sewerage | shinbone | shuffler | silkweed |
| sex angle | shingled | shut-down | silkworm |
| sexology | shingles | sibilant | sillabub |
| sextuple | ship-load | sibilate | Silurian |
| sexually | shipmate | sick-list | silverly |
| sforzato | shipment | sickness | simoniac |
| shabbily | shipping | sickroom | simperer |
| shabrack | ship's boy | side-arms | simplify |
| shaddock | ship-worm | side-dish | simulate |
| shades of | ship-yard | side-drum | Sinaitic |
| shafting | shirring | sidekick | sinapism |
| shagreen | shirting | sideline | sinciput |
| shalloon | shivaree | sidelong | sinecure |
| shamanic | shocking | sidereal | sinfonia |
| shambles | shoe-horn | siderite | sinfully |
| shameful | shoelace | sideshow | singsong |
| shamrock | shoeless | sidesman | singular |
| shanghai | shoetree | sidesmen | sinister |

sink-hole
Sinn Fein
sinology
siphonal
siphonic
sirenian
sisterly
sitology
sit tight
situated
sitz-bath
sixpence
sixpenny
sixtieth
sizeable
sjambock
skean-dhu
skeletal
skeleton
skerries
sketcher
skewbald
skid-road
skilless
skillful
skim-milk
skimming
skin-deep
skinhead
skinless
ski-pants
skipjack
ski-plane
skipping
skirmish
skirting
skirtles
ski stick
skittish
skittles

skive off
skua gull
skylight
slab-cake
slapdash
slashing
slattern
slaverer
Slavonic
sleepily
sleeping
slightly
slime-pit
slimming
slimness
sling mud
slipcase
slip-dock
slipknot
slippage
slippery
slip road
slipshod
slipslop
slobbery
sloe-eyed
slope off
slop-shop
slothful
slovenly
slow fuse
slowness
slow-worm
sluggard
sluggish
sluttery
sluttish
smacking
smallage
small fry

smallpox
smart ass
smart set
smash hit
smashing
smelling
smeltery
smidgeon
smithery
smocking
smoke box
smoothen
smoothie
smoothly
smothery
smoulder
smuggler
smugness
smut-ball
smuttily
snappish
snapshot
snarling
snatcher
sneaking
sneezing
snivelly
snobbery
snobbish
snobbism
snowball
snowbird
snow-boot
snow-clad
snow-cold
snowdrop
snowfall
snowless
snow-line
snowshoe

snow-show
snow-slip
snow tyre
snowy owl
snub-nose
snuffbox
snuffler
snuggery
snugness
soapwort
sobriety
sob-story
so-called
sociable
sociably
socially
Socinian
sock it to
Socratic
sodomite
softball
soft-core
softener
softness
soft porn
soft sell
soft-soap
soft spot
software
softwood
soil-pipe
solar day
solarium
solatium
solderer
soldiery
solecise
solecism
solecist
solecize

| | | | |
|---|---|---|---|
| solemnly | soul mate | spectate | splinter |
| soleness | sound-box | spectral | split pea |
| solenoid | sounding | spectrum | splitter |
| solipede | souped-up | specular | splotchy |
| solidify | sourness | speculum | splutter |
| solidity | sourpuss | speed cop | spoliate |
| solitary | southern | speedily | spondaic |
| solitude | southing | speeding | sponsion |
| solstice | southpaw | speedway | spontoon |
| solution | souvenir | spelaean | spookish |
| solvable | sowbread | spelling | spoonful |
| solvency | soya bean | spell out | sporadic |
| somatism | soy sauce | sperm oil | sporidia |
| somatist | space age | sphagnum | sportful |
| sombrely | space-bar | sphenoid | sporting |
| sombrero | spaceman | spherics | sportive |
| sombrous | spacemen | spheroid | spotless |
| somebody | spacious | spherule | spot-weld |
| some such | spadeful | sphygmic | spray gun |
| sometime | spalpeen | spicatto | sprigged |
| somewhat | spandrel | spicular | springer |
| somnific | spangled | spiffing | sprinkle |
| songbird | Spaniard | spikelet | spritzer |
| songless | spanking | spilikin | sprocket |
| songster | span-roof | spillway | sprucely |
| son-in-law | sparable | spinelle | spun silk |
| sonobuoy | spar deck | spinifex | spur-gall |
| sonority | sparerib | spinster | spur gear |
| sonorous | sparkish | spiracle | spurious |
| soothing | sparkler | spirally | spurrier |
| sopranos | sparsely | spirelet | spyglass |
| sorcerer | spathose | spiricle | squabble |
| sordidly | spavined | spirilla | squadron |
| soreness | speaking | spirited | Squamata |
| sorority | spearman | spiteful | squamate |
| sortable | spearmen | spitfire | squamous |
| sortment | specific | spittoon | squander |
| souchong | specimen | splatter | squarely |
| soul food | specious | splendid | square up |
| soulless | speckled | splenius | squatter |

squeaker
squeegee
squeezer
squiggle
squirrel
stabling
stablish
staccato
stagnant
stagnate
stair-rod
stairway
stake-net
stakeout
stalking
stallage
stallion
stalwart
stamened
staminal
Stamp Act
stampede
stamping
stamp tax
stancher
stanchly
standard
standing
standish
stand-off
stanhope
stannary
stannous
stanzaic
stapella
starched
starcher
stardust
starfish
star-gaze

starkers
starless
starlike
starling
star sign
Star Wars
statedly
statical
statuary
steadily
stealing
stealthy
steaming
steam-tug
stearine
steatite
stedfast
steeling
steenbok
steepled
steerage
steering
stellary
stellate
stem leaf
stemless
stenosis
step on it
sterling
stibnite
stitcher
stickler
stifling
stiletto
stimulus
stingily
stinging
sting-ray
stipular
stirless

stirring
stockade
stock car
stocking
stockman
stockmen
stockpot
stoicism
stoicist
stomatic
Stone Age
stooping
stop bath
stopcock
stop dead
stop-over
stoppage
stopping
storeman
storemen
stormful
Storting
stowaway
straddle
straggle
straight
strained
strainer
straiten
straitly
stranger
strangle
strapper
strategy
stratify
streamer
strength
striated
stricken
strickly

strictly
strident
striking
stringed
stringer
stripper
strobile
stroller
strongly
strontia
strophic
struggle
strummer
strumose
strumous
strumpet
strung up
strutter
stubbled
stubborn
stuck for
stud-book
studious
stuffing
stultify
stumbler
stunning
stuntman
stuntmen
stupidly
stuprate
sturgeon
subacrid
subacute
subclass
suberose
suberous
subgenus
subhuman
sublease

| | | | |
|---|---|---|---|
| sublunar | summoner | swastika | tabulate |
| submerge | sunbaked | sweeping | taciturn |
| submerse | sunbathe | sweet bay | tackling |
| suborder | sunburnt | sweeting | tacksman |
| suborner | sunburst | sweetish | tacksmen |
| subovate | sun-dried | sweet-pea | tactical |
| subpoena | sunlight | sweet-sop | tactless |
| subpolar | sunshade | swelling | taenioid |
| subserve | sunshine | swimming | tafferel |
| subsonic | sunshiny | swim-suit | taffrail |
| subtitle | superadd | swindler | Tahitian |
| subtlety | superbly | swinging | tailback |
| subtonic | superego | sword-arm | tail-coat |
| subtotal | superior | sybarite | tail-gate |
| subtract | superman | sycamine | tailless |
| subulate | supinely | sycamore | tail-pipe |
| suburban | supplant | syllabic | tail-race |
| succinct | supplier | syllable | tail-spin |
| succinic | supposed | syllabub | tail-wind |
| succubus | supposer | syllabus | take a bow |
| suchlike | suppress | symbolic | takeaway |
| suchwise | surcease | symmetry | take over |
| suckling | sure-fire | sympathy | take-over |
| sudatory | surgical | symphony | take part |
| suddenly | surmiser | symposia | take root |
| sufferer | surmount | syndrome | takingly |
| suffrage | surplice | synonymy | talisman |
| suicidal | surprise | synopsis | talk-show |
| suitable | surround | synoptic | talliage |
| suitably | surtitle | synovial | tallness |
| suitcase | surveyor | syphilis | tallower |
| sukiyaki | survival | systemic | tall ship |
| sulcated | survivor | systolic | tally-man |
| sullenly | suspense | syzygies | tally-men |
| sulphate | suzerain | | Talmudic |
| sulphite | swan-dive | **T** | tamandua |
| sulphoid | swannery | tabbinet | tamarack |
| sulphury | swanskin | tabby-cat | tamarind |
| sultanic | swansong | tableaux | tamarisk |
| summitry | swashing | tabouret | tamboura |

| | | | |
|---|---|---|---|
| tameable | taxodont | template | thalline |
| tameless | taxology | temporal | thallium |
| tameness | taxonomy | tempting | thanedom |
| tamperer | tax-payer | temulent | thankful |
| tan-balls | tea-caddy | tenacity | thank you |
| tandoori | tea-chest | tenantry | thatcher |
| tangency | teaching | tendance | thearchy |
| tangible | tea-cloth | tendency | theistic |
| tangibly | team-mate | tenderly | thematic |
| tanistry | teamster | tenement | theocrat |
| tannable | team-work | tenesmic | theodicy |
| tantalum | tear-away | tenesmus | theogony |
| tantalus | tear-drop | tenon-saw | theology |
| tap-dance | tearless | tentacle | theories |
| tape deck | teaseler | tent-wise | theorise |
| tape-line | teaspoon | teocalli | theorist |
| tapestry | tea towel | tephrite | theorize |
| tapeworm | technics | terebene | therefor |
| taphouse | tectonic | terminal | thereout |
| tarboosh | teenager | terminus | thermion |
| targeted | tee-shirt | termless | thespian |
| tarlatan | teething | terrapin | theurgic |
| tarragon | teetotal | terrazzo | thiamine |
| tartaric | teetotum | terrible | thick ear |
| tartness | tegument | terribly | thickish |
| tartrate | telecast | terrific | thick-set |
| task-work | telecoms | tertiary | thievery |
| tastable | telefilm | tesserae | thievish |
| taste bud | telegram | testator | thinking |
| tasteful | telemark | test case | thin line |
| tattered | Teletext® | testicle | thinness |
| tattling | telethon | test-tube | thinnish |
| tattooer | Teletype® | tetanoid | thin time |
| taunting | televise | tetragon | thirster |
| taverner | tellable | tetrapod | thirteen |
| tawdrily | telltale | tetrarch | thole pin |
| tawny owl | tellural | Teutonic | thoracic |
| taxation | telluric | textbook | thorinum |
| tax exile | temerity | text-hand | thorough |
| tax haven | tempered | thalamus | thousand |

| | | | |
|---|---|---|---|
| thraldom | tillable | toil-worn | totality |
| thrasher | timbered | tokenism | totemism |
| threaten | time-ball | tolbooth | totterer |
| threnode | time-bill | tolerant | touchily |
| threnody | time-bomb | tolerate | touching |
| thresher | time-fuse | tollable | touch off |
| thriller | timeless | toll call | toughish |
| thriving | time-worn | toll-gate | touristy |
| thrombin | time zone | tomahawk | tournure |
| thrombus | timidity | tomatoes | tovarich |
| throstle | timorous | tombless | tovarish |
| throttle | tincture | tomentum | towardly |
| thrummer | tinkling | tommy-gun | toweling |
| thuggery | tinnitus | tommy rot | towering |
| thumb-nut | tin miner | tom-noddy | town hall |
| thumbs up | tin-plate | tomorrow | township |
| thumping | tinsmith | to my mind | townsman |
| thundery | tintless | tonality | town-talk |
| thurible | tipstaff | tone-deaf | townward |
| thurifer | tiramisu | toneless | toxaemia |
| Thursday | tireless | tone poem | toxicant |
| thwarter | tiresome | tonicity | toymaker |
| thwartly | Titanian | tonsured | tracheal |
| thyroxin | titanium | tool-room | trachoma |
| tickling | tithable | toothful | trachyte |
| ticklish | tithe-pig | top-boots | trackage |
| tick over | titivate | top brass | tractate |
| tick-tock | titmouse | top-dress | traction |
| tide-gate | titulary | top-heavy | tractive |
| tideless | toad-fish | topnotch | trade gap |
| tidemark | toad-flax | topology | trade-off |
| tide-mill | toad-spit | toponomy | traducer |
| tidesman | toadyism | toreador | tragical |
| tidesmen | to and fro | toreutic | tragopan |
| tide wave | to be sure | tortilla | trail-net |
| tidiness | toboggan | tortious | training |
| tie-break | together | tortoise | train-oil |
| tiger-cat | toiletry | tortuose | trampler |
| tiger-eye | toilless | tortuous | tram-road |
| tigerish | toilsome | torturer | tranquil |

| | | | |
|---|---|---|---|
| transact | tribrach | truckler | turnsole |
| transept | tribunal | true-blue | turnspit |
| transfer | trichina | true-born | turreted |
| transfix | trichoma | true-bred | tutelage |
| tranship | trichord | true-love | tutelary |
| transmit | trickery | trueness | tutorage |
| transude | tricking | truffled | tutoress |
| trap-ball | trickish | trumpery | tutorial |
| trap-door | tricycle | truncate | twaddler |
| trapezia | trifling | trunnion | tweezers |
| trappean | trifocal | trussing | twelvemo |
| trapping | triglyph | trustful | twilight |
| Trappist | trigonal | trustily | twin-born |
| trash-can | trigraph | truthful | twinling |
| trashily | trillion | tsaritsa | twitcher |
| travails | trimaran | tubercle | twocking |
| traverse | trimeter | tuberose | two-cycle |
| travesty | trimming | tuberous | two-edged |
| trawling | trimness | tubewell | two-faced |
| trawl-net | triplane | tubiform | twopence |
| treasure | tripping | tubulose | twopenny |
| treasury | triptote | tubulous | two-piece |
| treating | triptych | tug of war | tympanic |
| treatise | tripwire | tumbling | tympanum |
| trecento | triumvir | tumidity | typecast |
| tree-fern | trivalve | tuneless | typeface |
| tree-frog | trochaic | tungsten | typifier |
| treeless | trochoid | tungstic | typology |
| tree line | trolldom | tunicate | tyrannic |
| treenail | trolling | tuppence | Tyrolean |
| tree toad | trombone | Turanian | Tyrolese |
| trembler | troopial | turbaned | tzatsiki |
| trencher | trophied | turbofan | |
| trephine | trophies | turbojet | U |
| trespass | tropical | turgidly | ubiquity |
| trial run | troubler | turmeric | udometer |
| triander | trousers | turncoat | ugliness |
| triangle | troutlet | turncock | ulcerate |
| triarchy | trouvere | turn-over | ulcerous |
| Triassic | truckage | turnpike | ulterior |

| | | | |
|---|---|---|---|
| ultimate | underact | unicycle | unseeded |
| ultraism | underage | unifilar | unseemly |
| ultraist | underarm | unionise | unsettle |
| umbonate | underbid | unionism | unshaken |
| umbrella | underbuy | unionist | unshapen |
| umpirage | undercut | unionize | unshroud |
| unabated | underdog | unipolar | unsifted |
| una corda | underlay | uniquely | unslaked |
| unallied | underlie | unitedly | unsocial |
| unatoned | underpin | univalve | unsoiled |
| unavowed | undersea | universe | unsought |
| unawares | undertow | univocal | unsoured |
| unbeaten | underway | unjustly | unspoken |
| unbelief | undreamt | unkennel | unstable |
| unbiased | undulate | unkindly | unsteady |
| unbidden | unearned | unlawful | unstring |
| unbolted | uneasily | unleaded | unstrung |
| unbought | unending | unlikely | unsuited |
| unbroken | unenvied | unlimber | unswathe |
| unbuckle | unerring | unlisted | untangle |
| unbundle | unevenly | unloosen | untasted |
| unburden | unfading | unlovely | untaught |
| unburied | unfairly | unmanned | unthread |
| unburned | unfasten | unmeetly | unthrift |
| unbutton | unfetter | unmuffle | untidily |
| uncalled | unfilial | unmuzzle | untimely |
| uncandid | unforgot | unpathed | untinged |
| uncasual | unformed | unpeople | untiring |
| unchased | unfreeze | unperson | untitled |
| unchurch | unfunded | unpitied | untoward |
| unciform | ungainly | unplaced | unvalued |
| uncinate | ungentle | unpoetic | unvaried |
| Uncle Sam | ungently | unpolite | unversed |
| Uncle Tom | unglazed | unproved | unvoiced |
| unclothe | ungulate | unreason | unwanted |
| uncomely | unhanged | unrepaid | unwarily |
| uncommon | unharmed | unriddle | unwarped |
| uncouple | unheeded | unsaddle | unwashed |
| unctuous | unholily | unsafely | unwashen |
| undecked | uniaxial | unsealed | unwieldy |

unwisdom
unwisely
unwished
unworthy
upgrowth
upheaval
upholder
up in arms
uplander
upmarket
upper cut
uprising
upspring
upstairs
upstream
upstroke
up-to-date
urbanite
urbanity
urethral
urgently
uric acid
uroscopy
Ursuline
urticate
usefully
usufruct
usurious
uxorious

**V**

vacation
vaccinal
vaccinia
vagabond
vaginate
vagrancy
vainness
valerian
Valhalla

validate
validity
Valkyrie
valorise
valorize
valorous
valuable
valuator
valvelet
valvular
vambrace
vanadium
Vandalic
vanguard
vanquish
vaporise
vaporish
vaporize
vaporose
vaporous
vapourer
variable
variably
variance
varicose
varietal
variform
variolar
variorum
varletry
vascular
vasculum
Vaseline®
vasiform
vassalry
vastness
vaulting
vavasour
vavassor
vegetate

vegetive
vehement
veilless
veinless
velarium
velleity
velocity
vena cava
venality
venation
vendetta
vendible
vendibly
venerate
venereal
Venetian
vengeful
venially
venomous
venosity
venturer
veracity
verandah
veratrin
verbally
verbatim
verbiage
verdancy
verderer
verditer
verdured
verifier
verjuice
vermouth
veronica
versicle
vertebra
vertexes
vertical
vertices

verticil
verticle
vesicant
vesicate
vespiary
vestment
vestured
Vesuvian
veterean
vexation
vexillar
vexillum
*via media*
viaticum
vibrator
vibrissa
viburnum
vicarage
vicarate
vicarial
vicenary
vicinage
vicinity
victoria
victress
Viennese
View-data®
viewless
vigilant
vigneron
vignette
vigoroso
vigorous
vileness
vilifier
vilipend
villager
villainy
vincible
vinculum

vine-clad
vinegary
vineyard
vinosity
vintager
vintnery
violable
violator
violence
viperine
viperish
viperous
virginal
viridity
virtuoso
virtuous
virulent
viscacha
visceral
viscount
Visigoth
visional
visitant
visiting
vitalise
vitalism
vitalist
vitality
vitalize
vitellin
vitellus
vitiator
vitreous
vituline
vivacity
vivarium
viva voce
vivisect
vixenish
vizcacha

vocalise
vocalist
vocality
vocalize
vocation
vocative
voiceful
voidable
voidance
voidness
volatile
volcanic
volitant
volition
volitive
voltaism
volution
vomiting
vomitive
vomitory
voracity
vorticel
vortices
votaress
votaries
votarist
votively
voussoir
vowelise
vowelism
vowelize
vowelled
voyageur
vulgarly
vulvitis

**W**

wagonage
wagon-lit
wainscot

waitress
Walhalla
walk-over
walker-on
walk tall
Walkyrie
wallaroo
wall-eyed
wallower
wanderer
wanderoo
wannabee
wantonly
war crime
war-dance
wardenry
wardress
wardrobe
ward-room
wardship
warfarin
war-horse
wariness
warmness
war-paint
warplane
war-proof
warranty
warrener
war-whoop
washable
wash-bowl
washed-up
wash-room
wasteful
watch-dog
watchful
watchman
watchmen
water-bed

water-dog
water-gas
water-hen
water-ice
watering
waterman
water-pot
water-pox
water-ram
water-rat
waterway
wattling
wave-band
waveless
wave-worn
wax-cloth
waxed-end
waxiness
wax-light
wax-paper
wayfarer
weakling
weakness
weanling
weaponed
weaponry
wearable
weeklies
weeviled
weevilly
welcomer
weldable
welladay!
wellaway!
well-born
well-bred
well done
well-head
well-knit
well-nigh

| | | | |
|---|---|---|---|
| well-read | whitecap | windowed | wood-lark |
| well-room | whitefly | windpipe | woodpile |
| well-to-do | white-hot | windrose | wood-pulp |
| well up on | white leg | wind-sail | woodruff |
| well-worn | white lie | wind sock | woodshed |
| werewolf | whitener | windward | woodsman |
| Wesleyan | white-out | wineskin | woodwind |
| westerly | white tie | wing-case | woodwork |
| westmost | whizz-kid | wingding | woodworm |
| westward | whodunit | wingless | wool-dyer |
| wet dream | whole hog | wingspan | wool-fell |
| wet-nurse | whomever | winnower | woolpack |
| whacking | whoredom | winterly | woolsack |
| wharfage | whoreson | wiredraw | woolward |
| whatever | wickedly | wireless | word-book |
| wheat-ear | wickered | wire-rope | word-play |
| wheat-fly | wide-eyed | wireworm | workable |
| wheedler | wideness | wire-wove | workably |
| wheelman | wifehood | wiriness | workaday |
| wheelmen | wifelike | wiseacre | workbook |
| wheel nut | wigmaker | wiseness | worked-up |
| whenever | wild-boar | wishbone | workhand |
| wherever | wild card | wistaria | workload |
| wherries | wild-eyed | wisteria | workmate |
| whey-face | wild-fire | witch-elm | workroom |
| whiffler | wildfowl | witchery | workshop |
| whiggery | wildlife | witching | wormcast |
| whiggish | wildness | withdraw | wormling |
| whimbrel | wild oats | withhold | wormwood |
| whimsies | wild rice | woefully | worrying |
| whinchat | Wild West | wolf-call | worthily |
| whip-cord | wild-wood | womanise | wrangler |
| whip-hand | wilfully | womanish | wrappage |
| whiplash | wiliness | womanize | wrapping |
| whipping | windburn | wonderer | wrathful |
| whipster | windfall | wondrous | wreckage |
| whirring | wind-gall | woodbine | wrestler |
| whistler | windlass | woodcock | wretched |
| white ant | windless | woodenly | wriggler |
| Whiteboy | windmill | woodland | wrinkled |

wrinklie
wristlet
write off
wrongful
wrongous

**X**
xanthein
xanthine
xanthoma
xanthous
xenogamy
xenolith
xylocarp

**Y**
yachting
Yale® lock
yarmulke
yataghan
yeanling
yearbook
yearling
year-long
yearning
yeomanly
yeomanry
yielding
yokemate

youngish
yourself
youthful
yuletide

**Z**
zamindar
zarzuela
zealotry
zemindar
zenithal
zeolitic
Zeppelin
zero hour

zigzaggy
zodiacal
zoolatry
zoom lens
zoophile
zoophily
zoophyte
zoosperm
zoospore
zootomic
zoot suit
zucchini
zwieback
zymology

# Nine-letter words

**A**
abandoned
abandoner
abashment
abatement
abbotship
abdominal
abduction
aberrance
abhorrent
abhorring
abidingly
abjection
abnegator
abolisher
abolition
abominate
aborigine
about face
about turn
Abrahamic
abreption
abruption
absconder
absinthic
*absit omen*
absorbent
absorbing
abstainer
abstinent
absurdity
abundance
abusively
Acalephae

acanthine
a cappella
accentual
accessary
accession
accessory
accidence
accipiter
acclimate
acclivity
acclivous
accompany
accordant
according
accordion
accretion
accretive
accumbent
accusable
acescence
acetifier
acetylene
aciculate
acid house
acidifier
acidulate
acidulent
acidulous
aciniform
acoustics
acquiesce
acquittal
acrobatic
acronical

acronycal
acropolis
acrospire
actualise
actualist
actuality
actualize
acuminate
a cut above
acuteness
adaptable
addiction
addressed
addressee
addresser
adducible
adduction
ademption
adenotomy
adherence
*ad hominem*
adiabatic
ad interim
adipocere
adjacence
adjacency
adjective
adjoining
adjutancy
admeasure
adminicle
admirable
admirably
admiralty

admission
admixtion
admixture
admonitor
ad nauseam
adoptable
adoration
adoringly
adornment
adsorbent
adulation
adulterer
adultness
adumbrant
adumbrate
ad valorem
advantage
Adventist
Adventual
adventure
adverbial
adversary
adversely
adversity
advertent
advertise
advertize
advisable
advisably
advisedly
advocator
aegophony
Aepyornis
aerialist

| | | | |
|---|---|---|---|
| aerodrome | agony aunt | allegoric | amazement |
| aerometer | agreeable | alleluiah | amazingly |
| aerometry | agreeably | allemande | amazon-ant |
| aerophyte | agreement | alleviate | Amazonian |
| aeroplane | aimlessly | All-hallow | amazonite |
| aerospace | air-cooled | alligator | amber-tree |
| aesthetic | air-engine | allograph | ambergris |
| aetiology | air-jacket | allopathy | ambiguity |
| affecting | air letter | allotment | ambiguous |
| affection | air pocket | allotropy | ambitious |
| affective | airworthy | allowable | amblyopia |
| affianced | aitchbone | allowably | ambrosial |
| affidavit | aitiology | allowance | ambrotype |
| affiliate | alabaster | alma mater | ambulacra |
| affirmant | alack a day! | almandine | ambulance |
| afflicter | alarm-bell | alms-giver | ambuscade |
| affluence | albatross | almshouse | amendable |
| aforehand | albescent | aloes wood | amendment |
| aforesaid | alburnous | alongside | americium |
| aforetime | alchemise | alpenglow | amianthus |
| a fortiori | alchemist | alpenhorn | amidships |
| Afrikaans | alchemize | altar-tomb | amino acid |
| Afrikaner | alcoholic | altar-slab | amoebaean |
| after-care | ale-conner | altar-wise | amorously |
| after-crop | alertness | alterable | amorphous |
| after-damp | algarroba | altercate | ampersand |
| after-glow | algebraic | alternant | amphibian |
| afterlife | algorithm | alternate | amphibole |
| after-mast | alienable | altimeter | amphiboly |
| aftermath | alienator | altimetry | amphigory |
| aftermost | alignment | altiscope | amphioxus |
| afternoon | alimental | altissimo | Amphipoda |
| after-note | aliphatic | aluminium | ampleness |
| afterward | alivewith | aluminous | amplified |
| aggravate | alla breve | alveolate | amplifier |
| aggregate | allantoic | amaryllis | amplitude |
| aggressor | allantoid | amassment | amusement |
| agitation | allantois | amatorial | amusingly |
| agonistic | allayment | amaurosis | amusively |
| agonizing | allegedly | amaurotic | amygdalin |

amylopsin
anabiosis
anabolism
anabranch
anacrusis
analectic
analeptic
analgesia
analgesic
analogise
analogism
analogist
analogize
analogous
analysand
analytics
anamnesis
anandrous
ananthous
anaplasty
anarchism
anarchist
anastatic
anatomise
anatomism
anatomist
anatomize
anatropal
ancestral
anchorage
anchorite
anchorman
anchylose
anciently
ancillary
ancipital
andantino
anecdotal
anemology
angel cake

angel dust
angel-fish
angelical
angiology
angle-iron
anglicise
anglicism
anglicize
Anglophil
angularly
angulated
anhydride
anhydrite
anhydrous
animalise
animalism
animality
animalize
animating
animation
animistic
animosity
ankylosis
annotator
announcer
annoyance
annuitant
annularly
annulment
anoestrus
anomalous
anonymity
anonymous
anopheles
Anschluss
antalkali
Antarctic
ante-choir
antelucan
antemetic

antenatal
antennary
antennule
anthelion
antheroid
anthodium
anthology
anthozoan
anthropic
antichlor
antidotal
antimonic
antipapal
antipasti
antipasto
antipathy
antiphony
antipodal
antipodes
antiquary
antiquity
antiserum
antitoxin
antitrade
anti-trust
antivenin
any old how
anxiously
apartheid
apartment
apathetic
aperiodic
aperitive
apetalous
aphyllous
apiculate
apishness
apivorous
aplanatic
apocopate

apocrypha
apodictic
apologise
apologist
apologize
apophysis
apostolic
apothecia
appalling
apparatus
apparitor
appellant
appellate
appendage
appendant
appertain
appetence
appetency
appetizer
apple-cart
apple-jack
apple-john
appliance
applicant
appointed
appointee
apportion
appraisal
appraiser
apprehend
approbate
April fool
aquaplane
aqua regia
aquarelle
aqua vitae
aquilegia
arabesque
arachnida
arachnoid

| | | | |
|---|---|---|---|
| aragonite | arrowroot | assurable | attribute |
| araucaria | arrowwood | assurance | attrition |
| arbitrage | arsenical | assuredly | aubergine |
| arbitrary | arsenious | assurgent | aubrietia |
| arbitrate | artemisia | asthmatic | *au courant* |
| arboreous | arthritic | astraddle | audacious |
| arboretum | arthritis | astrakhan | audiphone |
| archangel | arthropod | astrodome | augmenter |
| archducal | artichoke | astrolabe | augurship |
| archduchy | articular | astrology | *au naturel* |
| arch-enemy | artificer | astronaut | Aunt Sally |
| archetype | artillery | astronomy | auricular |
| archfiend | artlessly | Astroturf® | auriscope |
| archimage | arty-farty | astucious | austerely |
| architect | asafetida | asymmetry | austerity |
| archivist | asbestine | asymptote | authentic |
| archivolt | ascendant | asyndetic | authoress |
| archstone | ascendent | asyndeton | authorial |
| Arctic fox | ascension | at a low ebb | authorise |
| arcuation | ascertain | at a stroke | authority |
| arduously | Ashkenazi | atheistic | authorize |
| areometer | ashlaring | athenaeum | autoclave |
| Areopagus | asparagus | athletics | autocracy |
| Argentine | aspartame | atmolysis | autocrime |
| argentine | aspermous | atmometer | autocross |
| argillite | aspersion | atomicity | autograph |
| argy-bargy | aspersive | atonement | autolysis |
| armadillo | asphaltic | at one time | automatic |
| armillary | aspirator | at one with | automaton |
| armistice | asplenium | atrocious | automaton |
| army-corps | assailant | attainder | autopilot |
| aromatise | assembler | attendant | autoroute |
| aromatize | assertion | attention | autotoxic |
| arraigner | assertive | attentive | autotoxin |
| arresting | assiduity | attenuant | auxiliary |
| arrhizous | assiduous | attenuate | available |
| arris-wise | assistant | at the helm | avalanche |
| arriviste | associate | Attic salt | avocation |
| arrogance | assonance | attollent | avoidable |
| arrowhead | assuasive | attracter | avoidance |

avuncular
awakening
awe-struck
awfulness
awkwardly
axiomatic
ayatollah
azedarach
azimuthal

**B**
Babbittry
babirussa
baby-break
baby grand
bacchanal
bacchante
bacciform
bacillary
backbiter
backboard
backpedal
backslide
backspace
backstage
backstair
backsword
backtrack
backwater
backwoods
bacterium
badminton
bagatelle
bailiwick
*bain-marie*
bakehouse
baksheesh
balaclava
balalaika
balconied

bald eagle
bald-faced
baldachin
balefully
balladist
ballerina
ballistic
ballot box
ball-valve
balsam-fir
bamboozle
banderole
bandicoot
bandoleer
bandolier
bandoline
band-stand
band-wagon
bandwidth
baneberry
banefully
bank stock
bannister
banqueter
banquette
baptismal
baptistry
barbarian
barbarise
barbarism
barbarist
barbarity
barbarize
barbarous
barcarole
bare-faced
bargainer
Barmecide
barn dancc
barnstorm

barograph
barometer
baronetcy
baroscope
barracuda
barrelled
barricade
barrister
base-metal
bashfully
basic slag
basilican
bas-relief
bastinado
bastioned
Bath brick
Bath chair
Batrachia
battalion
battle-axe
battle-cry
bawdiness
bay-window
beachhead
beaconage
bean feast
bean-goose
bear-berry
beardless
bear fruit
bear it out
beastings
beatitude
*beau geste*
*beau idéal*
beau-monde
beauteous
beautiful
beccafico
becquerel

bed-fellow
bedlamite
bedraggle
bed-ridden
bed-sitter
bedspread
beechmast
beef-eater
beekeeper
Beelzebub
beer-money
beestings
beetle off
befitting
beginning
behaviour
beleaguer
belemnite
*bel esprit*
believing
bell-glass
bell tower
bellicose
bell-metal
bell-punch
belly flop
belly-ache
belly-band
belonging
belvedere
bench-mark
beneficed
benighted
benignant
benignity
berberine
bergamask
berkelium
berserker
berylline

beryllium
beseecher
beseeming
besetting
bespangle
bespatter
bespeckle
bestially
betel palm
bête noire
betrothal
betrothed
better off
bevel-gear
bewitcher
biangular
bibacious
biblicist
bicameral
bicipital
biconcave
bicyclist
bidentate
bifarious
bifoliate
bifurcate
big dipper
bigotedly
big screen
bilabiate
bilateral
bilge-keel
bilharzia
bilingual
bilirubin
biliteral
billabong
bill-board
billiards
billy goat

bilocular
bimonthly
bindingly
binervate
binocular
binominal
binturong
binuclear
biography
biologist
bionomics
biorhythm
biosphere
bipartite
bipennate
bipinnate
birch-wine
bird-brain
bird-organ
bird's-foot
bird's-nest
birthmark
birth rate
bisection
bisegment
bishopric
bismuthic
bisulcate
bitter end
bitterish
blackball
black band
black belt
blackbird
black body
black book
black-cock
black-fish
black flag
black game

black-head
black hole
black iron
black-jack
blacklead
blacklist
blackmail
black mass
blackness
black spot
bladdered
blade-bone
blaeberry
blameless
blandness
blankness
blaspheme
blasphemy
blast-pipe
bleachers
bleachery
bleakness
blear-eyed
blessedly
blind date
blind-fish
blindfold
blindness
blind spot
blind-worm
blockader
blockhead
block vote
blond lace
blondness
blood bank
blood bath
blood cell
blood clot
blood-heat

bloodless
bloodshed
bloodshot
blood test
blood type
blossomed
blow-torch
blue blood
blue-grass
Blue Peter
blueprint
blue rinse
bluestone
blue whale
bluffness
blunderer
bluntness
blush wine
blusterer
board game
board-room
board rule
board-walk
boat-house
boatswain
boat-train
bobsleigh
body clock
bodyguard
body shell
body spray
bog-butter
bold-faced
bolection
bolometer
Bolshevik
boltsprit
bomb-ketch
bomb-proof
bombardon

bombastic
bombazine
bomb-shell
bombsight
bona fides
bond-slave
bond-stone
boneblack
bone china
bone-earth
*bon vivant*
bon voyage
booby-trap
bookishly
book louse
book-maker
book-plate
book-stall
boomerang
boondocks
boorishly
boot-black
boot-maker
bordereau
bore stiff
boric acid
born again
bossa nova
botanical
bottle out
bottoms up!
boulevard
boundless
bounteous
bountiful
bourgeois
bower-bird
bow-legged
bowstring
bow-window

box girder
Boxing Day
box-office
boycotter
boyfriend
brachiate
Brachyura
bracteate
Brahmanic
brain dead
brainless
brain-sick
brain-wash
brain-wave
brake shoe
brambling
branchiae
branchial
branchlet
brand-iron
brandling
brand name
brass band
brasserie
brassière
brass neck
bratwurst
braveness
brazil-nut
bread-corn
bread line
breakable
break a leg!
break a way
break-away
break down
breakdown
break even
breakfast
break-neck

breastpin
breathing
Brechtian
breeching
bressomer
bric-a-brac
brick-clay
brick-kiln
brickwork
bride-cake
bridesman
bridewell
brief-case
briefless
briefness
brier-root
brigadier
brilliant
brimstone
briquette
briskness
Britannia
Britannic
Briticism
Britisher
broad bean
broadbrim
broadcast
broadloom
broadness
broad seal
broadside
brochette
broiderer
brokerage
bronchial
Bronze Age
broom-corn
broom-rape
brotherly

brown bear
brown coal
brownness
brown rice
brush up on
brushwood
brushwork
brusquely
brutalise
brutality
brutalize
brutishly
bubble-gum
buccaneer
Bucentaur
buckboard
bucketful
buck-hound
buckthorn
bucktooth
buckwheat
buffet car
buffeting
buff-stick
buff-wheel
bugle-horn
bugle-weed
buhrstone
Bulgarian
bulkiness
bulldozer
bullfight
bullfinch
bull-trout
bully beef
bumbailif
bumblebee
bumbledom
bump-start
bumptious

buoyantly
burlesque
burliness
burnisher
bursiform
bushiness
bush-metal
bushwhack
bussu palm
butter-bur
buttercup
butterfly
butterine
butter-nut
by-product
byssolite
bystander
by the book
Byzantine

**C**
caballero
caballine
cabbalism
cabbalist
cablegram
cable-laid
cabriolet
cachaemia
cacholong
cacodemon
cacoethes
cacophony
cadastral
cadaveric
cadetship
Caesarean
Caesarism
cafeteria
cafetière

Cainozoic
cairngorm
calaboose
calabrese
calamanco
calcaneum
calcedony
calcimine
calculary
calculate
calculous
calendrer
calendula
calenture
calibrate
caliphate
calla lily
callipers
call names
callosity
callously
calmative
calorific
Calvinism
Calvinist
calvities
calycinal
calyculus
camarilla
cambistry
camcorder
camel-hair
camembert
cameraman
camera-shy
camerated
campagnol
campanero
campanile
campanula

camphoric
camp-stool
Canaanite
Canada Day
cancerous
candidate
Candlemas
candle-nut
candytuft
cane-brake
cane-chair
canescent
cane-sugar
canker-fly
cankerous
cannelure
cannonade
cannoneer
canonical
cantabile
cantaloup
canticles
Cantonese
cantorial
canvasser
capacious
capacitor
caparison
capillary
capillose
cap in hand
capitally
capitular
capitulum
caponiere
capriccio
Capricorn
capriform
capsaicin
capsicine

capsulate
capsulise
capsulize
captaincy
captivate
captivity
carabiner
carambola
carambole
carbineer
carbolise
carbolize
carbonado
carbonate
carbonise
carbonize
carbuncle
carburise
carburize
carcinoma
cardboard
card-sharp
careenage
careerist
carefully
caretaker
Caribbean
carinated
Carmelite
carnalist
carnality
carnalise
carnalize
carnation
carnelian
Carnivora
carnivore
*carpe diem*
carpenter
carpentry

carpet-bag
carpeting
carpet-rod
carpingly
carpology
carrageen
carronade
carron oil
carrousel
Cartesian
cart-horse
cartilage
cartogram
cartouche
cartridge
cartulary
cartwheel
caryopsis
case-knife
casemated
case study
cashew-nut
Cassandra
cassareep
cassation
casserole
cassimere
cassocked
cassonade
cassowary
Castalian
castanets
castellan
castigate
Castilian
castor oil
cast-steel
casualism
casualist
casual sex

casuarina
casuistic
casuistry
cataclysm
catalepsy
catalogue
catalysis
catamaran
catamenia
catamount
cataplasm
cataplexy
catarrhal
catatonia
catchment
catchpole
catchpoll
catchword
catechise
catechism
catechist
catechize
caterwaul
catharist
catharsis
cathartic
cathedral
cat litter
catoptric
cat-silver
cattle-man
cattle-men
Caucasian
causality
causation
causative
causeless
cautelous
cauterise
cauterize

cautioner
cavalcade
cavernous
cease fire
ceaseless
cebadilla
celandine
celebrant
celebrate
celebrity
celestial
celestine
celestite
cellarage
cellarman
cellphone
cellulite
celluloid
cellulose
Celticism
Celticist
cenobitic
censorial
centenary
center-bit
centering
centigram
centipede
centrally
centrical
centurial
centurion
cephalate
cephaloid
ceraceous
ceratodus
ceraunite
Cerberean
cercarian
cerebrate

cerecloth
cerograph
certainly
certainty
certifier
certitude
cespitose
cessation
cetaceous
cevadilla
cha-cha-cha
chafferer
chaffinch
chain-gang
chain-mail
chain-pier
chain-pump
chain-shot
chair lift
Chaldaean
challenge
chalybite
chambered
chamberer
chameleon
chamomile
champagne
champaign
champerty
champlevé
chanceful
chandlery
changeful
chaparral
chaperone
character
chariness
charioted
charivari
charlatan

charlotte
chartered
charterer
charwoman
charwomen
chastener
chastiser
chatoyant
chatterer
chauffeur
chaw-bacon
cheap-jack
cheapness
cheatable
check-list
checkmate
check-rein
cheek-bone
cheerless
cheese-fly
Chekovian
chelonian
chemistry
chemitype
chequered
cherimoya
cherisher
cherry-pit
chevalier
chevelure
chevronel
chibouque
chicanery
chickadee
chickaree
chickling
chickweed
chidingly
chieftain
chihuahua

chilblain
child care
childhood
childless
childlike
chiliarch
chillness
china-clay
china-root
china-rose
Chinatown
china-ware
chincapin
chinchona
chin-cough
chinkapin
chipboard
chirology
chiropody
chiselled
chitlings
chivalric
chlorosis
chlorotic
chock-full
chocolate
choke-bore
choke-damp
choke-full
cholaemia
choleraic
Chomskyan
chondrify
chop-house
chorister
chorology
Christian
Christmas
chromatic
chromatin

chrome red
chromogen
chronicle
chrysalid
chrysalis
chthonian
Chubb® lock
chub-faced
churching
churchism
churchman
churchmen
cicatrise
cicatrize
cigarette
Cimmerian
cinctured
cineraria
cinerious
Cingalese
circadian
circinate
circuitry
circulate
cirrhosis
cirripede
cisalpine
citizenry
city-state
civilised
civiliser
civilized
civilizer
clack-dish
claimable
clamorous
clamourer
clap-board
claret cup
clarifier

clarionet
classable
classical
classless
class-mate
classroom
claustral
clavicorn
claviform
clay-slate
clay-stone
cleanness
clearance
clearness
cleavable
clemently
clepsydra
clergyman
clergymen
clericism
clerkship
cleverish
clientage
clientele
climatise
climatize
climbable
Clingfilm®
clinquant
clipboard
clip joint
cloak-room
clockwise
clockwork
clog-dance
cloisonné
cloistral
close call
closeness
close-time

cloth hall
cloth-yard
cloudless
cloud nine
clove-pink
clubbable
clubhouse
coach-hire
coadjutor
coadunate
coagulant
coagulate
coal-black
coal-brass
coal-field
coal-fired
coalition
coal-plant
coast-line
coastwise
coaxingly
cocainise
cocainism
cocainize
coccolite
coccolith
coccygeal
cochineal
cochleate
cock-a-hoop
cockaigne
cocked hat
cock-fight
cock-horse
cockle-hat
Cockneyfy
cockroach
cockscomb
cockswain
cocoa-bean

cocoonery
coemption
coenobite
coenosarc
coequally
coercible
coeternal
coffee-bag
coffee bar
coffee-pot
coffer-dam
co-founder
cogitable
cognation
cognisant
cognition
cognitive
cognizant
coheiress
coherence
Cointreau®
colcannon
colchicum
colcothar
cold-blast
cold cream
cold frame
cold front
cold sweat
coleopter
collation
collative
colleague
collected
collector
collegial
collegian
colligate
collimate
collinear

collision
collocate
collodion
colloidal
collotype
collusion
collusive
collyrium
colocynth
colonelcy
coloniser
colonizer
colonnade
colophony
colosseum
colostomy
colostrum
colour bar
colourful
colouring
colourise
colourist
colourist
colourize
colourman
coltishly
coltsfoot
colubrine
columbary
Columbian
columbine
columbite
columbium
columella
columnist
combatant
combative
come clean
come in for
come of age

come off it
comforter
comically
comic book
commander
commendam
commender
commensal
commenter
commingle
comminute
commissar
committal
committed
committee
committer
commodity
commodore
commonage
common law
commotion
communard
communion
communism
communist
community
compactly
companion
compeller
competent
complaint
complexly
complexus
compliant
component
composite
composure
comprador
comradery
concavely

concavity
concealer
conceited
concentre
concerned
concerted
concierge
conciliar
concisely
concision
concocter
concoctor
concordat
concourse
concreate
concubine
condemner
condenser
condiment
condition
con dolore
conducive
conductor
condyloid
conferree
conferrer
confessed
confessor
confidant
confident
confiding
configure
confirmed
confirmee
confirmer
confluent
conformer
Confucian
confusion
congenial

conger-eel
congeries
congested
congruent
congruity
congruous
conically
conjugate
connature
connector
connexion
connivent
connubial
conqueror
conscious
conscript
consensus
conserver
consignee
consigner
consignor
consonant
conspirer
constable
constancy
constrain
constrict
construct
consulate
consulter
consuming
contagion
contagium
container
contemner
contender
contented
conticent
continent
continual

continued
continuer
continuum
contorted
contralto
contrived
contriver
contumacy
contumely
contusion
conundrum
convector
converter
convertor
convexity
convivial
convocate
convolute
cook-chill
cookhouse
cooperage
cooperant
cooperate
copartner
cope-stone
coping-saw
copiously
coppering
copperish
coprolite
coprology
copsewood
copyright
coralline
corallite
coralloid
coral reef
coral tree
coral-wood
corbeille

corbicula
cordately
cordelier
cordially
cordiform
coreopsis
coriander
corkscrew
cormorant
corn-crake
cornelian
cornetist
cornfield
cornflour
cornopean
corn poppy
corn-stalk
corollary
corolline
coroneted
corozo nut
corporate
corporeal
corposant
corpulent
corpuscle
correctly
corrector
correlate
corrodent
corrosion
corrosive
corrugate
corrupted
corrupter
corruptly
corticate
corticose
cortisone
coruscant

| | | | |
|---|---|---|---|
| coruscate | covetable | crenature | crosswise |
| corymbose | cowardice | crenulate | crossword |
| coseismal | cow-feeder | crepitant | crotchety |
| coseismic | coxcombry | crepitate | crowberry |
| cosmogony | crab-apple | crescendo | Crown land |
| cosmology | crabbedly | crestless | crownless |
| cosmonaut | crab-louse | cretinism | crown-work |
| cosmorama | crabstick | cribellum | crow-quill |
| cost a bomb | crack down | cricketer | crow's-bill |
| costively | crackdown | crimeless | crow's-feet |
| cost price | crack-head | criminate | crow's-foot |
| costumier | crackling | criminous | crow's nest |
| cotangent | cracksman | crinoline | crucifier |
| cothurnus | craftless | crippling | cruciform |
| cotillion | craftsman | crispated | crudeness |
| co-trustee | craftsmen | crispness | crush room |
| cottaging | cramp-iron | cristated | Crustacea |
| cotter-pin | cranberry | criterion | cryometer |
| cottonade | crank-case | criticise | cryptical |
| cotton-gin | crankness | criticism | cryptogam |
| cotyledon | crapulent | criticize | cryptonym |
| cough drop | crapulous | crocodile | ctenidium |
| countable | crash dive | croissant | cubbyhole |
| countdown | crash-land | Cro-Magnon | cubically |
| countless | crassness | crookedly | cubicular |
| countship | cravatted | crop-eared | cubiculum |
| coup d'état | cravingly | croquette | cuckoldly |
| courgette | craziness | crosiered | cuckoldom |
| courteous | cream-cake | cross-bill | cuckoldry |
| courtesan | cream-laid | cross-bred | cucullate |
| court hand | cream-wove | cross-eyed | cudgeller |
| courtling | creatable | crossfire | cullender |
| court-roll | creatress | cross-head | culminate |
| courtship | credendum | crossness | culpatory |
| courtyard | credulity | crossover | cultivate |
| couturier | credulous | cross-road | cultrated |
| cover-girl | creep-hole | cross-talk | cumbrance |
| cover-slip | cremation | cross-tree | cuneiform |
| coverture | crematory | cross-ways | cunningly |
| covertway | crenation | cross-wind | cupbearer |

curdiness
curettage
curiosity
curiously
curliness
currently
curry-comb
cursorial
cursorily
curstness
curtailer
curtilage
curvature
cushioned
cuspidate
custodial
custodian
custodier
customary
cutaneous
cut it fine
cut-throat
cuttingly
cyanamide
cyanotype
cybercafé
cyberpunk
cycloidal
cyclopean
cyclorama
cyclotron
cylindric
cymbalist
cymophane
cynegetic
cynically
cyprinoid
cystiform
cystocele
cystolith

cystotomy
cytherean
cytoblast
cytoplasm

**D**

dachshund
dairy farm
dairy-maid
Dalai Lama
dalliance
Dalmatian
damascene
damaskeen
damnation
damnatory
dampishly
damp squib
damselfly
dandelion
dandiprat
dangerous
dapple-bay
Dardanian
dare-devil
dark horse
dart-board
Darwinian
Darwinism
dashboard
dash-wheel
dastardly
dasymeter
dauntless
davenport
Davy Jones
day-labour
day-school
day-spring
deaconess

dead-drunk
deadening
dead-house
dead-light
dead march
dead set on
deafening
death-bell
death-blow
death duty
death-fire
deathless
deathlike
death-mask
death rate
deathsman
death trap
death wish
debarment
debatable
debauched
debauchee
debaucher
debenture
debutante
decachord
decadence
decadency
decagonal
decalcify
decalitre
decalogue
decametre
decapodal
decastyle
decathlon
deceitful
decennial
decennium
deception

deceptive
decidable
decidedly
deciduate
deciduous
decilitre
decillion
decimally
decimator
decimetre
deck-cargo
deck-chair
declaimer
declinate
declining
declivity
declivous
decoction
decollate
*décolleté*
decomplex
decompose
decontrol
decorated
decorator
decoy-duck
decrement
decretist
decretive
decretory
decumbent
decurrent
decussate
dedicated
dedicatee
dedicator
deducible
deducibly
deduction
deductive

| | | | |
|---|---|---|---|
| Deep South | delta wing | depicture | dessicant |
| deep space | deludable | depletion | destinate |
| deer-hound | demagogic | depletive | destinist |
| deer-mouse | demagogue | depletory | destitute |
| defalcate | demandant | deposable | destroyer |
| defaulter | demanding | depositor | desuetude |
| defeatism | demantoid | depravity | desultory |
| defeatist | demarcate | deprecate | detection |
| defection | demeanour | depredate | detective |
| defective | demi-devil | depressed | detention |
| defendant | demi-lance | depressor | detergent |
| defensive | demi-monde | depurator | determent |
| defensory | demisable | de rigueur | determine |
| deference | demission | derisible | deterrent |
| deferment | demi-tasse | derivable | detersion |
| deficient | demiurgic | derivably | detersive |
| definable | democracy | dermatoid | dethroner |
| definably | demulcent | derring-do | detonator |
| deflation | demurrage | derringer | detracter |
| deflected | demystify | descanter | detractor |
| deflector | dendritic | descender | detriment |
| deflorate | denigrate | describer | detrition |
| defluxion | denotable | desecrate | detrusion |
| defoliant | denouncer | desertion | deuterium |
| defoliate | denseness | deserving | devaluate |
| deformity | dentately | desiccate | devastate |
| defrauder | dentiform | designate | developer |
| degrading | dentistry | designing | deviation |
| dehiscent | dentition | desirable | devil-fish |
| dehydrate | denyingly | desirably | devilment |
| deiparous | deodorant | desmology | devil's bit |
| dejection | deodorise | desolated | devilship |
| delftware | deodorize | desolater | deviously |
| delicious | deoxidate | desolator | devisable |
| delighted | deoxidise | despairer | devisably |
| delineate | deoxidize | desperado | devitrify |
| deliquium | departure | desperate | devonport |
| deliriant | depasture | despoiler | devotedly |
| delirious | dependant | desponder | dewlapped |
| deliverer | dependent | despotism | dexterity |

dexterous
dextrorse
diablerie
diabolise
diabolism
diabolize
diabrosis
diachylon
diachylum
diaconate
diacritic
diactinic
diaeresis
diagnosis
dialectal
dialectic
dialogise
dialogism
dialogist
dialogize
dial-plate
diametral
diametric
diamonded
diandrous
dianoetic
diaphragm
diarrhoea
diastolic
diathermy
diathesis
diathetic
diatomite
dicastery
dichogamy
dichotomy
dichroism
dichromic
dicky-bird
dicoelous

dictation
dictatory
dictatrix
dictature
didactics
didactile
Didelphia
didelphic
die-sinker
dietarian
dietetics
dietetist
different
difficult
diffident
diffluent
diffusion
diffusive
digastric
digenesis
digestion
digestive
digitalin
digitalis
digitated
dignified
dignitary
dilatable
diligence
dimension
dimidiate
dimissory
dimyarian
dine out on
dinginess
dining-car
Dinoceras
dinothere
dioecious
dionysiac

dionysian
dioptrics
diphthong
diphycerc
diplomacy
dipterous
direction
directive
directory
directrix
direct tax
direfully
dirigible
dirt-cheap
dirtiness
disaccord
disaffect
disaffirm
disappear
disarming
disavouch
disavowal
disavower
disbelief
disburden
disburser
discalced
disc brake
discerner
discharge
dischurch
discoidal
discolour
discomfit
discommon
discourse
discovert
discovery
discredit
discusser

disembark
disembody
disenable
disengage
disenroll
disentail
disentomb
disesteem
disfavour
disfigure
disforest
disgorger
disgracer
disguiser
dish-cloth
dish-clout
dishonest
dishonour
dish-towel
dish-water
disinfect
disinhume
disk drive
dislocate
dismantle
dismember
dismissal
disnature
disoblige
disorient
disparage
disparate
disparity
dispauper
dispeller
dispenser
dispeople
dispersal
disperser
displayer

displease
dispondee
disposure
dispraise
disproval
disputant
disregard
disrelish
disrepair
disrepute
dissector
disseisin
disseisor
disseizin
disseizor
dissemble
dissenter
dissident
dissipate
dissolute
dissolver
dissonant
distantly
distemper
distiller
*distingué*
distorted
distraint
disturbed
disturber
disusance
dithyramb
diurnally
divergent
diversely
diversify
diversion
diversity
diverting
dividable

divisible
divisibly
divorcive
divulsion
divulsive
Dixieland
dizziness
doctorate
doctrinal
dodecagon
dog-collar
dog eat dog
dogmatics
dogmatise
dogmatism
dogmatist
dogmatize
dog-paddle
dolabrate
dolefully
dominator
dominical
Dominican
do one's bit
do one's nut
door-plate
dormitive
dormitory
doss-house
doubleton
doubtable
doubtless
doughtily
dowerless
downgrade
downiness
downright
downscale
downstage
downthrow

down train
down under
downwards
draconian
draftsman
dragonfly
dragonish
drag queen
drainable
drainpipe
draintrap
dramatics
dramatise
dramatist
dramatize
dramaturg
draperied
Dravidian
dray-horse
dreadless
dreamland
dreamless
dress-coat
driftless
driftwood
drinkable
driveller
dromedary
droppings
drop-press
drop-scene
dropsical
drugstore
druidical
drum-major
drumstick
dry as dust
drysalter
dualistic
dubiously

duck-board
ductilely
ductility
duffel bag
duffle bag
dulcamara
dumb cluck
dumbfound
duodecimo
duodenary
duplicate
duplicity
Duralumin®
dura mater
duskiness
dust-brand
dust-cover
Dutch oven
duteously
dutifully
dyer's-weed
dynamical
dynamiter
dyscrasia
dysentery
dysgenics
dyspepsia
dyspeptic
dysphagia
dysphasia
dysphoria
dystrophy
dziggetai

**E**

eagerness
eagle-eyed
eaglewood
ealdorman
ear-cockle

earliness
early bird
early days
earnestly
earth-born
earthfast
earthling
earthward
earth-wolf
earthwork
earth-worm
easterner
easy as ABC
easy as pie
easy chair
easy-going
easy-peasy
easy rider
eavesdrop
ebullient
eccentric
echinated
eclampsia
economics
economise
economist
economize
ecosphere
ecosystem
ecstasied
ectoblast
ectomorph
ectoplasm
edelweiss
edibility
edificial
editorial
education
Edwardian
educative

eel-basket
effective
effectual
efficient
effluence
effluvial
effluvium
effluxion
effodient
effulgent
eglantine
egotheism
egotistic
egregious
egression
eiderdown
eiderduck
eidograph
eightfold
eightieth
eirenicon
ejaculate
ejectment
elaborate
elaterium
elbow-room
eldership
elder-wine
electoral
electrify
electrode
electuary
elegantly
elemental
elevation
elevatory
eliminate
ellipsoid
Elmo's fire
elocution

Elohistic
elopement
eloquence
elsewhere
elucidate
elutriate
emaciated
emanation
embarrass
embattled
embayment
embellish
Ember days
Ember-tide
Ember week
embezzler
emblement
embracery
embrasure
embrocate
embroider
embryonal
embryonic
embryotic
emendator
emergence
emergency
eminently
Emmenthal
emollient
emolument
emotional
empathise
empathize
emphasise
emphasize
emphysema
empirical
emptiness
empyreuma

emulation
emulative
emulatory
emulously
emunctory
enactment
enamelist
encaustic
enchanted
enchanter
enchorial
enclosure
encomiast
encompass
encounter
encourage
encrimson
encrinite
endearing
endeavour
endecagon
endeictic
endemical
endlessly
endocrine
endolymph
endomorph
endoplasm
endoplast
endoscope
endosperm
endosteum
endostome
endowment
endurable
endurably
endurance
energetic
energical
enfeebler

| | | | |
|---|---|---|---|
| engineman | ephemeral | eradicate | ethically |
| engiscope | ephemeris | erasement | Ethiopian |
| Englishry | ephemeron | erectness | ethmoidal |
| engrailed | epicentre | eremitism | ethnicism |
| engrained | epiclinal | ergometer | ethnology |
| engrainer | Epicurean | eriometer | etiquette |
| engraving | epicurism | eristical | etymology |
| engrosser | epidermal | erogenous | Eucharist |
| engyscope | epidermic | eroticism | euchology |
| enhydrous | epidermis | erroneous | Euclidean |
| enigmatic | epidictic | erstwhile | eulogical |
| enjoyable | epigenous | eruditely | euphemise |
| enjoyment | epigraphy | erudition | euphemism |
| enlighten | epigynous | eruginous | euphemize |
| enlivener | epileptic | erythrite | euphonium |
| en passant | epilogise | escalator | Euphorbia |
| enrapture | epilogize | escapable | Eurotrash |
| enrolment | epiphragm | escheator | evaginate |
| entelechy | epiphysis | esclandre | evangelic |
| enteritis | epiphytal | Eskimo dog | evaporate |
| entertain | epiphytic | esophagus | evasively |
| enthymeme | episcopal | esoterism | eventuate |
| entoblast | episodial | Esperanto | evergreen |
| entomical | epistaxis | espionage | everybody |
| entophyte | epistolic | esplanade | evidently |
| entourage | epitaphic | essential | evocation |
| entreater | epitomise | establish | evocative |
| entrechat | epitomist | estafette | evolution |
| entrecôte | epitomize | estaminet | evolutive |
| entremets | epizootic | estate car | exactness |
| entrochal | eponymous | estimable | examinant |
| entropium | Epsom-salt | estimably | examining |
| enucleate | equalness | estimator | exanimate |
| enumerate | equipment | estuarial | exanthema |
| enunciate | equipoise | estuarine | exarchate |
| enviously | Equisetum | estuarine | Excalibur |
| envoyship | equitable | esurience | excavator |
| eparchate | equitably | esuriency | exceeding |
| epaulette | equivocal | etceteras | excellent |
| ephedrine | equivoque | eternally | excelsior |

excentric
excepting
exception
excessive
exchanger
exchequer
excipient
excisable
exciseman
excisemen
excitable
excitably
exclaimer
exclusion
exclusive
excoriate
excrement
excretion
excretive
excretory
exculpate
excurrent
excursion
excursive
excusable
excusably
execrable
exccrably
cxecutant
execution
executive
executory
executrix
exegetics
exegetist
exemplary
exemplify
exemption
exequatur
exerciser

exfoliate
exhalable
exhausted
exhibiter
exhibitor
existence
ex officio
exogamous
exogenous
exonerate
exorciser
exosmosis
exosmotic
expansile
expansion
expansive
expatiate
expectant
expedient
expensive
expertise
expiation
expiatory
expirable
expiscate
explainer
expletive
expletory
explicate
exploiter
explosion
explosive
expositor
expounder
expressly
expulsion
expulsive
expurgate
exquisite
exsertile

exsiccant
exsiccate
extempore
extensile
extension
extensity
extensive
extenuate
externals
extirpate
extortion
extractor
extradite
extravert
extremely
extremist
extremity
extricate
extrinsic
extrorsal
extrovert
extrusion
exuberant
exuberate
exudation
eyebright
eye-opener
eye shadow

**F**

fabaceous
fabricate
facetious
face value
facsimile
factitive
factorage
factorial
factorize
factsheet

faff about
faggoting
faintness
fairy-land
fairy-ring
fairy-tale
faith cure
faithless
Falangist
falcation
falciform
falconine
faldstool
Fallopian
falsehood
falseness
falsifier
faltering
fanatical
fanciless
fancy fair
fancy-free
fancy work
fantasise
fantasist
fantasize
fantastic
farandole
farmhouse
farmstead
far-seeing
far-sought
fasciated
fascicled
fascicule
fascinate
fashioner
fastening
fast track
fatefully

fatidical
fattiness
fatty acid
faultless
faveolate
favourite
fearfully
feathered
febricula
febrifuge
feculence
fecundate
fecundity
feelingly
feignedly
fellowman
felonious
fenestral
Fenianism
fenugreek
feoffment
feracious
feringhee
ferocious
ferrotype
ferry-boat
fertilely
fertilise
fertility
fertilize
fervently
fervidity
festinate
festively
festivity
fetichism
feticidal
fetidness
fetishism
fetlocked

fettucine
fettucini
feudalise
feudalism
feudalist
feudality
feudalize
feudatory
*feu de joie*
fibriform
fibrinous
fictional
fiddle-bow
fiduciary
field-book
fieldfare
field-work
fieriness
fife-major
fifteenth
figurable
figurante
filaceous
filiation
filigreed
filleting
fillister
filminess
filoplume
filter-tip
fimbriate
financial
financier
fine-drawn
fin-footed
finger-dry
fingering
finically
finicking
fire-alarm

firebrand
firebreak
fire-brick
fire-eater
fireguard
fire-irons
fireplace
fire-power
fire-proof
fire-water
firmament
first-born
first-hand
First Lady
firstling
first-rate
fisherman
fishiness
fish-joint
fish-louse
fish-plate
fish-slice
fish-spear
fish stick
fish-woman
fistulose
fistulous
fittingly
fixedness
flabellum
flaccidly
flagellum
flageolet
flagrancy
flagstaff
flagstone
flag-waver
flakiness
flammable
flap-eared

flashback
flashbulb
flatterer
flatulent
flaunting
flavorous
flavoured
flay-flint
fleckless
fledgling
fleetness
flesh-hook
fleshings
fleshless
flesh-meat
flexitime
flightily
flint-lock
flippancy
flocculus
flood-gate
flood-mark
flood-tide
floor plan
floorshow
floreated
floriated
floridity
floscular
floss-silk
flotation
flouncing
flowchart
flowering
flowerpot
fluctuant
fluctuate
fluoresce
fluorspar
fluxional

fly-bitten
fly-fisher
flying fox
flyweight
foeticide
fogginess
fog-signal
foliation
folic acid
folk music
following
food chain
foodstuff
foolhardy
foolishly
foolproof
foot-board
foot-cloth
foot-fault
footloose
foot-pound
footprint
foot-stalk
foot-stall
footstool
foppishly
forasmuch
forbearer
forbidden
force-feed
forceless
forcemeat
force-pump
foreclose
forecourt
forefront
foregoing
foreigner
forejudge
forenamed

foresheet
foreshore
foresight
forestall
forestine
foretaste
foretoken
foretooth
forewoman
forfeiter
forficate
forgather
forgetful
forgiving
forgotten
forlornly
formalise
formalism
formalist
formality
formalize
formation
formative
formicary
formulary
formulate
formulism
formulize
fornicate
forsythia
forthwith
fortifier
fortitude
fortnight
fortunate
forty-five
forwardly
fossilise
fossilize
fossorial

fosterage
foster-son
foundling
foundress
foundries
four flush
fourpence
fourscore
foveolate
foxhunter
fractions
fractious
fragrance
fragrancy
framework
franchise
francolin
frangible
frankness
fraternal
fraudless
free-board
free fight
free house
freelance
Freemason
free-range
freesheet
freestone
freestyle
free trade
free verse
free-wheel
freezable
freeze-dry
freighter
Frenchify
Frenchman
frequency
freshness

fretfully
friar bird
fricassee
fricative
frightful
frigidity
frivolity
frivolous
frock-coat
frogmarch
front door
frontless
frontward
frost-bite
frost-work
frowardly
fructuous
frugality
fruiterer
fruitless
frustrate
fruticose
fruticous
fugacious
fulgurate
fulgurite
fulgurous
full-blown
full-dress
full house
full-scale
fulminant
fulminate
fulsomely
fundament
fungicide
fungiform
fungology
funicular
funiculus

funnelled
funny-bone
furbisher
furcation
furfurous
furiously
furnished
furnisher
furniture
furtherer
furtively
fusillade
fussiness
fustigate
fustiness

**G**
gabardine
gaberdine
gabionage
gainsayer
galantine
Galatians
galenical
galingale
gallantly
gallantry
galleries
Gallicise
Gallicism
Gallicize
gallinule
gallivant
galliwasp
gallooned
gallopade
gallowses
gallstone
galvanise
galvanism

galvanist
galvanize
gambadoes
game point
gamma rays
ganglions
gang-plank
gannister
gardening
gargarism
garibaldi
garmented
garnishee
garnisher
garniture
garreteer
garrotter
garrulity
garrulous
gasconade
gas-holder
gasometer
gasometry
gaspingly
gastritis
gastropod
gatehouse
gathering
gaucherie
gaudeamus
gaudiness
gaugeable
gavelkind
gazetteer
gear shift
gear-wheel
gelignite
gelsemium
geminated
gemmation

genealogy
generable
generally
generator
generical
genetical
geniality
genitival
genteelly
gentility
gentleman
gentlemen
genuflect
genuinely
geodesist
geography
geologian
geologise
geologist
geologize
geomancer
geomantic
geometric
geophagia
geoponics
georgette
georgical
gerfalcon
geriatric
germander
Germanise
Germanism
germanium
Germanize
germicide
germinant
germinate
gerundial
gerundive
gestation

get-at-able
get down to
get shot of
get wind of
ghost town
giantship
gibberish
gibbosity
gibbously
giddiness
gilt-edged
ginger-ale
ginglymus
girandola
girandole
Girl Guide
Girl Scout
Girondist
gladiator
gladiolus
glamorise
glamorize
glandered
glandular
glass-ware
glass-wort
glaucosis
glengarry
glissando
globulous
glomerate
glomerule
glomosity
glossitis
glowingly
glueyness
glutinate
glutinous
glyceride
glycerine

| | | | |
|---|---|---|---|
| glyptodon | go to earth | gravy-boat | ground-ivy |
| gnathonic | goutiness | great-aunt | ground-nut |
| gnomonics | governess | great-coat | groundsel |
| gnomonist | graceless | Great Dane | groveller |
| go bananas | grace-note | greatness | gruelling |
| go-between | gracility | Greek fire | gruffness |
| godfather | gradation | Greek gift | guacamole |
| godlessly | gradatory | greenback | guarantee |
| godliness | gradually | green bean | guarantor |
| godmother | graduator | green belt | guardable |
| go down big | gramineal | green-eyed | guardedly |
| godparent | grammatic | greengage | guard-rail |
| goffering | grandaunt | greenhorn | guardsman |
| gogglebox | Grand Duke | greenmail | guard's van |
| go haywire | grandiose | greenness | guerrilla |
| going over | grand jury | green-room | guess-work |
| golden age | grandmama | Green-sand | guest-room |
| golden boy | grandness | greenwood | guide-book |
| golden-rod | grandpapa | Gregorian | guideless |
| gold-field | Grand Prix | grenadier | guide-line |
| goldfinch | grandsire | grenadine | guide-post |
| gold-plate | grand slam | greybeard | guild-hall |
| goldsmith | grand tour | greyhound | guileless |
| golf-links | granitoid | greywacke | guillemot |
| golliwogg | grantable | grievance | guilloche |
| gondolier | granulate | grill-room | guiltless |
| Gongorism | granulite | grimalkin | guinea-pig |
| gonophore | granulose | griminess | gum arabic |
| gonorrhea | granulous | gripingly | gumminess |
| goosander | grapeshot | grisaille | gun-cotton |
| goose-neck | grape-vine | groceries | gunpowder |
| goose-step | graphical | groomsman | gushingly |
| gorgonian | grassland | gropingly | gustation |
| gorgonise | gratifier | grosgrain | gustatory |
| gorgonize | gratitude | gros point | guttering |
| go sky high | gratulate | gross-beak | gymnasial |
| gospeller | graveless | grossness | gymnasium |
| gossamery | graveness | grotesque | gymnastic |
| gossipped | graveyard | ground-hog | gymnogene |
| Gothicism | gravitate | grounding | gynoecium |

gynopathy
gynophore
gyrfalcon
gyroscope

# H
habergeon
habitable
habituate
hackberry
hacked off
hackneyed
haematite
haematoid
haggardly
hagiology
hailstone
hailstorm
hairiness
hair-piece
hairstyle
half-baked
half-caste
halfpence
halfpenny
half-title
half-track
half-truth
halitosis
Hallowe'en
Hallowmas
Hallstatt
halophyte
haloscope
hamadryad
hamadryas
hamburger
ham-fisted
ham-handed
hammerman

hamstring
handiness
handiwork
handlebar
hand-shake
hand-spike
handstand
hansom cab
haphazard
happening
happy hour
haranguer
harbinger
harborage
harbourer
hardboard
hard facts
hardihood
hardiness
hard lines
hard stuff
harlequin
harmattan
harmfully
harmonica
harmonics
harmonise
harmonist
harmonium
harmonize
harmotome
harnesser
harpooner
harquebus
harshness
hartbeest
hartshorn
harvester
hastiness
hatch-back

hatchment
hatefully
hats off to
haughtily
have a ball
have a word
have had it
haversack
have words
hawse-hole
hay-making
hazardous
headboard
head-dress
head-first
headiness
headlight
headphone
headpiece
headstall
head start
headstone
healthful
healthily
heartache
heartbeat
heartburn
heartfelt
heartland
heartless
heart-sick
heartsome
heartwood
heathenry
heaviness
heavy-duty
heavy spar
Hebraical
Hebridean
hectogram

heedfully
hegemonic
heinously
heliostat
heliotype
hellebore
Hellenian
Hellenise
Hellenism
Hellenist
Hellenize
hellishly
Helvetian
hemicycle
hemiplegy
hemistich
hem-stitch
hendiadys
hepatical
hepatitis
heptaglot
heptarchy
herbalist
herbarium
herbicide
herbivore
Herculean
hereabout
hereafter
heretical
hereunder
heritable
heritably
hermitage
hermitary
heroic age
heronshaw
hesitancy
hesitator
Hesperian

| | | | |
|---|---|---|---|
| hetaerism | histology | hopscotch | humdinger |
| heterodox | historian | horehound | humectate |
| heteronym | hit and run | horologer | humiliate |
| heteropox | hitch-hike | horometry | humourist |
| heuristic | hit the hay | horoscope | humungous |
| hexachord | hoar-frost | horoscopy | hunch-back |
| hexagonal | hoariness | horseback | hundredth |
| hexameter | hobgoblin | horse-hair | Hungarian |
| hexastyle | hobnailed | horseplay | hunky-dory |
| Hexateuch | hodiernal | horseshoe | hurricane |
| hibernate | hodometer | horsetail | hurriedly |
| Hibernian | hoidenish | horse-whip | hurtfully |
| hide-bound | hoi polloi | hortation | husbandly |
| hideously | hold forth | hortative | husbandry |
| hiemation | hold out on | hortatory | hush money |
| hierarchy | hold water | hostilely | huskiness |
| hierogram | hollyhock | hostility | hybridise |
| hierology | holocaust | hot button | hybridism |
| hifalutin | holograph | hot potato | hybridity |
| high-class | Holy Ghost | Hottentot | hybridize |
| high-flier | Holy Grail | hound-fish | hydrangea |
| high-flown | holystone | hour-glass | hydraulic |
| high-flyer | home-grown | house-boat | hydrocele |
| high jinks | Home Guard | household | hydrofoil |
| highlight | homestead | houseleek | hydrology |
| high-power | home truth | houseless | hydrolyze |
| high water | homewards | housemaid | hydropath |
| hilarious | homeyness | house-room | hydrosoma |
| hill billy | homicidal | housewife | hydrozoan |
| hilliness | homiletic | house-work | hyetology |
| Hindooism | homograph | howsoever | hygienism |
| hindrance | homologue | huckaback | hygienist |
| hindsight | homophone | hue and cry | hylozoism |
| hippiatry | homuncule | huffiness | hymnology |
| hippocras | honeycomb | hum and | hypallage |
| hirundine | honeymoon | haw | hyperbola |
| hispidity | honky-tonk | humankind | hyperbole |
| histamine | honorabic | humanness | hypethral |
| histogeny | honorific | humble-bee | hyphenate |
| histogram | hopefully | humble pie | hypnotise |

hypnotism
hypnotize
hypocaust
hypocrisy
hypocrite
hypogeous
hyponasty
hypostyle
hysterics

**I**
ibuprofen
ice hockey
Icelander
Icelandic
ichneumon
ichnolite
ichnology
ichthyoid
iconology
idealizer
identical
ideograph
ideologue
idiocrasy
idiograph
idiomatic
idiopathy
idiotical
ignitable
ignitible
ignoramus
ignorance
iguanodon
ill at ease
illegally
illegible
illegibly
ill-gotten
illiberal

illicitly
illogical
imaginary
imbalance
imbricate
imbroglio
imbuement
imitation
imitative
immanence
immanency
immediacy
immediate
immensely
immensity
immersion
immigrant
immigrate
imminence
immodesty
immolator
immorally
immovable
immovably
immutable
immutably
impartial
impassion
impassive
impatiens
impatient
impeacher
impedance
impellent
impendent
imperator
imperfect
imperious
impetrate
impetuous

impingent
impiously
impleader
implement
implicate
impliedly
impolitic
important
importune
imposable
imposture
impotence
impotency
impounder
imprecate
imprecise
improbity
impromptu
improving
improvise
imprudent
impudence
impulsion
impulsive
imputable
in a bad way
inability
in a lather
inamorata
inamorato
inanimate
inanition
inaudible
inaugural
inbreathe
incapable
incarnate
incaution
incentive
inception

inceptive
incessant
incidence
incipient
inclement
inclosure
inclusive
incognita
incognito
income tax
incommode
incorrect
incorrupt
increment
incubator
incubuses
inculcate
inculpate
incumbent
incurable
incurably
incurious
incursion
incurvate
indecency
indecorum
indelible
indelibly
indemnify
indemnity
indenture
indexical
indicator
indiction
indigence
indignant
indignity
indispose
indolence
indraught

inducible
inductile
induction
inductive
induement
indulgent
indweller
in earnest
inebriant
inebriate
inebriety
inebrious
ineffable
ineffably
inelastic
inelegant
inequable
inertness
infantile
infantine
infatuate
infection
infective
inferable
inference
infertile
infielder
infirmary
infirmity
inflation
inflexion
influence
influenza
influxion
informant
in full cry
infuriate
infusible
infusoria
ingenious

ingenuity
ingenuous
ingle-nook
ingluvies
ingrained
ingrowing
inhabiter
inherence
inherency
inheritor
inhumanly
injection
injurious
injustice
in line for
inner city
innermost
inner tube
innervate
innkeeper
innocence
innocency
innocuous
innovator
innoxious
innuendos
inoculate
inodorous
inorganic
in-patient
inquiline
inquiries
inquiring
insatiate
insectary
insensate
insertion
in-service
inside job
inside out

insidious
insincere
insinuate
insistent
in so far as
insofar as
insolence
insoluble
insolvent
insomniac
inspector
instanter
instantly
instigate
institute
insularly
insulator
insulting
insurable
insurance
insurgent
integrant
integrate
integrity
intellect
intendant
intensely
intensify
intension
intensity
intensive
intention
*inter alia*
intercede
intercept
interdict
interface
interfere
interfuse
interject

interlace
interlard
interleaf
interline
interlink
interlock
interlope
interlude
interment
internist
internode
interplay
interpose
interpret
interrupt
intersect
intervene
interview
interwind
intestacy
intestate
intestine
in the club
in the dark
in the know
in the pink
in the soup
in the swim
in the wars
in the wind
intortion
intricacy
intricate
intriguer
intrinsic
introduce
introvert
intrusion
intrusive
intuition

intuitive
intumesce
inunction
inurement
inutility
invective
invention
inventive
inventory
inversely
inversion
invidious
inviolate
invisible
invisibly
involucel
involucre
involuted
inwreathe
inwrought
ipso facto
irascible
irascibly
Irish bull
Irish moss
Irish stew
irksomely
iron-bound
iron horse
iron-smith
iron-stone
ironworks
irradiant
irradiate
irregular
irriguous
irritable
irritably
irruption
irruptive

isinglass
isoclinal
isoclinic
isolation
isomerism
isometric
isosceles
isotheral
Israelite
issueless
italicise
Italicism
italicize
itchiness
itching to
iteration
iterative
itineracy
itinerant
itinerary
itinerate

**J**

jaborandi
jacaranda
jackfruit
jack-knife
jack-snipe
Jacobinic
Jacobitic
jam-packed
janissary
Jansenism
Jansenist
jargonise
jargonize
jaundiced
jealously
jeeringly
jellyfish

jenneting
jequirity
jerfalcon
jessamine
Jesuitism
jet engine
jet stream
jettiness
jewellery
jitter-bug
job-seeker
jobsworth
jockstrap
jocularly
jocundity
Joe Public
jolliness
joss-stick
journeyer
joviality
joylessly
joy-riding
judgement
judgeship
judicable
judicator
judiciary
judicious
juiceless
juiciness
jump-start
juniorate
juniority
junketeer
juridical
jurywoman
justiciar
justifier
juvenilia
juxtapose

**K**

kalsomine
Kamasutra
karabiner
keep at bay
kentledge
keratitis
kerb-stone
kernelled
key-stroke
kick-start
kidnapper
killingly
kilocycle
kilohertz
kilolitre
kilometre
kinematic
king-craft
king-sized
kinswoman
kinswomen
kissagram
kitchener
kittenish
kittiwake
kiwi fruit
knavishly
knife-edge
knightage
knock back
knockback
knock down
knock-down
knot-grass
knowingly
know-it-all
knowledge
krummhorn
kymograph

**L**
labialise
labialize
laborious
labouring
labyrinth
lacerable
lacerated
lacertian
lacertine
lachrymal
laciniate
laconical
lactation
lactifuge
lacunaria
lacustral
ladies' man
laevigate
laevulose
lager lout
laid paper
Lambrusco
laminated
lamp-black
lancewood
landamman
landaulet
landgrave
land of Nod
landowner
landscape
landslide
langouste
*langue d'oc*
lanthanum
Laodicean
largeness
larghetto
larviform

laryngeal
laryngean
lassitude
last ditch
lastingly
last laugh
last rites
last straw
latecomer
laterally
latter-day
laudation
laudative
laudatory
laughable
laughably
launch-pad
laundress
laurelled
lawgiving
lawlessly
lawnmower
lay figure
lay reader
lay sister
lay to rest
lazarette
lazaretto
lazy-bones
leadglass
leafiness
leakiness
learnedly
leaseback
leasehold
leastways
leave cold
lecherous
left-overs
legendary

legionary
legislate
leisurely
leitmotif
lend a hand
lengthily
leniently
lentiform
leprosity
leprously
lethargic
letter-box
lettering
leukaemia
leukocyte
leukotomy
levantine
levelling
levelness
leviathan
levigable
Levitical
lexically
liability
libellous
liberally
liberator
libertine
librarian
libration
libratory
lichenous
lickerish
lie in wait
lienteric
life-blood
life cycle
life event
lifeguard
life style

ligatured
lightness
lightning
lightship
lightsome
lights out
light-year
lign-aloes
ligniform
ligulated
like a shot
lily-white
limaceous
limelight
limestone
limitable
limitedly
limitless
limnology
limousine
limpidity
limpingly
lineament
lineation
lineolate
lingering
lingulate
lintwhite
lippitude
liquation
liquefier
liquidate
liquidise
liquidity
liquidize
liquorice
Listerism
literally
literatim
litheness

lithesome
lithoidal
lithology
lithotomy
lithotypy
litigable
litigator
litigious
litter-bug
liturgics
liturgies
liturgist
live in sin
live rough
liverwort
liveryman
liverymen
livestock
lividness
lixiviate
lixivious
loadstone
loathsome
lobscouse
lock horns
locksmith
locomotor
lodestone
lodgement
loftiness
logarithm
logically
logistics
logograph
logogriph
logomachy
logomania
logorrhea
loincloth
longcloth

longevity
longevous
longicorn
longingly
longitude
long johns
long-lived
long-range
longshore
look-alike
look sharp
look small
look smart
loop-holed
looseleaf
looseness
loquacity
Lord Mayor
lorgnette
loricated
lose heart
lose sleep
lost cause
lotophagi
love-child
loving-cup
low-budget
low comedy
lower-case
lowermost
Lowlander
lowliness
lubricant
lubricate
lubricity
lucidness
luckiness
lucrative
lucubrate
ludicrous

Luftwaffe
lumbering
lumbrical
lumpishly
lunar year
lunisolar
lunulated
lustfully
lustiness
luxuriant
luxuriate
luxurious
lymphatic
lymph node
lyonnaise

**M**
macadamia
macaronic
macaronis
Maccabean
macedoine
machinate
machinery
macintosh
macrocosm
macrurous
madeleine
madrepore
maelstrom
magdalene
magically
magistral
magnalium
magnesian
magnesium
magnetics
magnetise
magnetism
magnetize

magnifico
magnifier
magnitude
Maharajah
Maharanee
mahlstick
Mahomedan
Mahometan
mail order
mainframe
mainsheet
majordomo
majorship
majuscule
make a pass
make merry
make my day
makeshift
make use of
malachite
maladroit
malanders
malarious
*malgré lui*
malicious
malignant
malignity
malleable
mallemuck
malleolar
malleolus
malvoisie
mammalian
mammalogy
mammogram
mammonism
mammonist
mammonite
man and boy
man-at-arms

Mancunian
mandatary
mandatory
mandoline
manducate
man Friday
manganate
manganese
manganite
manhandle
Manichean
manifesto
manipular
manliness
mannequin
mannerism
mannerist
manoeuvre
manometer
manticore
manyplies
many-sided
marcasite
marchpane
Mardi Gras
mare's-nest
mare's-tail
margarine
margarite
marginate
marihuana
marijuana
marked man
marketing
marmalade
marmoreal
marmorean
marquetry
marrowfat
marsupial

marsupium
martially
Martinmas
martyrdom
martyrise
martyrize
masculine
masculism
masculist
masochism
massagist
massé shot
massiness
massively
mass media
masterful
masticate
matchable
matchless
matchlock
match play
matchwood
maternity
matriarch
matricide
matrimony
matronage
matronise
matronize
matutinal
maulstick
maunderer
mausolean
mausoleum
mavournin
mawkishly
maxillary
mayoralty
mealiness
meaningly

meanwhile
meatiness
mechanics
mechanise
mechanism
mechanist
mechanize
medallion
medallist
mediaeval
mediately
mediation
mediatise
mediative
mediatize
medicable
medically
medicinal
medullary
megabucks
megacycle
megahertz
megaphone
megaspore
megastore
megathere
melanosis
melaphyre
Meliboean
meliorate
meliorism
melodious
melodrama
meltingly
meltwater
memoirist
memorable
memoranda
memoriser
memorizer

menagerie
men-at-arms
mendacity
Mendelism
mendicant
mendicity
meniscoid
menopause
Menshevik
menstrual
menstruum
mentality
mentation
mercenary
mercerise
mercerize
merciless
mercurial
mercurous
merganser
merriment
mescaline
mesentery
mesmerise
mesmerism
mesmerist
mesmerize
mesoblast
mesophyll
mesophyte
messenger
messianic
messieurs
metalline
metallise
metallist
metallize
metalloid
metameric
metaplasm

meteorite
meteoroid
metheglin
methodise
Methodism
Methodist
methodize
methought
methylene
methystic
metonymic
metrology
metronome
mezzanine
mezzotint
miasmatic
micaceous
microbial
microbian
microchip
microcosm
microcyte
microfilm
micrology
micropyle
microtome
microwave
microzoon
microzyme
micturate
middle age
middleman
midsummer
midwifery
midwinter
migration
migratory
milestone
militancy
milkiness

milkround
milk-teeth
milk-tooth
millboard
millenary
millepede
millepore
milligram
millinery
millionth
millipede
millstone
Miltonian
mimetical
mincemeat
mindfully
minefield
mine-layer
miniature
mini-skirt
minorship
mint-julep
minute-man
minute-men
mirifical
mirthless
misbehave
misbelief
mischance
miscreant
misdemean
misdirect
misemploy
miserable
miserably
misgiving
misgovern
misguided
misinform
mismanage

misreport
misshapen
missioner
mistiness
mistletoe
mizen-mast
mnemonics
mobocracy
mockingly
modelling
moderator
modernise
modernism
modernist
modernize
modillion
modulator
moistness
molecular
mollifier
momentary
momentous
monachism
monadelph
monadical
monarchal
monarchic
monastery
monatomic
monecious
monergism
monergist
moneyless
Mongolian
monitress
monkeyism
monk's-
hood
monobasic
monochord

monocline
monocular
monodrama
monograph
monologue
monomania
monoplane
monoptote
monosperm
monostich
monotreme
Monsignor
monstrous
monticule
moodiness
moonlight
moonraker
moonshine
moonshiny
moonstone
moraliser
moralizer
morbidity
mordacity
Mormonism
Mormonist
Mormonite
Morse code
mortality
mortgagee
mortgager
mortgagor
mortician
mosaicist
moschatel
mossiness
moth-eaten
motorbike
motor-boat
motorcade

motor
mould
mous
mouth
Mrs
mucr
mudd
mulli
multi

| | | | |
|---|---|---|---|
| | ...ness | neologise | nictitate |
| multiform | name names | neologism | niggardly |
| multiplex | nameplate | neologist | night-club |
| multitude | nanny-goat | neologize | nightfall |
| mumchance | narcissus | neoplasty | night-gown |
| mummy's boy | narcotise | neoterise | nightless |
| mumpishly | narcotism | neoterism | night-life |
| mundanely | narcotize | neoterize | night-long |
| municipal | narration | nepenthes | nightmare |
| murderess | narrative | nephalism | nightspot |
| murderous | naseberry | nephalist | night-time |
| muricated | nastiness | nepheloid | nightward |
| murmuring | natrolite | nephology | nigritude |
| muscadine | nattiness | nephritic | Nilometer |
| muscavado | naturally | nephritis | ninetieth |
| muscology | naughtily | Neptunian | nisi prius |
| muscovado | naumachia | neptunium | nobleness |
| Muscovite | nautiloid | nervation | noctiluca |
| musically | navigable | nerve cell | nocturnal |
| musketeer | navigably | nerveless | noiseless |
| musketoon | navigator | nervously | noisiness |
| musk melon | near thing | nescience | noisomely |
| Mussulman | necessary | Nestorian | nominally |
| mustachio | necessity | neuralgia | nominator |
| mustiness | neck-cloth | neuralgic | nonce-word |
| mutilator | necrology | neurility | nonentity |
| muttering | nectareal | neuroglia | nonillion |
| mydriasis | nectarean | neurology | nonlethal |
| mydriatic | nectarial | neuropter | nonpareil |
| myography | nectarine | neurotomy | non-profit |
| myriorama | nectarous | neutrally | normalise |
| myrobalan | needfully | never more | normalize |

nose-bleed

nostalgia
nostalgic
nostology
notabilia
notepaper
not guilty
notochord
notoriety
notorious
not proven
nourisher
novelette
novelties
novennial
novitiate
nowhither
no worries
noxiously
nucleolus
nullifier
nullipara
nullipore
number one
Number Ten
numbskull
numerable
numerally
numerator
numerical
numero uno
nummulary
nummulite

nux vomica
nystagmus

# O

oast-house
obbligato
obconical
obcordate
obedience
obeisance
obeseness
obfuscate
objectify
objection
objective
objet d'art
objurgate
obliquely
obliquity
oblivious
obnoxious
obscenity
obscurant
obscurely
obscurity
obsecrate
obsequies
observant
observing
obsession
obstetric
obstinacy

occipital
occlusion
occultism
occupancy
ocellated
octachord
octagonal
octameter
octastyle
octennial
octillion
octopuses
odalisque
Odd Fellow
odd man out
odontalgy
odorously
odourless
oenanthic
oestrogen
off colour
offensive
offertory
officiant
officiate
officinal
officious
off-limits
offspring
off-the-peg
of no avail
Ogen melon

Oligocene
olive drab
ombudsman
ominously
omissible
omophagic
on a string
on balance
onerously
onomastic
on one's tod
onslaught
on the ball
on the make
on the mend
on the move
on the rack
on the side
on the trot
on the wane
oogenesis
open doors
open-ended
operation
operative
opercular
operculum
operosely
operosity
ophiology
opportune

opposable
oppressor
oppugnant
optically
optimates
optometer
opulently
orangeade
Orangeism
Orangeman
Orangemen
orang-utan
orbicular
orchestra
orderless
ordinance
organical
organised
organiser
organized
organizer
organzine
orgiastic
orientate
oriflamme
originate
orlop deck
orography
orphanage
orris root
orthodoxy
orthoepic
orthogamy
orthopter
orthoptic
Orwellian
osbcenely
oscillate
oscitancy
osmometry

ossifrage
osso bucca
ostensive
osteology
osteotome
osteotomy
ostiolate
ostracean
ostracise
ostracism
ostracize
Ostrogoth
otherness
otherwise
otologist
otorrhoea
oubliette
ourselves
out and out
outermost
outfitter
outgrowth
outnumber
out of date
out of hand
out of turn
outrigger
outskirts
outspoken
outspread
outwardly
oven-ready
overblown
overboard
overbuild
overcloud
overcrowd
overdraft
overdress
overdrive

overgorge
overgrown
overissue
overjoyed
overmatch
overnight
overpower
overreach
overreact
overshoot
oversight
oversized
oversleep
overspend
overstate
overstock
overthrow
overtrade
overtrain
overtrump
overvalue
overweigh
overwhelm
overwrite
oviferous
ovigerous
oviparous
ovulation
ownership
oxidation
oxygenate
oxygenise
oxygenize
oxygenous
ozocerite
ozokerite
ozone hole

**P**
pacemaker

pachyderm
packaging
packed out
packhorse
pademelon
paedagogy
paedology
pageantry
paillasse
painfully
paintball
palaestra
palankeen
palatable
palatably
palfreyed
Palladian
palladium
palletise
palletize
palliasse
palmately
palmister
palmistry
palpation
palpebral
palpiform
palpitate
palsgrave
palustral
panatella
panderess
panderism
pandurate
panegyric
panelling
panellist
panhandle
panoplied
pantalets

pantaloon
pantheism
pantheist
pantihose
pantomime
panty hose
paparazzo
paperback
paperwork
papeterie
papillary
papillate
papillote
parabasis
parabolic
parachute
paraclete
paragogue
paragraph
paralysis
paralytic
paramatta
paramedic
parameter
paramount
paranymph
parapeted
parapodia
parataxis
parbuckle
parcenary
parchment
paregoric
parentage
parenting
pargeting
parhelion
*pari passu*
parochial
parodical

paronymic
parotitis
parquetry
parrakeet
parricide
Parseeism
parsimony
parsonage
partially
partition
partitive
partridge
party line
pas de deux
passenger
passerine
passional
passively
passivity
pasticcio
pastorale
pastorate
pasturage
patchouli
patchouly
patchwork
paternity
pathogeny
pathology
patiently
patriarch
patrician
patricide
patrimony
patriotic
patristic
patrolman
patronage
patroness
patronise

patronize
paulownia
pauperise
pauperism
pauperize
paymaster
peaceable
peaceably
peace camp
peace pipe
peasantry
pea-souper
peccantly
peccaries
pectinate
peculator
pecuniary
pedagogic
pedagogue
pederasty
pedicular
pedometer
peer group
peevishly
Pekingese
Pelasgian
pellitory
pemphigus
penal code
pencilled
pendently
pendragon
pendulate
pendulous
peneplain
peneplane
penetrant
penetrate
peninsula
penitence

penniless
penny-wise
pennywort
pensioner
pensively
penstemon
pentaglot
pentagram
pentangle
pentarchy
Pentecost
penthouse
penultima
penurious
pepperoni
peptonize
per capita
perceiver
perchance
percheron
percolate
perdition
peregrine
perennial
perfecter
perfectly
perfervid
perforate
performer
perfumery
periclase
perimeter
peripetia
periphery
periscope
perisperm
perispore
peristome
peristyle
permanent

permeable
permeably
permitter
perpetual
persecute
persevere
persimmon
personage
personate
personify
personnel
persuader
pertinent
perturber
pertusion
pervasive
perverted
perverter
pessimism
pessimist
pessimize
pesticide
pestilent
petardeer
petardier
petechiae
petechial
petersham
petiolate
petit four
petroleum
petrology
petticoat
pettiness
pettishly
pettitoes
petulance
petulancy
phaenogam
phagocyte

phalanger
phalanges
phalanxes
phalarope
pharisaic
pharology
pharyngal
phenology
pheromone
philander
philately
philippic
philogyny
philology
philomath
philomela
phlebitis
phocacean
phonation
phone book
phone call
phonecard
phonetics
phonetist
phonogram
phonology
phonotype
phonotypy
phosphate
phosphene
phosphide
phosphite
photocall
photocell
photocopy
photology
Photostat®
phototype
phototypy
phrenetic

phrenitis
phycology
phyllopod
phylogeny
physician
physicism
physicist
phytogeny
phytotomy
pick-a-back
pick clean
pickthank
pictorial
piecemeal
piecework
pier table
pietistic
piggy-back
piggy-bank
pigheaded
pigmental
pikestaff
pillar-box
pilloried
pimpernel
pinchbeck
pineapple
pinnately
PIN number
pinstripe
pipe-dream
piping hot
pipistrel
pipsqueak
piquantly
piratical
pirouette
piscatory
pisciform
pisolitic

pissed off
pistachio
pitch-dark
pitchfork
pitchpine
pitchpipe
piteously
pithecoid
pithiness
pitifully
pituitary
pituitous
pityingly
pixilated
pizzicato
placeless
placement
place-name
placental
placidity
plainness
plainsman
plainsong
plaintiff
plaintive
planarian
planetary
planetoid
plantless
plaquette
plasmatic
plastered
plasterer
platinise
platinize
platinoid
platinous
platitude
Platonism
Platonist

| | | | |
|---|---|---|---|
| plausible | poignancy | pomposity | practical |
| plausibly | pointedly | pompously | practiced |
| played out | pointless | ponderous | practised |
| playfully | pointsman | pontonier | practiser |
| playhouse | poison gas | poorhouse | pragmatic |
| plaything | poison ivy | popliteal | prayerful |
| pleasance | poisonous | poppycock | preachify |
| plenarily | poker-face | popularly | preaching |
| plenitude | polar bear | porbeagle | prebendal |
| plenteous | polarizer | porcelain | precative |
| plentiful | polemical | porcupine | precatory |
| pleuritic | pole vault | porringer | precedent |
| pleuritis | policeman | porterage | preceding |
| plication | policemen | portfolio | precentor |
| plicature | politesse | porticoed | preceptor |
| plimsoles | political | porticoes | precipice |
| plimsolls | politicly | portioner | precisely |
| ploughboy | pollenise | portrayal | precision |
| ploughman | pollenize | portrayer | precocity |
| plumbeous | pollinate | possessed | precursor |
| plumeless | pollution | possessor | predatory |
| plumpness | polonaise | posterior | predicant |
| plunderer | polo shirt | posterity | predicate |
| pluralise | polyandry | post-haste | predictor |
| pluralism | polyarchy | postilion | predigest |
| pluralist | polybasic | postnatal | prefatory |
| plurality | polyester | postulant | preferrer |
| pluralize | polygonal | postulate | prefigure |
| plutocrat | polygonum | posturist | prefixion |
| Plutonian | polygraph | potassium | pregnable |
| plutonist | polymorph | pot-boiler | pregnancy |
| plutonium | polyphone | potentate | prejudice |
| pneumatic | polyphony | potential | prelatist |
| pneumonia | polypidom | pot-hunter | prelature |
| pneumonic | polyscope | potpourri | prelector |
| pocketful | polystyle | poulterer | prelusive |
| poenology | polythene | pourboire | premature |
| poetaster | polyzonal | poussette | premonish |
| poeticule | pomaceous | powerless | preoccupy |
| pogo stick | pompadour | pozzolana | preordain |

prepotent
preputial
prerecord
presbyter
preschool
prescient
prescribe
prescript
preselect
presentee
presenter
presently
preserver
president
presidium
press-gang
press-mark
presuming
pretended
pretender
preterite
pretermit
prettyish
prevalent
preventer
prevision
priceless
priestess
primarily
primatial
prime time
primipara
primitive
princedom
principal
principia
principle
printable
priorship
prismatic

privateer
privately
privation
privatise
privative
privatize
privilege
proactive
probation
probative
probatory
proboscis
procedure
processor
pro-choice
proclitic
proconsul
procreant
procreate
procuracy
prodigies
profanely
profanity
professed
professor
profferer
profilist
profiteer
profusely
profusion
prognosis
programme
projector
prolepsis
proleptic
proletary
prolixity
prolusion
promenade
prominent

promising
promotion
promotive
pronation
proneness
pronounce
prooemium
proofread
propagate
*pro patria*
propeller
propellor
prophetic
proponent
propriety
proptosis
prorogate
proscribe
prosector
prosecute
proselyte
prose poem
prosiness
prosodial
prosodian
prosodist
prostrate
protector
protester
prothorax
prototype
protozoal
protozoan
protozoon
proudness
Provençal
provender
provident
providing
provision

provisory
provoking
proximate
proximity
prudently
prudishly
prurience
pruriency
psalmodic
pseudonym
psoriasis
psychical
psychosis
psychotic
ptarmigan
pterosaur
pterygoid
Ptolemaic
pubescent
publicise
publicist
publicity
publicize
publisher
puerilely
puerilism
puerility
puerperal
puffiness
pugnacity
puissance
pullulate
pulmonary
pulpiness
pulpiteer
pulsatile
pulsation
pulsative
pulsatory
pulseless

pulverise
pulverize
pulverous
pulvinate
pumiceous
punchball
punch-bowl
punch-card
punchline
punctated
punctilio
punctuate
pungently
punishing
pupillage
pupillary
puppeteer
purchaser
purgation
purgative
purgatory
puritanic
purloiner
purposely
purposive
purpureal
pursuance
purulence
purulency
pushchair
pushingly
pussyfoot
pustulate
pustulous
put on airs
put paid to
putridity
puzzolana
pyorrhoea
pyramidal

pyramidic
pyrethrum
pyritical
pyrogenic
pyrolater
pyrolysis
pyromania
pyrometer
pyroxylic
pyroxylin
pyrrhonic
pythoness
pythonism
pythonist

**Q**

quadratic
quadrifid
quadrille
quadruped
quadruple
quaffable
Quakeress
Quakerish
Quakerism
qualified
qualifier
qualities
quarryman
quarrymen
quartered
quarterly
quartette
quartzite
quartzose
quebracho
queen-cake
queenhood
queerness
querulous

quickener
quicklime
quickness
quicksand
quick-step
quiescent
quietness
quintette
quintuple
quitclaim
quittance
quixotism
quizzical
quodlibet
quotation
quotidian

**R**

rabbinate
rabidness
race-horse
racetrack
racialism
rackarock
racketeer
raconteur
radial-ply
radiantly
radiately
radiation
radically
radicchio
radiogram
radiology
radio wave
railingly
rain-check
rain-gauge
raininess
rainproof

raise Cain
Rajahship
rampantly
rancheria
rancherie
rancidity
rancorous
randomise
randomize
rantipole
rapacious
rapidness
raptorial
rapturous
rare earth
raree-show
rascaldom
rascalism
rascality
raspberry
ratepayer
rationale
rauwolfia
ravishing
razor-bill
razor-clam
reachable
reachless
readdress
readiness
readjourn
ready-made
realistic
realities
reanimate
reappoint
rearguard
rearlight
rearrange
reasoning

reattempt
rebaptise
rebaptism
rebaptize
rebellion
rebounder
rebuilder
rebukeful
recapture
receiving
recension
reception
receptive
recession
recessive
*réchauffé*
recherché
recipient
reckoning
reclinate
reclusely
reclusive
recognise
recognize
recollect
recommend
reconcile
recondite
reconduct
reconquer
recording
recordist
recoverer
recreancy
recrement
recruiter
rectangle
rectifier
rectitude
rectorate

rectorial
recumbent
recurring
recurvate
recusance
recusancy
recycling
redaction
redbreast
red carpet
reddition
redeliver
red-handed
red-letter
red mullet
redolence
redolency
redoubted
red pepper
red salmon
reducible
reduction
redundant
re-educate
refection
refectory
referable
reference
referment
refinedly
refitment
reflation
reflected
reflector
reflexion
reflexive
reforming
refortify
refractor
refresher

refulgent
refurbish
refurnish
refusable
refusenik
refutable
regardant
regardful
regarding
regenesis
regicidal
regiminal
registrar
regretful
regularly
regulator
rehearsal
rehearser
reimburse
reimplant
reimprint
reinforce
reinspect
reinspire
reinstall
reinstate
reinsurer
reiterate
rejection
rejoicing
rejoinder
relay race
relevance
relevancy
relief map
relieving
religious
reliquary
reluctant
remainder

remigrate
remindful
reminisce
remission
remissive
remissory
remittent
removable
renascent
rendering
rendition
renewable
renitence
renitency
renouncer
renovator
reparable
reparably
repayable
repayment
repeating
repellent
repentant
repercuss
repertory
reperusal
replenish
repletion
repletory
replicant
reportage
reporting
reposeful
repossess
reprehend
represent
re-present
represser
reprimand
reprobate

reproduce
reptatory
reptilian
republish
repudiate
repugnant
repulsion
repulsive
reputable
reputedly
requisite
rescuable
resection
resentful
reserpine
reservist
reservoir
residence
residency
residuary
resilient
resistant
resolvent
resonance
resonancy
resonator
respecter
restfully
restiform
restively
restraint
resultant
resumable
resurgent
resurrect
retaining
retaliate
retardant
retention
retentive

reticence
reticulum
retinitis
retiredly
retractor
retrieval
retriever
retrocede
retroussé
revaluate
reverence
reversely
reversion
reversive
revetment
revivable
revocable
revolting
revulsion
revulsive
rewarding
rhachitis
rhapsodic
rheometer
rheumatic
Rhine wine
rhinolith
rhinology
rhizodont
rhymeless
rhythmics
rice-paper
riddlings
ridge-pole
righteous
right hand
rightness
right wing
rigidness
rigmarole

ring a bell
ringleted
riotously
ritualism
ritualist
rivalship
riverside
roadblock
road house
road-metal
road movie
roadstead
rocambole
rockiness
rock 'n' roll
roguishly
roisterer
rokambole
role model
romancist
romanizer
Roman nose
rompishly
roominess
root-stock
Roquefort
rosaceous
rosewater
rostellum
rostrated
rotundity
rough-cast
rough-neck
roughness
rough ride
roughshod
roundelay
Roundhead
roundness
round trip

roundworm
royal blue
rubberise
rubberize
rubescent
ruddiness
ruffianly
ruination
ruinously
ruminator
run across
run around
runcinate
rusticate
rusticity
rustiness
ruthenium

**S**

sabadilla
saccharic
saccharin
sacciform
sackcloth
sacrament
sacred cow
sacrifice
sacrilege
sacristan
saddle-bag
saddle-bow
Sadducean
safeguard
safe-house
safety net
safety-pin
safflower
sagacious
sage-brush
sagittate

| | | | |
|---|---|---|---|
| sailboard | *sans doute* | scapiform | scioptric |
| sail-borne | sans-serif | scapolite | scirrhoid |
| sailcloth | *sans souci* | scapulary | scirrhous |
| sailoring | sapan-wood | scarecrow | sclerosis |
| sailplane | sapidness | scarf-skin | sclerotic |
| saint's day | sapiently | scarifier | scoliosis |
| sainthood | sapodilla | scarpines | scombroid |
| saintship | sappiness | scatheful | scorbutic |
| salacious | sarcastic | scatology | scorching |
| salad days | sarcocarp | scattered | score card |
| salangane | sargassum | scatterer | scorpioid |
| saleratus | sarmentum | scaup-duck | Scotch egg |
| salesroom | sartorial | scavenger | Scotchman |
| sales talk | sartorius | scene-dock | Scotchmen |
| salicylic | sassafras | scentless | Scots pine |
| saliently | Sassenach | sceptical | scoundrel |
| salimeter | satanical | scheelite | scraggily |
| salmonoid | satellite | schematic | scrambler |
| saloon bar | satiation | schemeful | scrapbook |
| saltation | satin-wood | schilling | scrap-heap |
| saltatory | saturable | schistose | scratcher |
| salt-marsh | saturated | schistous | screaming |
| saltpeter | saturnian | schlemiel | screening |
| saltpetre | saturnine | schlieren | screwball |
| salt-water | sauciness | schnauzer | screw-pine |
| salubrity | saunterer | schnitzel | scribbler |
| salvation | savourily | schnorkle | scrimmage |
| Samaritan | saxifrage | schnozzle | scrimshaw |
| sanctuary | saxophone | scholarly | scriptory |
| sandalled | say 'cheese' | scholiast | scripture |
| sandarach | scagliola | schoolboy | scrivener |
| sand-blast | scaliness | schooling | scroll-saw |
| sand-glass | scallawag | schoolman | scrum half |
| sandiness | scalloped | sciatical | scrummage |
| sandpaper | scallywag | sciential | scrutoire |
| sandpiper | Scansores | scientism | sculpture |
| sandstone | scantling | scientist | scumbling |
| sand-storm | scantness | scintilla | scummings |
| sand wedge | scapegoat | sciomachy | scutcheon |
| sangfroid | scapement | sciomancy | scutellum |

scutiform
scuzz ball
scytheman
sea-anchor
sea-breeze
sea-change
sea-faring
seamy side
searching
seasoning
sea-urchin
seaworthy
sebaceous
secateurs
secernent
secession
seclusion
seclusive
secondary
secretary
secretion
secretive
secretory
sectarian
sectional
secularly
secundine
securable
sedentary
seditious
seducible
seduction
seductive
seed-coral
seediness
seed-money
see double
seed-pearl
seemingly
see reason

see things
segmental
segregate
seigneury
seigniory
selachian
selection
selective
selenious
self-abuse
self-drive
self-image
selfishly
Sellotape®
sell short
selvedged
semaphore
semblance
semibreve
semicolon
semifinal
semifluid
semilunar
semiology
semiotics
semirigid
semisolid
semitonic
semivowel
senescent
seneschal
seniority
sensation
senseless
sensitise
sensitive
sensitize
sensorial
sensorium
sensually

sentencer
sentiment
sentry-box
separable
separably
separates
separator
September
septenary
septuplet
sepulchre
sepulture
sequester
seraskier
serenader
sergeancy
sergeanty
serialise
serialism
seriality
serialize
sericeous
serigraph
seriously
sermonise
sermonize
serotonin
serration
serrature
serricorn
serviette
servilely
servility
servitude
sessional
setaceous
set-square
set theory
set up shop
sevenfold

seven seas
seventeen
seventhly
severable
severally
severance
sex appeal
sexennial
sex object
sextuplet
sexualise
sexuality
sexualize
sforzando
sgraffito
shadiness
shadow-box
shake a leg
shake-down
shakiness
shallowly
shamanism
shamateur
shambling
shambolic
shameless
Shangri-la
shapeable
shapeless
sharkskin
sharpener
sharpness
shaveling
shearling
sheathing
sheep-cote
sheep-fold
sheep-hook
sheepskin
sheep-walk

sheer-legs
sheet bend
sheldrake
shelf-life
shell-duck
shellfish
shell suit
shemozzle
shiftless
shingling
ship-board
shipowner
shipshape
shipwreck
shirt-tail
shock-jock
shock wave
shoe-black
shoemaker
shop-floor
shoreless
shoreline
shortfall
shorthand
short head
shorthorn
short-list
shortness
short-term
short-time
short wave
shovelful
shoveller
show house
showiness
show-piece
show-place
shrinkage
shrubbery
shuffling

sibilance
sibilancy
sibylline
siccation
siccative
sickening
sick leave
sickle-man
sideboard
sidelight
siderosis
sideswipe
sidetrack
sidewards
sighingly
sightless
sight-read
sigmoidal
signalise
signalize
signalman
signatory
signature
signboard
signitary
signorina
siliceous
silicious
silicosis
siliquose
silkiness
silliness
silver-fox
silvering
silverise
silverize
similarly
simpatico
simpering
simpleton

simulator
simulcast
sincerely
sincerity
sinewless
singleton
Sinhalese
sinistral
sinlessly
sinologue
sinuation
sinuosity
sinuously
sinusitis
siphonage
siphuncle
situation
sixteenmo
sixteenth
sixty-nine
sizarship
skedaddle
skeptical
sketchily
skew-whiff
skilfully
skin flick
skinflint
skingraft
skintight
sky-diving
sky-rocket
slackness
slakeness
slanderer
slantwise
slap-happy
slapstick
slatiness
slaughter

slave-ship
slavishly
Slavonian
sleaze-bag
sleekness
sleepless
sleep with
slenderly
slide rule
slighting
sliminess
slingback
sling-shot
slippered
slivovitz
slivovitz
sloppy joe
slouch hat
slouching
slowcoach
slow-match
slumberer
slumbrous
slush fund
small-arms
small beer
smallness
small talk
small-time
smart alec
smartarse
smart card
smartness
smatterer
smear test
smell a rat
smilingly
smokeless
smokiness
smuggling

| | | | |
|---|---|---|---|
| snake-root | sojourner | sorriness | speakeasy |
| snakeskin | solar cell | sorrowful | spearhead |
| snake-weed | solar pond | sortilege | spearmint |
| snare drum | solar wind | sottishly | specially |
| sniveller | solar year | sotto voce | specialty |
| snowberry | soldering | soubrette | spectacle |
| snow-blind | soldierly | soul music | spectator |
| snow-bound | solemness | soundable | speculate |
| snow-drift | solemnise | sound bite | speculums |
| snowflake | solemnity | soundings | speechify |
| snow-goose | solemnize | soundless | speedball |
| snow-limit | solfatara | soundness | speed trap |
| snow-storm | solfeggio | sour cream | speedwell |
| snow-white | solicitor | sourdough | spelunker |
| snub-nosed | solidness | Southdown | spermatic |
| soapberry | soliloquy | south-east | spermatid |
| soap opera | solipsism | southerly | spherical |
| soapstone | solitaire | southmost | sphincter |
| soberness | solo whist | South Pole | spice-bush |
| sobriquet | someplace | southward | spiciness |
| socialise | something | south-west | spiculate |
| socialism | sometimes | sou'wester | spikenard |
| socialist | somewhere | sovereign | spillikin |
| socialite | sommelier | sovietism | spin a yarn |
| sociality | somnolent | spaced out | spindrift |
| socialize | sonic boom | spaceship | spineless |
| societies | sonneteer | space-suit | spininess |
| sociology | sonnetise | spacewalk | spinnaker |
| sociopath | sonnetize | spadework | spinneret |
| soda bread | sonometer | spaghetti | spinosity |
| soda water | sootiness | spareness | spirillum |
| soft-cover | sophister | spare tyre | spiritual |
| soft drink | sophistic | sparingly | splash out |
| softening | sophistry | sparkling | spleenful |
| soft focus | sophomore | spark-plug | spleenish |
| soft goods | soporific | sparteine | splendent |
| soft-paste | sopranino | spasmodic | splendour |
| soft-pedal | sopranist | spatially | splenetic |
| soft touch | sorceress | spatulate | splenitis |
| *soi-disant* | sore point | speakable | splintery |

spokesman
spokesmen
spoliator
sponge bag
spongiole
spoon-bill
sporangia
sporidium
sporocyst
sporozoan
sportsman
sportsmen
spot check
spotlight
spoutless
sprightly
springbok
springing
springlet
sprinkler
spritsail
spuminess
sputterer
squalidly
squarrose
squeamish
stabilise
stability
stabilize
stableboy
stableman
stage-door
stage left
stagnancy
stag party
staidness
stainless
staircase
stairwell
stalactic

stalemate
staleness
Stalinism
stalkless
stalworth
staminate
stammerer
stamp duty
stanchion
standpipe
stand up to
starboard
starchily
staringly
starlight
startling
stateless
statement
state-room
stateside
statesman
statesmen
stational
stationer
statistic
statuette
status quo
statutory
staymaker
St Bernard
steadfast
steamboat
steam iron
steel band
steel grey
steel wool
steelyard
steepness
steersman
stegosaur

stellated
stellular
stepchild
steradian
sterilise
sterility
sterilize
sternmost
sternness
stevedore
stewartry
sticky end
stiffener
stiffness
stigmatic
stillborn
still life
stillness
stimulant
stimulate
stink bomb
stinkhorn
stinkweed
stinkwood
stintless
stipitate
stipulate
stitching
stockdove
stockpile
stockyard
stoically
stolidity
stomachal
stomacher
stomachic
stone-cold
stone-dead
stone-deaf
stonefish

stonewall
stoniness
stoplight
stop-press
stop-watch
store card
Storthing
stoutness
straggler
strangely
strangles
strangury
strapping
stratagem
strategic
straw poll
streamlet
streetcar
strenuous
stretcher
striation
stricture
strike off
strike oil
strike-pay
stringent
string tie
strip club
stripling
strobilus
strong-arm
strongbox
strontium
structure
struggler
strychnia
stuck with
studiedly
stupefier
stupidity

| | | | |
|---|---|---|---|
| stutterer | subtilise | sunniness | swallower |
| stylishly | subtilize | sunrising | swansdown |
| stylistic | subtitles | sunstroke | swarthily |
| stylobate | subtorrid | superable | swear word |
| suability | subverter | supercool | sweat band |
| suasively | succeeder | superfine | sweat-shop |
| subaerial | successor | superglue | sweepings |
| subalpine | succotash | superheat | sweetcorn |
| subaltern | succourer | supernova | sweetener |
| subarctic | succulent | superpose | sweetmeat |
| subatomic | succursal | supersede | sweetness |
| subcostal | suctorial | superstar | sweet-talk |
| subdeacon | sudorific | supervene | swept-back |
| subdivide | suffering | supervise | swept-wing |
| subduable | suffixion | suppliant | swiftness |
| subeditor | suffocate | supporter | swimmeret |
| subereous | suffragan | suppurate | swindling |
| subfamily | suffusion | supremacy | swineherd |
| subgenera | sugar-beet | supremely | swingeing |
| subjacent | sugar-cane | surcharge | swing-wing |
| subjudice | suggester | surcingle | swinishly |
| subjugate | sulcation | sure thing | Swiss roll |
| sublessee | sulkiness | surf-board | sword-fish |
| sublimate | sulphuret | surgeoncy | sword-play |
| sublimely | sulphuric | surliness | swordsman |
| sublimity | sultanate | surmising | swordsmen |
| sublunary | sultaness | surmullet | sybaritic |
| submarine | summaries | surpliced | sycophant |
| submersed | summarily | surprisal | syllabify |
| subnormal | summarise | surprised | syllogise |
| subregion | summarist | surrender | syllogism |
| subscribe | summarize | surrogacy | syllogize |
| subscript | summation | surrogate | symbiosis |
| subsidies | summerset | surtitles | symbiotic |
| subsidise | summing up | surveying | symbolise |
| subsidize | summonses | suspender | symbolism |
| substance | sumptuary | suspensor | symbolist |
| subsultus | sumptuous | suspicion | symbolize |
| subtenant | sunflower | sustainer | symbology |
| subtilely | sun lotion | swaggerer | symmetric |

symphonic
symphysis
symposiac
symposium
synagogue
synchrony
synclinal
syncopate
syncopize
syndicate
syneresis
synergist
synizesis
synodical
synonymic
synovitis
syntactic
synthesis
synthetic
syphilise
syphilize
systaltic
systemise
systemize

**T**
tabasheer
tablature
table-land
tableware
tabularly
tabulator
tacamahac
tactician
taeniasis
tail-board
tail-light
tailoress
tailoring
tailplane

tail rotor
tail-stock
taintless
take after
take amiss
take a part
take heart
taken with
take sides
take steps
take stock
Talegalla
talkative
talking to
talk radio
tall order
tall story
Talmudism
Talmudist
tambourin
tangerine
tantalise
tantalize
Taoiseach
tarantism
tarantula
taraxacum
tarbouche
tardiness
tarentola
targeteer
targetier
tarnisher
tarpaulin
Tartarean
tartarise
tartarize
tartarous
tasimeter
task force

Tasmanian
tasselled
tasteless
tattooing
tauriform
tautology
tawniness
taxidermy
taximeter
taxonomic
tax return
teachable
techiness
technical
technique
tectonics
teddy-bear
tediously
tegulated
telegenic
telegraph
telemeter
telemetry
teleology
telepathy
telephone
telephony
telesales
telescope
telescopy
tell tales
tellurian
tellurium
temazepam
temperate
tempering
temporary
temporise
temporize
temptable

temptress
temulence
tenacious
tenaculum
tenderise
tenderize
tendinous
tenebrous
tenor-clcf
tenseness
tensility
tentacled
tentative
tepidness
terebinth
termagant
terminate
termitary
terrarium
territory
terrorise
terrorism
terrorist
terrorize
terseness
tessellar
tessitura
testacean
testament
testatrix
testifier
testimony
testiness
test match
test pilot
tête à tête
tetralogy
tetrarchy
textorial
textually

thallogen
thanatoid
thanehood
thaneship
thankless
thatching
that's that
theandric
theatrics
the masses
theme park
theme song
theocracy
theocrasy
theogonic
theologic
theomachy
theomancy
theophany
theoretic
theoriser
theorizer
theosophy
thereaway
therefore
therefrom
thereinto
thereupon
therewith
thermally
thesaurus
theurgist
thickhead
thickness
thigh-bone
thinkable
think-tank
thin on top
third-rate
thirstily

thirtieth
thrashing
threefold
threesome
threnetic
threshing
threshold
thriftily
thrilling
throbless
throttler
throwaway
throwback
throw over
throwster
thumbless
thumb-nail
thumb-tack
thunderer
thylacine
thyristor
thyroxine
ticked off
tidal wave
tidewater
tie-dyeing
tiger-lily
tiger-moth
tiger's-eye
tight-knit
tightness
tightrope
timbering
time clock
time flies
time-frame
time-piece
time-share
timetable
timidness

timocracy
tinder-box
tip one off
tipsiness
tiredness
tit for tat
titillate
title-deed
title page
title-rôle
titration
tittivate
tittlebat
titularly
toadstool
tolerable
tolerably
tolerance
tolerator
tollbooth
tombstone
tomentose
tomentous
tonguelet
tonka bean
to no avail
tonometer
tonsillar
tonsorial
toolmaker
toothache
toothless
toothpick
toothsome
top drawer
top-flight
topiarian
topically
top-secret
torch-song

tormenter
tormentil
tormentor
tornadoes
torpedoes
torpidity
torquated
torridity
torsional
tortility
tortricid
to speak of
totalness
totem-pole
to the fore
to the good
to the life
touchable
touch-down
touch-line
touchmark
touchtype
touch wood
touchwood
toughness
tourmalin
tournedos
towelette
towelling
town house
townsfolk
townwards
trabecula
traceable
traceably
tracheary
trachytic
trackless
track shoe
tracksuit

| | | | |
|---|---|---|---|
| tractable | triatomic | trivalent | turn round |
| tractably | tribalism | trivially | turnstile |
| trademark | tribesman | trochlear | turnstone |
| tradesman | tribesmen | troop-ship | turntable |
| tradesmen | tribology | tropology | turpitude |
| trade-wind | tribunate | troublous | turquoise |
| tradition | tributary | trousered | tussilago |
| tragedian | tributory | trousseau | tutorship |
| trainable | trichosis | troutling | twentieth |
| traitress | tricksome | truceless | twenty-one |
| transcend | trickster | truculent | twinkling |
| trans fats | triclinic | truepenny | twinscrew |
| transform | tricolour | trumpeter | two a penny |
| transfuse | tricuspid | truncated | two-handed |
| transient | tridental | truncheon | two-stroke |
| translate | triennial | trunk-line | typically |
| transmute | triennium | trunk road | tyrannise |
| transpire | trifacial | trustless | tyrannize |
| transport | trifloral | truthless | tyrannous |
| transpose | triforium | try-square | |
| trapezium | trigamist | tsetse fly | **U** |
| trapezoid | trigonous | tubercled | Ugli® fruit |
| trappings | trihedral | tubulated | ugly as sin |
| trattoria | trihedron | tufaceous | Ulsterman |
| traumatic | trilinear | tug of love | ultimatum |
| travelled | trilithic | tulip-tree | umbellate |
| traveller | trilithon | tulip-wood | umbilical |
| traverser | trilobate | tumble-dry | umbilicus |
| travertin | trilobite | tumescent | unabashed |
| treachery | trilogies | tumidness | unadorned |
| treadmill | trimerous | tunefully | unadvised |
| treasurer | trimester | tunicated | unalloyed |
| treatment | trinketry | turbidity | unamiable |
| trebuchet | trinomial | turbinate | unanimity |
| trematode | triserial | turboprop | unanimous |
| trematoid | triteness | turbulent | unassured |
| trembling | tritheism | turfiness | unavenged |
| tremulous | triturate | turgidity | unbeknown |
| trenchant | triumphal | Turkey red | unbending |
| triathlon | triumpher | turn about | unbiassed |

unblessed
unbounded
unbridled
unceasing
uncertain
uncharted
uncivilly
uncleanly
unclouded
unconcern
uncorrupt
uncourtly
uncouthly
uncovered
uncrossed
uncrowned
undaunted
undecagon
undeceive
undecided
undefined
underbred
undercoat
underdone
underfelt
under fire
underfoot
undergrid
underhand
underhung
underline
underling
undermine
undermost
underpass
underplay
underplot
underprop
underrate
underseal

undersell
undershot
underside
undersign
undertake
undertone
underwear
underwent
underwood
undesired
undiluted
undivided
undoubted
undreamed
undressed
undulated
undutiful
unearthly
uneatable
unendowed
unengaged
un-English
unequable
unequally
unexpired
unexposed
unfailing
unfeeling
unfeigned
unfitness
unfitting
unfledged
unfounded
ungallant
ungenteel
unguarded
unguiform
unhandily
unhappily
unharness

unhealthy
unheard of
unheedful
unheeding
unhopeful
unifacial
uniformly
uninjured
uninvited
Union Jack
uniparous
uniserial
unisexual
unisonant
unisonous
Unitarian
unit trust
univalent
univalved
universal
unjointed
unknowing
unlearned
unlimited
unluckily
unmatched
unmeaning
unmerited
unmindful
unmixedly
unmortise
unmusical
unnatural
unnoticed
unopposed
unpitying
unplumbed
unpopular
unquietly
unreality

unwarlike
unwatched
unwatered
unwearied
unweighed
unwelcome
unwilling
unwinking
unwitting
unwomanly
unworldly
unwounded
unwritten
unwrought
up-country
updraught
upholster
upper case
upper hand
uppermost
uprightly
up the ante
up the wall
urceolate
Uriah Heep
urticaria
use-by date
uselessly
usherette
ushership
utilities
utricular
utterable
utterance
uttermost

**V**

vacancies
vaccinate
vacillate

vade mecum
vagueness
vainglory
valentine
valiantly
vallation
vallecula
valuation
valueless
vampirism
vandalise
vandalism
vandalize
vanity box
vapidness
vaporable
vaporific
vapourish
variation
varicella
variegate
varieties
variolate
variolite
varioloid
variolous
variously
varnisher
vasculose
vasectomy
vasomotor
vassalage
veeringly
vegetable
vehemence
vehemency
vehicular
vellicate
velveteen
velveting

venatical
veneering
venerable
venerably
venerator
vengeance
veniality
ventilate
ventricle
venturous
veracious
veratrine
verbalise
verbalism
verbalist
verbalize
verbosely
verbosity
verdantly
verdigris
veridical
veritable
veritably
vermicide
vermiform
vermifuge
vermilion
verminate
verminous
vernation
verrucose
verrucous
versatile
versifier
*vers libre*
vertebrae
vertebral
Very light
vesicular
vestibule

vestigial
vestryman
vetchling
vexatious
vexillary
viability
vibracula
vibratile
vibration
vibrative
vibratory
vibrissae
vicariate
vicarious
vicarship
vicennial
viceregal
vice-reine
vice versa
viciously
victimise
victimize
victoress
Victorian
victories
victorine
victualer
vide infra
videlicet
videotape
vide supra
viewpoint
vigesimal
vigilance
vigilante
villiform
villosity
vimineous
vinaceous
vindicate

vingt-et-un
violation
violently
violinist
virescent
Virgilian
virginity
virgulate
virtually
virtuosos
virulence
viscerate
viscidity
viscosity
viscounty
visionary
visual aid
visualise
visuality
visualize
vitelline
vitiation
vitrified
vitriform
vitriolic
Vitruvian
vivacious
vividness
vizierate
vizierial
vocalness
Vodaphone®
voiceless
voice-over
vol au vent
volcanise
volcanism
volcanist
volcanize
volcanoes

volte-face
voltmeter
volumeter
voluntary
volunteer
voodooism
voracious
vorticism
vorticose
vouchsafe
vox humana
vox populi
vulcanian
vulcanise
vulcanism
vulcanite
vulcanize
vulgarian
vulgarise
vulgarism
vulgarity
vulgarize
vulnerary
vulpicide
vulpinite
vulturine
vulturish
vulturous
vulviform

**W**

waggishly
Wagnerian
wagonette
wailingly
waist-band
waistcoat
waistline
wakefully
Waldenses

walk-about
walk on air
wallabies
walloping
wallpaper
wandering
wapenshaw
wapentake
warble-fly
warehouse
warm front
warmonger
warningly
warrantee
warranter
warrantor
wash-basin
wash-board
wash-cloth
washed out
washiness
washing up
wash-stand
waspishly
wasp-waist
wassailer
wasteland
wasteness
waste-pipe
watchband
watch-case
watchword
water-bird
waterbuck
water-cure
water down
waterfall
water-flea
waterfowl
water-hole

water-jump
waterless
water-lily
water-line
water-main
watermark
water-mill
water-polo
watershed
waterside
water-worn
waveguide
wayfaring
waywardly
weak-kneed
wealthily
weariness
wearisome
weathered
weatherly
Wednesday
week-night
weepingly
weevilled
weighable
weightily
weirdness
well-being
well-found
well-known
well out of
well-woman
westering
westerner
westwards
whalebone
wheatfree
wheatgerm
wheatmeal
wheedling

wheelbase
wherefore
whereinto
whereness
whereunto
whereupon
wherewith
wherryman
whetstone
whichever
whimperer
whimsical
whiningly
whinstone
whip-round
whip-stock
whirligig
whirlpool
whirlwind
whiskered
whisperer
whitebait
white flag
white gold
Whitehall
white heat
white hope
white lead
white meat
whiteness
whitewash
white wine
white-wood
whodunnit
wholefood
wholemeal
wholeness
wholesale
wholesome

whoop it up
whosoever
wide-angle
wideawake
widowhood
wieldable
willingly
willpower
wind-blown
windbreak
windchill
windiness
windingly
window-box
windswept
wineglass
winepress
wing chair
winningly
win the day
wisecrack
wistfully
witchhunt
with a will
withdrawn
withering
withstand
witlessly
witnesser
witticism
wittiness
wittingly
woebegone
wofulness
wolfhound
wolfishly
wolverine
womanhood
womankind

womanlike
womenfolk
wonderful
woodchuck
woodcraft
woodentop
woodiness
wood-louse
wood-nymph
wood-screw
wood smoke
wordiness
workbench
workforce
workhorse
workhouse
workmanly
work of art
workwoman
worldling
World War I
world-wide
worm-eaten
worriment
worrisome
worse luck
worst-case
worthless
woundable
wrestling
wristband
wrongdoer
wrongness
wrynecked

**X**
Xanthippe
xanthosis
xenophile

xeroderma
xerophyte
xylograph
xylophone

**Y**
yachtsman
Yankeeism
yardstick
yellowish
yerba maté
yesterday
yester-eve
Yggdrasil
yo-heave-
ho!
Yom Kippur
youngling
youngness
youngster
ytterbium
yuppie flu

**Z**
zealously
zeitgeist
zemindary
Zeuglodon
zeugmatic
zirconium
zoography
zoologist
zoophytic
zootomist
zucchetto
zumbooruk
zygomatic
zygospore
zymometer

# Ten-letter words

## A

abbreviate
abdication
abdominous
aberdevine
aberration
abhorrence
abiogenist
abjectness
abjuration
abjuratory
able-bodied
able-seaman
abnegation
abnormally
abominable
abominably
aboriginal
aborigines
abortively
above board
abranchial
abridgment
abrogation
abrogative
abruptness
abscission
absentment
absinthian
absinthism
absolutely
absolution
absolutism
absolutory

absorbable
absorbedly
absorption
absorptive
abstemious
abstention
abstergent
abstersion
abstinence
abstracted
abstractly
abstrusely
absurdness
abundantly
Abyssinian
academical
accelerate
accentuate
acceptable
acceptably
acceptance
acceptancy
accessible
accessibly
accidental
accipitral
accomplice
accomplish
accordance
*accoucheur*
accountant
accounting
accredited
accrescent

accubation
accumbency
accumulate
accurately
accusation
accusative
accusatory
accustomed
acephalous
acetabulum
acetanilid
acetarious
acetic acid
acetimeter
acetometer
achievance
achromatic
aciculated
acidimeter
acinaceous
acorn shell
acotyledon
acoustical
acquainted
acquirable
acroamatic
acrobatics
acrogenous
acromegaly
acronychal
acrophobia
acroterium
actiniform
actinolite

actinozoan
actinozoon
actionable
active duty
activeness
act of faith
act the goat
*ad absurdum*
adactylous
Adam's apple
adamantine
adaptation
adder's-meat
additional
addle-pated
adduceable
adequately
adherently
adhesively
adhibition
adiactinic
adjacently
adjectival
adjudgment
adjudicate
adjunction
adjunctive
adjuration
adjuratory
adjustable
adjustment
admeasurer
administer
admiration
admiringly
admissible
admissibly
admittable
admittance
admittedly

admonisher
admonition
admonitive
admonitory
adolescent
adrenaline
adroitness
adsorption
adulterant
adulterate
adulteress
adulterine
adulterous
adventurer
advertence
advertency
advertiser
adzuki bean
aeriferous
aerobatics
aerogramme
aerologist
aeronautic
aerostatic
aeruginous
aesthetics
affability
affectedly
affettuoso
affiliable
affirmable
afflicting
affliction
afflictive
affronting
aficionado
aforenamed
Africander
Afrikander
afrormosia

after-birth
after-grass
after-hours
after-image
after-pains
after-piece
after-shave
aftertaste
afterwards
agapanthus
aggrandise
aggrandize
aggravated
aggression
aggressive
agony uncle
agronomics
agrypnotic
aid and abet
aide-de-camp
air-bladder
air-cushion
air hostess
air vesicle
alarm clock
alarmingly
albescence
albumenise
albumenize
albuminoid
albuminous
alcoholise
alcoholism
alcoholize
alcoometer
aldermanry
aldermanic
aldermanly
alexanders
algebraist

| | | |
|---|---|---|
| alienation | altruistic | analytical |
| alimentary | amalgamate | analyzable |
| allegation | amanuensis | anamniotic |
| allegiance | amateurish | anaplastic |
| allegorise | amazedness | anarthrous |
| allegorist | ambassador | anastigmat |
| allegorize | ambidexter | anastomose |
| allegretto | ambivalent | anastrophe |
| allergenic | ambulacrum | anatomical |
| alleviator | ambulation | ancestress |
| All-Hallows | ambulatory | anchoretic |
| alliaceous | ambushment | anchor-hold |
| alligation | ameliorate | anchylosis |
| alliterate | amendatory | ancipitous |
| allocation | amenorrhea | andalusite |
| allocution | amerceable | androecium |
| allopathic | amercement | androgynal |
| all-purpose | Amerindian | anecdotist |
| all the best | ametabolic | anelectric |
| all the rage | amiability | anemograph |
| all the same | ammoniacal | anemometer |
| allurement | ammunition | anemometry |
| alluringly | Ampelopsis | anemoscope |
| allusively | amphibious | anesthesia |
| almond cake | amphibrach | anesthetic |
| almond-milk | amphimacer | aneurismal |
| alms-giving | amphimixis | angiosperm |
| alongshore | amputation | Anglo-Irish |
| alpenstock | amygdalate | Anglo-mania |
| alphabetic | amygdaline | Anglophile |
| alphameric | amygdaloid | Anglophobe |
| altar-bread | amylaceous | Anglo-Saxon |
| altar-cloth | anabaptism | angora wool |
| altar-ledge | anabaptist | angularity |
| altar-piece | anacamptic | angulation |
| altazimuth | anaclastic | anhungered |
| alteration | anadromous | animadvert |
| alterative | anaerobium | animalcule |
| alternator | anagogical | anisomeric |
| altogether | analysable | annexation |

annihilate
Anno Domini
annotation
annual ring
annulation
annunciate
anointment
an open book
answerable
answerably
answerless
antagonise
antagonism
antagonist
antagonize
antecedent
antechapel
antepenult
anteriorly
anthracene
anthracite
anthropoid
antibiotic
Antichrist
anticipant
anticipate
anticlimax
anticlinal
antiemetic
antifreeze
antilithic
antimasque
antimatter
antimonous
Antinomian
antiphonal
antipyrine
antiquated
anti-Semite
antiseptic

anti-social
antistatic
antithesis
antithetic
aphaeresis
aphoristic
apiculture
aplacental
apocalypse
apocarpous
apochromat
apocryphal
apodeictic
apolitical
apologetic
apologiser
apologizer
apophthegm
apoplectic
apostatise
apostatize
apostolate
apostrophe
apothecary
apothecium
apotheosis
apparently
apparition
appealable
appearance
appeasable
appendicle
appetising
appetitive
appetizing
applausive
apple sauce
applicable
applicancy
applicator

appositely
apposition
appositive
appreciate
apprentice
approacher
approvable
apterygial
aquafortis
aquamarine
aquiferous
arachnidan
arbitrator
arbor vitae
archbishop
archdeacon
archeology
archer-fish
archetypal
architrave
archpriest
arctogaeal
arc welding
arefaction
arenaceous
areolation
areopagite
argumental
aristocrat
arithmetic
Armageddon
armipotent
arrestment
arrogantly
arrogation
artfulness
articulate
artificial
art nouveau
arty-crafty

asafoetida
asbestosis
ascendable
ascendancy
ascendency
asceticism
ascomycete
ascribable
ascription
aspersions
asphyxiate
aspidistra
aspiration
aspiringly
assailable
assemblage
assentient
assessable
assessment
asseverate
assibilate
assignable
assignment
assimilate
assistance
associable
assortment
assumption
assumptive
asteriated
asteroidal
astomatous
astonished
astounding
astragalus
astringent
astrolatry
astrologer
astrometer
astrometry

astronomer
astronomic
astuteness
asymmetric
at all costs
at a premium
at full tilt
Athanasian
atmosphere
at odds with
atomic bomb
atrabiliar
atramental
attachable
attachment
attackable
attainable
attainment
attendance
at the stake
Attic order
attraction
attractive
auctioneer
audibility
audiometer
auditorium
augustness
auriculate
auriferous
aurigation
auscultate
auspicious
Australian
australoid
authorship
autochthon
autocratic
autogenous
autography

automation
automatism
automatous
automobile
automotive
autonomous
autoplasty
autoptical
autostrada
auto-teller
avant-garde
avant-guard
avanturine
avaricious
aventurine
averseness
aviculture
avouchment
awakenment
axe to grind

**B**
babblement
babe in arms
babiroussa
baby boomer
baby-farmer
Babylonian
backgammon
background
back-handed
back-hander
back-number
backslider
backstairs
back-stitch
back-stroke
back to back
backwardly
bafflingly

bag of bones
baked beans
baking soda
balderdash
ballistics
ballooning
balloon jib
balneology
balustrade
banana skin
banderilla
band-master
banishment
bankruptcy
bannerette
baptistery
Barbary ape
barbed wire
barbershop
Barbie Doll®
barcarolle
bare-backed
bare-footed
bare-handed
bare-headed
barge-board
barkentine
barking mad
barley-corn
barmecidal
bar mitzvah
barometric
baronetage
barrel-bulk
barrenness
base-minded
basketball
basket-hilt
basset-horn
bassoonist

bastardise
bastardize
bat-fowling
bathing-box
bathometer
bathymetry
batrachian
battledore
battle-line
battlement
battleship
Beach-la-Mar
beach music
beadleship
bean sprout
bear down on
bear-garden
bear in mind
beat hollow
Beaujolais
beautician
beautifier
beauty shop
beauty-spot
bêche-de-mer
becomingly
bedchamber
bed-clothes
bed of nails
bed of roses
beefburger
beef tomato
beer-engine
beforehand
behind bars
behindhand
believable
believably
belladonna
bell-flower

bell-hanger
bell-ringer
bell the cat
bell-turret
bell-wether
belly dance
belongings
benedicite
Benedictus
benefactor
beneficent
beneficial
benevolent
benumbment
bequeather
besottedly
besprinkle
bestialise
bestiality
bestialize
bestiarian
bestseller
better half
betterment
bettermost
betterness
bewitchery
bewitching
biblically
bibliology
bibliopegy
bibliophil
bibliopole
bichloride
bichromate
bicornuate
bicorporal
biennially
Big Brother
bijouterie

bilge-water
bilinguist
biliverdin
bill-broker
billet-doux
bill of fare
billposter
biloculate
bimaculate
bimetallic
binary star
binoculars
binucleate
biogenesis
biogenetic
biographer
biometrics
biophysics
bioplasmic
bipartisan
bird cherry
bird of prey
bird-spider
birostrate
birthnight
birthplace
birthright
birthstone
bismuthite
bissextile
bisulphate
bisulphite
bit of fluff
bit of stuff
bitterness
bituminise
bituminize
bituminous
blackamoor
blackberry

blackboard
black bread
Black Death
black friar
black frost
blackguard
black magic
Black Maria
black power
black sheep
Blackshirt
blacksmith
blackthorn
black widow
blamefully
blancmange
blandisher
blanketing
blank verse
blasphemer
blastoderm
blazonment
bleary-eyed
blind alley
blind-story
blissfully
blistering
blitheness
blithering
blithesome
blitzkrieg
blockhouse
blonde lace
blood count
blood donor
blood group
blood-horse
bloodhound
bloodiness
blood-money

blood sport
blood-stain
blood stock
blood-stone
bloody flux
Bloody Mary
bloomingly
blow by blow
blubber-lip
blue bonnet
blue-bottle
blue cheese
blue-collar
blue-devils
bluejacket
blue ribbon
bluishness
blushingly
blustering
blusterous
board-wages
boastfully
boastingly
boat people
body-colour
body-warmer
bog-trotter
boiler-suit
boisterous
boll-weevil
Bolshevism
bombardier
bomb-vessel
bond-holder
bondswoman
bone-setter
bone-spavin
booby-prize
book-hunter
book-keeper

book-marker
bookseller
bootlessly
boot-licker
borderland
border-line
bored stiff
bothersome
botryoidal
bottle bank
bottle-neck
bottle-nose
bottle-tree
bottomless
bottom line
bouts-rimés
bow-compass
bowdlerise
bowdlerize
bowie-knife
boyishness
brachiopod
brachylogy
brachyural
brachyuran
bracketing
bracteated
braggingly
Brahmanism
brain child
brain death
brain drain
brain-fever
brain storm
branchiate
branchless
brass tacks
brawlingly
brawniness
brazenness

braziletto
brazil-wood
bread-fruit
bread-stuff
break of day
breakwater
brcast-bone
breast-deep
breast-feed
breast-knot
breast-wall
breastwork
breathable
breathless
brent-goose
bricklayer
bridegroom
bridesmaid
bridge-deck
bridgehead
bridgework
bridle-hand
bridle-path
bridle-rein
bridle-road
brigandage
brigandism
brigantine
brightness
brightsome
brilliance
brilliancy
bring round
Britishism
broad arrow
broad-cloth
broadsheet
broadsword
brocatelle
broken-down

brokenness
broken reed
broken wind
brome grass
bromic acid
bronchitis
brontosaur
broomstaff
broomstick
browbeater
brown bread
browned off
brown-shirt
brown-stone
brown study
brown sugar
brusquerie
bubble bath
bubonocele
buccinator
Buchmanism
buck-basket
bucket-seat
bucket-shop
buck-jumper
buck-passer
Buddhistic
budgerigar
buffer zone
buffoonery
buffoonish
bulk buying
bull-headed
bullionist
bull-necked
bumfreezer
bunglingly
Bunsen lamp
burdensome
bureaucrat

burglarise
burglarize
burrow-duck
bush-harrow
bushmaster
bushranger
bush shrike
butlership
butter-bean
butter-bird
butter-boat
buttermilk
butter-tree
butterwort
buttery bar
buttonhole
buttonhook
button push
buttonwood
by and large
by a whisker
by-election

**C**
cabin staff
cachinnate
cack-handed
cacodaemon
cacography
cadaverous
caespitose
*café au lait*
cajolement
calamander
calamitous
calcareous
calceiform
calceolate
calcinable
calc-sinter

calculable
calculated
calculator
Caledonian
caliginous
call it a day
calumniate
calumnious
calyciform
calyptrate
camel's hair
camelopard
Cameronian
camouflage
campaigner
campestral
camphorate
cancellate
cancellous
candescent
candidness
candle-coal
candle-fish
candlewick
candy-floss
candy-sugar
canephorus
cankerworm
cannel-coal
cannelloni
cannon-ball
cannon-shot
can of worms
canonicals
canonicity
cantaloupe
cantatrice
Canterbury
cantilever
cantonment

canvasback
canzonetta
caoutchouc
capability
capacitate
capitalise
capitalism
capitalist
capitalize
capitation
capitulary
capitulate
capnomancy
cappuccino
capreolate
capricious
capsulated
captiously
carabineer
carabinier
caramelise
caramelize
caravaneer
carbazotic
carbonated
carbon-copy
carbuncled
carcinogen
cardialgia
cardiogram
cardiology
carelessly
careworker
caricature
carmagnole
carnallite
Carolinian
carpellary
carpellate
carpophore

carragheen
Carthusian
cartwright
cascarilla
case-bottle
case-harden
casemented
cassia-bark
Cassiopeia
cassolette
castigator
castration
*casus belli*
catabolite
catabolism
catafalque
catalectic
cataleptic
catamenial
cataphract
catarrhine
cat burglar
catch-penny
catechetic
catechumen
categorise
categorize
catenarian
catenation
catenulate
cathode ray
catholicon
catoptrics
Cat scanner
cat's cradle
cattle grid
cattle-show
caulescent
causticity
cautionary

cautiously
cavalierly
celebrated
celebrater
Cellophane®
cellulated
censorious
censorship
censurable
censurably
centaurian
centennial
centesimal
centigrade
centilitre
centimetre
centipedal
centralise
centralism
centrality
centralize
centrefold
centricity
centrifuge
cephalagia
cephalitis
cephalopod
cerebellar
cerebellum
cerebritis
ceremonial
certiorari
ceruminous
cessionary
cestracion
chain-cable
chain-smoke
chain-store
chalcedony
chalkiness

chalkstone
challenger
chalybeate
Chamaeleon
chamber-pot
Chambertin
*champignon*
champignon
chancellor
chandelier
changeable
changeably
changeless
changeling
changeover
channelled
chaparejos
chap-fallen
chaplaincy
chargeable
charge card
charioteer
charitable
charitably
Charleston
charmingly
chartreuse
chartulary
chasteness
chatelaine
chatterbox
Chaucerian
chauvinism
chauvinist
cheapskate
check digit
checkpoint
cheek pouch
cheek-tooth
cheerfully

cheeriness
cheeringly
cheesecake
cheesed off
cheesiness
cheiropter
Chekhovian
chemically
chemisette
cheque-book
chersonese
cherubimic
chess-board
chevrotain
chewing gum
chew the cud
chew the fat
chicken-pox
chiff-chaff
chiffonier
child abuse
childbirth
childishly
child's-play
chiliastic
chilliness
chillingly
chimerical
chimney-pot
chimney-top
chimpanzee
china aster
chinchilla
chinquapin
chip-bonnet
chirognomy
chirograph
chiromancy
chirurgeon
chiselling

chivalrous
chloralism
chloridate
chloridise
chloridize
chlorinate
chlorodyne
chloroform
chlorophyl
chocaholic
choiceless
cholagogue
choliambic
Chomskyite
chop-fallen
chopsticks
choriambus
chorus girl
Christhood
Christless
Christlike
chromatics
chromosome
chronicler
chronogram
chronology
chrysolite
chubbiness
chuck-wagon
church-goer
churchless
church-rate
churchyard
churlishly
Ciceronian
cinchonine
cinchonism
cinenchyma
cinerarium
cinquefoil

cinquepace
circensian
circuitous
circulable
circularly
circulator
circumcise
circumflex
circumfuse
circummure
circumvent
cismontane
Cistercian
citizeness
citizenise
citizenize
citric acid
citronella
city editor
clack-valve
clamminess
clangorous
clannishly
clapped-out
Clarenceux
claspknife
classicism
classicist
classified
clavichord
clavicular
claw-hammer
clay-pigeon
cleansable
clean slate
clear as mud
clear-story
clerestory
clergiable
cleverness

clientship
clingstone
clinically
clinkstone
clinometer
clod-hopper
cloistered
cloisterer
closed book
closed shop
close ranks
close shave
close-stool
close thing
clothes-pin
cloudberry
cloud-built
cloud-burst
cloudiness
clove hitch
cloven hoof
cloverleaf
clownishly
club-footed
clumsiness
Clydesdale
coach-wheel
coadjutrix
coagulable
coagulator
coalescent
coal-heaver
coal-master
coaptation
coarseness
coastguard
coastwards
coat-armour
coathanger
coatimundi

coat of arms
coat of mail
cobalt blue
cobalt bomb
cochleated
cockalorum
cock a snook
cockatrice
cock-chafer
cockneydom
cockneyish
cockneyism
coconut shy
codswallop
coelacanth
coequality
coercively
coetaneous
coeternity
coexecutor
coexistent
coffee-bean
coffee-mill
coffee-room
coffee shop
coffin-bone
cogitation
cogitative
cognisable
cognisably
cognisance
cognizable
cognizably
cognizance
cognominal
coherently
cohesively
coincident
cold chisel
cold turkey

coleorhiza
collar-beam
collarbone
collarless
collatable
collateral
collection
collective
collegiate
collimator
collingual
colliquate
collocutor
colloquial
colloquise
colloquist
colloquium
colloquize
coloration
coloratura
colorature
colourable
colourably
colour-code
colour-fast
colourless
colporteur
combatable
combinable
combinedly
combustion
comedienne
comedietta
come hither
comeliness
comestible
come to life
come to rest
come to that
comforting

comicality
comic opera
comic strip
commandant
commandeer
commanding
commentary
commentate
commercial
commissary
commission
commissure
commitment
commixture
commodious
commonable
commonalty
commonness
common time
commonweal
communiqué
commutable
commutator
company car
comparable
comparably
comparison
compassion
compass-saw
compatible
compatibly
compatriot
compelling
compendium
compensate
competence
competency
competitor
complacent
complainer

complement
completely
completion
completive
completory
complexion
complexity
compliance
compliancy
complicacy
complicate
complicity
compliment
composedly
compositor
compounder
comprehend
compressed
compressor
compromise
compulsion
compulsive
compulsory
computable
concentric
conception
conceptual
concerning
concertina
concertino
concession
concessive
conchoidal
conchology
conciliate
concinnity
conclavist
concluding
conclusion
conclusive

concoction
concordant
concretely
concretion
concurrent
concussion
concussive
condescend
condolence
conduction
conductive
confection
conference
confervoid
confession
confidante
confidence
confinable
confiscate
conflation
confluence
conformist
conformity
confounded
confounder
confusedly
confutable
congeneric
congenital
congestion
congestive
conglobate
congregate
congruence
coniferous
conjecture
conjointly
conjugally
conjunctly
connascent

connatural
connection
connective
conniption
connivance
connivency
conquering
conscience
consecrate
consensual
consequent
considered
consistent
consistory
consociate
consolable
consonance
consonancy
consortium
conspectus
conspiracy
con spirito
constantly
constipate
constitute
constraint
constringe
consubsist
consuetude
consulship
consultant
consulting
consultive
consumable
consumedly
consummate
contactual
contagious
contention
contestant

contextual
contexture
contiguity
contiguous
continence
contingent
continuant
continuity
continuous
contortion
contraband
contrabass
contracted
contractor
contradict
contraflow
contrarily
contravene
contribute
contritely
contrition
controller
controvert
convalesce
convection
convective
convenable
convenance
convenient
convention
conventual
convergent
conversant
conversely
conversion
convexness
conveyable
conveyance
conviction
convincing

convoluted
convulsion
convulsive
cool-headed
cooperator
coordinate
coparcener
Copernican
copperhead
coprolitic
copulation
copulative
copulatory
copyholder
copy-writer
coquettish
coradicate
cordiality
cordillera
cordon bleu
cordwainer
co-relation
co-relative
coriaceous
Corinthian
cork-cutter
corking-pin
cork-jacket
corn circle
corn-cockle
corn-cutter
corned beef
cornerwise
cornettist
corn-factor
cornflakes
cornflower
cornstarch
cornucopia
coronation

coroniform
corporally
corporator
corporeity
corpulence
correction
corrective
correctory
correspond
corrigenda
corrigible
corroboree
corrodible
corrugated
corrugator
corruption
corruptive
corseleted
corsetière
corticated
coryphaeus
cosmically
cosmogonal
cosmoramic
costliness
cothurnate
cottierism
cotton-seed
cottontail
cotton-tree
cottonwood
cotton wool
cotyliform
cotyloidal
couch-grass
cough syrup
councillor
councilman
councilmen
council tax

counsellor
counteract
countryman
countrymen
county road
county town
courageous
court-baron
court-dress
courthouse
courtwards
cousinhood
cousinship
covenantee
covenanter
covenantor
covered-way
covetingly
covetously
cow-catcher
cow-parsley
cow-parsnip
cow-puncher
crack a joke
cradle-song
craftiness
cragginess
crane's-bill
craniology
craniotomy
crankshaft
crapulence
craquelure
crassament
crassitude
crawlingly
cream-faced
creaminess
creational
credential

creditable
creditably
credit card
crenellate
crenulated
crepe paper
crescented
crescentic
Cretaceous
cribriform
criminally
cringeling
criosphinx
crispation
criss-cross
critically
criticizer
crop circle
cross-bones
cross-breed
cross-check
cross-cloth
crosshatch
crosspatch
crosspiece
cross-staff
cross-stone
cross-trees
crow-flower
crown-glass
Crown lands
crown-wheel
cruet-stand
crumb-brush
crumb-cloth
crustacean
crustation
crustiness
cryogenics
cryophorus

cryptogamy
cryptogram
cryptology
Ctenophora
cuckoo-pint
cuckoo-spit
cucullated
cucurbital
cuddlesome
cuirassier
cultivable
cultivator
culturable
cumberless
cumbersome
cumbrously
cummerbund
cumulation
cumulative
curability
curateship
curmudgeon
curriculum
cursedness
curvaceous
cussedness
customable
cut corners
cuttlebone
cuttlefish
cut up rough
cyanic acid
cyathiform
cyberspace
cyclometer
cyclopedia
cyclopedic
cylindroid
cystoscope
czarevitch

**D**
daggletail
daily bread
daily dozen
daily round
daintiness
daisy-chain
daisy-wheel
dallymoney
damageable
damask plum
damask rose
dandy-brush
Danish blue
dapple-grey
dark-browed
daughterly
dauphiness
day-dreamer
dazzlingly
deaconhood
deaconship
deactivate
dead letter
dead-lights
deadliness
dead-nettle
dead ringer
dead weight
dear-bought
deaspirate
death-angel
death's door
death's head
death watch
debasement
debauchery
debentured
debilitate
debonairly

debonnaire
debouchure
decagynian
decagynous
decahedral
decahedron
decalogist
decampment
decandrian
decandrous
decangular
decapitate
decapodous
deceivable
decelerate
Decemberly
Decembrist
decemviral
decimalise
decimalize
decimation
decipherer
decisively
deckle-edge
declaimant
declarable
declarator
declaredly
declassify
declension
declinable
declinator
decolonise
decolonize
decolorant
decolorate
decolorise
decolorize
decompound
decompress

decoration
decorative
decorously
decreeable
decrescent
decumbence
decumbency
decurrence
decurrency
dedication
dedicatory
deductible
deep-freeze
deep-rooted
deep-seated
de-escalate
defacement
defalcator
defamation
defamatory
defeasance
defeasible
defecation
defendable
defensible
deficience
deficiency
defilement
definitely
definition
definitive
definitude
deflagrate
deflection
deflowerer
deformedly
defrayment
degeneracy
degenerate
degradable

degression
dehiscence
dehumanise
dehumanize
dejectedly
dejudicate
del credere
delectable
delectably
delegation
deliberate
delicately
delightful
delimitate
delineator
delinquent
deliquesce
delocalise
delocalize
delphinium
delusively
demagogism
demandable
demi-quaver
demobilise
demobilize
democratic
demodulate
demogorgon
demography
demoiselle
demolisher
demolition
demonetise
demonetize
demoniacal
demonology
demoralise
demoralize
demureness

demurrable
dendriform
dendrolite
dendrology
denegation
denisation
denization
denominate
denotation
denotation
denotative
dénouement
densimeter
dentifrice
denudation
denunciate
deobstruct
deodoriser
deodorizer
deontology
department
dependable
dependably
dependence
dependency
depilation
depilatory
deplorable
deplorably
deployment
depolarise
depolarize
depopulate
deportment
depositary
deposition
depository
depravedly
deprecator
depreciate

depredator
depressant
depression
depressive
depuration
depuratory
deputation
deracinate
derailleur
deregulate
deridingly
derisively
derivation
derivative
dermatitis
derogation
derogatory
desalinate
descendant
descendent
descending
descension
desecrator
deservedly
deshabille
desiccator
desiderate
designator
designedly
desolately
desolation
despairing
despatcher
despicable
despicably
despisable
despiteful
despondent
despotical
desquamate

destructor
desudation
detachable
detachment
detainment
detectable
detectably
detergence
detergency
determined
determiner
detestable
detestably
detonating
detonation
detraction
detractive
detractory
detruncate
deutoplasm
devastator
devilishly
devil's dust
devitalise
devitalize
devolution
devotement
devotional
devourable
diabetical
diabolical
diacaustic
diacoustic
diaglyphic
diagnostic
diagonally
dialectics
dialogical
diapedesis
diaphanous

diaphonics
diaskeuast
diathermal
diathermic
diatribist
dichloride
dichogamic
dichroitic
Dictaphone®
dictatress
dictionary
Dictograph®
didactical
didelphian
didynamous
dielectric
dietetical
difference
difficulty
diffidence
difformity
diffusible
digestible
digestibly
digitately
digitation
digitiform
digression
digressive
dijudicate
dilacerate
dilapidate
dilatation
dilatorily
dilettante
diligently
dilly-dally
dilucidate
diminisher
diminuendo

diminution
diminutive
dimorphism
dimorphous
dining-room
dinner-hour
dinnerless
dinner-time
dioptrical
dipetalous
diphtheria
diphtheric
diphyllous
diphyodont
diplodocus
diplomatic
diprotodon
dipsomania
directness
directoire
directress
disability
disanimate
disapparel
disappoint
disapprove
disarrange
disastrous
disbelieve
disburthen
discerning
discharger
discipline
disc jockey
disclaimer
disclosure
discomfort
discommend
discommode
discompose

disconcert
disconnect
discontent
Discophora
discordant
discounter
discourage
discourser
discoverer
discreetly
discrepant
discretion
discretive
discursive
discussion
discussive
discutient
disdainful
disembogue
disembosom
disembowel
disembroil
disenchant
disengaged
disennoble
disenslave
disenthral
disentitle
disfeature
disfigurer
disfurnish
disgustful
disgusting
dishabille
dish aerial
disharmony
dishearten
dishonesty
dishwasher
disincline

disinherit
disjointed
disloyally
disloyalty
dismalness
dismission
dismissive
dismissory
disomatous
disordered
disorderly
disownment
disparager
dispassion
dispensary
dispensing
dispeopler
dispermous
dispersion
dispersive
dispirited
displeased
displeaser
disposable
dispossess
disputable
disqualify
disrespect
disruption
disruptive
dissatisfy
dissecting
dissection
dissembler
dissension
dissenting
dissertate
disservice
dissidence
dissilient

dissimilar
dissipated
dissociate
dissoluble
dissolvent
dissonance
dissuasion
dissuasive
dissymetry
distension
distensive
distention
distichous
distillate
distillery
distinctly
distortion
distortive
distracted
distrainee
distrainer
distrainor
distraught
distressed
distribute
disulphate
disulphide
disyllable
ditheistic
ditto marks
divagation
divaricate
dive-bomber
divergence
divergency
divination
divineness
diving-bell
diving-suit
divisional

do away with
docimastic
doctorship
documental
doggedness
dogmatical
dogmatiser
dogmatizer
dog's dinner
dolorously
domination
donkey-work
door-keeper
do the trick
double-back
double-bass
double-dyed
double-lock
doubleness
double park
double star
double-take
doubtfully
down-and-out
down-at-heel
down-looked
down-market
downstairs
draft board
dragon tree
dramatical
dramaturge
dramaturgy
draw a blank
drawbridge
drawing-pin
drawlingly
drawstring
dreadfully
dreadlocks

dreaminess
dreariness
dressmaker
drink-drive
droopingly
drop a brick
drop-hammer
drosometer
drossiness
drowsiness
drudgingly
drug addict
drupaceous
dry as a bone
drysaltery
dubitation
duck-billed
duffel coat
duffle coat
dull-witted
dumbwaiter
dunderhead
duniwassal
duodecimal
dupability
duplicator
durability
duster coat
dust-jacket
Dutch treat
Dutch uncle
duumvirate
dwarfishly
dynamitard
dysenteric
dysprosium

E
earth-bound
earthiness

earth-plate
earthquake
earth-shine
earthwards
ear-trumpet
ear-witness
easterling
Eastertide
éboulement
ebracteate
ebullience
ebulliency
ebullition
ecchymosis
ecclesiast
eccoprotic
echinoderm
economical
ecthlipsis
ecumenical
eczematous
edaciously
edentulous
edibleness
edifyingly
editorship
educatable
edulcorate
effaceable
effacement
effectible
effectless
effectuate
effeminacy
effeminate
effervesce
efficiency
effloresce
effortless
effrontery

effulgence
egocentric
Egyptology
eighteen-mo
eighteenth
eisteddfod
elaborator
elasticity
elbow-chair
elderberry
elecampane
electorate
electrical
electronic
elementary
elenchical
Eleusinian
eliminable
eliquation
elliptical
elongation
eloquently
elucidator
emaciation
emancipate
emarginate
emasculate
embankment
embassador
ember-goose
Ember weeks
emblazoner
emblazonry
emblematic
emblements
embodiment
embolismal
embolismic
embonpoint
embossment

embouchure
embroidery
embryogeny
embryology
embryonary
embryotomy
emendation
emendatory
emergently
emery board
emery-paper
emetically
emigration
emmetropia
emphatical
empiricism
employable
employment
enamellist
enantiosis
encampment
encephalic
encephalon
enchanting
enclitical
encourager
encrinital
encrinitic
encroacher
encyclical
encystment
endearment
endemicity
endermatic
endogamous
endogenous
endopleura
endorhizal
endorsable
endosmosis

endosmotic
endostitis
end product
enduringly
energetics
enervation
enforcible
engagement
engagingly
Englishman
enharmonic
enigmatist
enjoinment
enlacement
enlistment
enormously
enrichment
enrockment
ensanguine
ensignship
entailment
enterocele
enterolite
enterolith
enterotomy
enterprise
enthronise
enthronize
enthusiasm
enthusiast
enticeable
enticement
enticingly
entireness
entombment
entomology
entophytic
entrochite
entry money
Entryphone®

enumerator
enunciable
enunciator
epaulement
epauletted
epenthesis
epenthetic
epexegesis
ephemerist
epicycloid
epideictic
epidemical
epigastric
epigenesis
epigenetic
epiglottic
epiglottis
epigraphic
epileptoid
epilogical
epiloguise
epiloguize
epirhizous
episcopacy
episcopate
episiotomy
episodical
epispastic
epistolary
epistolise
epistolist
epistolize
epistrophe
epitaphian
epitaphist
epithelial
epithelium
epitomator
epitomiser
epitomizer

epoxy resin
eprouvette
Epsom salts
equability
equanimity
equanimous
equatorial
equestrian
equitation
equivalent
equivocate
eradicable
eradicator
erectility
eremitical
erethistic
ergonomics
ericaceous
erotomania
erpetology
erubescent
eructation
eruptional
erysipelas
escapement
escarpment
escharotic
escritoire
Esculapian
escutcheon
esophagous
espadrille
especially
esteemable
estimation
estivation
esuriently
eternalise
eternalist
eternalize

ethereally
etheriform
ethnically
ethnologic
etiolation
etymologic
eucalyptol
eucalyptus
eudemonism
eudemonist
eudiometer
eudiometry
euhemerism
eulogistic
euphonical
euphonious
euphorbium
euphuistic
eurhythmic
Eurocheque
Euro-tunnel
eurythmics
Eustachian
euthanasia
evacuation
evaluation
evanescent
evangelise
evangelism
evangelist
evangelize
evaporable
even-handed
eventually
ever-living
everything
everywhere
evidential
eviscerate
evolvement

exacerbate
exactitude
exaggerate
exaltation
examinable
examinator
exasperate
ex cathedra
excavation
excellence
excellency
excerption
excitation
excitative
excitatory
excitement
excititive
excogitate
excrescent
excruciate
excusatory
excuseless
execration
execrative
execratory
executable
exegetical
exegitical
exhalation
exhalement
exhausting
exhaustion
exhaustive
exhibition
exhibitive
exhibitory
exhilarant
exhilarate
exhumation
exorbitant

exoterical
expansible
expansibly
expatiator
expatriate
expectance
expectancy
expedience
expediency
expedition
expellable
expendable
experience
experiment
expertness
expiratory
explicable
explicably
explicitly
exploitage
explorable
exportable
exposition
expositive
expository
expression
expressive
expressway
expurgator
exsanguine
exsiccator
extendable
extendible
extensible
extenuator
exteriorly
externally
extincteur
extinction
extinguish

extirpable
extirpator
extraction
extractive
extra-mural
extraneous
extricable
extricably
exuberance
exuberancy
exulcerate
exultation
exuviation
eyeglasses
eyelet-hole
eye-servant
eye-service
eyewitness

**F**
fabricator
fabulosity
fabulously
face-saving
facileness
facilitate
factionary
factionist
factiously
factitious
factorship
faggot-vote
Fahrenheit
fairground
fair-minded
fair-spoken
fairy story
faithfully
fallacious
fallow-deer

false alarm
false start
familiarly
family name
family tree
famishment
fanaticise
fanaticism
fanaticize
fancifully
fancy dress
fancy-woman
fantoccini
fan-tracery
farcically
far-fetched
farmership
far-sighted
fasciation
fascicular
fasciculus
fastidious
fastigiate
fatalistic
fat-brained
fatherhood
fatherland
fatherless
fathership
fathomable
fathomless
faultiness
favourable
favourably
fearlessly
fear-naught
fear-nought
featherbed
feathering
febrifugal

federalise
federalism
federalist
federalize
federation
federative
feebleness
feel at home
felicitate
felicitous
fell-monger
fellow-heir
fellowship
felspathic
feme covert
femininely
femininity
fenestrate
fer-de-lance
fertiliser
fertilizer
fervidness
fetterless
fetterlock
fettuccine
feuilleton
feverishly
fibreglass
fibrillose
fibrositis
fictionist
fictitious
fiddle-head
field event
fieldmouse
fifth wheel
fifty-fifty
figuration
figurative
figurehead

filibuster
fimbriated
finger-bowl
fingerling
fingernail
finger-post
fire-engine
fire-escape
fire-raiser
fire-screen
firewarden
firing-line
first-class
first night
fish finger
fishing-rod
fishmonger
fissipedal
fisticuffs
flabellate
flagellant
flagellate
flagitious
flamboyant
flapdoodle
flashboard
flash flood
flashlight
flashpoint
flat-footed
flatulence
flatulency
flavescent
flavouring
flea-bitten
flea market
fledgeling
flesh-wound
fleur de lis
fleur de lys

flick-knife
flight deck
flightless
flint glass
floatation
flocculant
flocculent
floodlight
floorboard
floppy disk
Florentine
floribunda
fluid ounce
fluoridate
fluorinate
fluviatile
fly-by-night
flycatcher
fly-fishing
flying boat
flying fish
fly the coop
fly-tipping
foliaceous
*folie à deux*
fontanelle
fool around
foot-bridge
footlights
forbidding
fore-and-aft
foreboding
forecastle
forechoose
forefather
forefinger
foregather
foreground
forehanded
foreignism

foreordain
forerunner
foreshadow
foreteller
forfeiture
forgivable
formic acid
formidable
formidably
fornicator
forte piano
forthgoing
forthright
fortissimo
fortuitous
for two pins
forty-niner
forty winks
fosterling
foudroyant
foundation
fourchette
four-handed
four-poster
four-square
four-stroke
fourteenth
fox-terrier
fractional
fragmental
fragrantly
framboesia
Franciscan
frangipane
frangipani
fraternise
fraternity
fraternize
fratricide
fraudfully

fraudulent
fraxinella
freakishly
freebooter
free-for-all
free-handed
freeholder
free-living
freemartin
free-spoken
freightage
freight-car
French horn
French roof
frenziedly
frequenter
freshwater
fricandeau
frictional
friendless
friendship
Frigid Zone
frigorific
friskiness
fritillary
froghopper
frolicsome
front bench
frontwards
frostiness
frothiness
frowningly
fruiteress
fruitfully
fruit salad
frustrable
frutescent
fucivorous
fuddy-duddy
fugitively

fulfilment
fuliginous
full-bodied
fumatorium
fumigation
functional
fund-holder
funereally
fungaceous
funny money
furbelowed
futuristic
futurology

**G**
gabionnade
gadolinite
gadolinium
gain ground
galimatias
galloglass
Gallup Poll®
galvaniser
galvanizer
gamekeeper
game theory
ganglionic
gangrenous
garage sale
gargantuan
garishness
garnishing
gas chamber
gas-guzzler
gasteropod
gastralgia
gastrology
gastronome
gastronomy
gate-keeper

Gatling-gun
gelatinate
gelatinise
gelatinize
gelatinoid
gelatinous
gemination
gemmaceous
gendarmery
generalise
generality
generalize
generation
generative
generatrix
generosity
generously
genethliac
genialness
geniculate
gentlefolk
gentleness
geocentric
geodetical
geognostic
geographer
geological
geometrise
geometrize
geophagism
geophysics
geoponical
geoselenic
geothermal
geothermic
geotropism
geriatrics
get a look in
get a move on
get knotted

| | | |
|---|---|---|
| get nowhere | goat's-beard | gramineous |
| get round to | goatsucker | grammarian |
| get stuffed | go beetroot | gramophone |
| get the boot | gobsmacked | granadilla |
| get the chop | God-fearing | grandchild |
| get the sack | go down hill | grandniece |
| get up and go | goggle-eyed | grand opera |
| get up steam | go-go dancer | grand piano |
| ghost-write | gold-digger | grandstand |
| giant panda | golden calf | granduncle |
| ginger beer | golden mean | grangerise |
| ginger snap | golden rule | grangerism |
| gingivitis | gold-filled | grangerize |
| girl Friday | goldilocks | granny-knot |
| girlfriend | golf-course | grapefruit |
| give a leg up | goniometer | graphology |
| glacialist | gonorrhoea | graphotype |
| glaciation | good as gold | graph paper |
| glamourise | Good Friday | graptolite |
| glamourize | goodliness | grassiness |
| glancingly | goody-goody | grass roots |
| glandiform | gooseberry | grass-snake |
| glandulous | goose-bumps | grass widow |
| glassiness | goose-flesh | gratefully |
| glimmering | goose-grass | gratifying |
| glitterati | gopherwood | gratuitous |
| globularly | gorgeously | graveolent |
| gloriously | gorgoneion | gravestone |
| glossarial | Gorgonzola | gravigrade |
| glossarist | gormandise | gravimeter |
| glossiness | gormandize | gravy train |
| glossology | go straight | greasiness |
| glottology | go to pieces | great-niece |
| glucosuria | go to the bad | great-uncle |
| glumaceous | governance | Greco-Roman |
| gluttonise | government | Greek cross |
| gluttonize | gracefully | greenfinch |
| glycosuria | graciously | green heart |
| Gnosticism | graduation | greenhouse |
| goal-keeper | grama grass | green light |

Greenpeace
greenshank
greenstone
greensward
green thumb
gregarious
gressorial
grey matter
grievously
grim reaper
grindstone
grittiness
grogginess
groundless
ground rule
groundsill
groundsman
groundsmen
groundwork
grovelling
grudgingly
guardhouse
guesthouse
guillotine
guiltiness
guinea-fowl
Gulf Stream
gunning for
gun-running
gunslinger
gutturally
gymnasiums
gymnastics
gymnosperm
gynandrous
gynecology
gyrational

**H**
habiliment

habilitate
habitation
habitually
hackmatack
haematosis
haematozoa
haematuria
hagiocracy
hair-spring
halberdier
half-nelson
half-sister
half-volley
Hallelujah
hammer-head
handicraft
hand in hand
hand-maiden
hand-picked
handspring
hand-to-hand
hang-glider
hanky-panky
happy event
harassment
harbourage
hard-bitten
hard-boiled
hard cheese
hard done by
hard-headed
hark back to
harmlessly
harmonious
hartebeest
hatchet job
hatchet-man
haustellum
have a nerve
headbanger

head honcho
headmaster
headstrong
head waiter
headwaters
health-care
health farm
hearing aid
heartbreak
heartiness
heart's-ease
heart-throb
heart-whole
heathenish
heathenism
heavenward
heavy cream
heavy-going
heavy-laden
heavy metal
heavy water
hebdomadal
hectically
hectograph
heedlessly
helianthus
helicoidal
helicopter
heliograph
heliolatry
heliometer
heliotrope
heliotropy
heli-skiing
helminthic
hematology
hemihedral
hemihedron
hemiplegia
hemipteran

hemipteron
hemisphere
hemistitch
henceforth
hendecagon
henotheism
heptagonal
heptameter
heptarchic
Heptateuch
herbaceous
herbescent
hereabouts
hereditary
heresiarch
heretofore
hermetical
herpetical
hesitation
Hesperides
heterodoxy
heterodyne
heterogene
heterotopy
heulandite
hexagynian
hexahedral
hexahedron
hexametric
hexandrian
hiddenness
hierarchal
hierocracy
hieroglyph
hierophant
high and dry
High Church
high ground
high-handed
highjacker

Highlander
high-minded
high priest
high-roller
high school
high season
high-strung
highwayman
highwaymen
Himyaritic
hinderance
hindermost
Hindustani
hinterland
hippodrome
hippogriff
hippogryph
hippophagy
hippophile
historical
histrionic
hithermost
hitherward
hit the mark
hit the road
hit the roof
hoarseness
hobby-horse
hocus pocus
hodge-podge
hoity-toity
hokey-pokey
hollow-eyed
hollowness
holography
holohedral
holophotal
holus-bolus
Holy Spirit
home and dry

homeliness
homeopathy
homiletics
homogenise
homogenize
homologous
Homoousian
homophobia
homophobic
homosexual
homotonous
homunculus
honorarium
honourable
honourably
hopelessly
hopping mad
horizontal
hornblende
horography
horologist
horoscopic
horrendous
horse brass
horse-flesh
horse-laugh
horse-leech
horse-power
horse-sense
horse-trade
horsewoman
hospitable
hospitably
hot-blooded
hotch-potch
hot-housing
housebound
House music
house-party
house-plant

house-proud
housewives
hovercraft
how do you do?
hubba-hubba
hullabaloo
human being
humbleness
humoralism
humoralist
humoresque
humoristic
humorology
humorously
humourless
humoursome
humpbacked
hurdy-gurdy
hurly-burly
husbandman
husbandmen
hydraulics
hydrolysis
hydromancy
hydromania
hydrometer
hydropathy
hydrophane
hydrophone
hydrophyte
hydroplane
hydroscope
hygrometer
hygroscope
hylotheism
hymenopter
hypaethral
hyperbolic
hyperdulia
hypermeter

hypersonic
hypnotiser
hypnotizer
hypocorism
hypodermal
hypodermic
hypogynous
hypostasis
hypostatic
hypotenuse
hypothesis
hypothetic
hypsometer
hypsometry
hysteresis
hysterical

**I**
ice-breaker
ichthyosis
iconoclasm
iconoclast
iconolatry
ideography
ideologist
idiopathic
idiot board
idolatrous
idoloclast
ignipotent
ignorantly
ill-advised
illatively
illegality
ill-founded
illiteracy
illiterate
ill-natured
ill-starred
illuminant

illuminate
illuminati
illuminism
illustrate
imaginable
imaginably
imbecility
imbibition
imbricated
immaculate
immanation
immaterial
immaturely
immaturity
immemorial
immersible
immiscible
immobilise
immobility
immobilize
immoderate
immodestly
immolation
immorality
immortelle
immunology
impalpable
impalpably
impanation
impartible
impassable
impassible
impatience
impeccable
impeccably
impediment
impenitent
imperative
imperially
impersonal

impervious
implacable
implacably
implicitly
importable
importance
imposingly
imposition
impossible
impossibly
imposthume
impotently
impoundage
impoverish
impregnate
impresario
impression
impressive
imprimatur
improbable
improbably
improperly
imprudence
impudently
impugnable
impuissant
imputation
imputative
*in absentia*
inaccuracy
inaccurate
inactively
inactivity
inadequate
inapposite
inaptitude
inartistic
inaugurate
in bad odour
incandesce

incapacity
incasement
incautious
incendiary
incestuous
inchoately
inchoative
incidental
incinerate
incivility
inclinable
includible
incoherent
incomplete
inconstant
incredible
incredibly
increscent
incubation
incubative
incumbency
indagation
indecently
indecision
indecisive
indecorous
indefinite
indelicacy
indelicate
Indian corn
Indian file
indication
indicative
indictable
indictment
indigenous
indirectly
indiscreet
indiscrete
indisposed

indistinct
inditement
individual
indocility
inducement
inductance
indulgence
induration
industrial
indwelling
inebriated
ineducable
inelegance
ineligible
ineloquent
inequality
in evidence
inevitable
inevitably
inexorable
inexpiable
inexplicit
*in extremis*
infallible
infallibly
infamously
infatuated
infectious
infeftment
infelicity
inferiorly
inferrable
inferrible
infidelity
infighting
infiltrate
infinitely
infinitive
infinitude
inflatable

inflection
inflective
inflexible
inflexibly
infliction
inflictive
informally
infraction
infrasonic
infrequent
infusorial
infusorian
inglorious
in good nick
in good time
ingratiate
ingredient
ingulfment
inhabitant
inhalation
inharmonic
inherently
inheritrix
inhibition
inhibitory
in hot water
inhumanity
inhumation
inimically
inimitable
iniquitous
initialise
initialize
initiation
initiative
initiatory
injudicial
injunction
injury time
in memoriam

in name only
innateness
innocently
innominate
innovation
innuendoes
innumerate
innumerous
inoculable
inoculator
inodourous
inofficial
in one's cups
inoperable
inordinate
inosculate
inquietude
inquisitor
insalivate
insalutary
ins and outs
insaneness
insanitary
insatiable
insatiably
insecurely
insecurity
inseminate
insensible
insensibly
insentient
insinuator
insipidity
insobriety
insolation
insolently
insolvable
insolvency
insouciant
inspection

inspirable
inspissate
instalment
instigator
instilment
institutor
instructor
instrument
insufflate
insularity
insulation
intangible
intangibly
integrator
integument
intendancy
intendment
interbreed
intercross
interested
interferon
intergrade
interleave
interloper
interlunar
intermarry
intermezzo
intermural
internally
interplead
interspace
interstate
interstice
intertwine
interweave
intestable
intestinal
in the black
in the clear
in the event

in the frame
in the money
in the wrong
intimately
intimation
intimidate
intinction
intonation
intoxicant
intoxicate
intramural
intrepidly
introducer
introspect
in tune with
in two minds
in two ticks
inundation
invaginate
invalidate
invalidity
invaluable
invariable
invariably
inventible
inventress
inveracity
investment
inveterate
invigorate
invincible
inviolable
invitation
invitatory
invitingly
invocation
invocatory
involucral
involucrum
involution

inwardness
in your face
ionosphere
iridaceous
iridescent
iridosmium
iron maiden
ironmonger
irradiance
irradiancy
irrational
irrelative
irrelevant
irreligion
irremeable
irresolute
irreverent
irrigation
irritating
irritation
isagogical
Ishmaelite
isochronal
isodynamic
isomerical
isometrics
isoseismal
isoseismic
Israelitic
Italianate
itinerancy
I told you so
ivory tower

## J

jackanapes
jack-rabbit
Jack the lad
jaggedness
jam session

janizaries
jardinière
jargonelle
jaw-breaker
jeopardise
jeopardize
jeopardous
jerry-built
Jesuitical
Jesus freak
jiggermast
jinrikisha
job-sharing
jocularity
joint stock
jolly along
Jolly Roger
jolter-head
journalese
journalise
journalism
journalist
journalize
journeyman
jovialness
joyfulness
joyousness
jubilation
Judaically
judgmental
judicatory
judicature
judicially
juggernaut
jump the gun
juncaceous
junior miss
jury-rigged
justiciary
just in time

just the job
juvenility
juxtaposit

**K**
Kafkaesque
keep in with
keep posted
keep tabs on
kerchiefed
kerseymere
kettledrum
Kewpie doll®
keyboarder
khidmutgar
kibbutznik
kick boxing
kidney bean
kieselguhr
kilogramme
kindliness
kinematics
kinetic art
kingfisher
kingliness
King-of-Arms
kinnikinic
kiss of life
knackwurst
knick-knack
knighthood
knobkerrie
knock about
knock-kneed
knottiness
kookaburra
kriegspiel

**L**
labionasal

laboratory
laceration
lachrymose
laciniated
lackadaisy
lacklustre
laconicism
lactescent
lactic acid
lactometer
lactoscope
lacustrine
ladder back
ladies' room
lady-killer
lady's-smock
lambdacism
lambdoidal
lambrequin
lamentable
lamentably
lamination
lanceolate
lancet arch
land-holder
landlocked
land-lubber
land-spring
languorous
laniferous
lanigerous
lansquenet
lantern jaw
lanthanide
laparotomy
lardaceous
large-scale
laryngitis
lascivious
Lassa fever

last hurrah
last minute
Last Supper
laughingly
Laundromat
laureation
law-abiding
lawbreaker
lawfulness
lawn tennis
lawrencium
leaderette
leadership
leading man
lead the way
lebensraum
lectionary
lederhosen
ledger-line
left-handed
left-hander
legateship
legislator
legitimacy
legitimate
legitimise
legitimist
legitimize
leguminous
lemon grass
lengthways
lengthwise
lentamente
lenticular
leprechaun
lethargise
lethargize
let one in on
letter bomb
letterhead

leucopathy
leucorrhea
levigation
levitation
lexicology
liberalise
liberalism
liberality
liberalize
liberation
liberatory
libidinist
libidinous
librettist
licentiate
licentious
lie heavy on
lieutenant
life-jacket
lifelessly
life-saving
ligamental
lighterage
lighthouse
light opera
likelihood
likeliness
likeminded
limberness
limitation
linguiform
linguistic
linseed-oil
lion-hunter
lion's share
lip service
liquescent
liquidator
liquidiser
liquidizer

literalism
literalist
literality
literalize
literature
lithograph
lithologic
lithophyte
lithotrity
litigation
littleness
liturgical
livelihood
liveliness
liverwurst
living-room
living wage
living will
locker room
locomotion
locomotive
loculament
loganberry
logan-stone
loggerhead
logistical
logography
log-rolling
Lollardism
loneliness
lonesomely
long-headed
long-winded
look down on
loquacious
lord it over
lordliness
lorication
loss leader
lotus-eater

love-affair
loveliness
love-making
lovey-dovey
lower class
Lower House
low-tension
loxodromic
lubricator
lucifugous
lucklessly
luculently
lugubrious
lumber-jack
luminosity
luminously
lumpsucker
lunar month
lusciously
lustration
lustreless
lustreware
lute-string
luxuriance
lycopodium
lymphocyte

**M**
macadamise
macadamize
maceration
machinator
machine-gun
Mach number
mackintosh
macrobiote
macrospore
maculation
magistracy
magistrate

Magna Carta
magnetiser
magnetizer
magnifical
Magnificat
magnum opus
maidenhair
maidenhead
maidenhood
maiden name
maiden over
mainspring
mainstream
maintainer
maisonette
make amends
make a stand
make do with
make eyes at
make much of
make no odds
make tracks
makeweight
malacology
malapropos
malcontent
malefactor
maleficent
malevolent
malignance
malignancy
malingerer
malodorous
Malpighian
Malthusian
malvaceous
mammillary
mammillate
manageable
management

manageress
managerial
manchineel
mandibular
mandragora
manfulness
mangosteen
maniacally
Manicheism
manifestly
manifoldly
manipulate
mannerless
manoeuvrer
man of straw
manservant
mansuetude
manuscript
maraschino
marcel wave
marcescent
marginalia
marginally
margravate
margravine
marguerite
Mariolatry
marionette
marketable
marlaceous
marmorated
marquisate
marrow-bone
marrowless
marshaller
marshiness
martial law
martingale
marvellous
mascarpone

masquerade
massasauga
mastectomy
masterless
mastermind
mastership
masterwork
masticable
masticator
mastodynia
masturbate
matchboard
matchmaker
materially
maternally
mathematic
matriarchy
matronhood
matronymic
maturation
maturative
matureness
mavourneen
maxilliped
Maximalist
mayonnaise
meadow-lark
meagreness
meal ticket
measurable
measurably
meat market
mechanical
medallurgy
meddlesome
medicament
medication
mediocrity
meditation
meditative

meerschaum
megalithic
megalosaur
melanaemia
melancholy
melting-pot
membership
membranous
memorandum
menacingly
mendacious
mendicancy
meningitis
menstruate
menstruums
mensurable
mensurably
mephitical
mercantile
merchantry
mercifully
meridional
mesenteric
mesmeriser
mesmerizer
mesolithic
mesothorax
metabolise
metabolism
metabolize
metacarpal
metacarpus
metacentre
metallurgy
metaphoric
metaphrase
metaphrist
metaphysic
metastasis
metatarsal

metatarsus
metathesis
metathorax
metempiric
methodical
Methuselah
methylated
meticulous
metrically
metrograph
metronymic
metropolis
mettlesome
Michaelmas
Mickey Finn
microfarad
microfiche
micrograph
micrometer
micrometry
microphone
microphyte
microscope
microscopy
microseism
Midas touch
Middle Ages
midshipman
midshipmen
mightiness
mignonette
militarise
militarism
militarist
militarize
militiaman
millennial
millennium
millesimal
millilitre

millimetre
millwright
mimeograph
minatorial
mineralise
mineralize
mineralogy
minestrone
minimalism
miniseries
ministrant
minorities
minstrelsy
minuteness
miraculous
mirthfully
misadvised
misarrange
misbelieve
miscellany
misconduct
misericord
misery-guts
misfortune
misleading
mismeasure
misogamist
misogynist
misprision
missionary
mistakable
mistakenly
mizzen-mast
mnemonical
mock-heroic
moderately
moderation
moderatism
moderniser
modernizer

modernness
modifiable
modishness
modulation
Mohammedan
moisturise
moisturize
molybdenum
monandrous
monarchism
monarchist
monastical
monasticon
monetarism
money talks
mongrelise
mongrelize
moniliform
monitorial
monkey suit
monocarpic
monochrome
monochromy
monoculous
monoecious
monogamist
monogamous
monolithic
monologist
monomaniac
monophobia
monophonic
monoplegia
monopolise
monopolize
monotheism
monotheist
monotonous
monovalent
monsignore

monstrance
monumental
moon-flower
moonshiner
moonstruck
mopishness
moratorium
morbidness
mordacious
morganatic
moroseness
morphinism
morphology
mortifying
mosaically
motherhood
motherland
motherless
motionless
motivation
motor-cycle
motor-mouth
mouldiness
mountebank
mournfully
mousseline
mouth-organ
mouthpiece
movability
mozzarella
mucedinous
muckraking
mucousness
muliebrity
mulishness
multi-level
multimedia
multiplane
multiplier
multivalve

mumblingly
mumbo-jumbo
munificent
Murphy's law
musicology
mutability
mutilation
mutinously
mycologist
myocardium
myrtaceous
mystagogue
mysterious
mythically
mythologic
mythopoeic
myxomycete

**N**

nail polish
namby-pamby
namelessly
name the day
naphthalic
Napoleonic
narcissism
nasturtium
natatorial
nativeness
natterjack
natural gas
naturalise
naturalism
naturalist
naturalize
natural law
nautically
navigation
Neapolitan
nebulosity

necrolatry
necromancy
necropolis
nectareous
needlework
ne'er-do-well
negatively
neglectful
negligence
negligible
negotiable
negotiator
neological
neoplastic
neoterical
nephralgia
nephrology
nephrotomy
nethermost
nettle-rash
networking
neurectomy
neuropathy
neurotonic
neutralise
neutrality
neutralize
never-never
New England
newfangled
news-letter
newsmonger
newsworthy
next door to
nidamental
nidificate
night-dress
night-glass
night-light
nightshade

night-shirt
night-stick
night-watch
nigrescent
nihil ad rem
nihilistic
nimbleness
nincompoop
nineteenth
nit-picking
nitric acid
Nobel prize
noble-woman
no-man's land
nom de plume
nominalism
nominalist
nominately
nomination
nominative
nomography
nomothetic
non-aligned
nonchalant
non-ferrous
non-starter
northerner
northwards
nosography
nosologist
nosy parker
notability
notarially
not cricket
noteworthy
not half bad
noticeable
noticeably
notifiable
not much cop

not one's day
nourishing
noviceship
nubiferous
nuciferous
nucleonics
nudge-nudge
nudibranch
nulla-nulla
numberless
numeration
numerology
numerously
numismatic
nunciature
nurseryman
nurserymen
nutcracker
nutritious
nyctalopia
nympholept

O
obdurately
obediently
object-ball
objectless
objuration
oblateness
obligation
obligatory
obligement
obligingly
obliterate
obsequious
observable
observably
observance
obsidional
obsoletely

obstetrics
obstructor
obtainable
obtainment
obturation
obtuseness
occasional
occultness
occupation
occurrence
oceanarium
ocean-going
ochlocracy
ochraceous
octahedral
octahedron
octandrian
octangular
octodecimo
octogenary
octohedron
odiousness
odontalgic
odontology
oesophagus
officially
officiator
off-licence
off-putting
off-roading
off-the-cuff
off the hook
off-the-wall
oftentimes
Oireachtas
Old Country
Old English
oleaginous
oleraceous
oligarchic

oligoclase
olivaceous
omnifarous
omnigenous
omnipotent
omniscient
omnivorous
omophagous
on all fours
on a par with
oneirology
one's own man
onomastics
on red alert
on the cards
on the house
on the level
on the loose
on the rocks
on the shelf
on the wagon
ontologist
on your bike
oojamaflip
opalescent
open-handed
open letter
open-minded
open secret
open sesame
opera-house
operameter
ophthalmia
ophthalmic
oppositely
opposition
oppression
oppressive
opprobrium
oppugnancy

opsiometer
optatively
optimistic
optionally
oracularly
oratorical
orbiculate
orchestral
orchideous
ordainable
ordainment
ordination
Ordovician
oreography
organogeny
organology
originally
originated
originator
ornamental
ornamenter
orogenesis
orographic
orological
orphanhood
orthoceras
orthoclase
orthodoxly
orthoepist
orthogonal
orthopraxy
oscillancy
oscillator
osculation
osculatory
ossiferous
ossivorous
ostensible
osteoblast
osteocolla

osteologic
osteopathy
osteophyte
otherwhere
other-while
ottava rima
outbalance
outer space
outgeneral
outlandish
out of order
out of sorts
out of touch
out on a limb
out-patient
outpouring
outrageous
out-station
outstretch
out to lunch
ovariotomy
overactive
overbridge
overburden
overcanopy
overcharge
overexpose
overgrowth
overmasted
overmaster
overshadow
overslaugh
overstrain
overstrung
over the top
overturner
overweight
overwisely
ovipositor
oxalic acid

oxidisable
oxidizable
oxygen tent
ozone layer
ozonoscope

**P**

pachymeter
pacifiable
pack animal
packsaddle
paddymelon
paediatric
pagination
paideutics
painkiller
painstaker
Palaeozoic
palatalise
palatalize
palatinate
palimpsest
palindrome
palinodist
pall-bearer
palliation
palliative
pallidness
palmaceous
Palm Sunday
palpitated
paltriness
paludinous
pancratium
pancreatic
pancreatin
panegyrise
panegyrist
panegyrize
pangenesis

paniculate
panjandrum
Pan-Slavism
pantograph
paperknife
paper-money
paper tiger
papistical
papyrology
paraboloid
paradisiac
paralipsis
parallelly
paralogism
paranomasy
paranormal
paraphrase
paraplegia
parapodium
paraselene
parasitise
parasitism
parasitize
paratroops
pardonable
pardonably
parenchyma
parentless
pari-mutuel
Parisienne
parking lot
parliament
Parnassian
paroecious
paronymous
paroxysmal
paroxysmic
paroxytone
parramatta
parrot-fish

partiality
participle
particular
parturient
party piece
pasigraphy
pasquinade
passageway
passionary
passionate
pasteboard
pastellist
pasteurise
pasteurize
pastmaster
patentable
pathfinder
pathologic
patisserie
patriarchy
patriciate
patriotism
patristics
patroniser
patronizer
patronymic
pave the way
pawnbroker
pay court to
Peace Corps
peacefully
peacemaker
peace talks
pearl-diver
peashooter
peccadillo
peculation
peculiarly
pedantical
pedestrian

pediatrics
pediculous
pedophilia
peduncular
peeping Tom
peerlessly
peirameter
pejorative
pellicular
penalty box
pendentive
penetrable
penetrably
penetralia
penetrator
penguinery
penicillin
penmanship
pennyroyal
pennyworth
pensionary
pentachord
pentagonal
pentameter
pentastyle
Pentateuch
pentathlon
pentatonic
peppercorn
peppermill
peppermint
pepperwort
percentage
perception
perceptive
perchloric
percipient
percolator
percurrent
percussion

percussive
percutient
perdurable
perdurably
peremptory
perfection
perfidious
perfoliate
perforator
performing
perihelion
perilously
periodical
periosteal
periosteum
peripheral
periphrase
peripteral
periscopic
perishable
peritoneal
peritoneum
periwinkle
perlaceous
permafrost
permanence
permanency
permeation
permission
permissive
pernicious
pernickety
peroration
perpetrate
perpetuate
perpetuity
perplexing
perplexity
perquisite
perruquier

| | | |
|---|---|---|
| persiennes | phlegmasia | pig-sticker |
| persiflage | phlegmatic | pile-driver |
| persistent | phlogistic | pilgrimage |
| persistive | phlogiston | piliferous |
| personable | phlyctaena | pillow-case |
| personably | Phoenician | pillow-slip |
| personally | phone freak | pill-popper |
| personalty | phonetical | pilot-light |
| personator | phonograph | pincushion |
| perstringe | phonometer | pine-marten |
| persuasion | phosphoric | pinnatifid |
| persuasive | phosphorus | pistillary |
| pertinence | photogenic | pistillate |
| perversion | photograph | pitch-black |
| perversity | photometer | pitchiness |
| perversive | photometry | pitilessly |
| pestilence | photophone | pityriasis |
| Peter-see-me | phrasebook | plagiarise |
| petitioner | phrenology | plagiarism |
| petit point | phylactery | plagiarist |
| petroglyph | phyllotaxy | plagiarize |
| petrolatum | phylloxera | planchette |
| pettichaps | physically | planimeter |
| petulantly | physiocrat | planimetry |
| phagedaena | physiology | planometer |
| phalangeal | phytophagy | plantation |
| phallicism | pianissimo | plasmodium |
| phanerogam | pianoforte | plasmolyse |
| phantasmal | picaresque | plasmolyze |
| pharisaism | piccalilli | plastering |
| pharmacist | pickpocket | plasticity |
| pharyngeal | picric acid | plate-glass |
| pheasantry | pictograph | plate-layer |
| phenacetin | pied-à-terre | platyrhine |
| phenomenal | pierceable | plauditory |
| phenomenon | piercingly | playfellow |
| philistine | piezometer | playground |
| philosophe | pigeonhole | play possum |
| philosophy | pigeon post | playwright |
| phlebotomy | pigeon-toed | pleadingly |

pleasantly
pleasantry
plebiscite
pleonastic
plesiosaur
Plexiglass®
pleximeter
plexometer
ploddingly
ploughable
plough back
plumassier
pluperfect
plutocracy
pneumatics
poachiness
pocket-book
poculiform
poephagous
poetically
poignantly
poinsettia
point-blank
polar angle
poles apart
politeness
politician
pollutedly
polyanthus
polyatomic
polycarpic
polychaete
polychrome
polychromy
polyclinic
polydactyl
polygamist
polygamous
polygenous
polygraphy

polyhedral
polyhedron
polymerise
polymerism
polymerize
polynomial
polyphonic
polyporous
polytheism
polytheist
Pomeranian
pomiferous
pomologist
ponderable
ponderably
pontifical
popularise
popularity
popularize
population
populously
porousness
porphyrite
porraceous
portamento
portcullis
portentous
portliness
Portuguese
positional
positively
positivism
positivist
possession
possessive
possessory
postal card
post-chaise
posthumous
postillion

postliminy
postmaster
post-mortem
post office
postscript
potentiate
potentilla
pour-parler
powerfully
power-house
power plant
pozzuolana
practising
praemunire
praetorium
pragmatics
pragmatism
prairie-dog
pratincole
prayerless
pre-Adamite
prearrange
prebendary
precarious
precaution
precedence
precedency
preceptive
precession
preciously
preclusion
preclusive
precocious
preconcert
precursory
predaceous
predacious
predecease
predestine
predicable

predicably
prediction
predictive
predispose
pre-eminent
pre-emption
pre-emptive
prefecture
preferable
preferably
preference
preferment
pre-glacial
prehensile
prehension
pre-history
prelatical
premarital
premonitor
prepayment
prepossess
prepotency
prep school
presbyopia
presbytery
prescience
presentive
presidency
presignify
pressed for
pressingly
pressurise
pressurize
presumable
presumably
presuppose
pretension
prevailing
prevalence
prevenient

prevention
preventive
priesthood
priestlike
prima donna
prima facie
prime mover
primevally
primordial
princeling
principled
private eye
privileged
prize-fight
proceeding
procession
proclivity
proclivous
procoelian
procreator
proctorial
procumbent
procurable
procurator
prodigious
producible
productile
production
productive
profession
proficient
profitable
profitably
profitless
profligacy
profligate
profundity
progenitor
prognathic
prognostic

projectile
projection
projective
prolocutor
Promethean
prominence
prominency
promissory
promontory
promptness
promulgate
pronominal
pronounced
propagable
propaganda
propagator
propellant
propellent
propensity
properness
proper noun
propertied
propitiate
propitious
proportion
proprietor
propulsion
propulsive
propylaeum
proscenium
proscriber
prosecutor
prospector
prospectus
prosperity
prosperous
prosthesis
prostitute
protection
protective

protectrix
*pro tempore*
Protestant
prothallus
protophyte
protoplasm
protoplast
protracted
protractor
protrusile
protrusion
protrusive
provenance
proverbial
providence
provincial
prudential
psalmodise
psalmodist
psalmodize
pseudocarp
psittacine
psychiatry
psychology
psychopath
pubescence
publicness
publishing
pugilistic
pugnacious
puissantly
pulsimeter
pulsometer
pulveriser
pulverizer
pulvinated
punctually
punishable
punishment
pupilarity

pupiparous
pupivorous
purblindly
Puritanism
purposeful
pursuivant
purulently
purveyance
push-button
putrescent
put to sleep
puzzlement
pycnometer
pyracantha
pyramidion
pyrogenous
pyrometric
pyrophoric
pyrotechny
Pyrrhonism
Pyrrhonist
pythogenic

**Q**

quadrangle
quadrantal
quadratics
quadrature
quadricorn
quadrivial
quadrivium
Quadrumana
quadruplet
quandaries
quarantine
quarriable
quarterage
quartering
quaterfoil
quaternary

quaternion
quaternity
quatrefoil
queasiness
quenchable
quenchless
quercitron
questioner
quid pro quo
quiescence
quintuplet
quixotical
quizmaster

**R**
rabbinical
rabblement
racecourse
radarscope
radicalism
radiograph
radiometer
radiosonde
ragamuffin
rain forest
rain shadow
ramblingly
Ramboesque
ram-raiding
ramshackle
rancidness
rangership
ransomable
ransomless
ranunculus
ratability
rattlewort
ravenously
ravishment
razor-shell

razzmatazz
reactively
readership
reafforest
real estate
realisable
realizable
real number
real tennis
reapproach
reasonable
reasonably
reassemble
rebellious
rebukingly
recallable
receivable
recentness
receptacle
recidivism
recidivist
recipiency
reciprocal
recitation
recitative
recklessly
recommence
recompense
reconciler
reconquest
reconsider
recoupment
recreantly
recreation
recreative
recrudesce
rectorship
recumbency
recuperate
recurrence

recylcable
red admiral
red-blooded
redeemable
redelivery
redemption
red herring
rediscover
redressive
redundance
redundancy
referendum
referrible
refinement
reflecting
reflection
reflective
reflexible
reformable
refracting
refraction
refractive
refractory
refragable
refreshing
refringent
refulgence
refulgency
refutation
refutatory
regalement
regardless
regelation
regeneracy
regenerate
regentship
regimental
registered
regression
regressive

regularise
regularize
regulation
regulative
rejuvenate
relational
relatively
relativity
relaxation
relaxative
releasable
relegation
relentless
relievable
relinquish
relishable
reluctance
reluctancy
remarkable
remarkably
remarriage
remedially
remediless
rememberer
remissible
remissness
remittance
remonetise
remonetize
remorseful
remoteness
remunerate
renascence
renascency
rencounter
renderable
rendezvous
renownedly
reorganise
reorganize

| | | |
|---|---|---|
| repairable | resilience | revengeful |
| reparation | resiliency | reverencer |
| reparative | resistance | reversible |
| repatriate | resolution | reversibly |
| repealable | resonantly | revertible |
| repeatable | resounding | reviewable |
| repeatedly | respectful | revitalise |
| repellence | respecting | revitalize |
| repellency | respective | revivalism |
| repentance | respirable | revivalist |
| repertoire | respirator | revocation |
| repetition | respondent | revolution |
| repetitive | responsive | rewardable |
| repiningly | responsory | rhabdoidal |
| replevisor | restaurant | rhapsodise |
| reportable | rest-harrow | rhapsodist |
| report card | restlessly | rhapsodize |
| reportedly | restorable | rhetorical |
| reposition | restrained | rheumatism |
| repository | restrainer | rheumatoid |
| repression | restricted | rhinestone |
| repressive | resultless | rhinoceros |
| reproacher | resumption | rhinoscope |
| reprobater | resumptive | rhomboidal |
| reproducer | resurgence | riboflavin |
| reprovable | retainable | rickettsia |
| reprovably | retardment | ridiculous |
| republican | reticulate | riding high |
| repudiator | retirement | rift valley |
| repugnance | retractile | right-angle |
| repurchase | retraction | rightfully |
| reputation | retractive | right of way |
| requitable | retrochoir | rigorously |
| reschedule | retrograde | rinderpest |
| rescission | retrospect | ring-finger |
| researcher | retrovirus | ring-leader |
| resentment | returnable | ringmaster |
| reservedly | revanchism | rip-roaring |
| reshipment | revealable | risibility |
| residenter | revelation | rising damp |

river basin
river front
river-horse
roadrunner
robustness
rockabilly
rock-bottom
rock garden
rolling pin
Romanesque
roof garden
rootedness
roquelaure
rosaniline
rose-window
Rotary Club
rotational
rotisserie
rottenness
rough house
rough stuff
rough trade
roundabout
round-house
round robin
rowing-boat
royal flush
royal jelly
rubberneck
rubber tree
rubbishing
Rubenesque
rubiginous
Rubik's cube®
rubricator
ruby orange
rudimental
ruefulness
ruffianish
ruffianism

ruggedness
rumination
rumpy-pumpy
runner bean
runologist
run short of
run the show
run through
run to earth
ruthlessly

# S

sabbatical
sabre-tache
saccharide
saccharify
saccharine
sacerdotal
sacredness
sacrificer
sacrosanct
saddle soap
saddle-tree
safari park
safari suit
safe period
safety belt
safety-lamp
salamander
sales clerk
salineness
salivation
sallenders
sallowness
salmagundi
salmagundy
salmonella
salmon pink
salopettes
saltcellar

salt-shaker
salubrious
salutarily
salutation
salutatory
Samian ware
sanatorium
sanctified
sanctifier
sanctimony
sandalwood
sand-castle
sanderling
sand-martin
sanguinary
sanguinely
sanitarian
sanitarium
sanitation
Santa Claus
sapphirine
saprogenic
saprophyte
sarcolemma
sarcophagi
sash-weight
sash-window
satisfying
saturation
saturnalia
satyagraha
satyriasis
sauerkraut
Sauropsida
savageness
save the day
savourless
saxicavous
saxicoline
saxicolous

say the word
scabbiness
scandalise
scandalize
scandalous
scantiness
scapegrace
scarabaeid
scaramouch
scarceness
scarlatina
scatheless
scattering
scepticise
scepticism
scepticize
schematise
schematize
schemingly
scherzando
schismatic
schizocarp
scholastic
schoolgirl
schoolmate
schoolroom
sciagraphy
scientific
sciography
sciolistic
scirrosity
scoffingly
scoreboard
scornfully
scorzonera
Scotch mist
Scotch tape®
scotograph
Scotticism
scowlingly

scrambling
scratch-pad
screenings
screenplay
scrimpness
scrimshank
scriptural
scrofulous
scrupulous
scrutineer
scrutinise
scrutinize
scrutinous
scullionly
sculptress
sculptural
sculptured
scurrility
scurrilous
scurviness
sea-anemone
sealed-beam
sealing-wax
seamanship
seamstress
searchable
searchless
searedness
sea-serpent
seasonable
seasonably
seasonless
sebiferous
seborrhoea
second-best
second-hand
second-rate
second wind
secretaire
secretness

secularise
secularist
secularize
secureness
sedateness
seducement
sedulously
seed-oyster
seed-potato
seed-vessel
seemliness
see one's way
seersucker
see-through
seguidilla
seismology
selectness
self-acting
self-denial
self-esteem
self-regard
self-rising
self-styled
sell-by date
semeiology
semeiotics
semiannual
semicircle
semiquaver
semiyearly
sempstress
senatorial
sense-organ
sensualise
sensualist
sensualize
separately
separation
separatism
separatist

septennial
septicidal
septic tank
septillion
Septuagint
sepulchral
sequacious
sequential
Serbo-Croat
sereneness
serio-comic
serpentine
serviceman
servomotor
sestertius
set the pace
settlement
seventieth
sewage farm
sexagenary
Sexagesima
sex hormone
sextillion
shadowless
shagginess
shamefaced
shampooing
shandygaff
shanty-town
shearwater
sheep's eyes
sheepshank
sheet-glass
sheet-metal
sheet music
shell-proof
shell-shock
shenanigan
shibboleth
shieldless

shillelagh
shipmaster
shipwright
shirt-dress
shirtwaist
shish kebab
shockingly
shock-proof
shoemaking
shoe-string
shoot a line
shopaholic
shopkeeper
shoplifter
shop-soiled
shop-walker
shortbread
shortening
short-lived
short-range
shovel-head
shrewdness
shrewishly
shrievalty
shrillness
shrink-wrap
Shrovetide
shuddering
shut up shop
sialogogue
Siamese cat
sibilatory
sick as a dog
sickliness
sick-making
side by side
side effect
side glance
siderostat
sidesaddle

side-stroke
sidewinder
Sigillaria
signet ring
silentness
silhouette
silk-cotton
silk-screen
silver-gilt
silver-side
silverware
silver-weed
similarity
similitude
simnel-cake
simoniacal
simplicity
simplistic
simulacrum
simulation
simulatory
sinecurist
*sine qua non*
sinfulness
Singhalese
single file
singles bar
singularly
sinisterly
sinistrous
sinologist
sinsemilla
sisterhood
sisterless
six-shooter
sixth sense
skateboard
skin-diving
skittishly
skulkingly

skyscraper
sky-writing
slack water
slanderous
slantingly
Slave State
slave-trade
sleep rough
sleepy-head
sleetiness
sleeveless
slightness
slipperily
slip-stitch
slipstream
slit-trench
sloppiness
slothfully
slow-motion
sluggishly
slumberous
sluttishly
small hours
small print
small-scale
smart-aleck
smart-money
smattering
smoke alarm
smokestack
smoothbore
smuttiness
snail-paced
snail's pace
snake-stone
snapdragon
snappishly
sneakingly
sneeringly
sniffer dog

snivelling
snobbishly
snowblower
snowmobile
snow-plough
snuff movie
snuff video
social work
sociologic
sociometry
Socratical
soda siphon
soft-boiled
soft-headed
soft option
soft palate
solacement
solar flare
solar month
solar panel
solar power
soldiering
solecistic
solemniser
solemnizer
solicitant
solicitous
solicitude
solidarity
solid state
solitarily
solstitial
solubility
somatology
somatotype
sombreness
somersault
somewheres
somnolence
sonorously

soothingly
soothsayer
sordidness
sororicide
soubriquet
soundboard
sound-proof
sound-track
sour grapes
southerner
spacecraft
space probe
spaciously
spadiceous
Spanish-fly
sparseness
specialise
specialism
specialist
speciality
specialize
speciation
speciously
spectacled
spectrally
speculator
speechless
speleology
spellbound
spermaceti
spermicide
sperm whale
sphalerite
sphenogram
sphenoidal
sphericity
spheroidal
spider-crab
spiderwort
spinal cord

spin doctor
spinescent
spirit away
spiritedly
spiritless
spirituous
spirograph
spirometer
spissitude
splanchnic
splashdown
spleen-wort
splendidly
splenology
split hairs
split-level
split shift
spoilsport
spokeshave
spoliation
spondaical
sponge-cake
sponginess
sponsorial
spoonerism
sporangium
sportscast
spotlessly
spring roll
springtail
spring tide
springtime
sprinkling
spruceness
spumescent
spuriously
squadroned
squalidity
square deal
square meal

squareness
square root
square up to
squeezable
squeeze-box
squirehood
squireship
stabiliser
stabilizer
stableness
stag-beetle
stage-coach
stage-craft
stage right
staggering
stagnantly
stagnation
stalactite
stalagmite
staminated
stamineous
stammering
stand in for
stand-point
standstill
stand up for
staphyloma
starriness
starry-eyed
start a hare
starvation
starveling
statecraft
statehouse
statically
stationary
stationery
statistics
statoscope
statuesque

statutable
statutably
Statute Law
staurolite
stay-at-home
steadiness
steakhouse
stealthily
steaminess
stelliform
stenciller
stenograph
stentorian
step by step
stepfather
step-ladder
stepmother
step-parent
stepsister
stercorate
stereotype
steriliser
sterilizer
stertorous
stewardess
stickiness
stick up for
stiffening
stigmatise
stigmatist
stigmatize
stipulator
stirrup cup
stochastic
stock-still
stolidness
stomatitis
stony-broke
stoopingly
storehouse

storksbill
storm-bound
storyboard
strabismus
strabotomy
straighten
stramonium
strategist
strathspey
stratified
stratiform
strawberry
streamline
street cred
streetwise
strengthen
strepitoso
strictness
stridulate
stridulous
stringency
striptease
stroganoff
stroke play
stronghold
strongroom
strong suit
structural
structured
struthious
strychnine
stubbornly
studiously
stuffiness
stultifier
stupendous
stupidness
sturdiness
subaquatic
subaqueous

subclavian
subculture
subduction
subheading
subjection
subjective
subjoinder
subjugator
subkingdom
sublimable
subliminal
sublingual
submersion
submission
submissive
subprefect
subroutine
subscriber
subsection
subsequent
subsidence
subsidiary
subsistent
subspecies
substitute
substratum
subtangent
subterfuge
subtleness
subtleties
subtracter
subtrahend
subvention
subversion
subversive
succedanea
succeeding
successful
succession
successive

succinctly
succulence
succulency
succussion
successive
such as it is
sudatorium
suddenness
sufferable
sufferably
sufferance
sufficient
suffragist
sugar-daddy
sugariness
suggestion
suggestive
suicidally
sui generis
sullenness
sulphurate
sultanship
sultriness
Sunday best
sunglasses
sunsetting
supercargo
supergiant
supergrass
superhuman
superlunar
superpower
supersonic
superstore
supertonic
supervisal
supervisor
supination
supperless
supplanter

supplement
suppleness
suppletory
suppliance
supplicate
supposable
supposedly
suppressor
suprarenal
sure enough
sure-footed
suretyship
surface-man
surf the net
surgically
surpassing
surplusage
surprising
surrealism
susceptive
suscipient
suspension
suspensive
suspensory
suspicious
sustenance
suzerainty
swaggering
swan around
sweat blood
sweatiness
sweatshirt
sweepingly
sweepstake
sweetbread
sweet-brier
sweetening
sweetheart
sweet tooth
sweltering

swimmingly
swine-fever
Swiss chard
switchback
Switch card
sword dance
swordstick
sybaritism
sycophancy
syllabical
symbolical
symmetrise
symmetrize
sympathise
sympathize
syncarpous
synchronal
syncretism
synecdoche
syngenetic
synonymist
synonymous
synthesise
synthesize
syphilitic
systematic
systemless

**T**
tabernacle
table-cloth
table d'hote
tablespoon
tabula rasa
tabularise
tabularize
tabulation
tachograph
tachometer
tachymeter

taciturnly
tactically
tailor-made
take as read
take ill out
take in hand
take it easy
taken aback
take the air
take the rap
take to task
take up arms
take up with
talent show
talismanic
talk down to
talk turkey
Talmudical
tambourine
tangential
tank engine
tannic acid
tantamount
tape player
tarantella
tardigrade
tartareous
taskmaster
tastefully
tattletale
tauntingly
tauromachy
tautologic
tawdriness
taxability
tax evasion
taxidermic
tax shelter
T-bone steak
team spirit

tear-jerker
tea-service
tea-tree oil
technetium
technician
technology
telegraphy
teleologic
teleostean
telepathic
telescopic
television
tellership
telpherage
temperable
temperance
temporiser
temporizer
temptation
temptingly
tenability
tenantable
tenantless
tenderfoot
tenderloin
tenderness
tendrilled
tenebrific
tenemental
tensimeter
tentacular
tenterhook
teratology
terracotta
terra firma
tessellate
testicular
tetchiness
tetrachord
tetragonal

tetrameter
tetrastich
tetrastyle
textualist
thankfully
theatrical
themselves
theocratic
theodicean
theodolite
theogonist
theologian
theologise
theologize
theophanic
theoretics
theosopher
theosophic
thereabout
thereafter
thereunder
theriotomy
thermionic
thermistor
thermostat
thermotics
the thing is
the three Rs
the year dot
thickening
thievishly
thimbleful
thinkingly
think twice
third-class
third party
Third World
thirteenth
thoroughly
thoughtful

thousandth
threadbare
threadworm
threatener
three-pence
threepenny
threescore
thriftless
thrift shop
thrivingly
thrombosis
throneless
throughout
throughput
throughway
thumb a lift
thumb index
thumbscrew
thumbs down
thundering
thunderous
ticker-tape
ticking off
ticklishly
tie-breaker
tie in knots
tiger shark
tiger snake
timber line
timber-wolf
time-keeper
timeliness
time-server
timorously
tinctorial
Tinseltown
tip the wink
tiresomely
titularity
to cap it all

tocopherol
toe the line
toilsomely
tolerantly
toleration
tomfoolery
tomography
tongue-lash
tongueless
tongue-tied
tonic sol-fa
to one's cost
to one's name
toothbrush
toothpaste
top-gallant
topography
topsy-turvy
top the bill
tormenting
torpidness
torrential
torrentine
torridness
tortellini
tortuously
torturable
touch and go
touchiness
touchingly
touch judge
touchpaper
touchstone
tourmaline
tournament
tourniquet
tower block
townhouse
toxicology
trabecular

tracheitis
track event
Tractarian
trade cycle
tradesfolk
trade union
trafficker
tragacanth
tragically
traitorous
trajectory
trammelled
trammeller
tramontane
trampoline
tranquilly
transactor
transcribe
transcript
transducer
transferee
transgress
transience
transiency
transistor
transition
transitive
transitory
translator
translucid
translunar
transplant
transposal
transposer
transputer
transverse
trashiness
traumatism
travailing
travelling

travelogue
travertine
tread water
tread-wheel
treasuries
treble clef
tremendous
trench-coat
trench-foot
trepanning
trespasser
triangular
tricennial
trichiasis
trichology
trichotomy
trickiness
triclinium
tricostate
tridentate
tridentine
trifarious
triflingly
trifoliate
trifurcate
trigeminal
trigrammic
trilateral
trilingual
triliteral
trilocular
trimestral
trimmingly
trimorphic
trinervate
trinoctial
tripartite
triphthong
tripinnate
triple jump

triplicate
trippingly
triradiate
trisection
triskelion
trisulcate
triternate
triturable
triumphant
triviality
trochanter
troglodyte
trolley bus
trolley-car
tropaeolum
tropically
tropopause
troubadour
trousering
troy weight
truculence
truculency
trunnioned
trustfully
trustiness
trustingly
truthfully
tryptophan
tsarevitch
tubercular
tuberculin
tuberosity
tub-thumper
tubuliform
tuitionary
tumbledown
tumblerful
tumbleweed
tumultuary
tumultuous

tungstenic
tuning-fork
turbidness
turbulence
turbulency
turgescent
turgidness
turkey-cock
turn turtle
turpentine
turtle-dove
turtle-neck
Twelfth Day
twelfth man
twelve-tone
twittering
twittingly
two of a kind
tympanites
tympanitic
tympanitis
typescript
typewriter
typography
tyrannical

**U**

ubiquitous
ulceration
ulnar nerve
ultimately
ultrafiche
ultra-short
ultrasonic
ultrasound
ultravirus
ultroneous
umbellifer
umbilicate
umbrageous

unaffected
unAmerican
unaspiring
unassisted
unassuming
unattached
unattended
unattested
unavailing
unbalanced
unbearable
unbeatable
unbecoming
unbeliever
unblushing
unbuttoned
unchanging
unchastity
unclerical
uncoloured
uncommonly
unconfined
uncritical
unctuosity
undecaying
undefended
undeniable
undeniably
underbelly
underbrace
underbrush
underclass
undercover
underdrain
underlying
underneath
underpants
underproof
underscore
undersexed

undershirt
undershoot
undershrub
undersized
underskirt
underslung
understand
understate
understudy
undertaker
undervalue
underwater
underwhelm
underworld
underwrite
undeterred
undismayed
undisposed
undisputed
undulating
undulation
undulatory
uneasiness
uneconomic
unedifying
uneducated
unemployed
unenclosed
unenviable
unequalled
unerringly
unevenness
uneventful
unexamined
unexampled
unexecuted
unexpected
unexplored
unfairness
unfaithful

unfamiliar
unfathered
unfatherly
unfeminine
unfettered
unfinished
unflagging
unforeseen
unforgiven
ungenerous
ungoverned
ungraceful
ungracious
ungrateful
ungrounded
ungrudging
unhallowed
unhampered
unhandsome
unhistoric
unholiness
unhonoured
unicameral
unicostate
uniflorous
uniformity
unilateral
unilocular
unimagined
unimpaired
unimposing
unimproved
uninclosed
uninspired
uninviting
unisonance
university
univocally
unkindness
unlamented

unleavened
unlettered
unlicensed
unmannerly
unmeasured
unmerciful
unmolested
unmotherly
unnameable
unnumbered
unoccupied
unofficial
unpleasant
unpleasing
unpoetical
unpolished
unpolluted
unprepared
unprovided
unprovoked
unpunctual
unpunished
unreadable
unrecorded
unredeemed
unreformed
unregarded
unreliable
unrelieved
unrepealed
unrepented
unrequited
unreserved
unresisted
unresolved
unrestored
unrevenged
unrewarded
unrivalled
unromantic

unruliness
unsaleable
unschooled
unscramble
unseasoned
unseconded
unsisterly
unsmirched
unsociable
unsociably
unsteadily
unstrained
unsuitable
unsuitably
unswerving
untameable
untempered
untenanted
unthankful
unthinking
untidiness
untillable
untowardly
untroubled
untruthful
unwariness
unwavering
unwearable
unwieldily
unwontedly
unworthily
unyielding
up a gum-tree
up and about
up and doing
upbraiding
upbringing
up for grabs
upholstery
up in the air

upper class
upper crust
upper house
uppishness
uproarious
upside-down
upstanding
up the creek
up the spout
up to a point
up to no good
urethritis
urinalysis
urinoscopy
urogenital
urtication
usefulness
usurpation
utriculate
uxoriously

**V**

vacationer
vagus nerve
valorously
valvulitis
vampire bat
vanity case
vanquished
vanquisher
varicocele
varicosity
variegated
variolitic
Vaticanism
vaticinate
vaudeville
vauntingly
vegeburger
vegetality

vegetarian
vegetation
vegetative
vehemently
vehiculary
velocipede
velocities
velutinous
veneration
vengefully
venialness
venomously
ventilator
ventricose
ventricous
verifiable
verifiably
vermicelli
vermicular
vermillion
vernacular
versicolor
vertebrata
vertebrate
vertically
vesication
vesicatory
vesiculate
vesiculose
vesiculous
vespertine
vestibular
veterinary
vibraculum
vibraphone
vice-consul
vicegerent
Vichy water
victorious
victualler

video nasty
view-finder
vigilantly
vigorously
villainous
villanella
villanelle
villeinage
vinaigrous
vindicator
vindictive
viniferous
violaceous
virescence
virtueless
virtuously
virulently
viscometer
viscountcy
visibility
visitation
vitrescent
vitriolate
vitriolise
vitriolize
vituperate
vivandière
viviparity
viviparous
vivisector
vocabulary
vocational
vociferant
vociferate
vociferous
volatilise
volatility
volatilize
volitional
volley-ball

voltameter
volubility
volumetric
voluminous
voluptuary
voluptuous
vomitories
vorticella
vowel-point
voyageable
vulnerable

**W**

waffle-iron
wage earner
wainwright
walk of life
walky-talky
wallflower
Wall Street
wall to wall
wanderlust
wapinschaw
wardenship
warming pan
wastefully
waste paper
watched pot
watchfully
watchmaker
watch-night
watch-tower
water-borne
water-clock
water craft
water-cress
waterfront
water-glass
wateriness
water-level

water-melon
water-power
waterproof
water-spout
water-table
watertight
water-tower
water-wheel
water-wings
water-works
wavelength
waveringly
weak-minded
weather-eye
weathering
weatherman
weather-map
weaver-bird
weed-killer
well-heeled
wellington
well-spoken
well-wisher
Welsh corgi
Wendy house®
westernise
westernize
westwardly
wet blanket
wharfinger
whatsoever
wheel-chair
wheel clamp
wheelie bin
whensoever
whereabout
whispering
whistle for
white dwarf
white goods

White House
white light
white metal
white noise
white paper
white sauce
white slave
white water
white whale
Whit-Sunday
whizzingly
whole-wheat
whorehouse
wickedness
widespread
widow's peak
wildebeest
wilderedly
wilderment
wilderness
wilfulness
willow-herb
willy-nilly
wind-jammer
windowpane
windowsill
windscreen
windshield
wind-tunnel
wine-cellar
wine-cooler
wine-grower
wing-collar
wingspread
wire-haired
wishy-washy

witchcraft
witch hazel
withdrawal
withholder
witness box
woefulness
wolframite
womanishly
wonderland
wonderment
wondrously
wood-cutter
wooden-head
woodpecker
wood-pigeon
woolly-bear
workaholic
working-day
work to rule
world-class
world music
world power
World War II
world-weary
worry beads
worryingly
worshipful
worshipper
worthiness
worthwhile
wrathfully
wretchedly
wrist-watch
writership
wrongfully
wunderkind

**X**
xanthopsia
xenophobia
xerodermia
xerography
xerostomia
xylography
xylotomous

**Y**
yackety-yak
yard-master
yawnsville
yearningly
yeastiness
yellow spot
yellowwood
yestereven
yestermorn
Yggdrasill
ylang-ylang
yourselves
youthfully

**Z**
zabaglione
Zend-Avesta
zero option
Zimbabwean
zincograph
*Zollverein*
zoomorphic
zoophagous
zootomical
zygodactyl

# Eleven-letter words

**A**
Aaron's beard
abandonment
abbreviator
abecedarian
abhorrently
abiogenesis
ablactation
abnormality
abolishable
abomination
abortionist
above-ground
abracadabra
abranchiate
abridgement
absentation
absenteeism
absolvatory
abstinently
abstraction
abstractive
abusiveness
academician
acarpellous
acatalectic
acaulescent
accelerando
accelerator
acceptation
accessional
accessorial
accessorily
accipitrine

acclamation
acclamatory
acclimatise
acclimatize
accommodate
accompanier
accompanist
accordantly
accordingly
accoucheuse
accountable
accountably
accountancy
account book
accumulator
acetanilide
achievement
achromatise
achromatize
acidifiable
acinaciform
acknowledge
aclinic line
acoustician
acquiescent
acquirement
acquisition
acquisitive
acquittance
acrimonious
acrocarpous
acrylic acid
actinometer
acumination

acupressure
acupuncture
acute accent
Adam's-needle
addle-headed
adiaphorous
adiathermic
ad infinitum
adjectively
adjournment
adjudicator
adminicular
admiralship
adolescence
adolescency
adumbration
adumbrative
advancement
adventuress
adventurous
adverbially
adversarial
adversative
adverseness
advertently
advertising
advertizing
advertorial
advisedness
Aeolian harp
aerological
aeronautics
aerostatics
aerostation

Aesculapian
aesthetical
aestivation
a far cry from
affectation
affectingly
affectioned
affiliation
affirmation
affirmative
affranchise
afterburner
after-effect
agatiferous
agglomerate
agglutinant
agglutinate
aggrandiser
aggrandizer
aggravating
aggravation
aggregately
aggregation
agnosticism
agnus castus
agonizingly
agony column
agoraphobia
agrarianism
agriculture
agrostology
*aguardiente*
ahead of time
aide-memoire
aiguillette
ailurophobe
aimlessness
albuminuria
alchemistic
alexandrian

alexandrine
alkalescent
alkalimeter
alkalimetry
all-American
allegorical
alleviation
alleviative
All Fools' Day
allineation
all of a piece
allopathist
allophylian
allotropism
All Souls' Day
all that jazz
alphabetise
alphabetize
altar-screen
altercation
alternately
alternation
alternative
alto-relievo
alto-rilievo
amalgamator
amaranthine
amativeness
Amazon stone
ambiguously
ambitiously
ambrosially
amelanchier
ameliorator
amenorrhoea
amentaceous
Amer-English
Americanise
Americanism
Americanize

amethystine
amiableness
amici curiae
amontillado
amorousness
*amor patriae*
*amour propre*
amphetaminc
amphibology
amphisbaena
amplexicaul
amyl nitrite
anacanthous
anachronism
anacoluthia
anacoluthon
anacreontic
anadiplosis
anaesthesia
anaesthetic
anagnorisis
analogously
anaphylaxis
anaplerotic
anastomosis
anastomotic
anchoritess
anchor-stock
anchor-watch
anchovy pear
ancientness
androgenous
androgynous
androsphinx
anecdotical
anemography
anemophilus
anfractuous
angelically
angelolatry

angelophany
angiography
angioplasty
Anglicanism
Anglo-French
Anglo-Indian
Anglo-Norman
Anglophobia
animalcular
animalculum
animatingly
annihilable
annihilator
anniversary
annunciator
anomalistic
anonymously
antecedence
antechamber
antemundane
antenuptial
antepaschal
antependium
anteriority
anthologise
anthologize
anthracitic
antibilious
anticyclone
antifebrile
anti-federal
antinuclear
antioxidant
antiphonary
antiphrasis
antipyretic
antiquarian
antiqueness
antirrhinum
antispastic

antistrophe
antitypical
antonomasia
anxiousness
anything but
aphrodisiac
apocalyptic
apologetics
aponeurosis
apopetalous
aposiopesis
a posteriori
apostleship
apostrophic
apotheosise
apotheosize
appallingly
appellation
appellative
apple blight
apple-brandy
apple-pie bed
application
applicative
applicatory
appointment
apportioner
appreciable
appreciably
apprehender
approbation
appropriate
approvingly
approximate
appurtenant
aquaculture
aquiculture
arbitrament
arbitrarily
arbitration

arboraceous
arborescent
archaeology
archangelic
archdiocese
archduchess
archegonium
Archimedean
archipelago
arduousness
aristocracy
armed forces
Arminianism
armour plate
arraignment
arrangement
arrow-headed
arsenic acid
arterialise
arterialize
arteriotomy
articulator
artillerist
artiodactyl
artlessness
artsy-fartsy
ascensional
ascertainer
ascititious
aspergillus
aspersorium
asportation
assassinate
assemblyman
assentation
assentingly
assertively
assessorial
assiduously
assignation

association
associative
assuagement
assuredness
Assyriology
astigmatism
astonishing
astringency
at a discount
at a loose end
at face value
athermanous
athleticism
atmidometer
atmospheric
atomisation
atomization
atrabilious
atrociously
attaché case
attemptable
attentively
attenuation
attestation
at the double
attitudinal
attractable
attribution
attributive
*au contraire*
audaciously
audibleness
audiotypist
audiovisual
auditorship
auricularly
auscultator
austereness
autoerotism
autogenesis

autographic
avoirdupois
awestricken
awkwardness

**B**

bacchanalia
bacciferous
baccivorous
bacilliform
back-bencher
back-draught
bactericide
badderlocks
bag of nerves
bag of tricks
baker's dozen
bald as a coot
balefulness
ball-bearing
balletomane
balloon sail
banana split
bandy-legged
bank account
bank holiday
barbarously
barbiturate
barefacedly
barge-couple
barge-course
barley sugar
barley water
barn swallow
barquantine
barquentine
barrel-organ
barrier-reef
bar sinister
barycentric

bashfulness
bashi-bazouk
basset hound
bastard-wing
bathyscaphe
bathysphere
battle-field
battle-royal
beach-comber
beam compass
bear-baiting
bearing-rein
bear's-breech
bear's-grease
beastliness
beat the band
beat the drum
beauteously
beautifully
beauty salon
beauty sleep
bedizenment
bed of thorns
beguilement
believingly
bell-founder
belligerent
bellows-fish
bellybutton
below stairs
Benedictine
benediction
benedictive
benefaction
beneficence
beneficiary
benevolence
Bengal light
benignantly
bereavement

bergschrund
beseemingly
beta-blocker
bewitchment
beyond a joke
biauricular
bibliolater
bibliolatry
bibliomancy
bibliomania
bibliophile
bibliotheca
bicarbonate
bicentenary
bicephalous
bifurcation
big business
biliousness
bill-sticker
bimetallism
bimetallist
binucleated
biodynamics
biofeedback
biogenesist
bipartition
biquadratic
birdwatcher
bishop's-weed
bite the dust
bittersweet
bituminated
black-beetle
black bryony
black comedy
black-letter
black market
black Monday
bladder-fern
bladder-wort

blamelessly
blameworthy
blank cheque
blasphemous
blaze a trail
bleach-field
blepharitis
blessedness
blind as a bat
blind-storey
block-buster
block-letter
block-system
blood-bought
blood-guilty
bloodlessly
bloodstream
blood-sucker
blood-vessel
blow one's top
blow the gaff
blue-coat boy
blue-eyed boy
blunderbuss
board-school
body politic
body popping
body-servant
Bohemianism
bolting mill
bolt upright
bombardment
bonapartist
bonnet rouge
book-binding
bookishness
book-keeping
book-learned
book of words
book-selling

boorishness
booster shot
boracic acid
borborygmus
botanically
botheration
bottle-brush
bottle-glass
bottle-green
bottle-nosed
boulder-clay
bounden duty
boundlessly
bounteously
bountifully
bourgeoisie
boutonniere
boxer shorts
boxing glove
boxing match
boysenberry
brabblement
brace and bit
brachiopoda
braggadocio
brain teaser
branchiopod
brazen-faced
bread basket
breadthways
breadthwise
bread-winner
break the ice
breast-plate
breast-wheel
breech birth
breech-block
breeze-block
bricklaying
bridge-board

brilliantly
brine-shrimp
bring home to
bring to book
bring to heel
brise-soleil
bristliness
brittleness
Broad Church
broad-minded
bronchocele
bronchotomy
bronze steel
brotherhood
brotherless
brucellosis
brush turkey
brusqueness
brutishness
bucket-wheel
buffalo-robe
buffer state
Buggins' turn
build on sand
built-up area
bulbiferous
bulk carrier
bull-baiting
Bulldog clip®
bullet-proof
bull-fighter
bull-terrier
bums on seats
bureaucracy
burgess-ship
burglarious
burgomaster
burnt-sienna
bushwhacker
business end

businessman
businessmen
busybodyism
butcher-bird
butter-knife
butter-print
butter-stamp
butyraceous
butyric acid
bye-election
byssiferous

**C**
cabbage-moth
cabbage-palm
cabbage-rose
cabbage-tree
cabbage-worm
cabbalistic
cable-stitch
cacogastric
cacophonous
cakes and ale
Calabar bean
calceolaria
calciferous
calcination
calculating
calculation
calculative
calefacient
calefaction
calefactory
calibration
californium
calligraphy
calling-crab
calling-hare
call it quits
callousness

call the tune
calorimeter
calorimetry
calumniator
Calvinistic
camaraderie
camel's-thorn
camera-ready
campanology
campanulate
camphor tree
camp-meeting
Canada goose
canary-grass
cancellated
canceration
candelabrum
candescence
candidature
candleberry
candlelight
candle-power
candlestick
cannibalise
cannibalism
cannibalize
canonically
cantharides
cantharidin
capaciously
capacitance
capillament
capillarity
capilliform
capital gain
capitulator
capriccioso
captainship
captivating
caravansary

carbon-paper
Carborundum®
carbuncular
carburetted
carburettor
carcinology
cardinalate
cardiograph
card-sharper
career woman
carefulness
caressingly
carminative
carnationed
carnivorous
Carolingian
carriage dog
carriageway
carrick bend
carrick bitt
carrier wave
carrion crow
carry the can
carry the day
carry weight
cartography
carunculate
carvel-built
case history
cash machine
cassiterite
castellated
castigation
castigatory
Castile soap
casting vote
catacaustic
catachresis
cataclysmal
cataclysmic

catadromous
cataphonics
catastrophe
catch-phrase
catch the sun
catchweight
catechetics
categorical
cater-cousin
caterpillar
cathedratic
catheterise
catheterize
cathode rays
catholicise
Catholicism
catholicity
catholicize
catoptrical
cat's whisker
caught short
cauliflower
causatively
causativity
causelessly
caustically
caustic soda
caveat actor
cave-dweller
cavernulous
cavo-rilievo
ceaselessly
celebration
celestially
celliferous
cementation
centenarian
centigramme
central bank
centre-board

centre-piece
centrically
centrifugal
centripetal
centrobaric
cephalalgic
cephalaspis
cephalotomy
cerebralism
cerebration
cerebriform
ceremonious
ceroplastic
certainness
certificate
chafing-dish
chain-bridge
chain-stitch
chalcedonic
chalcedonyx
chamberlain
chambermaid
championess
chancellery
chancellory
changefully
change hands
chanterelle
chanticleer
chaos theory
chaotically
chaperonage
charlatanic
charlatanry
chartaceous
chastisable
check-string
cheek by jowl
cheer-leader
cheerlessly

cheese-cloth
cheese-press
*chef-d'oeuvre*
chemin de fer
chequer-work
cherry-stone
chess-player
cheval-glass
chiaroscuro
chicken-feed
chicken-wire
chieftaincy
chieftainry
chiffonnier
child labour
chinoiserie
Chippendale
chirography
chiromancer
chiromantic
chiropodist
chirurgical
chitterling
chloric acid
chlorometer
chlorophyll
chock-a-block
choirmaster
choir-screen
cholesterin
cholesterol
chondrology
choreograph
chorography
chrismatory
Christendom
christening
Christianly
Christology
chromatrope

chrome-green
chronograph
chronologer
chronologic
chronometer
chronometry
chronoscope
chrysoberyl
chrysocolla
chrysoprase
church-court
church-going
churchwoman
churchwomen
cicatricule
cineraceous
cineritious
cinnabarine
cinquecento
Cinque Ports
circularise
circularity
circularize
circular saw
circulating
circulation
circulative
circulatory
circumpolar
circumspect
circumvolve
citizenship
city fathers
city slicker
civil rights
Civvy Street
clairvoyant
clamorously
clandestine
class-fellow

classically
clean-handed
clean-limbed
cleanliness
clear-headed
clear-starch
clear the air
cleft palate
cleistogamy
cleptomania
clericalism
clever-clogs
cliff-hanger
climacteric
climatology
clinometric
close at hand
close-fisted
close-handed
close-hauled
close season
close to home
clothes-line
clothes-moth
cloud-capped
clover-grass
coach office
coagulation
coagulative
coalescence
coal-measure
coal-whipper
cobblestone
cochin-china
cock-a-leekie
cock-and-bull
cockle-shell
cocoa butter
coconut palm
codicillary

cod-liver oil
coeducation
coefficient
coessential
coeternally
coexistence
coextensive
coffee-berry
coffee-house
coffee table
cognoscente
cognoscible
coincidence
cold-blooded
cold comfort
cold-hearted
cold-storage
coleopteran
collaborate
collapsable
collapsible
collectable
collectanea
collectedly
collectible
colligative
collimation
collocation
collusively
colonialism
colonialist
colorimeter
colour-blind
columbarium
columnarity
combination
combustible
come in handy
comet-finder
come to grief

come to light
come unstuck
comeuppance
comfortable
comfortably
comfortless
comic relief
commandment
*comme il faut*
commemorate
commendable
commendably
commendator
commendment
commentator
commination
comminatory
comminution
commiserate
commissural
commonality
common chord
commonplace
common sense
common touch
communalise
communalism
communalist
communalize
communicant
communicate
communistic
commutation
commutative
compact disc
compact disk
compactness
comparative
compartment
compassable

compass-card
compellable
compendious
compensator
competently
competition
competitive
compilation
complacence
complacency
complainant
complaisant
compliantly
complicated
comportment
compositely
composition
compossible
compound eye
compression
compressive
compressure
compromised
compromiser
comptroller
compunction
compurgator
computation
computerate
computerise
computerize
comradeship
concatenate
concealable
concealment
conceitedly
conceivable
conceivably
concentrate
conceptacle

concernment
conciliable
conciliator
conciseness
concomitant
concordance
concubinage
concubinary
concurrence
condemnable
condensable
conditional
conditioned
conditioner
condolatory
condolement
condominium
condonation
condottiere
condottieri
conductance
conductible
conductress
confabulate
confederacy
confederate
conferrable
confessedly
confidently
confidingly
confinement
confirmable
confiscable
confiscator
conflagrate
conflicting
confliction
conformable
conformably
conformance

confutation
congealable
congelation
Congressman
congruously
conirostral
conjectural
conjugality
conjugation
conjunction
conjunctiva
conjunctive
conjuncture
conjuration
connectedly
connoisseur
connotation
connotative
connubially
conquerable
consanguine
consciously
consecrator
consecution
consecutive
consentient
consequence
conservable
conservancy
conservator
considerate
considering
consignment
consilience
consistence
consistency
consolation
consolatory
consolidant
consolidate

consonantal
consortship
conspicuous
conspirator
constellate
consternate
constituent
constituter
constrained
constrainer
constricted
constrictor
constructer
constructor
consumately
consumerism
consumption
consumptive
contact lens
containable
containment
contaminate
contemplate
contentedly
contentious
contestable
continental
continently
contingence
contingency
continuable
continually
continuance
continuator
continuedly
contour line
contrabasso
contractile
contraction
contractive

contractual
contra-dance
contraption
contrariant
contrariety
contrarious
contra-tenor
contravener
contrayerva
contredanse
contretemps
contributor
contrivable
contrivance
controlment
controversy
conurbation
convenience
conveniency
conventicle
convergence
conversable
conversably
convertible
convertibly
conveyancer
convincible
convivially
convocation
convolution
convolvulus
convulsible
cookery book
cool tankard
cooperation
cooperative
coparcenary
copiousness
copperplate
coppersmith

coprophilia
coquilla nut
coralliform
coram populo
corbel-table
cornerstone
corniculate
cornigerous
corporality
corporately
corporation
corporeally
corpulently
corpuscular
correctable
correctness
correlation
correlative
corrigendum
corroborant
corroborate
corrosively
corrugation
corruptible
corruptibly
corruptless
corruptness
coruscation
cosignatory
cosmogonist
cosmography
cosmologist
cosmopolite
cost a packet
costiveness
coterminous
cotoneaster
cotton candy
cotton-grass
cotton-plant

cotton-press
cotyledonal
couch potato
counselling
countenance
counterfeit
counterfoil
counterfort
countermand
countermark
countermine
countermove
counterpane
counterpart
counterplot
counterseal
countersign
countersink
countervail
counterwork
countrified
country club
country code
countryfied
countryside
coup de grâce
courteously
courtesy car
courtliness
cover charge
coxcombical
crabbedness
crackerjack
Cracovienne
craniometer
craniometry
cranioscopy
crap-shooter
crash helmet
crateriform

cream-cheese
creationism
creatorship
credentials
credibility
credulously
crematorium
crenellated
creophagous
crepe rubber
crepitation
crepuscular
crestfallen
crime-writer
criminalist
criminality
crimination
criminative
criminology
criticaster
crocidolite
crocodilian
crook-backed
crookedness
cross-action
cross-legged
cross-stitch
cross swords
crotcheteer
Crown Colony
crown prince
cruciferous
crucifixion
crucigerous
cruelty-free
crustaceous
crying shame
cryosurgery
cryptogamic
cryptograph

crystalline
crystallise
crystallize
crystalloid
cubicalness
cuckoo clock
cuir-bouilli
culmiferous
culmination
culpability
cultivation
cunnilingus
cupellation
cupriferous
curatorship
curly-headed
currant wine
curry powder
cursoriness
curtailment
curtain call
curvilineal
curvilinear
customarily
custom-built
custom-house
cut and dried
cut both ways
cutting edge
cybernetics
cyberphobia
cycadaceous
cyclopaedia
cyclopaedic
cynophilist
cyperaceous
cytogenesis

**D**

dactylogram

dactylology
dairy cattle
dampishness
dancing-girl
danger money
dangerously
data-capture
dauntlessly
day in, day out
day-labourer
dead as a dodo
deaf as a post
death-rattle
death-struck
debarkation
debauchment
debs' delight
decarbonate
decarbonise
decarbonize
deceitfully
decemvirate
deceptively
declamation
declamatory
declaration
declarative
declaratory
declination
declinatory
declinature
decollation
décolletage
decolourise
decolourize
decommunise
decommunize
decomposite
decorticate
decrepitate

decrepitude
decrescendo
decumbently
decurrently
decussately
decussation
deductively
deep-freezer
deep-mouthed
deerstalker
defalcation
defectively
defenceless
defensively
deferential
defiantness
defibrinate
defibrinise
defibrinize
deficiently
deflagrator
defloration
defoliation
deforcement
deformation
deglutinate
deglutition
deglutitory
degradation
degradingly
dehortation
dehortative
dehortatory
dehydration
dehypnotise
dehypnotize
deictically
deification
deistically
delectation

deleterious
deliciously
delightedly
delightless
delightsome
delineation
delinquency
deliriously
delitescent
deliverable
deliverance
demagnetise
demagnetize
demagogical
demagoguery
demarcation
demarkation
demesmerise
demesmerize
demi-bastion
demi-cadence
democratise
democratize
demographic
demoniacism
demonolater
demonolatry
demonologic
demonstrate
denizenship
denominable
denominator
dental floss
denticulate
deniability
dentigerous
denunciator
deobstruent
deoxidation
depauperate

depauperise
depauperize
dependently
dephlegmate
depopulator
deportation
depravation
deprecation
deprecative
deprecatory
depredation
depredatory
deprivation
deprivement
de profundis
depth-charge
derangement
dereliction
dermatology
descendable
descendible
describable
description
descriptive
desecration
desegregate
deservingly
desiccation
desideratum
designation
designative
desperately
desperation
despisingly
despoilment
despondence
despondency
destination
destitution
destroyable

destruction
destructive
desultorily
deteriorate
determinant
determinate
determinism
determinist
detestation
detrimental
deuterogamy
Deuteronomy
Deutschmark
devastation
developable
development
deviousness
devolvement
devotedness
dexterously
diacritical
diadelphous
diagnostics
dialectical
dialogistic
diamagnetic
diametrical
diamond-back
diaphaneity
diaphoresis
diaphoretic
diarthrosis
diatessaron
diathermous
dicephalous
dichogamous
dichotomous
dichromatic
dichroscope
dicotyledon

dictatorial
didactylous
die laughing
die the death
differentia
differently
difficultly
diffidently
diffraction
diffractive
diffuseness
diffusively
digitigrade
dilapidated
dilapidator
diluvialist
dimensional
dimensioned
dinner-table
dinosaurian
Dinotherium
diphthongal
diphycercal
diplomatics
diplomatise
diplomatist
diplomatize
diprismatic
dipsomaniac
direct debit
directional
directorate
directorial
direfulness
dirty old man
disaccustom
disaffected
disafforest
disapproval
disarmament

disbandment
disbeliever
discernible
discernibly
discernment
discography
discontinue
discordance
discordancy
discotheque
discourager
discourtesy
discrepance
discrepancy
discussable
disembitter
disencumber
disentangle
disenthrone
disentrance
disgraceful
disgruntled
disguisedly
dish antenna
dishevelled
dishonestly
dish the dirt
disillusion
disinclined
disinterest
disjunction
disjunctive
dislocation
dismastment
disobedient
disobliging
disorganise
disorganize
dispensable
dispersedly

dispiriting
displeasing
displeasure
disposition
disputation
disputative
disquieting
disquietude
dissectible
disseminate
dissentient
dissepiment
dissertator
dissilience
dissimulate
dissipation
dissolutely
dissolution
dissolvable
dissyllabic
dissyllable
dissymmetry
distaff line
distaff side
distasteful
distempered
distensible
distillable
distinction
distinctive
distinguish
distracting
distraction
distressful
distressing
distributor
distrustful
disturbance
dithyrambic
diversified

divertingly
diving board
diving-dress
divining-rod
divorceable
divorcement
do a good turn
doctrinaire
doctrinally
documentary
do justice to
dolabriform
dolefulness
domesticate
domesticity
domiciliary
domiciliate
domineering
done to a turn
donkey's ages
do one's stuff
double agent
double cream
double-cross
double-Dutch
double-edged
double entry
double-faced
double first
double-quick
double-think
doughtiness
down payment
down to earth
downtrodden
doxological
dramaturgic
draughtsman
draughtsmen
drawing-room

draw the line
dreadnaught
dreadnought
dreamlessly
dress-circle
drilling rig
drive home to
driving test
drug therapy
drunkenness
dubiousness
duck and dive
ductileness
duplication
duplicative
duplicature
dust-wrapper
dutifulness
dynamically
dynamometer
dysfunction
dyslogistic

E
eager beaver
earnestness
earthenware
earthliness
easternmost
eccentrical
echo chamber
echo sounder
eclecticism
edification
editorially
educational
effectively
efficacious
efficiently
effoliation

effulgently
egalitarian
eglandulose
egregiously
eidoloclast
einsteinium
ejaculation
ejector seat
elaborately
elaboration
elaborative
elastically
elasticated
elbow-grease
electioneer
electorship
electric eel
electric eye
electrician
electricity
electrocute
electrolyse
electrolyte
electrolyze
electronics
electrotype
elementally
elephantine
elephantoid
eligibility
Elizabethan
ellipsoidal
ellipticity
elucidation
elucidative
elusoriness
elutriation
emancipator
emarginated
embarkation

embarrassed
emblematise
emblematist
emblematize
embowelment
embracement
embrocation
embroilment
embryologic
emmenagogic
emmenagogue
Emmenthaler
empirically
emplacement
empty-handed
empty-headed
emulatively
emulsionise
emulsionize
enarthrosis
encapsulate
encephaloid
encephalous
enchainment
enchantment
enchantress
encomiastic
encouraging
encumbrance
encystation
endemically
endlessness
endocardiac
endocardium
endorhizous
endorsement
endosmosmic
endospermic
endothelium
energetical

energy drink
enfeoffment
enforceable
enforcement
enfranchise
engineering
engorgement
engrailment
engrossment
enhancement
enigmatical
enlargement
enlightened
enlivenment
enneagynous
enneahedral
enneahedron
ennoblement
enouncement
enslavement
entablature
entablement
enteropathy
entertainer
enthralment
entomologic
entozoology
entrance fee
entreatable
entwinement
enucleation
enumeration
enunciation
enunciative
enunciatory
envelopment
environment
epidermical
epidiascope
epigastrium

epigraphics
epilogistic
epipetalous
epiphyllous
epiphytical
episcopally
epistolical
epithalamic
epithelioma
epithetical
equableness
equiangular
equidistant
equilateral
equilibrate
equilibrist
equilibrium
equinoctial
equipollent
equivalence
equivalency
equivocally
equivocator
eradication
eradicative
Erastianism
eremacausis
erratically
erroneously
erubescence
erythematic
erythrocyte
eschatology
escheatable
esotericism
essentially
established
establisher
estate agent
Eternal City

eternal rest
etherealise
ethereality
etherealize
ethnography
ethnologist
etymologise
etymologist
etymologize
eucharistic
eudaemonism
eudaemonist
euphemistic
eurhythmics
Europeanise
Europeanize
Eurosceptic
evanescence
evangelical
evaporation
evaporative
eventuality
eventuation
everlasting
evolutional
exaggerator
examination
exceedingly
excellently
exceptional
excessively
exclamation
exclamatory
exclusively
exclusivism
excoriation
excorticate
excrescence
exculpation
exculpatory

excursively
ex-directory
executioner
executorial
exemplarily
exemplifier
exfoliation
exhaustible
exhaustless
exhaust pipe
exhortation
exhortative
exhortatory
existential
exoneration
exonerative
exorbitance
exorbitancy
exoskeletal
exoskeleton
exotericism
expansively
expatiation
expatiatory
expectation
expectative
expectorant
expectorate
expediently
expeditious
expenditure
expensively
experienced
expiscation
explanation
explanative
explanatory
explication
explicative
explicatory

exploitable
exploration
explorative
exploratory
explosively
exponential
exportation
exposedness
ex post facto
expostulate
expressible
expropriate
expurgation
expurgatory
exquisitely
extemporary
extemporise
extemporize
extensively
extenuation
extenuatory
exteriorise
exteriority
exteriorize
exterminate
externalise
externalism
externality
externalize
extirpation
extirpatory
extortioner
extractible
extradition
extrapolate
extravagant
extravagate
extravasate
extrication
extrinsical

exuberantly
eye-catching

**F**
fabrication
facetiously
facsimilist
factory farm
factory ship
facts of life
facultative
faddishness
faggot-voter
fair-weather
faithlessly
fallibility
falteringly
familiarise
familiarity
familiarize
fanatically
fanfaronade
fantastical
farinaceous
far-reaching
farthermore
farthermost
farthingale
fasciculate
fascinating
fascination
fashionable
fast-forward
fastigiated
father-in-law
fat transfer
faugiferous
faultlessly
faussebraie
faussebraye

favouritism
fearfulness
feasibility
feather-edge
feather-head
featherless
featureless
febriculose
febriferous
fecundation
feloniously
felspathose
*femme fatale*
fenestrated
fermentable
ferociously
ferriferous
Ferris wheel
ferruginous
ferulaceous
fibre-optics
fiddle-de-dee
fiddlestick
fidgetiness
field events
field hockey
fifth column
filamentary
filamentoid
filamentose
filamentous
fillibuster
fill the bill
fimetarious
financially
*fin de siècle*
finger-board
fingerprint
finger-stall
finicalness

fire-brigade
firecracker
firefighter
fire-lighter
fire station
firing-squad
firmamental
first-fruits
first person
fish-eye lens
fissiparous
flabbergast
flaccidness
flannelette
flatulently
flavourless
flexibility
flightiness
flip one's lid
flirtatious
flocculence
flog to death
florescence
florilegium
flourishing
floweriness
fluctuating
fluctuation
fluorescent
fluoroscope
flying squad
flying start
focal length
fomentation
foolishness
fool's-errand
foot the bill
foppishness
foraminated
foraminifer

forasmuchas
forbearance
forced entry
forcipation
for dear life
foreclosure
foreignness
forepayment
foreshorten
forestaller
forestation
forethought
fore-topmast
forevermore
forfeitable
forget-me-not
forgiveness
forlorn hope
formicarium
formication
formularise
formularize
formulation
fornication
forthcoming
for the birds
fortifiable
fortnightly
fortunately
forwardness
foul-mouthed
fountain pen
four-flusher
fractionate
fractionise
fractionize
fractiously
fragileness
fragmentary
frankfurter

frantically
fraternally
fratricidal
fraudlessly
fraudulence
free as a bird
freebooting
freedom food
freemasonry
free radical
freethinker
freeze-frame
French bread
French chalk
French doors
French fries
French leave
French toast
fretfulness
frigate-bird
frightfully
frigidarium
frivolously
front-runner
frowardness
frugivorous
fruitlessly
frustration
fulguration
full-blooded
full-frontal
full of beans
fulminating
fulmination
fulsomeness
funambulist
functionary
functionate
fundamental
fund-holding

fungivorous
furiousness
furnishings
furtherance
furthermore
furthermost

**G**
gaff-topsail
gainfulness
gall-bladder
Gallicanism
gallimaufry
gallowglass
gambrel-roof
games theory
gamogenesis
garnishment
garrulously
gastronomer
gate-crasher
gay Lothario
gemmiparous
gendarmerie
genealogist
generalship
generically
gene therapy
genetically
genetic code
geniculated
genteelness
gentlemanly
gentlewoman
gentlewomen
genuflexion
genuineness
geometrical
geopolitics
germination

germinative
germ warfare
gerontology
gerrymander
gesticulate
get cold feet
get cracking
get even with
get one's goat
get straight
get the drift
get together
ghastliness
ghostliness
gigantesque
gild the lily
gillyflower
gingerbread
girlishness
give and take
give the bird
give the boot
give the slip
give what for
glaucescent
globeflower
globigerina
globularity
glomeration
glumiferous
glyptotheca
goatishness
goddaughter
God-forsaken
godlessness
go great guns
gold-beating
golden eagle
golden hello
go like a bird

gonfalonier
good innings
good-looking
good-natured
go overboard
Gordian knot
gormandiser
gormandizer
gory details
go the rounds
go to the dogs
go to the wall
go up in smoke
gourmandise
gourmandize
go with a bang
gracelessly
gradational
grammatical
grandfather
grandiosity
grandmaster
grandmother
grandnephew
grandparent
graniferous
granitiform
granivorous
granulation
graphically
graphic arts
grasshopper
gratulation
gratulatory
graven image
gravimetric
gravitation
gravitative
greasepaint
greasy spoon

Great Divide
great-nephew
greengrocer
green pepper
griddlecake
gristliness
grizzly bear
grotesquely
grotesquery
ground cover
ground floor
ground rules
ground-sheet
ground-swell
guaniferous
guardedness
guelder rose
guesstimate
guilelessly
guiltlessly
guipure lace
gullibility
gum ammoniac
gummiferous
gurgitation
gutta-percha
guttersnipe
guttiferous
gutturalise
gutturalize
gynaecology
gynaeolatry
gyro-compass

# H
haberdasher
habituation
haemoglobin
haemophilia
haemoptysis

haemorrhage
hagiography
hagiologist
hair-breadth
hairdresser
hairpin bend
hair-raising
hairweaving
halcyon days
half-and-half
half-brother
half-hearted
half-measure
half the time
hallucinate
hand-breadth
handicapped
handicapper
hand in glove
hand to mouth
handwriting
happy medium
harbourless
hard and fast
hard as nails
hard-hearted
hard-hitting
hard-pressed
hard put to it
hare-brained
harmfulness
harpsichord
harum-scarum
harvest moon
hatefulness
haughtiness
haustellate
Havana cigar
have a down on
have a hand in

have a stab at
have it in for
have it in one
have kittens
have one's ear
hazardously
head-on crash
health foods
healthfully
healthiness
heart attack
heartbroken
hearthstone
heartlessly
heavenwards
heavy-handed
heavyweight
hebdomadary
heedfulness
heinousness
Heliochrome®
heliochromy
heliography
Hellenistic
hellishness
helminthoid
helpfulness
helping hand
hemeralopia
hemihedrism
hemipterous
hemispheric
hemitropous
heptagynian
heptagynous
heptahedral
heptahedron
heptamerous
heptandrous
heptangular

herbivorous
hereditable
hereditably
hereinafter
heresiology
heretically
hermeneutic
heroic verse
herpetology
herring-bone
hesperornis
heteroclite
heterophemy
hexagonally
hibernation
Hibernicism
hide-and-seek
hideousness
hiding place
hierarchism
hierarchist
highfalutin
highlighter
high-pitched
high-powered
high treason
Highway Code
hippocampus
Hispanicism
historicity
historiette
histrionics
histrionism
hobbledehoy
hold one's own
holoblastic
holographic
holothurian
home stretch
homiletical

hominy grits
homocentric
homoeopathy
homogeneity
homogeneous
homogenesis
homogenetic
homoiousian
homomorphic
homophonous
homoplastic
Homo sapiens
honeysuckle
honours list
Hooray Henry
hopefulness
hornswoggle
horological
horoscopist
hors d'oeuvre
horseradish
hose-pipe ban
hospitalise
hospitality
hospitalize
hospitaller
house arrest
house-broken
householder
housekeeper
house martin
housemaster
housewifely
housewifery
huckleberry
hucksterage
Hudibrastic
huff and puff
hullaballoo
human shield

humectation
humiliation
humming-bird
hunchbacked
hundredfold
hurtfulness
hyacinthine
hyalography
hydrocarbon
hydrocyanic
hydrogenate
hydrogenous
hydrography
hydrometric
hydropathic
hydrophobia
hydrophobic
hydroponics
hydrosphere
hydrostatic
hydrothorax
hyetography
hygrometric
hygroscopic
hymnography
hyperactive
hyperbolise
hyperbolism
hyperbolize
hyperborean
hypercritic
hypermetric
hypersthene
hypertrophy
hypnologist
hypocycloid
hypogastric
hypoglossal
hypostasise
hypostasize

hypostatise
hypostatize
hypothecate
hypothermia
hypothesise
hypothesize
hysterotomy

**I**
ichthyoidal
ichthyolite
ichthyology
ichthyornis
ichthyosaur
iconography
icosahedral
icosahedron
identically
ideographic
idiomatical
idiomorphic
idiotically
ignition key
ignobleness
ignominious
ignoramuses
ill-disposed
I'll eat my hat
ill-favoured
ill-humoured
illiberally
illimitable
ill-mannered
illogically
illuminator
illusionism
illusionist
illustrator
illustrious
I'm a Dutchman

imagination
imaginative
imbrication
imitability
imitatively
immediately
immenseness
immigration
immortalise
immortality
immortalize
impartation
impartially
impassioned
impassively
impatiently
impeachable
impeachment
impecunious
impedimenta
impenitence
imperfectly
imperforate
imperialise
imperialism
imperialist
imperialize
imperiously
impermanent
impermeable
impermeably
impersonate
impertinent
impetuosity
impetuously
impiousness
implacental
implausible
implemental
implication

implicative
imploration
imploratory
importantly
importation
importunate
importunity
impractical
imprecation
imprecatory
impregnable
impregnably
impressible
impressibly
impressment
impropriate
impropriety
improvement
improvident
imprudently
impulsively
inadvertent
inadvisable
inalienable
inalienably
inalterable
inalterably
in a nutshell
inattention
inattentive
inaugurator
incalescent
incantation
incantatory
incarcerate
incarnadine
incarnation
inceptively
incertitude
incessantly

incinerator
inclemently
inclination
inclusively
incogitable
incognisant
incognizant
incoherence
incoherency
in cold blood
incompetent
incongruent
incongruity
incongruous
inconsonant
inconstancy
incontinent
incorporate
incorporeal
incorrectly
incorrupted
increasable
incredulity
incredulous
incremental
incrimation
incriminate
inculcation
inculpation
inculpatory
incumbrance
incunabulum
incuriously
incurvation
incurvature
indeciduate
indeciduous
in deep water
indefinable
indefinably

indehiscent
indentation
independent
index finger
indexterity
india-rubber
indifferent
indigestion
indigestive
indignantly
indignation
indirection
indirect tax
individuate
indivisible
indivisibly
indomitable
indomitably
indorsement
indubitable
indubitably
inductional
inductively
indulgently
in duplicate
industrious
inebriation
ineffective
ineffectual
inefficient
inelegantly
ineluctable
inequitable
inescapable
inessential
inestimable
inestimably
inexcusable
inexcusably
inexpedient

inexpensive
inexplosive
infanticide
infatuation
infecundity
inferential
inferiority
infertilely
infertility
infestation
infeudation
infinitival
inflammable
inflammably
inflexional
influential
informality
information
informative
informatory
infracostal
infrangible
infrangibly
infrequency
in full swing
ingathering
ingeniously
ingenuously
in good hands
in good heart
ingratitude
ingurgitate
inhabitable
inheritable
inheritably
inheritance
injudicious
injuriously
innavigable
innervation

innocuously
innoxiously
innumerable
innumerably
innutrition
inobservant
inobtrusive
inoculation
inoffensive
inofficious
in one's shoes
inoperative
inopportune
inorganized
*in perpetuum*
inquisition
inquisitive
insalubrity
insatiately
inscription
inscriptive
inscrutable
inscrutably
insecticide
insectivore
insensitive
inseparable
inseparably
insessorial
insidiously
insincerely
insincerity
insinuating
insinuation
insinuative
insouciance
inspiration
inspiratory
instability
installment

instigation
instinctive
instinctual
institution
institutive
instruction
instructive
insultingly
insuperable
insuperably
integration
intelligent
intemperant
intemperate
intenseness
intensively
intentional
intentioned
interaction
interactive
intercalary
intercalate
intercepter
interceptor
intercessor
interchange
intercostal
intercourse
interesting
interfacing
interfluent
interfusion
interiority
interjacent
interlineal
interlinear
interlining
intermeddle
intermedial
intermedium

interminate
intermingle
internality
internecine
internuncio
interocular
interpolate
interpreter
interracial
interregnum
interrelate
interrogate
interrupted
intersperse
intertribal
interviewee
interviewer
in the grip of
in the making
in the offing
in the saddle
in the wake of
intolerable
intolerably
intolerance
into thin air
in touch with
intractable
intractably
intravenous
intrepidity
intricately
intrinsical
intrusively
intuitional
intuitively
intuitivism
intuitonism
intumescent
in two shakes

invectively
inventively
inventorial
investigate
investiture
invidiously
inviolately
involuntary
involvement
ion exchange
ipecacuanha
iridescence
Irish coffee
irksomeness
iron curtain
ironmongery
iron rations
irradiation
irrecusable
irredentist
irreducible
irreducibly
irrefutable
irrefutably
irregularly
irrelevance
irrelevancy
irreligious
irremovable
irremovably
irreparable
irreparably
irretentive
irreverence
irrevocable
irrevocably
isochronism
isochronous
isometrical
isomorphism

isomorphous
Israelitish
itching palm
ithyphallic

**J**

Jacobitical
jactitation
jam tomorrow
Jesus Christ
*joie de vivre*
join the club
joylessness
judgemental
Judgment Day
judiciously
jugular vein
jumper cable
jungle juice
juridically
justiceship
justiciable
justifiable
justifiably
juvenescent

**K**

Kelvin scale
kick oneself
kidney stone
killer whale
kilocalorie
kind-hearted
kinematical
king's ransom
kiss and sell
kiss-and-tell
kiss of death
kitchenette
kleptomania

knavishness
knock for six
know by sight
kwashiorkor

**L**

labefaction
labiodental
laboriously
labradorite
laconically
lactescence
lactiferous
lamellicorn
lamelliform
lamentation
lammergeier
lammergeyer
lamp-lighter
lanceolated
lancinating
lancination
landaulette
landgravine
landing-gear
landscapist
langoustine
languidness
languishing
lapis lazuli
large as life
laryngology
laryngotomy
lasertripsy
latifoliate
latifolious
latifundium
latitudinal
laughing gas
launderctte

laurustinus
lawlessness
leading edge
leading lady
leaseholder
leather-back
Leatherette®
leather-neck
leave-taking
lecherously
lectureship
legal tender
legerdemain
legionnaire
legislation
legislative
legislature
lengthiness
lentiginous
lepidosiren
lese-majesty
lethargical
let off steam
letterpress
leucorrhoea
level-headed
libellously
libertarian
liberticide
libertinism
liberty hall
lichenology
lickerishly
lickspittle
lie-detector
lieutenancy
life of Riley
life science
ligamentous
light-headed

light-keeper
light-weight
lignum vitae
Lilliputian
lily-livered
limp-wristed
line-drawing
line printer
lingeringly
linguistics
lion-hearted
liposuction
liquefiable
liquescency
liquidambar
liquidation
lissomeness
listeriosis
literalness
lithography
lithosphere
lithotomist
lithotripsy
lithotritor
litigiously
littérateur
little woman
live-in lover
loadsa money
loathliness
loathsomely
locum tenens
logarithmic
logicalness
logographer
logomachist
London pride
longanimity
long-playing
long-sighted

look askance
look the part
loop the loop
loose cannon
loosestrife
Lord's Prayer
lose one's rag
lose one's way
lose track of
lotophagist
loudspeaker
love-handles
love-in-a-mist
low-spirited
lubrication
lucubration
ludicrously
luggage rack
luminescent
lumpishness
lustfulness
Lutheranism
luxuriantly
luxuriously
lycanthrope
lycanthropy
Lyme disease

**M**
machination
machine code
machine-tool
macrobiotic
macroscopic
made to order
magic circle
magisterial
magistratic
Magna Charta
magnanimity

magnanimous
magnetician
magnifiable
magnificent
magnificoes
Mahabharata
maidservant
maintenance
make a dent in
make a go of it
make a hash of
make a hole in
make a meal of
make-believe
make headway
make history
make light of
make one's day
make one's way
make or break
make strides
maladjusted
malapropism
malediction
*male entente*
maleficence
malevolence
malfeasance
malfunction
maliciously
malignantly
malposition
malpractice
mammiferous
mandarinate
mandibulate
manduction
manducatory
manganesian
Manichaeism

manipulator
mansard roof
manufactory
manufacture
manumission
marchioness
mare clausum
mare liberum
marginalise
marginalize
margraviate
marketplace
marlinspike
marmoration
marqueterie
marshalling
marshalship
marshmallow
martial arts
martyrology
masculinity
masquerader
masterpiece
mastication
masticatory
matchlessly
materialise
materialism
materialist
materiality
materialize
mathematics
matriarchal
matriculate
matrimonial
mawkishness
meadowsweet
meaningless
measureless
measurement

mechanician
mechanistic
mechanology
mediastinum
mediateness
mediatorial
medicinally
medievalism
medievalist
meet halfway
megalomania
megatherium
melancholia
melioration
melliferous
mellifluent
mellifluous
mellivorous
melodiously
memento mori
memorabilia
memorandums
memorialise
memorialist
memorialize
mendelevium
menorrhagia
menorrhagic
mensuration
mentionable
mercenarily
merchandise
merchantman
merchantmen
mercilessly
mercurially
meritocracy
meritorious
meroblastic
Merovingian

merry-making
mésalliance
mesophloeum
messiahship
metagenesis
metamorphic
metaphysics
meteorolite
meteorology
methodistic
methodology
metonymical
metrication
metric scale
Mexican wave
Mickey Mouse
micrococcus
microfloppy
micrography
microlithic
micrometric
microphonic
microscopic
microsystem
micturition
middle class
middy blouse
millenarian
milligramme
millionaire
mind-bending
mind-blowing
mindfulness
mineraliser
mineralizer
mineralogic
mine-sweeper
miniaturise
miniaturist
miniaturize

ministerial
ministering
minnesinger
misalliance
misanthrope
misanthropy
misbecoming
misbegotten
misbeliever
miscarriage
mischievous
misconceive
misconstrue
misdemeanor
misericorde
misfeasance
missing link
misspelling
miss the boat
mistrustful
mitigations
mitral valve
mixtilineal
mixtilinear
mobile phone
Möbius strip
mocking-bird
moiré effect
molestation
mollycoddle
momentarily
momentously
monarchical
monasticism
money for jam
money-lender
money market
money to burn
monocarpous
monodelphic

monogenesis
monogenetic
monographer
monographic
monomorphic
monophthong
monophysite
monopoliser
monopolizer
monospermal
Monotremata
Monseigneur
monstrosity
monstrously
moonlighter
Moravianism
morning coat
morning star
morning suit
morphologic
morris dance
mortar-board
mortise lock
moss-trooper
mother-in-law
mother's milk
mother's ruin
mountaineer
mountainous
movableness
multangular
multanimous
multifidous
multilineal
multinomial
multipotent
multiserial
multisonous
mumpishness
mum's the word

muncipalise
muncipalize
munificence
murderously
murmuringly
muscle-bound
Muscovy duck
muscularity
musculature
muskellunge
mutableness
mutton chops
mycological
myocarditis
myrmecology
mythologian
mythologise
mythologist
mythologize
mythopoetic

**N**
name-calling
naphthalene
narratively
narrow gauge
nationalise
nationalism
nationalist
nationality
nationalize
naturalness
naughtiness
Neanderthal
near-sighted
near the bone
necessarily
necessitate
necessitous
neck and neck

neckerchief
necrobiosis
necrologist
necromancer
necromantic
necrophilia
needfulness
needle-point
needle-woman
nefariously
negligently
negotiation
negotiatory
neighbourly
neotropical
nephritical
*ne plus ultra*
nerve centre
nether world
neuropathic
neuropteran
neutraliser
neutralizer
neutron bomb
neutron star
never say die
New Year's Day
New Year's Eve
nice-looking
Nicene Creed
nickelodeon
nictitation
night-flower
nightingale
night school
nimbiferous
nip in the bud
nitrogenise
nitrogenize
nitrogenous

nitrous acid
nitty-gritty
noble savage
noctilucous
noctivagant
nocturnally
noiselessly
noisomeness
nom de guerre
nomenclator
nominatival
nonchalance
nondescript
nonetheless
nonfeasance
nonpartisan
nonsensical
non sequitur
non-violence
north-easter
northwardly
north-wester
nosological
no such thing
not a bad sort
notableness
not a patch on
nothingness
nothing to it
notice-board
no time at all
notoriously
Nototherium
not up to much
nourishable
nourishment
nowhere near
noxiousness
nuclear bomb
nuclear test

nucleic acid
number plate
numerically
numismatics
numismatist
nuncupative
nuncupatory
nursing home
nutrimental
nutritively
nyctitropic
nympholepsy
nymphomania

# O

obediential
obfuscation
object-glass
objectively
objectivism
objectivity
objurgation
objurgatory
oblique case
obliqueness
obliviously
obnoxiously
obsceneness
obscuration
obscurement
obscureness
obsecration
obsecratory
observantly
observation
observative
observatory
obsolescent
obstetrical
obstinately

obstipation
obstruction
obstructive
obtestation
obtrusively
obviousness
occultation
ochlocratic
odds and ends
odds and sods
odoriferous
oecumenical
*oeil-de-boeuf*
oenophilist
oesophageal
off Broadway
offensively
officialdom
officialese
officialism
officiously
off one's head
off one's oats
off the rails
oil-painting
Old Catholic
old chestnut
olive branch
olla podrida
ominousness
omnifarious
omnipotence
omnipresent
omniscience
omnisciency
omphalotomy
on cloud nine
oneiromancy
one's ewe lamb
on no account

onomasticon
onomatology
on the bottle
on the carpet
on the fiddle
on the stocks
ontogenesis
ontological
opalescence
open and shut
open-hearted
open-mouthed
opera bouffe
operational
operatively
operoseness
opinionable
opinionated
opportunely
opportunism
opportunist
opportunity
opprobrious
optical disk
oral history
orange stick
orang-outang
orbicularly
orbiculated
orchestrate
orchestrion
orchidology
orderliness
organically
organisable
organizable
orientalise
Orientalism
Orientalist
orientalize

orientation
originality
original sin
origination
originative
ornamentist
ornitholite
ornithology
ornithopter
orthography
orthopaedia
orthopaedic
orthopteran
orthotropal
orthotropic
oscillating
oscillation
oscillatory
ostentation
osteography
osteologist
osteoplasty
ostreaceous
out and about
out-building
outdistance
out of pocket
out of the way
outstanding
over a barrel
overbalance
overbearing
overflowing
over the hill
over the moon
over the odds
overweening
overwrought
owner-driver
Oxford Group

oxygenation
oxyhydrogen

**P**

pacifically
pacificator
package tour
paediatrics
paedophilia
painfulness
painstaking
palaearctic
pale as death
palmiferous
palpability
palpigerous
palpitation
palsgravine
pampas-grass
pamphleteer
pampiniform
Pan-American
pandemonium
Pandora's box
panduriform
panegyrical
panhellenic
panic attack
panic button
panic-struck
paniculated
pantalettes
pantheistic
pantomimist
paperweight
papier maché
papyraceous
papyrograph
parabolical
paracentral

paracentric
paradoxical
paragenesia
paragenesis
paragogical
paragraphic
Paraguay tea
paraldehyde
paraleipsis
parallactic
parallelism
paramedical
parasailing
parasitical
parathyroid
parchedness
parentheses
parenthesis
parenthetic
parenticide
paresthesia
paripinnate
parishioner
parlour game
parochially
paronomasia
part company
partibility
participant
participate
participial
particulate
partitively
partnership
parturition
party pooper
parvanimity
passibility
passionless
Passion play

passiveness
past its best
pastureless
paternalism
paternoster
pathologist
patriarchic
patrimonial
patristical
patronising
patronizing
pay the piper
pearlaceous
pearl-button
pearl-oyster
Pearly Gates
peccability
pectination
peculiarity
pecuniarily
pedagogical
pedicellate
pedunculate
peevishness
Pelagianism
pelargonium
pellucidity
penalty area
penetrating
penetration
penetrative
penicillate
peninsulate
penitential
pennoncelle
pennyweight
pension plan
pensiveness
pentadactyl
pentagynian

pentagynous
pentahedral
pentahedron
pentamerous
pentandrous
pentangular
pentavalent
Pentecostal
penultimate
penuriously
peptic ulcer
perambulate
perceivable
perceivably
perceptible
perceptibly
percipience
percipiency
percolation
peregrinate
perennially
perestroika
perfectible
perfectness
perforation
perforative
performable
performance
perfumatory
perfunctory
pericardiac
pericardial
pericardium
pericarpial
pericranium
perigastric
periodicity
period piece
periosteous
periostitis

peripatetic
periphrases
periphrasis
peristaltic
peritonaeal
peritonaeum
peritonitis
permanently
permissible
permissibly
permutation
perpetrator
perpetuable
perpetually
persecution
persecutrix
persevering
persistence
persistency
persnickety
personalise
personalism
personality
personalize
personation
perspective
perspicuity
perspicuous
perspirable
persuadable
persuasible
pertinacity
pertinently
perturbable
perturbance
pervertible
pessimistic
pestiferous
pestilently
Peter's pence

petitionary
petrifiable
petrodollar
petrography
petrologist
pettifogger
phagedaenic
phantomatic
pharisaical
pharyngitis
phenomenism
phenomenist
philatelist
Philhellene
philologian
philologist
philomathic
philosopher
philosophic
phone phreak
phonetician
phonography
phosphorate
phosphorise
phosphorize
phosphorous
photochromy
photo-finish
photoglyphy
photography
photometric
photophobia
photosphere
phraseogram
phraseology
phthiriasis
phylacteric
phyllotaxis
physiognomy
physiolatry

physiologic
phytography
phytologist
pick holes in
pick-up truck
picrotoxine
pictorially
picturesque
piece of cake
pie in the sky
pietistical
pigsticking
pineal gland
pinnatisect
Pinteresque
piperaceous
pipistrelle
piratically
piscatorial
piscivorous
pitchblende
piteousness
pitifulness
placability
plagiostome
plain-spoken
plaintively
planetarium
planetoidal
planisphere
plano-convex
plantigrade
plasmolysis
plaster cast
platinotype
platyrrhine
play footsie
play for time
playfulness
playing card

play it by ear
play the game
pleasurable
pleasurably
plebeianise
plebeianism
plebeianize
Pleistocene
plenariness
plenipotent
plenteously
plentifully
plethorical
pleuritical
pliableness
ploughshare
plum pudding
pluriparous
plutocratic
pluviometer
pneumometer
pneumonitis
pocket-knife
pocket money
pococurante
podophyllin
pointedness
pointillism
pointillist
point of sale
poison dwarf
poisonously
polarimeter
polarisable
polariscope
polarizable
polemically
politically
pollination
poltergeist

poltroonery
polycarpous
polychromic
polygastric
polygenesis
polymorphic
polyonymous
polyphagous
polyphonism
polyphonist
polyplastic
polyrhizous
polyspermal
polysporous
polystyrene
polytechnic
pomegranate
pomiculture
pompelmoose
pompousness
ponderosity
ponderously
pontificate
poppet-valve
pornography
porphyritic
portability
porter-house
portmanteau
portraitist
portraiture
possibility
posteriorly
post-glacial
postulatory
potentially
powerlessly
practicable
practicably
practically

pragmatical
prairie wolf
prayerfully
preaudience
preceptress
precipitant
precipitate
precipitous
preciseness
precognosce
preconceive
precontract
predecessor
predicament
predication
predicative
predicatory
predictable
predictably
predominant
predominate
prehistoric
prejudgment
prejudicate
prejudicial
prelateship
prelibation
preliminary
prematurely
prematurity
premeditate
premiership
premonition
premonitory
preoccupied
preparation
preparative
preparatory
preposition
prepositive

prerogative
presagement
presbyteral
presentable
presentably
presentment
presentness
preservable
prestigious
prestissimo
presumption
presumptive
pretendedly
pretentious
preterition
preteritive
prevalently
prevaricate
preventable
prickliness
prickly heat
priestcraft
primateship
primigenial
primitively
principally
prismatical
privatively
probability
probationer
problematic
proboscides
proconsular
procreation
Procrustean
proctorship
procuration
procuratory
procurement
prodigality

profanation
profaneness
proficiency
profuseness
progenitive
prognathism
prognathous
progression
progressive
prohibition
prohibitive
prohibitory
prolegomena
proleptical
proletarian
proletariat
proliferate
proliferous
prominently
promiscuity
promiscuous
promisingly
promptitude
promulgator
pronouncing
propagation
propagative
prophetical
prophylaxis
propinquity
propitiable
propitiator
proposition
proprietary
proprieties
proprietrix
prorogation
prosaically
pros and cons
prosecution

prosecutrix
proselytise
proselytism
proselytize
prosenchyma
prosopopeia
prospection
prospective
prostitutor
prostration
protagonist
protectoral
protectress
proteolysis
protomartyr
protonotary
protractile
protraction
protractive
protrusible
protuberant
protuberate
providently
provisional
provocation
provocative
provokingly
provostship
proximately
prudishness
pruriginous
prussic acid
psalmodical
pseudomorph
pseudopodia
psittaceous
psittacosis
psychedelic
psychologic
psychomotor

psychopathy
pteridology
pterodactyl
publication
public works
publishable
pulchritude
pull one's leg
pull strings
pull through
pulverulent
pulviniform
punched card
Punchinello
punctilious
punctuality
punctuation
purchasable
purgatively
purgatorial
purgatorian
purificator
puritanical
purple patch
purple piece
purple prose
purposeless
put on the map
putrescence
putrescible
putrifiable
put the lid on
pyramidical
pyramidally
pyrotechnic
Pythagorean
Pythagorism

**Q**
quacksalver

quadrennial
quadrillion
quadrumanal
qualifiable
qualitative
quantum jump
quantum leap
quarrelsome
quarter-back
quarter-deck
quarter note
queen-mother
Queer Street
querulously
questionary
queue-jumper
quibblingly
quicksilver
quick-witted
quiescently
quincuncial
quindecagon
quinquereme
quintillion
quitch-grass
quiveringly
quo warranto

**R**
rabbit punch
Rabelaisian
racing green
racing model
rack-railway
radar beacon
radiant heat
radical sign
radioactive
radio beacon
radiocarbon

radiography
radiopaging
radio source
ragged robin
rah-rah skirt
rain or shine
raise a stink
*raison d'être*
rallentando
range-finder
rank and file
rant and rave
rapaciously
rapscallion
rapturously
rarefaction
Rastafarian
ratatouille
rate-capping
ratiocinate
rationalise
rationalism
rationalist
rationality
rationalize
rattlesnake
ravishingly
raw material
reactionary
reactionist
readability
readmission
realisation
realization
reanimation
rear-admiral
reassertion
reassurance
recantation
re-celebrate

receptivity
reciprocate
reciprocity
reclaimable
reclamation
reclination
recognition
recommender
recondition
reconnoitre
reconstruct
recoverable
recremental
recriminate
recruitment
rectangular
rectifiable
rectilineal
rectilinear
rectiserial
recumbently
Red Crescent
reddishness
rediscovery
redoubtable
redressible
red squirrel
redundantly
reduplicate
referential
reflectible
reflexively
reflexology
reformation
reformative
reformatory
refractable
refrainment
refrangible
refreshment

refrigerant
refrigerate
refulgently
regardfully
regimentals
regretfully
regrettable
regrettably
regular army
regurgitate
reinsertion
reinterpret
reintroduce
reiteration
reiterative
reliability
religionism
religionist
religiosity
religiously
reluctantly
remembrance
remigration
reminiscent
remonstrant
remonstrate
remorseless
remunerable
Renaissance
renegotiate
repentantly
repetitious
replacement
replenished
repleviable
replication
reportorial
reprehender
representer
repressible

repressibly
reproachful
reprobation
reprography
reprovingly
repudiation
repugnantly
repulsively
requirement
requisition
rescindment
resemblance
resentfully
reservation
residential
resignation
resourceful
respectable
respectably
respiration
respiratory
resplendent
respondence
respondency
responsible
responsibly
responsions
rest assured
restitution
restiveness
restoration
restorative
restriction
restrictive
restructure
resuscitate
retaliation
retaliative
retaliatory
retardation

retardative
retentively
reticularly
reticulated
retiredness
retractable
retranslate
retribution
retributive
retributory
retrievable
retrievably
retroactive
retrorocket
reverberant
reverberate
reverential
reverseless
reversioner
revoltingly
rhabdomancy
rhapsodical
rhetorician
rhinocerial
rhinoplasty
rhombohedra
ride shotgun
rifacimento
right as rain
righteously
right-handed
right-minded
right to life
rigor mortis
riotousness
risibleness
risk capital
ritualistic
rock-and-roll
rock crystal

rock the boat
rodomontade
role-playing
rollerskate
roller-towel
roll-top desk
Roman candle
romanticise
romanticism
romanticist
romanticize
rompishness
Rosicrucian
rotten apple
rubber glove
rubber plant
rubber stamp
rubefacient
rudimentary
rule of thumb
rumbustious
rummage sale
running mate
rustication

S
Sabbatarian
sacramental
sacrificial
saddle-cloth
Sadduceeism
safe-conduct
safe-cracker
safe-deposit
safe-keeping
safety glass
safety-match
safety-razor
safety-valve
sagaciously

Sagittarius
sailing-boat
salesperson
salinometer
salmon-trout
salvability
sal volatile
samurai bond
sandwich-man
sanguineous
sans-culotte
Sanskritist
saponaceous
saprogenous
Saracenical
sarcastical
sarcomatous
sarcophagic
sarcophagus
satellite TV
satirically
Saturnalian
saving grace
savings bank
savoir faire
savouriness
scaffolding
scale insect
scalpriform
scapularies
scaremonger
scenography
sceptically
schistosoma
schistosome
scholarship
scholiastic
schoolchild
schoolhouse
schottische

sciatically
science park
Scientology®
scintillant
scintillate
scirrhosity
scleritis
sclerobasic
scleroderma
sclerometer
sclerotitis
Scolopendra
scopiferous
scopolamine
Scotch broth
scoundrelly
scout-master
scragginess
scratch card
screw-driver
scrumptious
scrutiniser
scrutinizer
scuttlebutt
sea-cucumber
sea-lavender
searchingly
searchlight
search-party
secondaries
secondarily
second-class
second sight
secret agent
secretarial
secretariat
sectionally
secularness
sedentarily
sedimentary

seditionary
seditiously
seductively
see daylight
see the light
segregation
seigniorage
seigniorial
seismograph
seismometer
self-assured
self-centred
self-control
self-defence
self-evident
self-induced
selfishness
self-loading
self-raising
self-reliant
self-respect
self-seeking
self-service
self-serving
self-starter
self-winding
sell one a pup
semiography
semiskilled
semiskimmed
semitrailer
sempiternal
sensational
senselessly
sensibility
sensiferous
sensitively
sensitivity
sententious
sentimental

sentinelled
septicaemia
septiferous
sequestered
sequestrate
serendipity
sericulture
seriousness
serviceable
serviceably
service area
service road
sesquipedal
set the scene
set to rights
seventeenth
sexagesimal
sexennially
sexual abuse
shadowiness
shallowness
shamelessly
Shanks's mare
Shanks's pony
shapeliness
shareholder
share option
sharp-witted
sheath-knife
shed light on
sheet-anchor
shellacking
shelterless
shepherd dog
shepherdess
sheriffalty
sheriffship
shiftlessly
ship-biscuit
ship-builder

shirtsleeve
shiveringly
shock troops
shopkeeping
shoplifting
short-change
short-coming
short-handed
short shrift
shortwinded
showeriness
show-jumping
show of hands
show the door
shrinkingly
shrubbiness
shufflingly
shuttlecock
sick at heart
sideroscope
sightliness
sight-seeing
significant
silicon chip
silly season
silver birch
silver paper
silver plate
silversmith
simperingly
sinfonietta
single cream
single-entry
single-stick
singularity
sinistrally
sinistrorse
sinking-fund
sinlessness
Sino-Tibetan

sister-in-law
sitka spruce
sitting duck
sitting-room
skeleton-key
sketchiness
skilfulness
skimmed milk
skin and bone
skulduggery
Skye terrier
slaughterer
slave-driver
slave-holder
slave labour
sleep around
sleeping-bag
sleeping car
sleeplessly
sleep-walker
slenderness
sleuth-hound
slightingly
slipped disc
slot-machine
slumberless
small change
small-minded
small screen
small wonder
smithereens
smokescreen
smoky quartz
smooth-faced
smorgasbord
smut disease
snowed under
snow-leopard
sociability
socinianism

soft-hearted
soft landing
sojournment
solanaceous
solar plexus
solar system
soldatesque
soldiership
solemnities
soliloquies
soliloquise
soliloquize
solmisation
solmization
solubleness
solvability
somewhither
somnambulic
son of a bitch
soothsaying
sophistical
sorrowfully
soteriology
sottishness
soup-kitchen
southwester
sovereignty
sparklingly
spathaceous
spectacular
spectatress
spectrology
speculation
speculative
speedometer
spelling-bee
spend a penny
spendthrift
spermatozoa
spherically

spherometer
spice of life
spiciferous
spifflicate
spinabifida
spiniferous
spirit-level
spirochaete
split screen
split second
spoiling for
spondylitis
sponsorship
spontaneity
spontaneous
sports drink
spotted dick
spreadeagle
spreadsheet
spring-board
spring-clean
springiness
spring onion
spud-bashing
spumiferous
squalidness
square dance
squeamishly
squirearchy
stagefright
stage-manage
stage-struck
stagflation
staging area
staging post
stake a claim
stalactical
stalactitic
standardise
standardize

stand-offish
stand out for
staphylosis
starchiness
star-crossed
Star of David
star-studded
stateliness
stately home
state of play
state school
statistical
statute-book
statute mile
stay the pace
steadfastly
steam-engine
steam-roller
stearic acid
steeplejack
steerage-way
stegosaurus
St Elmo's fire
stenography
stepbrother
stephanotis
stereograph
stereoscope
stereoscopy
stereotrope
stereotyped
stereotyper
stereotypic
sternutator
stethometer
stethoscope
stethoscopy
stewardship
stichomancy
stichometry

stick insect
stickleback
stiff-necked
stigmatical
stimulating
stimulation
stimulative
stintedness
stipendiary
stipulation
stirrup-pump
stockbroker
stock-holder
stock market
stocktaking
stomach pump
stomatology
stone's throw
stone-washed
stool-pigeon
stop short of
storekeeper
straight man
straight-out
straightway
strait-laced
stramineous
strangeness
strangulate
strap-hanger
strategetic
strategical
stratopause
street value
strenuously
strikebound
stringently
stringiness
strip mining
stroboscope

strong drink
strong point
studentship
studio couch
stuntedness
stylishness
stylography
subaxillary
subcontract
subcontrary
subdeaconry
subdivision
subdominant
subglobular
subjugation
subjunctive
sublimation
sublimatory
sublimeness
submergence
submersible
submetallic
submultiple
subordinacy
subordinate
subornation
subscapular
subsensible
subsequence
subservient
subsistence
substantial
substantive
subtileness
subtraction
subtropical
suburbanite
succedaneum
succourless
sudden death

to advantage
toast-master
tobacconist
toffee-apple
toffee-nosed
toilet-paper
toilet water
tonsillitis
tooth-powder
topographer
topographic
torch-bearer
tormentille
torpedo-boat
torpescence
torturingly
totalisator
totalizator
to the letter
to the tune of
totipalmate
totteringly
touch a chord
tough-minded
*tour de force*
toxophilite
tracheotome
tracheotomy
tracklaying
tracklessly
track record
traditional
traducement
trafficator
traffic cone
trafficless
tragedienne
tragicomedy
trail-blazer
trailer park

tranquilise
tranquility
tranquilize
transaction
transalpine
transceiver
transcriber
transferrer
transfer-RNA
transfigure
transfixion
transfluent
transformer
transfusion
transfusive
transiently
transit camp
translation
translatory
translucent
transmarine
transmittal
transmitter
transparent
transported
transporter
transsexual
transuranic
transversal
trapeziform
trapezoidal
treacherous
tread on eggs
treasonable
treasonably
tree creeper
tree surgeon
tremblingly
tremulously
trencherman

trench-fever
trendsetter
trepidation
triangulate
tribulation
tribunician
tribunitial
tributaries
tributarily
tricapsular
trichinosis
trickle down
tricksiness
tricoloured
tricuspidal
triennially
trifoliated
trifurcated
trigeminous
trimestrial
Trinitarian
tripersonal
tripetalous
triphyllous
triquetrous
trisepalous
tristichous
trisyllabic
trisyllable
trituration
triturature
triumvirate
trivialness
troglodytic
troposphere
troublesome
truculently
true-hearted
truncheoned
trusteeship

trustworthy
trypanosome
tuberculate
tuberculine
tuberculise
tuberculize
tuberculose
tuberculous
tumble-dryer
tumefaction
tunableness
turbulently
turgescence
Turkish bath
tutti-frutti
twin-engined
two's company
typographer
typographic
tyrannicide
tyrannosaur
tyrannously

**U**
ulotrichous
ultramarine
ultraviolet
umbilicated
unabolished
unadvisable
unadvisably
unadvisedly
unalterable
unambiguous
unambitious
unapostolic
unaspirated
unavoidable
unbefitting
unbelieving

unblemished
uncalled for
uncanonical
unceasingly
uncertainty
unchristian
uncivilised
uncivilized
uncommitted
unconcealed
unconcerned
uncondemned
unconfirmed
unconnected
unconscious
uncontested
unconverted
uncorrected
uncourteous
uncouthness
undauntedly
undefinably
under a cloud
undercharge
underexpose
underground
undergrowth
underhanded
undersigned
understroke
undertaking
under the sun
underthings
underweight
undeserving
undesirable
undeviating
undignified
undisguised
undisturbed

undoubtedly
undutifully
unemotional
unendurable
unenlivened
unequivocal
unessential
unexercised
unexhausted
unfailingly
unfaltering
unfeelingly
unfeignedly
unfermented
unflappable
unflinching
unforgiving
unforgotten
unfortunate
unfulfilled
unfurnished
ungallantly
ungenteelly
ungodliness
unguardedly
unguiculate
unharboured
unhealthily
unheedfully
unicellular
unification
uniformness
unimportant
uninhabited
uninhibited
unipersonal
unipetalous
univalvular
universally
unknowingly

unluckiness
unmanliness
unmeaningly
unmelodious
unmindfully
unmitigable
unmitigated
unnaturally
unnecessary
unobservant
unobserving
unobtrusive
unoffending
unorganised
unorganized
unpalatable
unparagoned
unpatriotic
unperformed
unperverted
unpopularly
unpractical
unpractised
unpresuming
unprintable
unpromising
unprotected
unpublished
unqualified
unreadiness
unreasoning
unreclaimed
unredressed
unrelenting
unremitting
unrepentant
unresisting
unrighteous
unsatisfied
unsaturated

unseaworthy
unsectarian
unsentenced
unshrinking
unsmirching
unsolicited
unsoundness
unspeakable
unspeakably
unspecified
unspiritual
unsupported
unsurpassed
unsuspected
untarnished
unteachable
unthinkable
unthriftily
untinctured
untouchable
untraceable
untraceably
untractable
untractably
untravelled
unutterable
unutterably
unvarnished
unveracious
unwarranted
unwedgeable
unwholesome
unwillingly
unwitnessed
unwittingly
up against it
up and coming
upholsterer
up periscope
ups and downs

upsides with
up to scratch
up to the mark
uranography
urticaceous
uselessness
use one's loaf
utilitarian
utility room

**V**

vacationist
vaccination
vacillating
vacillation
vacuum flask
vagabondage
vagabondism
valediction
valedictory
vapour trail
variability
variegation
variety show
varsovienne
vascularity
vas deferens
vasodilator
vaticinator
vellication
vendibility
venesection
ventilation
ventricular
ventriloquy
venturesome
venturously
veraciously
verboseness
verisimilar

vermiculate
vermiculous
vermination
vermivorous
versatilely
versatility
versicolour
vertebrated
vertiginous
vespertinal
vesuvianite
vexatiously
vicariously
vice-admiral
viceregency
viceroyalty
viceroyship
vichyssoise
viciousness
vicissitude
vinaigrette
vincibility
vincristine
vindication
vindicative
vindicatory
vine-disease
vine-dresser
vinegarette
viniculture
vinificator
viola d'amore
violoncello
viridescent
viscountess
visibleness
visionaries
viticulture
vitrescence
vitrifiable

vituperable
vituperator
vivaciously
vivisection
vocal chords
volcanicity
volcanology
volubleness
voluntaries
voluntarily
voluntarism
voraciously
vortiginous
vulcanicity
vulcanology

**W**

waggishness
waiting game
waiting-list
waiting-room
wakefulness
walk through
Walter Mitty
wanderingly
want jam on it
warm as toast
warm-blooded
warm-hearted
war of nerves
warrantably
warts and all
washerwoman
washing soda
waspishness
water cannon
water-closet
water-colour
water-cooled
watercourse

water-hammer
watering-can
water-jacket
waterlogged
water-pistol
water-skiing
waxed jacket
waywardness
wealthiness
wear and tear
wearisomely
weasel words
weathercock
weathermost
weather-vane
wedding-cake
wedding-ring
weep buckets
weighbridge
weightiness
well-advised
well-founded
well-groomed
well-meaning
well-rounded
well-thumbed
Welsh rabbit
Wensleydale
Wesleyanism
westernmost
what have you
wheelbarrow
wheelwright
whereabouts
wheresoever
wherewithal
whichsoever
whimsically
whipping boy
whistle-stop

white-collar
white knight
white matter
white spirit
Whitsuntide
whole number
wholesomely
whoremaster
whoremonger
widdershins
willingness
wind-cheater
windfall tax
wind machine
wind-surfing
winsomeness
wintergreen
winter sport
wire service
wisdom tooth
wishfulness
witch-doctor
witenagemot
witheringly
withershins
withstander

witlessness
wolf-whistle
womanliness
wonderfully
wonderingly
wood alcohol
word for word
word-perfect
words fail me
workmanlike
workmanship
work station
world-beater
worldliness
worlds apart
worthlessly
wrapped up in
wrong-headed
wrought iron

**X**
xanthophyll
X-chromosome
xenomorphic
xerophilous
xylographer

xylographic
xylophagous
xylophilous
xylophonist

**Y**
yard-measure
Y-chromosome
yellow-belly
yellow fever
Yellow Pages®
Yellow Press
yesternight
youth hostel

**Z**
zealousness
zero gravity
zinciferous
zoantharian
zoomorphism
Zoroastrian
zygodactyle
zygomorphic
zymotically

# Twelve-letter words

**A**
abbreviation
abbreviatory
abolitionism
abolitionist
abortiveness
above oneself
above the salt
absent-minded
absoluteness
absorptivity
abstemiously
abstractedly
abstractness
abstract noun
abstruseness
academically
acanthaceous
acceleration
accelerative
acceleratory
accentuation
acciaccatura
acciaccature
accidentally
accommodator
accompanyist
accomplished
accomplisher
accouchement
accumulation
accumulative
accurateness
accusatorial

ace in the hole
Achilles' heel
achlamydeous
acknowledger
acoustically
acquaintance
acquiescence
acrocephalic
acrostically
adaptability
adder's tongue
addictedness
additionally
adhesiveness
adjudication
adjunctively
administrate
admonitorial
adorableness
adrenal gland
adscititious
adulteration
adulterously
advantageous
adventitious
Advent Sunday
adventureful
advocateship
aerodynamics
aeronautical
aerosiderite
aestheticise
aestheticism
aestheticize

aetiological
affectedness
affectionate
afflictingly
aforethought
Afro-American
Afrocentrism
after the fact
after-thought
agalmatolite
agamogenesis
agamogenetic
age of consent
agricultural
Aladdin's cave
alcohol abuse
alcoholmeter
alexipharmic
alienability
alimentation
alkalescence
alkalescency
all and sundry
all-important
all-inclusive
alliteration
alliterative
allomorphism
All Saints' Day
all steamed up
all systems go
all to the good
allusiveness
almightiness

alphabetical
alphanumeric
alterability
amalgamation
ambassadress
ambidextrous
amelioration
ameliorative
amenableness
amicableness
amicus curiae
amortisation
amortisement
amortization
amortizement
amphicoelous
amphistomous
amphitheatre
amygdaloidal
anabaptistic
anaerobiosis
anaesthetise
anaesthetist
anaesthetize
analogically
analytically
anamorphosis
anaphrodisia
anapodeictic
anathematise
anathematize
anatomically
*ancien régime*
and no mistake
anemophilous
angel of death
angel of mercy
angels' visits
angiocarpous
Angström unit

anguilliform
animalculine
animalculism
animalculist
animal rights
annihilation
annomination
announcement
Annunciation
annunciation
annunciatory
another-guess
another place
antagonistic
antarthritic
antasthmatic
antebrachial
antecedently
antediluvian
antemeridian
ante meridiem
antepileptic
anteprandial
anthelmintic
anthocarpous
anthological
anthropogeny
anthropology
anthropotomy
anti-aircraft
anticipation
anticipative
anticipatory
anticlerical
antidemocrat
anti-friction
antihypnotic
antimacassar
antimoniated
antiparallel

antiparticle
antipathetic
antiperiodic
antiphrastic
antistrophic
antitheistic
antivenereal
anything goes
aphorismatic
apostle-spoon
Apostolic See
apostrophise
apostrophize
apparitional
appassionato
appendectomy
appendicitis
appendicular
apperception
appoggiatura
appositional
appraisement
appreciation
appreciative
appreciatory
apprehension
apprehensive
approachable
approachably
appropriable
appropriator
appurtenance
April showers
aqueous humor
Arabian camel
arborescence
arborisation
arborization
archdeaconry
archipelagic

architecture
Arctic Circle
argillaceous
argue the toss
aristocratic
Aristotelean
Aristotelian
arithmetical
arithmometer
armour-bearer
armour-plated
aromatherapy
artesian well
articulately
articulation
artificially
artiodactyle
artistically
artsy-craftsy
Ascension Day
ascorbic acid
Ash Wednesday
asphyxiation
assassinator
assembly line
asseveration
assimilation
assimilative
assimilatory
astonishment
astringently
astrological
astronautics
astronomical
astrophysics
asymmetrical
asymptotical
at arm's length
at death's door
a tempo giusto

atheromatous
atmospherics
atomic energy
atomic number
atomic theory
atomic weight
at second hand
at the mercy of
at the outside
attitudinise
attitudinize
attorneyship
attractively
attributable
augmentation
augmentative
auld lang syne
auscultation
auspiciously
Australasian
authenticate
authenticity
autochthonal
avant-courier
avariciously
averruncator

**B**
babbit's metal
baby-carriage
baby-snatcher
bacchanalian
bachelorhood
bachelorship
back-breaking
back of beyond
backwardness
bacteriology
Bailey bridge
baking-powder

balance-sheet
balance-wheel
balladmonger
ball-point pen
Balm of Gilead
bamboo shoots
banderillero
bank discount
bantam-weight
barbette-ship
bare one's soul
basking-shark
basso-rilievo
battering-ram
battlemented
bay at the moon
bear the brunt
beat a retreat
beatifically
bedding-plant
beetle-browed
behaviourism
below the belt
below the salt
bench-warrant
bend sinister
benefactress
beneficently
beneficially
benevolently
bequeathable
bequeathment
Bermuda grass
beseechingly
besottedness
beta particle
better part of
betweentimes
bewilderment
bewitchingly

biarticulate
biauriculate
bibliography
bibliomaniac
bibliopolist
bicentennial
bide one's time
billingsgate
bill of health
biochemistry
biographical
biosynthesis
bird's-eye view
birth control
birthday-suit
black-and-blue
blackcurrant
black economy
blackguardly
black-hearted
black-mouthed
black-pudding
bladder-wrack
blamableness
blandishment
blarney-stone
blast-furnace
blatherskite
blennorrhoea
bletherskate
blissfulness
blister-steel
block-busting
blood-brother
blood-letting
blood-pudding
blood-sausage
bloodshedder
blood-stained
bloodthirsty

bloody-minded
blow one's mind
bluestocking
boarding pass
body-building
body language
body-snatcher
body-stocking
boiling-point
boisterously
boldface type
bolting-cloth
bomber jacket
boogie-woogie
book-learning
bootlessness
bottled water
bottle-holder
bottom drawer
boulevardier
boulevardist
bouquet garni
bow and scrape
bow-compasses
bowling-alley
bowling-green
brachygraphy
brackishness
branchiopoda
brass-founder
break dancing
break the bank
break the news
breakthrough
breast cancer
breast-plough
breast-stroke
breathalyser
breathalyzer
breathlessly

breathtaking
breeches-buoy
breech-loader
brevipennate
bride-chamber
bridging loan
brigade-major
brilliantine
bring to a head
bring to light
brinkmanship
Bristol-board
Bristol-stone
broken-winded
bronco-buster
Brontosaurus
brother-in-law
Brownie point
Brussels lace
buccaneering
buffle-headed
bull-fighting
bunch of fives
Bunsen burner
burdensomely
bureaucratic
burial ground
burning-glass
businesslike
butter-scotch
buttery-hatch
buyer's market
buzzard clock
by a short head

**C**

cabin cruiser
cabinet-maker
cachinnation
cadaverously

calabash-tree
calamitously
calisthenics
calligrapher
calligraphic
callisthenic
call of nature
call one names
call the shots
calorescence
calumniation
calumniatory
calumniously
calycifloral
camp-follower
Canada balsam
canaliculate
cancellarian
cancellation
candid camera
candle-holder
candy-striped
cannon-fodder
canonisation
canonization
Cantabrigian
cantankerous
cantharidine
capercaillie
capercailzie
capital goods
capitulation
capriciously
captiousness
caravanserai
carbohydrate
carbolic acid
carbonaceous
carbon-dating
carbonic acid

card-carrying
cardinal-bird
cardinalship
carelessness
caricaturist
Carlovingian
carpenter-ant
carpenter-bee
carpet-bagger
carpet-knight
carriageable
carte-blanche
Carthaginian
cartridge-box
case-hardened
case the joint
cash-and-carry
cash register
catachrestic
catacoustics
catadioptric
catallactics
catamountain
catastrophic
cat-o'-mountain
catch napping
catechetical
catelectrode
cat's whiskers
cattle-plague
causationism
cause célèbre
cautiousness
caveat emptor
cementitious
censoriously
centennially
centifolious
centuplicate
century plant

ceremonially
ceroplastics
chairmanship
chaise longue
chalcography
chalcopyrite
chamber music
championship
chance-medley
change colour
change of life
chaplainship
chapterhouse
characterful
characterise
characterize
Charles's-wain
charnel-house
charter-party
chartography
chastisement
chauvinistic
cheerfulness
cheeseburger
cheesemonger
cheese-paring
chemotherapy
chequer-board
cherry brandy
cherry laurel
cherry-pepper
cherry-picker
Chesterfield
chief justice
chieftainess
childbearing
childishness
child support
chilognathan
chimerically

chimney-piece
chimney-shaft
chimney-stack
chimney-stalk
chimney-sweep
Chinese white
chirographer
chirographic
chiropractic
chitterlings
chivalrously
chocolate-box
cholesterine
choreography
chrestomathy
Christ's-thorn
Christianise
Christianity
Christianize
Christmas-box
Christmas day
Christmas eve
chromatology
chrome-yellow
chromosphere
chronography
chronologist
chronometric
chrysophanic
church-warden
churlishness
chylifactive
cinéma vérité
circuitously
circumcision
circumfluent
circumfusion
circumgyrate
circumjacent
circumnutate

circumscribe
circumstance
cirrocumulus
cirrostratus
citizens' band
civil defence
civilisation
civilization
civil service
clairvoyance
clairvoyante
clannishness
classicalism
classicalist
classifiable
clear as a bell
clearing bank
clear-sighted
cleistogamic
climatically
climb the wall
clinging vine
clinker-built
closed season
cloth-binding
clothes-horse
cloud chamber
cloven-footed
cloven-hoofed
clownishness
club sandwich
coachmanship
coalitionist
coal-measures
coaxial cable
codification
coelenterate
cohabitation
cohesiveness
coincidental

coincidently
cold as marble
cold-shoulder
coleopterous
collaborator
collaterally
collectively
collectivise
collectivism
collectivist
collectivize
collectorate
colloquially
collywobbles
Cologne earth
Cologne water
colonisation
colonization
coloquintida
combinations
come a cropper
come in useful
commemorable
commemorator
commencement
commendation
commendatory
commensalism
commensality
commensurate
commentation
commentative
commercially
commiserator
commissarial
commissariat
commissioned
commissioner
commodiously
common market

commonwealth
communicable
communicably
communicator
companionway
compare notes
compellation
compensation
compensative
compensatory
complacently
complaisance
complemental
completeness
complexional
complexioned
complication
complicative
complimenter
composedness
compos mentis
comprehender
compressible
compulsively
compunctious
compurgation
computer game
concentrated
concentrical
concert party
concert pitch
concessioner
conchiferous
conchologist
conciliation
conciliatory
conclamation
conclusively
concomitance
concomitancy

concordantly
concremation
concrescence
concreteness
concupiscent
concurrently
condemnation
condemnatory
condensation
conditioning
conduplicate
confabulator
confectioner
conferential
confessional
confidential
confirmation
confirmative
confirmatory
confiscation
confiscatory
conformation
confoundedly
Confucianism
congeniality
conglobation
conglomerate
conglutinate
congratulant
congratulate
congregation
conic section
connectively
connectivity
conning tower
connubiality
conquistador
conscionable
conscionably
conscription

consecration
consecratory
consentience
consequently
conservation
conservatism
conservative
conservatory
considerable
considerably
consignation
consistently
consistorial
consociation
console table
consolidator
constabulary
constipation
constituency
constitution
constitutive
constriction
constrictive
constringent
construction
constructive
consultation
consultative
consultatory
consummation
consummative
contabescent
contagiously
containerise
containerize
contaminable
contemplator
contemporary
contemporise
contemporize

contemptible
contemptibly
contemptuous
conterminous
contestation
contiguously
contingently
continuation
continuously
contractedly
contractible
contradictor
contrapuntal
contrariness
contrariwise
contribution
contributive
contributory
contriteness
controllable
control panel
control tower
controverter
contumacious
contumelious
convalescent
convectively
conveniently
conventicler
conventional
conversantly
conversation
convexo-plane
conveyancing
conveyor belt
convincingly
convivialist
conviviality
convulsional
convulsively

cook the books
cooling tower
coordinately
coordination
coordinative
coprophagous
coprophilous
copulatively
copying-press
coquettishly
corallaceous
corduroy road
co-respondent
corn exchange
corn-marigold
corollaceous
corporalship
corporealism
corporealist
corporeality
corpse-candle
corradiation
correctional
correctitude
correlatable
corroborator
cosmographer
cosmographic
cosmological
cosmoplastic
cosmopolitan
costermonger
cost of living
cost the earth
cotyledonary
cotyledonous
council-board
counsellable
countenancer
counteragent

countercharm
countercheck
counterclaim
counterforce
countermarch
counterpoint
counterpoise
counterproof
counterscarp
countertenor
counterweigh
country-dance
country-house
country music
count the cost
coup de foudre
courageously
court-martial
court-plaster
cousin-german
covetousness
cowardliness
crack a bottle
crack-brained
crack the whip
craniologist
credibleness
credit rating
credit-worthy
creepy-crawly
cremationist
crenellation
crepe de Chine
crêpe suzette
cringe-making
criticisable
criticizable
Cro-Magnon man
cross-country
cross-current

cross-examine
cross-grained
cross-purpose
cross-section
crying out for
cryptogamous
cryptography
cucking-stool
culpableness
culture shock
cupboard-love
cupping-glass
cupuliferous
curling-irons
curling-stone
curling-tongs
currant jelly
curvirostral
custard-apple
cut and thrust
cutting-bench
cyclostomous
cylindriform

**D**
dactyliology
damnableness
danger-signal
Danish pastry
Darby and Joan
dating agency
Dead Sea fruit
deambulatory
death-warrant
debilitating
debilitation
debilitative
decapitation
decasyllabic
decasyllable

decentralise
decentralize
decimal point
decipherable
decipherment
decisiveness
declinometer
decoloration
decomposable
decongestant
deconsecrate
decreasingly
decrepitness
decrustation
dedicatorial
deducibility
deer-stalking
defamatorily
definiteness
definitional
definitively
deflagration
deforciation
deformedness
defraudation
degenerately
degeneration
degenerative
dejectedness
deliberately
deliberation
deliberative
delicateness
delicatessen
delightfully
delimitation
deliquescent
delitescence
delitescency
delusiveness

demilitarise
demilitarize
demimondaine
demoniacally
demonologist
demonstrable
demonstrably
demonstrator
demoralising
demoralizing
denaturalise
denaturalize
dendrologist
denomination
denominative
denouncement
denticulated
dentirostral
denunciation
denunciative
denunciatory
deontologist
departmental
depopulation
depravedness
depreciation
depreciative
depreciatory
depressingly
derivational
derivatively
dermatophyte
descensional
desiderative
designer drug
desirability
desolateness
despairingly
despitefully
despoliation

despondently
despotically
desquamation
desquamative
desquamatory
dessert-spoon
destructible
desulphurate
desulphurise
desulphurize
desynonymise
desynonymize
determinable
determinator
determinedly
dethronement
detonisation
detonization
detruncation
detumescence
deuteropathy
deuteroscopy
Deutsche Mark
devilishness
devil-may-care
devotionally
dextro-gyrate
diabolically
diagrammatic
dialectician
dialectology
dialling code
dialling tone
dialogically
diamagnetism
diamond-drill
diaphanously
diathermancy
diatomaceous
diatonically

dibranchiate
dichroscopic
dictatorship
didactically
dietetically
differential
digital clock
digital watch
digressional
digressively
dijudication
dilaceration
dilapidation
dilatability
dilatoriness
dilettantish
dilettantism
diminishable
diminutively
dinner-jacket
diphtheritic
diphthongise
diphthongize
diploblastic
diplomatical
directorship
disadvantage
disaffection
disaggregate
disagreeable
disagreeably
disagreement
disallowable
disallowance
disannulment
disappointed
disassociate
disastrously
disbursement
discerningly

discipleship
disciplinary
discomfiture
discommodity
discomposure
disconnected
disconsolate
discontented
discordantly
discountable
discouraging
discourteous
discoverable
discreetness
discretional
discretively
discriminate
discursively
disdainfully
diseasedness
disembarrass
disembellish
disempowered
disenchanted
disenchanter
disendowment
disestablish
disfranchise
disgorgement
disguisement
disgustingly
disharmonise
disharmonize
disincentive
disinfectant
disinfection
disingenuous
disintegrate
disinterment
dislodgement

disobedience
disorganised
disorganiser
disorganized
disorganizer
disorientate
dispauperise
dispauperize
dispensation
dispensatory
dispiritedly
displaceable
displacement
displeasedly
disputatious
disquisition
disquisitive
disregardful
disreputable
disreputably
dissatisfied
disseminator
dissenterism
dissertation
disseverance
dissimilarly
dissimulator
dissociation
dissociative
dissuasively
distillation
distillatory
distinctness
distractedly
distrainable
distribution
distributive
distributory
ditheistical
divarication

diverticulum
divertimento
divisibility
doctrinarian
dodecahedral
dodecahedron
dodecandrous
dogmatically
do-it-yourself
dolman sleeve
dolphinarium
Domesday Book
domestically
donkey-engine
donkey-jacket
donkey's years
doppelganger
dorsiventral
do the dirty on
do the honours
double-acting
double boiler
double-dagger
double-dealer
double-minded
doubtfulness
doughnutting
down the drain
dragon's-blood
dramatically
draught-board
drawing-board
drawing-paper
dreaded lurgy
dreadfulness
dressing-case
dressing-down
dressing-gown
dressing-room
driving-shaft

driving-wheel
drop a clanger
drop-in centre
droughtiness
drunk as a lord
ducking-stool
Dutch auction
Dutch courage
dwarfishness
dynamisation
dynamization

**E**
earnest money
ear-splitting
earth science
easy on the eye
eat humble pie
eat one's words
eau-de-Cologne
eavesdropper
eccentricity
ecclesiastic
ecclesiology
echo-location
eclectically
econometrics
economically
ecstatically
ectoparasite
educationist
eduction pipe
edulcoration
effectuation
effeminately
effervescent
efflorescent
effusiveness
egoistically
Egyptologist

elasmobranch
electrically
electric soup
electrolysis
electrolytic
electrometer
electrometry
electromotor
electron volt
electroplate
electroscope
electrotyper
eleemosynary
elementarily
elliptically
elocutionary
elocutionist
emancipation
emargination
emasculation
emasculative
emasculatory
embezzlement
embitterment
emblazonment
emblematical
embranchment
emigrational
emollescence
emotionalism
emotionalist
emphatically
empressement
empyreumatic
encephalitis
enchantingly
enclitically
encroachment
encumbrancer
encyclopedia

encyclopedic
endocarditis
end of the line
end of the road
endomorphism
endoparasite
endophyllous
endoskeleton
endosmometer
enfeeblement
enharmonical
entanglement
enterprising
entertaining
enthronement
enthusiastic
entomologist
Entomostraca
entrancement
entreatingly
entrepreneur
envisagement
epencephalon
epexegetical
ephemerality
ephemeridian
epicureanism
epicycloidal
epideictical
epidemiology
epigrammatic
episcopalian
episodically
epistemology
epithalamium
equalisation
equalization
equanimously
equatorially
equestrienne

equimultiple
equipollence
equipollency
equivalently
equivocatory
erythematous
escapologist
eschatologic
escort agency
escutcheoned
esoterically
essayistical
essentiality
essential oil
estrangement
etherisation
etherization
ethnographer
ethnological
etymological
euphoniously
Eurocentrism
evanescently
evangelicism
even-tempered
every man jack
evidentially
evisceration
evolutionary
evolutionist
exacerbation
exaggeration
exaggerative
exaggeratory
exalbuminous
exanthematic
exasperating
exasperation
exchangeable
exchange rate

excitability
exclusionism
exclusionist
excogitation
excruciating
excursionist
executorship
exercitation
exhaustively
exhibitioner
exhilaration
exhilarative
exophthalmic
exophthalmos
exophthalmus
exorbitantly
exoterically
expatriation
experiential
experimental
experimenter
expert system
explicitness
exploitation
expostulator
expressional
exsanguinate
exsanguinous
extemporiser
extemporizer
extensometer
exterminable
exterminator
extinguisher
extortionary
extortionate
extramarital
extramundane
extraneously
extravagance

extravagancy
extravaganza
extraversion
extroversion

**F**

factiousness
factitiously
faint-hearted
*fait accompli*
faithfulness
fallaciously
family circle
family credit
family doctor
family values
fancifulness
faradisation
faradization
farcicalness
fasciculated
fastidiously
fault-finding
*faute de mieux*
fearlessness
featherbrain
febrifacient
feeble-minded
feel the pinch
felicitation
felicitously
feminineness
fenestration
fennel-flower
ferae naturae
fermentation
fermentative
feverishness
fibrillation
fictitiously

fiddle-faddle
fiddlesticks
fidus Achates
field-glasses
fine and dandy
finnan-haddie
fissilingual
fissirostral
flabelliform
flagellation
flagelliform
flagitiously
flame-thrower
flatteringly
flexibleness
flittermouse
floriculture
fluorescence
flying doctor
flying picket
flying saucer
folding-chair
folding-stick
folding stuff
Foraminifera
for a rainy day
forbiddingly
*force majeure*
force of habit
forcibleness
fordableness
forebodement
foreknowable
formaldehyde
fornicatress
for one's pains
for the asking
for the record
fortuitously
foul one's nest

foundationer
fountain-head
fourth estate
Fourth of July
Frankenstein
frankincense
fraudulently
free-standing
French letter
French polish
frequentness
Freudian slip
friendly fire
frolicsomely
fromage frais
frondescence
frondiferous
frontispiece
fructescence
fructiferous
fruit machine
fugitiveness
fuller's earth
fully fledged
fulminic acid
functionally
furfuraceous
futilitarian

**G**

galactagogue
galactometer
galligaskins
gallinaceous
galvanometer
galvanometry
galvanoscope
gamesmanship
gamopetalous
gamophyllous

gamosepalous
gasification
gasp one's last
gastric juice
gastric ulcer
gastronomist
gate-leg table
gelatination
genealogical
general staff
geniculation
gentilitious
genuflection
geodesic dome
geographical
geologically
geometrician
Germanophile
Germanophobe
German silver
gerontocracy
gesticulator
get one's cards
get the bullet
get the hang of
get the wind up
getting on for
gift of the gab
give one stick
give the elbow
give the lie to
gladiatorial
gladiatorian
glandiferous
glass-blowing
glass ceiling
glaucomatous
globe-trotter
glockenspiel
gloom and doom

glossography
glossologist
glottologist
gluttonously
glyphography
glyptography
gobbledegook
gobbledygook
go by the board
go for a burton
go for nothing
go halves with
go hand in hand
Golden Fleece
gold standard
good-humoured
good riddance
good-tempered
goose-pimples
gossipmonger
go to one's head
go to the stake
governmental
governorship
go with a swing
gracefulness
graciousness
graduateship
grallatorial
grammaticise
grammaticize
grass-widower
gratefulness
gratuitously
Greek calends
green fingers
greenishness
gregariously
greylag goose
grey squirrel

grievousness
grind to a halt
grotesquerie
groundlessly
group therapy
growing pains
guiding light
gymnosophist
gynaecocracy

**H**
habeas corpus
haberdashery
habit-forming
hagiographer
hagiographic
hair of the dog
hair's-breadth
hallucinogen
handkerchief
hand over fist
hang one's head
happy as a lark
happy-go-lucky
hard shoulder
harlequinade
harmoniously
*haute couture*
haute cuisine
have a crack at
have a head for
have an eye for
have a nose for
have a stake in
have it coming
have no use for
headmistress
headquarters
headshrinker
health worker

heart and soul
heart-failure
heart-rending
heart-strings
heart-to-heart
heliocentric
heliogravure
heliotropism
henceforward
hereditament
hermeneutics
hermetically
herpetologic
hesitatingly
heterocercal
heterogamous
heterogeneal
heterogenous
heterologous
heteronomous
heterosexism
heterosexual
hibernaculum
Hibernianism
hidden agenda
hieroglyphic
highfaluting
high fidelity
highly strung
high-sounding
high-spirited
hindquarters
hippocentaur
hippophagism
hippophagist
hippophagous
hippopotamic
hippopotamus
hirepurchase
histogenesis

historically
histrionical
hit a bad patch
hit the bottle
hold to ransom
holidaymaker
holophrastic
Holy of holies
Holy Thursday
home from home
home straight
homoeopathic
homologation
homomorphism
homomorphous
horizontally
*hors de combat*
horticulture
housebreaker
house-husband
housekeeping
house-warming
hubble-bubble
hugger-mugger
humanitarian
humorousness
hunger strike
hydrocephaly
hydrochloric
hydrofluoric
hydrogen bomb
hydrographer
hydropathist
hydrostatics
hydrotherapy
hydrothermal
hygienically
hymenopteral
hymenopteran
hymnographer

hyperbolical
hypertension
hypertensive
hypnotherapy
hypnotisable
hypnotizable
hypochondria
hypocritical
hypogastrium
hypostatical
hypothecator
hypothetical
hysterectomy
hysterically

# I

iambographer
ichneumon-fly
ichthyolatry
ichthyopsida
identifiable
identifiably
identity card
idioelectric
idiosyncrasy
idolatrously
illegibility
illegitimacy
illegitimate
illiberality
illumination
illuminative
illustration
illustrative
immaculately
immatureness
immeasurable
immeasurably
immemorially
immensurable

immensurably
immersionist
immethodical
immoderately
immutability
impartiality
impenetrable
impenetrably
impenitently
imperatively
imperatorial
impercipient
imperfection
imperfective
imperforable
imperishable
imperishably
impersonally
impersonator
impertinence
impertinency
imperviously
impetiginous
imponderable
imposthumate
impressively
imprisonment
impropriator
improvidence
inaccessible
inaccessibly
inaccurately
in a cold sweat
inadequately
inadmissible
inadvertence
inadvertency
inapplicable
inapplicably
inappositely

inarticulate
inartificial
in at the death
inauspicious
incalculable
incalculably
incalescence
incandescent
incapacitate
incautiously
incendiarism
incidentally
incineration
inclinometer
incommodious
incommutable
incommutably
incomparable
incomparably
incompatible
incompatibly
incompetence
incompetency
incompletely
incomputable
inconclusive
inconformity
inconsequent
inconsistent
inconsolable
inconsolably
inconstantly
inconsumable
inconsumably
incorporeity
incorrigible
incorrigibly
incorrodible
incorruption
increasingly

incurability
indebtedness
indecisively
indeclinable
indeclinably
indecorously
indefeasible
indefeasibly
indefensible
indefensibly
indefinitely
indelibility
independence
independency
Indian summer
indicatively
indifference
indigestible
indigestibly
indirectness
indiscipline
indiscreetly
indiscretion
indisputable
indisputably
indissoluble
indissolubly
individually
indoctrinate
Indo-European
Indo-Germanic
induplicated
ineffaceable
ineffaceably
inefficiency
inelasticity
ineradicable
ineradicably
inexpedience
inexpediency

inexperience
inexpertness
inexplicable
inexplicably
inexpressive
inextensible
inextricable
inextricably
infectiously
infelicitous
infiltration
infinitively
inflammation
inflammatory
inflationary
inflationism
inflationist
inflectional
infrequently
infringement
infundibular
infusibility
inhabitation
inharmonious
inhospitable
inhospitably
in league with
innutritious
inobservance
in one's pocket
inosculation
insalubrious
insecureness
insolubility
inspectorate
inspissation
installation
instructress
instrumental
insufferable

insufferably
insufficient
insufflation
insurrection
integumental
intellection
intellective
intellectual
intelligence
intelligible
intelligibly
intemperance
intercession
interconnect
intercurrent
interdiction
interdictory
interdigital
interfemoral
interference
interglacial
interjection
interlineary
interlocutor
intermeddler
intermediacy
intermediary
intermediate
interminable
interminably
intermission
intermittent
intermixture
intermundane
internuncial
interoceanic
interorbital
interpellate
interpleader
interruption

interruptive
intersection
interstellar
interstitial
intertexture
intervention
intervocalic
in the balance
in the event of
in the hot seat
in the long run
in the running
in the teeth of
intimidation
intolerantly
intoxicating
intoxication
intracranial
intransigent
intransitive
intrapreneur
intrauterine
intrenchment
introduction
introductive
introductory
intromission
intromittent
introversion
intumescence
intumescency
intussuscept
invagination
invalidation
inveiglement
invertebrate
investigable
investigator
invisibility
involucellum

invulnerable
invulnerably
irascibility
ironicalness
ironing-board
irrationally
irredeemable
irredeemably
irreflective
irrefragable
irrefragably
irregularity
irremediable
irremediably
irremissible
irremissibly
irrepealable
irrepealably
irreprovable
irresistence
irresistible
irresistibly
irresolution
irresolvable
irrespective
irrespirable
irresponsive
irreverently
irreversible
irreversibly
irritability
isochromatic
isolationism
isolationist
it's a dog's life

**J**

Jack-in-office
jack-in-the-box
jack o' lantern

jigsaw puzzle
joint account
joint venture
journalistic
jump the queue
jurisconsult
jurisdiction
jurisdictive
jurisprudent
just like that
juvenescence

**K**

kaleidoscope
keep one's cool
keep one's head
keep one's word
keep the peace
Keynesianism
key signature
killing spree
kilowatt hour
kindergarten
kinnikinnick
kirschwasser
kleptomaniac
klipspringer
knight-errant
knocking copy
knocking-shop
know the ropes
know the score
Kyrie eleison

**L**

labour of love
lachrymatory
lady's slipper
laisser-faire
laissez-aller

laissez-faire
lance the boil
lancet window
landfill site
landing-craft
landing-stage
landing-strip
languishment
laryngoscope
lasciviously
laser printer
late in the day
latent period
laticiferous
laudableness
launching pad
laureateship
lay it on thick
leading light
learn by heart
legitimately
legitimation
legitimatise
legitimatize
leiotrichous
lenticularly
lepidopteral
lepidopteran
leptocardian
let oneself go
let well alone
level pegging
lexicography
lexicologist
libidinosity
libidinously
licence plate
licentiously
lickety-split
lick one's lips

lie of the land
lifelessness
life sentence
light-hearted
lightning-rod
ligniperdous
likeableness
like anything
like gold dust
lingua franca
liquefacient
liquefaction
listlessness
lithographer
lithographic
lithological
lithophagous
lithotripter
lithotriptor
little people
little tin god
liturgiology
localisation
localization
lollapalooza
lomentaceous
lonesomeness
long-distance
long-drawn-out
longitudinal
longshoreman
longshoremen
long-standing
looking-glass
loquaciously
lose one's cool
lose one's grip
lose one's head
Lower Chamber
low frequency

lugubriously
lukewarmness
lumbered with
luminiferous
luminousness
lunar eclipse
luncheon meat
lysergic acid

**M**
machicolated
Mackinaw coat
macrobiotics
macropterous
mad as a hatter
mademoiselle
magnetically
magnetic pole
magnetic tape
magnetisable
magnetizable
magnetometer
magnetometry
magnet school
magnificence
magniloquent
maidenliness
maiden speech
maiden voyage
maid of honour
maintainable
maitre d'hôtel
majestically
make a play for
make a point of
make ends meet
make good time
make it hot for
make mischief
make one's mark

make the grade
make up leeway
malevolently
malformation
malleability
malnutrition
maltreatment
malversation
man about town
mangel-wurzel
manifestable
manifestible
manipulation
manipulative
manipulatory
man of his word
manslaughter
manufacturer
market-making
mark one's card
marline-spike
marling-spike
marriageable
Marseillaise
marvellously
master-at-arms
master-stroke
materialness
mathematical
matter-of-fact
mealy-mouthed
mean business
meat and drink
mechanically
mediaevalise
mediaevalism
mediaevalize
mediaevalist
mediatorship
meditatively

megacephalic
Megalosaurus
melodramatic
melting-point
*ménage à trois*
mend one's ways
menstruation
mercantilism
mercantilist
merchantable
merchant bank
merchant navy
merchant ship
mercifulness
mercurialise
mercurialize
meretricious
meridionally
merry-go-round
merrythought
mesocephalic
mesogastrium
metamorphism
metaphysical
metempirical
meteorograph
methodically
metric system
metropolitan
mezzo-rilievo
mezzo-soprano
microbiology
microcircuit
microclimate
microgeology
microphonous
microscopist
middleweight
midsummer day
Midsummer Eve

miles per hour
mind-boggling
mine-detector
mineral water
minicomputer
ministration
ministrative
minstrel show
miraculously
mirthfulness
misadventure
misanthropic
misapprehend
misbelieving
miscalculate
misdemeanant
misdemeanour
misdirection
misinterpret
misplacement
mispronounce
misrepresent
misstatement
mistranslate
mitrailleuse
mixed doubles
mixed economy
mobilisation
mobilization
modification
modificatory
modus vivendi
moire antique
monadelphous
monastically
monetisation
monetization
money-changer
monkey-wrench
monodelphian

monographist
monomaniacal
monometallic
monomorphous
monopetalous
monophyllous
monosepalous
monospermous
monosyllabic
monosyllable
monumentally
moon-stricken
morality play
moral support
moral victory
morning after
morning-glory
morning watch
morphologist
motorcyclist
motor-scooter
motor vehicle
mountain bike
mournfulness
mucilaginous
mucopurulent
muddle-headed
mulligatawny
multiangular
multicostate
multifarious
multiformity
multilateral
multilingual
multipliable
multiplicand
multiplicate
multiplicity
multitubular
municipalise

municipality
municipalize
mysteriously
mythographer

**N**

name-dropping
namelessness
narcotically
narrow escape
narrow-minded
narrow squeak
national debt
national grid
National Park
naturalistic
nautical mile
navigability
necrophagous
nectocalyces
needlessness
neglectfully
neighbouring
neologically
Neoplatonism
Neoplatonist
nerve-racking
Nestorianism
neurasthenia
neurosurgery
nevertheless
Newfoundland
New Testament
nickel-silver
nidification
nightclothes
niminy-piminy
nitrous oxide
noctambulist
*nolens volens*

nomenclature
nominatively
nomothetical
nonagenarian
non-alcoholic
nonchalantly
non-combatant
non-committal
non-conductor
non-effective
none so pretty
none the wiser
non-flammable
non plus ultra
normal school
north-eastern
northernmost
north-western
notary public
not be oneself
not cut out for
not for toffee
not have a bean
nothing doing
notification
not one's scene
not turn a hair
nouveau riche
nuclear power
nuclear waste
Nunc dimittis
nursery rhyme
nursery slope
nutritionist
nutritiously
nuts and bolts
nyctitropism

**O**

obdurateness

obiter dictum
object-lesson
oblanceolate
obligatorily
obligingness
oblique angle
obliteration
obliterative
obscurantism
obscurantist
obsequiously
obsolescence
obsoleteness
obstreperous
occasionally
occidentally
oceanography
octane number
octane rating
octogenarian
octopetalous
octosyllable
octosyllabic
off one's guard
off-scourings
off the record
of the essence
oil the wheels
old-fashioned
old school tie
Old Testament
old wives' tale
oleomargarin
Olympic games
omnipotently
omnipresence
omnisciently
on a knife edge
on bended knee
one-hit wonder

one-horse race
one jump ahead
one's own thing
one-track mind
one-upmanship
onomatopoeia
onomatopoeic
on one's mettle
on one's uppers
on the qui vive
on the rampage
on the rebound
on the streets
on the up and up
on the warpath
opera-glasses
ophiophagous
opinionative
oppressively
optical fibre
optical glass
oratorically
organ-grinder
organisation
organization
organography
orienteering
ornamentally
ornithomancy
ornithoscopy
orographical
orthodontics
orthodontist
orthogenesis
orthogenetic
orthognathic
orthographer
orthographic
orthopaedics
orthotropism

orthotropous
oscilloscope
ossification
ostentatious
osteodentine
osteographer
osteomalacia
osteoporosis
other-worldly
out in the cold
outmanoeuvre
out of the blue
out on one's ear
outplacement
outrageously
overestimate
over one's head
overpowering
overwhelming
oxyacetylene

P

pack one's bags
palaeobotany
palaeography
palaeolithic
palette-knife
palingenesis
palpableness
panchromatic
Pan-Hellenism
pantisocracy
papistically
paracentesis
parachronism
paradisiacal
paraesthesia
paragraphist
paralipomena
paramilitary

parascending
parasiticide
parasitology
parenchymous
parenthesise
parenthesize
paridigitate
parisyllabic
parking-meter
parkinsonism
parochialise
parochialism
parochialize
paronomastic
parsimonious
participator
particularly
partisanship
part of speech
pasque-flower
passepartout
passion fruit
patent office
pathetically
pathogenesis
pathological
pat on the back
patriarchate
patriarchism
pay on the nail
peacefulness
peace process
peanut butter
pecking order
pedunculated
pellucidness
penitentiary
pentagonally
peradventure
perambulator

perceptivity
percutaneous
peregrinator
peremptorily
perfidiously
pergameneous
pericarditis
periodontics
peripherical
periphrastic
perivascular
perivisceral
permanganate
permeability
perpetration
perplexingly
perquisition
perseverance
persistently
*persona grata*
perspicacity
perspiration
perspiratory
persuasively
pertinacious
perturbation
pervicacious
pestilential
petrifaction
petrifactive
petrographer
petrographic
pettifoggery
pettifogging
petty larceny
petty officer
phaenogamous
phagocytosis
phanerogamic
pharmacology

pharyngology
pharyngotomy
Phi Beta Kappa
philanthropy
philharmonic
Philhellenic
philistinism
philosophise
philosophism
philosophist
philosophize
phlebotomise
phlebotomist
phlebotomize
phlegmatical
phonetically
phosphoresce
photographic
photogravure
phraseologic
phrenologist
phylogenesis
phylogenetic
physiocratic
physiography
phytogenesis
phytophagous
pick up the tab
pigmentation
pigs might fly
pip at the post
pisciculture
pitiableness
pitilessness
placableness
plain-clothes
plain sailing
plane sailing
planispheric
plano-concave

plaster-board
play ball with
playing field
pleasantries
plebiscitary
plenipotence
plenipotency
Plesiosaurus
Plimsoll line
Plimsoll mark
pluriliteral
plurilocular
pneumatology
Poet Laureate
polarisation
polarization
pole position
policyholder
pollutedness
polyanthuses
polyethylene
polymorphism
polymorphous
polyphyllous
polyspermous
polysyllabic
polysyllable
polysyndeton
polyurethane
pontifically
pop one's clogs
populousness
portableness
portentously
positiveness
possessively
postage-stamp
postdiluvial
postdiluvian
postgraduate

postliminium
postmeridian
post meridiem
postprandial
potentiality
power company
powerfulness
power-station
powers that be
practicality
practitioner
praiseworthy
praseodymium
precancerous
precedential
preceptorial
preciousness
precipitable
precisianism
precociously
precognition
pre-Columbian
precondition
predestinate
predetermine
predilection
prefabricate
preferential
prelatically
premaxillary
preoccupancy
preparedness
preponderant
preponderate
preposterous
prerequisite
presbyterial
Presbyterian
prescription
prescriptive

presentation
presentative
presentiment
preservation
preservative
presidential
presumptuous
prevailingly
preventative
pridefulness
pride of place
priestliness
primigenious
primogenitor
primrose path
primum mobile
principality
probationary
proboscidean
proboscidian
processional
proclamation
proclamatory
prodigiously
productivity
professional
professorate
professorial
profoundness
prolegomenon
proletariate
prolifically
prolificness
prolongation
promulgation
propaedeutic
propagandise
propagandism
propagandist
propagandize

propenseness
prophylactic
propitiation
propitiously
proportional
proscription
proscriptive
proselytiser
proselytizer
prosopopoeia
prosperously
prostitution
protactinium
protectorate
protestation
prothalamion
prothonotary
protoplasmic
protozoology
protractedly
protuberance
protuberancy
proverbially
providential
provisionary
prudentially
Prussian blue
pseudonymous
psychiatrist
psychologist
psychrometer
public health
public school
public sector
public spirit
pugnaciously
pulveraceous
pulverisable
pulverizable
pumpernickel

purblindness
purification
push one's luck
put a damper on
put a sock in it
put one wise to
put on the spot
putrefaction
putrefactive
put the bite on
put the boot in
pyroelectric
pyrometrical
pyrotechnics
pyrotechnist

**Q**

Quadragesmia
quadrangular
quadraphonic
quadrinomial
quadriplegia
quadrivalent
quadrumanous
qualmishness
quantitative
quaquaversal
quarter-bound
quarter-final
quarter light
quarter-staff
Quattrocento
querimonious
questionable
questionably
question mark
queue-jumping
quinquennial
quinquennium
quintessence

**R**

rabble-rouser
racing driver
radiocompass
radio control
radioelement
radioisotope
radiotherapy
rags to riches
rainbow trout
raise the ante
raise the wind
rambunctious
ramification
random access
ratification
razzle-dazzle
readjustment
readmittance
reannexation
reappearance
reassumption
rebelliously
recalcitrant
recapitulate
receivership
recensionist
receptacular
receptionist
reciprocally
recklessness
recognisance
recognizance
recollection
recollective
recommitment
reconcilable
reconstitute
reconveyance
recordership

record-player
recovery room
recrudescent
recuperation
recuperative
recuperatory
red blood cell
red corpuscle
redintegrate
redistribute
red-letter day
red-light area
reflectively
reflex camera
reform school
refractorily
refreshingly
refrigerator
refutability
regardlessly
regeneration
regenerative
regeneratory
registration
rehabilitate
reilluminate
reimposition
reindeer-moss
reinspection
reinstalment
reinvestment
reinvigorate
rejuvenation
relationless
relationship
relativeness
relentlessly
reliableness
religionless
relinquisher

remembrancer
reminiscence
remonstrance
remorsefully
removability
remuneration
remunerative
renewability
renouncement
renunciation
reparability
repercussion
repercussive
reprehension
reprehensive
repressively
reproachable
reproachably
reproduction
reproductive
reproductory
requiescence
residentiary
resiniferous
resistlessly
resoluteness
resolutioner
resolvedness
resourceless
respectfully
respectively
resplendence
resplendency
respondentia
responsively
restaurateur
restauration
restrainable
restrainedly
resurrection

resuscitable
resuscitator
reticulation
retractation
retrenchment
retrievement
retrocession
retroversion
return ticket
revengefully
reverberator
reverse video
rhesus factor
rhesus monkey
rheumatology
rhinoplastic
rhizophagous
rhododendron
rhodomontade
rhombohedral
rhombohedron
rhyming slang
rhythmically
rhythm method
ribonuclease
Richter scale
ride the tiger
ridiculously
right-hand man
ring-side seat
rip-off artist
risk one's neck
road junction
roaring drunk
rocking-chair
rocking-horse
rocking-stone
rolling-stock
rolling stone
Roman holiday

Roman numeral
romantically
rooming-house
rose-coloured
rough diamond
round the bend
rub shoulders
rule the roost
rumpty-pumpty
run its course
run of the mill
run the risk of
russophobist
ruthlessness

S
sacerdotally
sacramentary
sacrilegious
sacrosanctly
safari jacket
safe and sound
safe as houses
Saint Bernard
saleableness
sale or return
salesmanship
salmon-ladder
salubriously
salutariness
Salvationism
Salvationist
same old story
sanguiferous
sanguineness
sanguinolent
saponifiable
saprophagous
sarcophagous
sarsaparilla

satisfaction
satisfactory
*sauve qui peut*
save one's skin
savoy cabbage
scandalously
Scandinavian
scarificator
scarlatinous
scarlet fever
scarlet woman
scatter-brain
scenographer
scenographic
schismatical
schizomycete
schoolmaster
schorlaceous
sciatic nerve
scintigraphy
scissors kick
sclerenchyma
sclerodermic
scornfulness
scorpion-fish
Scotland Yard
scoundrelism
scraperboard
scratch video
screen-writer
scripturally
scriptwriter
scrofulously
scrophularia
scrupulosity
scrupulously
sculpturally
scurrilously
scutelliform
season ticket

secessionism
secessionist
second advent
second coming
second cousin
second fiddle
second nature
second person
second string
second to none
secretariate
secret police
sectarianise
sectarianism
sectarianize
security lock
security risk
sedge-warbler
sedulousness
see the back of
segmentation
seigniorship
seignorously
seismologist
selenography
self-catering
self-coloured
self-educated
self-employed
self-interest
self-portrait
self-reproach
selling plate
selling point
selling price
semeiography
semidetached
semiliterate
seminiferous
semiprecious

sempervirent
senatorially
sensibleness
sensifacient
sensitometer
separability
separateness
septennially
septuagenary
Septuagesima
sequestrator
seraphically
serial killer
serial number
seropositive
serpentiform
serum albumin
set one's cap at
sexagenarian
shamefacedly
shamefulness
share-cropper
sharp-shooter
sharp-tongued
shatter-proof
sheepishness
shepherd's pie
sheriff-court
Shetland pony
shilly-shally
ship's biscuit
ship-chandler
shirtwaister
shock therapy
shooting-star
shoot through
shopping list
shopping mall
short-circuit
short-sighted

short-staffed
shot in the arm
show business
show one's hand
show the ropes
shrewishness
shudderingly
shuffleboard
Siamese twins
siderography
side-whiskers
significator
sign language
silver lining
silver screen
silviculture
simoniacally
simple-minded
simultaneity
simultaneous
single-decker
single-handed
single market
single-minded
single ticket
siphon bottle
six of the best
skipping-rope
skullduggery
slanderously
slaughterous
sledgehammer
sleeping pill
sliding scale
slip one's mind
slipperiness
Sloane Ranger
slovenliness
slow handclap
sluggishness

sluttishness
small holding
smash-and-grab
smooth muscle
snake-charmer
snap fastener
snappishness
snobbishness
snooperscope
sociobiology
sock it to them
Socratically
soda-fountain
soixante-neuf
solicitation
solicitously
solidifiable
solisequious
solitariness
solvent abuse
somnambulate
somnambulism
somnambulist
son et lumière
song and dance
sonic barrier
sonorousness
sophisticate
soporiferous
sound barrier
sound effects
sounding-lead
sounding line
south-eastern
southernmost
south-western
space shuttle
space station
spaciousness
sparking-plug

speak too soon
speak volumes
specialities
specifically
spectrograph
spectrometer
spectroscope
spectroscopy
spermatocyte
spermatozoon
sphenography
sphenoid bone
sphragistics
sphygmograph
spick-and-span
spider-monkey
spinal column
spine-chiller
spiny lobster
spiral galaxy
spiritedness
spiritlessly
spiritualise
spiritualism
spiritualist
spirituality
spiritualize
spitefulness
splenomegaly
sporadically
sporogenesis
spotlessness
spuriousness
squeaky-clean
stage-manager
stage-whisper
stained glass
stalwartness
standing army
stand-up comic

stand-up fight
stanniferous
starting gate
starting grid
statesperson
station-house
stationwagon
statistician
status symbol
staying power
steal the show
steatopygous
steeplechase
steer clear of
stenographer
stenographic
stepdaughter
stereography
stereophonic
stereopticon
stereotypist
sternutation
sternutative
sternutatory
sticky wicket
stock-broking
stony-hearted
storm-trooper
stormy petrel
stout-hearted
straight away
straightedge
straight face
straightness
strait-jacket
stranglehold
straticulate
stratigraphy
stratosphere
strawberries

streetwalker
strengthener
streptomycin
stridulation
strike a chord
strike it rich
strip cartoon
strong-minded
stubbornness
studiousness
stuffed shirt
stupefacient
stupefaction
stupefactive
stupendously
stylographic
subcommittee
subconscious
subcontinent
subcutaneous
subdivisible
subepidermal
subfeudatory
subjectively
subjectivity
sublineation
submaxillary
submissively
suboccipital
subscription
subsequently
subservience
subserviency
subsidiarity
substantiate
substantival
substitution
substruction
substructure
subterranean

succedaneous
successfully
successional
successively
succinctness
sudoriferous
sufficiently
suffruticose
sugar the pill
suggestively
suitableness
suit one's book
sulphonamide
sulphuration
sulphuretted
summer school
Sunday school
sunshine roof
superannuate
superciliary
supercilious
supereminent
superhighway
supermundane
supernacular
supernaculum
supernatural
superstition
supplication
supplicatory
suppositious
suppressible
supramundane
supraorbital
Supreme Court
surmountable
surprisingly
surrejoinder
surroundings
surveillance

surveyorship
survivorship
susceptivity
suspiciously
sustentation
sweet-and-sour
sweet-william
swindle sheet
swing the lead
sycophantish
sycophantism
syllabically
symbolically
synantherous
synarthroses
synarthrosis
synonymously
synoptically
systematical

**T**

tabernacular
tachygraphic
take as gospel
take a shine to
take for a ride
take one's time
talcum powder
talismanical
talking point
tamelessness
tangentially
tangibleness
tape recorder
taramasalata
tartaric acid
tastefulness
tax avoidance
tax therapist
tear one's hair

technicality
technologist
techno-stress
teething ring
telaesthesia
telautograph
telegraphist
teleological
teleordering
teleprompter
teleshopping
tellurometer
temperaments
temporal lobe
temporalness
tenant-farmer
ten-gallon hat
tenuirostral
tercentenary
terebinthine
tergiversate
terribleness
terrifically
testosterone
test-tube baby
tetrapterous
thallogenous
thankfulness
thanksgiving
thaumatology
theatrically
the bare bones
the die is cast
the knowledge
theocratical
theorematist
theoretician
theosophical
therapeutics
therapeutist

thereagainst
the real McCoy
the red carpet
there's the rub
thermocouple
the very devil
the very thing
thick and fast
thick-skinned
thievishness
thitherwards
thoroughbred
thoroughfare
thoughtfully
three-quarter
thriftlessly
throw a wobbly
thunderstorm
thyrotrophin
ticklishness
time exposure
time-honoured
tip the scales
titaniferous
tittle-tattle
toggle-switch
toilet tissue
toothed whale
top of the tree
topographist
torrefaction
Torricellian
tortuousness
totalitarian
tourist class
tour operator
to wear motley
toxicologist
toxocariasis
trace element

tracing-paper
tradescantia
traditionist
traducianism
traducianist
traffic light
trailing edge
training-ship
train-spotter
train surfing
traitorously
tranquillise
tranquillity
tranquillize
tranquilness
transferable
transference
transfusible
transgressor
transhipment
transhumance
transitional
transitively
transitorily
translatable
translucence
translucency
transmigrant
transmigrate
transmission
transmogrify
transmutable
transmutably
transoceanic
transparence
transparency
transpicuous
transplanter
transpontine
transporting

transposable
transudation
transudatory
transumptive
transversely
transvestism
transvestite
travel agency
treasure hunt
triadelphous
triangularly
tricentenary
trichiniasis
trichomatose
trichromatic
trick-cyclist
trick or treat
tricuspidate
tridactylous
trigger-happy
trigonometry
trigrammatic
tripartitely
triphthongal
triumphantly
tropological
truncheoneer
truthfulness
truth will out
tubeless tyre
tuberculated
tuberculosis
tubular bells
tumultuously
tunnel vision
Turk's-cap lily
turning-point
turn of phrase
turn one's coat
turn one's head

turn up trumps
tu-whit tu-whoo
Twelfth Night
twenty-twenty
twist one's arm
two-way mirror
tympanic bone
typhoid fever
tyrannically

**U**
ubiquitously
ugly duckling
ultramontane
umbrageously
unacceptable
unaccustomed
unacquainted
unadulterate
unanswerable
unanswerably
unappealable
unappeasable
unaspiringly
unassailable
unassailably
unauthorised
unauthorized
unbecomingly
unbelievable
unbreathable
unchallenged
unchangeable
unchangeably
uncharitable
uncharitably
uncommercial
uncovenanted
unctuousness
uncultivated

undeceivable
undeclinable
underachieve
underclothes
undercurrent
underdressed
undergarment
underpinning
understratum
underwriting
undeservedly
undetermined
undiscerning
undischarged
unemployable
unexpectedly
unfaithfully
unfathomable
unfathomably
unfavourable
unfavourably
unfranchised
unfrequented
unfruitfully
ungenerously
ungovernable
ungovernably
ungracefully
ungraciously
ungratefully
unhandsomely
unhesitating
unhistorical
unimportance
unimpugnable
uninstructed
uninterested
Unitarianise
Unitarianism
Unitarianize

universalism
universalist
universities
universology
unkindliness
unlawfulness
unlikelihood
unlikeliness
unmanageable
unmarketable
unmercifully
unmistakable
unmistakably
unobservedly
unobstructed
unparalleled
unpatronised
unpatronized
unpleasantly
unpleasingly
unpoetically
unpopularity
unprejudiced
unpreparedly
unpretending
unprincipled
unprivileged
unproductive
unprofitable
unpropitious
unprosperous
unquenchable
unquenchably
unquestioned
unreasonable
unreasonably
unreconciled
unregeneracy
unregistered
unreservedly

unrestrained
unrestricted
unsanctified
unsatisfying
unscriptural
unscrupulous
unsearchable
unseasonable
unseasonably
unseemliness
unstableness
unsteadiness
unstratified
unsuccessful
unsuppressed
unsuspecting
unsuspicious
unsystematic
untenantable
unthinkingly
untowardness
untrammelled
untruthfully
unwieldiness
unwontedness
unworthiness
unwritten law
up one's street
uproariously
up to one's ears
up to one's eyes
urban renewal
urinogenital
user-friendly

**V**

vacuum bottle
vacuum-packed
vainglorious
valetudinary

valuableness
Vandyke beard
Vandyke brown
vanquishable
vaporisation
vaporization
variableness
varicoloured
vaticination
veggieburger
velocipedist
vendibleness
verification
vernacularly
versificator
vertebration
verticillate
vestal virgin
veterinarian
vice-chairman
victoria plum
victoriously
vigorousness
vilification
villainously
vindictively
*vin ordinaire*
viola da gamba
virgo intacta
viscosimeter
viscountship
visitatorial
visiting-card
visitor's book
vitalisation
vitalization
vitreous body
vitreousness
vitrifaction
vitrifacture

vitriolation
vituperation
vituperative
viviparously
vocabularies
vocalisation
vocalization
vociferation
vociferously
voluminously
voluntaryism
voluntaryist
voluptuaries
voluptuously
vomiturition
vote of thanks

**W**

walkie-talkie
walking-stick
wandering Jew
warehouseman
warehousemen
warning light
wasting asset
watchfulness
water-biscuit
water-blister
water-boatman
water-buffalo
water company
water-diviner
watering hole
water-soluble
water-spaniel
ways and means
weather-board
weather-bound
weather-glass
weatherproof

Welfare State
well-balanced
well-disposed
well-favoured
well-grounded
well-informed
Wellingtonia
well-mannered
Welsh dresser
Welsh rarebit
welterweight
whale of a time
what's cooking?
whatsitsname?
whencesoever
wherethrough
whimsicality
whipped cream
whip-poor-will
whisperingly
white feather
whole-hearted
whortleberry

wicket-keeper
willing horse
will-o'-the-wisp
winding-sheet
wind of change
wine-coloured
winter sports
wish one joy of
witching hour
within reason
with interest
with open arms
witness stand
womanishness
working-class
working party
world-shaking
World Wide Web
worm's-eye view
worshipfully
wranglership
wrathfulness
wretchedness

writer's cramp
writing-paper

**X**
xanthochroic
xiphisternum
xylobalsamum

**Y**
yellow-hammer
yellow-jacket
yellow streak
youthfulness

**Z**
zincographic
zoochemistry
zoogeography
zoologically
zoopathology
zoophytology
zygodactylic
zygomorphous

# Thirteen-letter words

**A**
above one's head
absorbability
accessibility
accidentalism
acclimatation
accommodating
accommodation
accommodative
accompaniment
accoutrements
acetabuliform
acetification
acidification
acquired taste
acquisitively
acrimoniously
active service
Addressograph®
admeasurement
administrator
admirableness
admissibility
adumbratively
adventurously
advertisement
advisableness
aesthetically
affirmatively
afforestation
affreightment
African violet
after a fashion
agglomeration

agglutination
agglutinative
aggravatingly
agreeableness
agree to differ
agriculturist
alcoholometer
algebraically
allegorically
alligator-pear
all in good time
all in one piece
allowableness
a long way after
alpha and omega
alpha particle
alternatively
aluminiferous
ambassadorial
ambidexterity
ambidexterous
American dream
amniocentesis
amphiprostyle
amplification
amplificative
amplificatory
amusement park
anachronistic
anagrammatise
anagrammatist
anagrammatize
analogue clock
analogue watch

anaphrodisiac
ancient lights
Ancient of Days
andropetalous
an eye for an eye
Anglo-American
Anglo-Catholic
angostura bark
angry young man
animadversion
animalisation
animalization
animal kingdom
animal spirits
annexationist
antaphroditic
anthropolatry
anthropologic
anthropometry
anthropopathy
anthropophagi
anthropophagy
antichristian
anticlimactic
anticlockwise
anticoagulant
anticorrosive
antiephialtic
antiepiscopal
antihistamine
antilogarithm
antimonarchic
antimonianism
antipersonnel

antiscorbutic
antispasmodic
antitypically
anybody's guess
apheliotropic
apogeotropism
Apostles' Creed
apostolically
appellatively
appendiculate
apple-pie order
applicability
apportionment
apprehensible
appropriately
appropriation
approximately
approximation
approximative
April-Fools' day
aqueous humour
Arabic numeral
arbitrariness
arboriculture
archaeologist
archaeopteryx
archbishopric
archidiaconal
archimandrite
architectonic
architectural
ardent-spirits
argentiferous
argilliferous
argumentation
argumentative
arithmetician
armed services
*arrière-pensée*
arundinaceous

ascertainable
ascertainment
ascriptitious
ask for the moon
assassination
assault course
assembly rooms
assiduousness
associateship
Assyriologist
asthmatically
astonishingly
at a snail's pace
at crack of dawn
at dead of night
at full stretch
atheistically
at one's service
at one's wits' end
atrociousness
attainability
attentiveness
at the bottom of
at the last gasp
attributively
auction bridge
audaciousness
authentically
authoritarian
authoritative
autobiography
autocephalous
autochondriac
autochthonous
autoeroticism
availableness
axiomatically

**B**

baccalaureate

back to the hilt
back to the wall
backwardation
bacteriolysis
Bactrian camel
bag and baggage
ballast-heaver
ball-cartridge
balsamiferous
bamboo curtain
baptism of fire
Barbour jacket
barefacedness
basso-profundo
battle-cruiser
be asking for it
beatification
Beaufort scale
beautifulness
beauty parlour
béchamel sauce
be curtains for
beetle-brained
before the fact
beginningless
believability
belles-lettres
Bermuda-rigged
Bermuda shorts
beside oneself
Bessemer-steel
be the making of
betweenwhiles
be up against it
be worlds apart
beyond compare
beyond one's ken
beyond the pale
bibliographer
bibliological

big bang theory
biodegradable
biotechnology
bird of passage
bite the bullet
black-and-white
blackguardism
blamelessness
blasphemously
blastogenesis
bleeding heart
blindman's-buff
blood-curdling
blood-pressure
blood-relation
blood-relative
bloodshedding
blood-spilling
blotting-paper
blow the lid off
boarding-house
Bob's your uncle
bombastically
booking-office
boot and saddle
Borstal system
bougainvillea
bouillabaisse
boundlessness
bountifulness
boustrophedon
brachypterous
break one's back
break one's duck
break one's neck
break the mould
breech-loading
breviloquence
brevirostrate
bring into play

brinksmanship
broad-spectrum
broken English
broken-hearted
bronchial tube
brotherliness
bubonic plague
bucketing down
bulletin-board
bumptiousness
burglariously
burning-mirror
burn one's boats
burnt offering
bush-telegraph
business class
butcher's-broom
butter-fingers
by all accounts

## C

calcification
calendar month
calico-printer
callisthenics
call one's bluff
calorifacient
camera obscura
campanologist
Campeachy wood
camphoraceous
campylobacter
candidateship
canonical hour
capaciousness
caprification
carbon dioxide
carboniferous
carbonisation
carbonization

cardboard city
cardiac arrest
carnification
carotid artery
carpet-bedding
carpenter-bird
carpenter-moth
carpet-sweeper
carrier pigeon
carte-de-visite
cartilaginous
cartridge-belt
cartridge-clip
cash dispenser
castle-builder
catastrophism
catch in the act
catchment-area
catch on the hop
catechistical
categorematic
categorically
cat-o'-nine-tails
causelessness
caustic potash
cauterisation
cauterization
Cayenne pepper
cellular radio
cephalic index
cephalisation
cephalization
cephalothorax
cerebral palsy
cerebrospinal
ceremonialism
ceremoniously
certification
cervical smear
chain reaction

chalcographer
challengeable
chammy leather
chancel-screen
chance one's arm
changeability
changefulness
change of heart
Channel Tunnel
characterless
charge account
chartographic
cheerlessness
cheiropterous
cheval de frise
chimney-corner
Chinese puzzle
chop and change
chopping-knife
chorepiscopal
chrematistics
Christian name
Christmas card
Christmas rose
Christmastide
Christmas tree
chromatophore
chronographer
chronological
chrysanthemum
chuck-farthing
churchmanship
church service
chylification
chymification
cicatrisation
cicatrization
cinchonaceous
cinematograph
cinnamon-stone

circumambient
circumduction
circumference
circumfluence
circumjacence
circumjacency
circumspectly
circumvallate
circumvention
circumventive
civil engineer
clamorousness
clandestinely
clarification
clearing house
clear one's name
clear the decks
cleistogamous
climatography
climbing-frame
clincher-built
clip one's wings
cloister-garth
closed circuit
coadjutorship
coarse-grained
cobelligerent
cochleariform
cocker spaniel
cock of the walk
coenaesthesis
coessentially
coextensively
cog in the wheel
cold as charity
collaborateur
collaboration
collectedness
colloquialism
colloquialist

combativeness
come to nothing
commandership
command module
commemorative
commensurable
commensurably
commercial art
commercialise
commercialism
commercialize
commiseration
commiserative
common measure
communication
communicative
community care
commutability
commutatively
companionable
companionably
companionless
companionship
comparatively
compassionate
compass points
compatibility
compendiously
complainingly
complaisantly
complementary
complex number
complimentary
comprehension
comprehensive
computer virus
concatenation
concavo-convex
conceitedness
concentration

concentrative
conceptualise
conceptualism
conceptualist
conceptualize
concomitantly
concretionary
concupiscence
concupiscible
condensed milk
condescending
condescension
conditionally
conduciveness
confabulation
confabulatory
confectionery
confederation
confederative
confessionary
confessorship
confidence man
confidingness
configuration
conflagration
confraternity
confrontation
congratulator
congressional
conjecturable
conjecturally
conjugational
conjunctional
conjunctively
consanguinity
conscientious
consciousness
consecutively
consentaneous
consequential

conservatoire
considerately
consideration
consolidation
conspicuously
conspiratress
constableship
constellation
consternation
constrainable
constrainedly
consumer goods
consumptively
contabescence
contamination
contaminative
contemplation
contemplative
contentedness
contentiously
contextualise
contextualize
continuity man
contortionist
contrabandism
contrabandist
contrabassoon
contraception
contraceptive
contractility
contradiction
contradictive
contradictory
contrapuntist
contrate-wheel
contravention
contributable
controversial
controvertist
convalescence

convalescency
conventionary
conventionist
*conversazione*
convexo-convex
convocational
convulsionary
cook one's goose
copartnership
coralliferous
corollifloral
corps de ballet
Corpus Christi
corpus delicti
correlatively
correspondent
corresponding
corresponsive
corroboration
corroborative
corroboratory
corrodibility
corrosiveness
corruptionist
corymbiferous
cosmopolitism
cost-effective
cottage cheese
cotton-spinner
counteraction
counteractive
counterattack
counterchange
countercharge
counterfeiter
countermotion
counterpoison
countersignal
counterstroke
counterweight

counting house
country cousin
county cricket
*coup de théâtre*
courteousness
coxcombically
craftsmanship
cranioscopist
crazy like a fox
cream of tartar
creditability
credulousness
crème de menthe
cross-breeding
cross-gartered
cross-hatching
cross one's mind
cross-question
crotchetiness
crown princess
cruise missile
cruiserweight
crustaceology
cry for the moon
cryptographer
cryptographic
crystal-gazing
cultured pearl
curtain-raiser
customariness
cut down to size
cut one's losses
cut to the quick
cylindrically
cytoscreening

# D
dactylioglyph
dactylography
daddy-long-legs

daguerreotype
dairy products
dancing-master
Dandie Dinmont
dangerousness
dastardliness
daughter-in-law
dauntlessness
dead and buried
dead as the dodo
dead reckoning
death-struggle
decaffeinated
deceitfulness
deceptiveness
decimal system
decomposition
deconcentrate
decontaminate
decortication
decrepitation
deep in thought
defectiveness
defencelessly
defensibility
deferentially
defibrination
deliciousness
deliquescence
delirifacient
deliriousness
dematerialise
dematerialize
demonstration
demonstrative
denationalise
denationalize
denticulately
denticulation
deodorisation

deodorization
deontological
depersonalise
depersonalize
dephosphorise
dephosphorize
deprecatingly
dermatologist
dermoskeleton
descriptively
desirableness
destructively
desultoriness
deterioration
determinately
determination
determinative
detrimentally
deus ex machina
deuteragonist
deuterogamist
developmental
devotionalism
devotionalist
devotionality
dexterousness
dialectically
dialogistical
diametrically
diaphragmatic
diathermanous
dice with death
dichlamydeous
dichotomously
dictatorially
diesel engine
differentiate
diffusibility
diffusiveness
digestibility

diphthongally
diplomatic bag
dipsomaniacal
direct current
disadvantaged
disappearance
disarticulate
disciplinable
discoloration
disconnection
discontinuity
discontinuous
discount store
discreditable
discreditably
discretionary
discriminator
disembarkment
disengagement
disfiguration
disfigurement
disgracefully
dishonourable
dishonourably
disintegrable
disinterested
disjunctively
dismemberment
disnaturalise
disnaturalize
disobediently
disobligement
disobligingly
disparagement
disparagingly
dispassionate
displantation
dispossession
disproportion
disrespectful

dissemination
dissimilarity
dissimilation
dissimilitude
dissimulation
dissolubility
dissoluteness
distastefully
distinctively
distinguished
distressfully
distressingly
distributable
distrustfully
diversifiable
do a double-take
domestication
domiciliation
double-dealing
double-hearted
double-jointed
double-meaning
double-tongued
Down's syndrome
draggle-tailed
draining board
dramatisation
dramatization
draughts-board
draw a veil over
drawing master
dressed to kill
dressing table
drill sergeant
drink-offering
dripping roast
driving mirror
dwelling-house
dyed-in-the-wool
dynamo-machine

dysmenorrhoea

**E**
earthly-minded
eat like a horse
eccentrically
Echinodermata
economisation
economization
educationally
effectiveness
effervescence
effervescible
efficaciously
efflorescence
egotistically
Egpytological
elaborateness
electric chair
electrifiable
electrocution
electromagnet
electrometric
electromotive
electrophorus
elephantiasis
embarrassment
embellishment
embryological
emigrationist
encephalogram
encomiastical
encompassment
encouragement
encouragingly
encyclopaedia
encyclopaedic
encyclopedist
endocrinology
endurableness

energetically
en grande tenue
enigmatically
enlightenment
entertainment
enter the lists
entomological
entomophagous
entomophilous
entozoologist
entrance money
epidermically
epigrammatise
epigrammatist
epigrammatize
epiperipheral
epiphenomenon
*e pluribus unum*
equestrianism
equidifferent
equidistantly
equilibration
equiponderant
equiponderate
equisetaceous
equitableness
equivocalness
erysipelatous
esprit de corps
establishment
estimableness
eucharistical
evangelically
even Homer nods
everlastingly
exanthematous
exceptionable
exceptionally
excitableness
exclusiveness

excommunicate
excortication
excusableness
exhibitionism
exhibitionist
exocrine gland
expansibility
expansiveness
expectoration
expectorative
expeditionary
expeditiously
expensiveness
experimentist
expostulation
expostulatory
expressionism
expressionist
expropriation
exquisiteness
extemporarily
extensibility
extensiveness
extermination
exterminatory
exterritorial
extragalactic
extrajudicial
extra-official
extraordinary
extravagantly
extravasation
extrinsically

**F**

Fabian Society
facetiousness
fall from grace
fall into place
fall off a lorry

Fallopian tube
falsification
fantastically
farinaceously
fast-fit centre
faultlessness
feather duster
feather-stitch
featherweight
*femme de chambre*
ferociousness
ferroconcrete
fertilisation
fertilization
figure of eight
figure skating
filibusterism
fine-tooth comb
finnan-haddock
fire insurance
fit like a glove
flashing point
flea in one's ear
flesh and blood
flesh-coloured
floating voter
floccillation
floricultural
flying colours
folk etymology
follow through
food poisoning
food processor
fool's paradise
foolhardiness
foot in the door
foraminiferal
forced landing
force one's hand
foreign office

foreknowledge
forementioned
forgetfulness
for good and all
forklift truck
formulisation
formulization
fortification
fortune-hunter
fortune-teller
fossiliferous
fossilisation
fossilization
fractiousness
freezing-point
French windows
frequentative
fresh as a daisy
fridge-freezer
frightfulness
fringe benefit
frivolousness
from the word go
frumentaceous
funambulation
functionalism
functionalist
fundamentally

**G**
galvanisation
galvanization
galvanoplasty
gasteropodous
gastrocnemius
gastroenteric
Geiger counter
generalissimo
general strike
generation gap

gentian violet
gentlemanlike
geometrically
German measles
gesticulation
gesticulatory
get in one's hair
get in on the act
get one's own way
get on one's wick
get the message
get to the point
get up one's nose
ghetto-blaster
give the bullet
give the creeps
global warming
glorification
glossographer
glossological
going a-begging
good-naturedly
good Samaritan
go the distance
go the whole hog
gracelessness
graminivorous
grammatically
granddaughter
grandiloquent
grandmotherly
grape-hyacinth
grappling-hook
grappling-iron
gratification
gravimetrical
grief-stricken
grin and bear it
grit one's teeth
grossulaceous

grotesqueness
ground control
gubernatorial
guided missile
guiltlessness
gum up the works
gymnastically
gymnospermous

**H**
hagiographist
hair-splitting
half the battle
hallucination
hallucinatory
hang by a thread
hanging matter
hang up one's hat
harbour-master
hard-luck story
hard of hearing
harmonisation
harmonization
have a field day
have a hold over
have a time of it
have high hopes
have it off with
have it out with
have no time for
have the edge on
head in the sand
head over heels
head restraint
heads will roll
healthfulness
health visitor
heart-breaking
heartlessness
hedge one's bets

heebie-jeebies
helminthology
helter-skelter
hemimetabolic
hemispherical
heritage trail
hermaphrodism
hermaphrodite
hermeneutical
heroic couplet
herpetologist
heterocarpous
heterogeneity
heterogeneous
heterogenesis
heteromorphic
heteroplastic
heteropterous
hieroglyphist
high and mighty
high-explosive
high-fibre diet
high frequency
Highland fling
high-water mark
hit rock bottom
hit the ceiling
hit the jackpot
Hobson's choice
hole-and-corner
hole-in-the-wall
holometabolic
Holy Communion
home economics
homoeopathist
homeward bound
horizontality
horripilation
horse chestnut
horticultural

housebreaking
human interest
hundredweight
hydriodic acid
hydrocephalus
hydrodynamics
hydrokinetics
hydrometrical
hymenopterous
hypercritical
hyperesthesia
hypermetropia
hypochondriac
hypophosphite
hypothecation

I

iatrochemical
ichthyologist
ichthyosaurus
ideographical
idiomatically
idiosyncratic
ignominiously
ill-considered
illegibleness
illustriously
immaterialise
immaterialism
immaterialist
immaterialize
immovableness
immutableness
imparipinnate
impartibility
impassibility
impassionable
impassiveness
impeccability
impecuniosity

imperceptible
imperfectness
imperiousness
impermissible
impersonality
impersonation
impertinently
imperturbable
impetuousness
implacability
importunately
impossibility
impracticable
impracticably
impregnatable
impressionism
impressionist
improbability
impropriation
improvability
improvisation
improvisatory
in a brown study
in a cleft stick
inadvertently
inappreciable
inappropriate
inattentively
in a weak moment
in cahoots with
incandescence
incarceration
incognoscible
in cold storage
incombustible
incommunicado
incompetently
inconceivable
inconceivably
incondensable

incondensible
incongruously
inconsequence
inconsiderate
inconsistence
inconsistency
inconspicuous
incontestable
incontestably
incontinently
inconvenience
inconvertible
inconvincible
incorporation
incorporeally
incorrectness
incorruptible
incorruptibly
incredibility
incredulously
incurableness
indefatigable
indefatigably
independently
indescribable
indeterminate
indeterminism
indifferently
indiscernible
indiscernibly
indispensable
indispensably
indisposition
indissociable
indissolvable
indistinctive
individualise
individualism
individualist
individuality

individualize
individuation
industrialise
industrialism
industrialist
industrialize
industriously
ineffectively
ineffectually
inefficacious
inefficiently
ineligibility
inexhaustible
inexhaustibly
inexpediently
inexpensively
inexperienced
inexpressible
inexpressibly
infallibilism
infallibilist
inferentially
infinitesimal
inflexibility
inflorescence
influentially
infundibulate
ingeniousness
inhospitality
injudiciously
inobservantly
inoffensively
in one's element
inopportunely
in Queer Street
inquisitional
inquisitively
inquisitorial
insatiability
insectivorous

insensibility
insidiousness
insignificant
insinuatingly
inspectorship
instantaneous
instinctively
institutional
instructively
insubordinate
insubstantial
insufficiency
insupportable
insupportably
insusceptible
insusceptibly
intangibility
integumentary
intelligencer
intelligently
intemperately
intensive care
intensiveness
intentionally
intercalation
intercellular
intercolonial
interdigitate
interestingly
intergalactic
interlacement
interlinearly
interlocution
interlocutory
intermarriage
intermediator
intermittence
intermuscular
international
interosculate

interpolation
interposition
interpretable
interrelation
interrogation
interrogative
interrogatory
interruptedly
intersidereal
interspersion
interstellary
interstratify
intertropical
in the abstract
in the dog-house
in the pipeline
in the region of
in the same boat
intraparietal
intratropical
intrinsically
introspection
introspective
intrusiveness
inventorially
inverted comma
investigation
investigative
invidiousness
invincibility
inviolability
invisibleness
involuntarily
irascibleness
irrationality
irreclaimable
irrecoverable
irrecoverably
irrefrangible
irreligiously

irreplaceable
irrepressible
irrepressibly
irresponsible
irresponsibly
irretrievable
irretrievably
irreverential
it is all up with
it's touch and go

**J**

Jekyll and Hyde
jet propulsion
jiggery-pokery
Job's comforter
jollification
judiciousness
jurisprudence
justification
justificative
justificatory
just the ticket

**K**

kaleidoscopic
kangaroo court
kapellmeister
keen as mustard
keep in the dark
keep one's end up
keep open-house
keep to oneself
kick the bucket
Kilroy was here
kinetic energy
kitchen-garden
knickerbocker
knit one's brows
knock-out drops

knock spots off
know backwards
knowledgeable
know one's place
know one's stuff
know what's what
knuckle-duster

**L**

lackadaisical
lady bountiful
lady-in-waiting
laevorotation
lance-corporal
languishingly
laryngoscopic
latchkey child
laughableness
laughing-stock
lay at one's door
lay down the law
lead by the nose
leap in the dark
learning curve
leatherjacket
lecherousness
Lepidodendron
lepidopterist
lepidopterous
lethargically
leucocythemia
level crossing
lexicographer
lexicographic
librarianship
licensing laws
lichenography
lickerishness
lick into shape
lick one's boots

life-preserver
light-fingered
lightsomeness
lignification
like clockwork
like grim death
line-engraving
linsey-woolsey
lipogrammatic
litigiousness
live like a lord
loathsomeness
logarithmical
long-suffering
look daggers at
Lord Privy Seal
lords temporal
lose one's nerve
lose one's touch
lose the thread
lottery ticket
lotus position
low technology
ludicrousness
lunatic fringe
luxuriousness
lyencephalous

**M**
Machiavellian
machicolation
macrocephalic
mad cow disease
magic mushroom
magisterially
magnanimously
magnetic field
magnetic north
magnetisation
magnetization

magnification
magnificently
magniloquence
make an issue of
make do and mend
make one's peace
make one's point
make the most of
malacostracan
maliciousness
malleableness
manifestation
man of the world
manufacturing
*marrons glacés*
marsipobranch
martello tower
martyrologist
masculineness
materfamilias
materialistic
materia medica
mathematician
matriculation
matrimonially
mediatorially
Mediterranean
meet one's match
megacephalous
meistersinger
mellifluently
mellifluously
melodiousness
melodramatist
membranaceous
mensurability
mercenariness
merchandising
mercilessness
meritoriously

mesencephalon
mesocephalous
metalliferous
metallography
metamorphosis
metaphysician
metempiricism
meteorologist
methodistical
metonymically
microcephalic
microcomputer
micrometrical
microorganism
microwave oven
mind-expanding
mineralogical
ministerially
mint condition
misanthropist
miscegenation
miscellaneous
mischievously
misconception
miserableness
misgovernment
mismanagement
misunderstand
misunderstood
mixed blessing
mixed marriage
mixed metaphor
moderatorship
modus operandi
Mohammedanism
mollification
momentariness
moment of truth
momentousness
monarchically

monochromatic
monocotyledon
monogrammatic
monographical
monometallism
monometallist
monothalamous
monotrematous
monstrousness
moral majority
morphinomania
mortality rate
mortification
mother-of-pearl
motion picture
mountainously
mouth-watering
muddle through
multangularly
multicapsular
multicoloured
multinational
multiplicable
multiplicator
multipresence
multisyllable
multitudinous
mummification
mystification
mythographist

**N**
name of the game
National Trust
natural number
nature-worship
necessitarian
necessitously
negotiability
neighbourhood

nervous system
neutron number
next to nothing
nickeliferous
niggardliness
nightwatchman
nitrification
nitroglycerin
no alternative
no great shakes
no holds barred
noiselessness
noli-me-tangere
nolle prosequi
nonconforming
nonconformist
nonconformity
nonjudgmental
nonsensically
Norfolk jacket
north-easterly
north-eastward
north-westerly
north-westward
not before time
not for a moment
not have any joy
not on your life
notoriousness
not see for dust
nuclear energy
nuclear family
nuclear fusion
nullification
nursery school

**O**
objectionable
objectionably
objectiveness

obliviousness
obnoxiousness
observational
obstinateness
obstructively
occasionalism
occidentalise
occidentalist
occidentalize
occluded front
odontoglossum
odoriferously
of a certain age
offensiveness
officiousness
off one's own bat
of unsound mind
old as the hills
old-boy network
oleomargarine
on a shoestring
once and for all
one for the road
one in a million
one night stand
onomatopoetic
on one's account
on pain of death
on shanks's pony
on tenterhooks
on the safe side
opéras bouffes
ophthalmology
opportuneness
oppositionist
opprobriously
orchestration
order of the day
ordinal number
organogenesis

organological
organotherapy
ornamentation
ornithichnite
ornithologist
orthocephalic
orthoepically
orthognathous
ostensibility
osteomyelitis
ostreiculture
other-directed
out at the elbow
out of one's head
out of one's mind
out of one's tree
out of the woods
outsettlement
overflowingly
overqualified
overstatement
oversubscribe
overvaluation
ovoviviparous
owner-occupier
oxyhemoglobin
oystercatcher

**P**
paediatrician
pain in the neck
paint-stripper
palaeographic
palaeontology
palaeotherium
palaeozoology
palatableness
pandiculation
panegyrically
panic-stricken

panspermatism
pantheistical
papaveraceous
parabolically
paradoxically
paragraphical
paralipomenon
parallelogram
paraphernalia
parasitically
parasynthesis
parenthetical
*par excellence*
Parkinson's Law
parliamentary
parrot-fashion
part and parcel
parthenocarpy
participation
participially
parti-coloured
particularise
particularism
particularist
particularity
particularize
passementerie
passion flower
Passion Sunday
patent-leather
paterfamilias
paternity suit
paternity test
pathognomonic
patrimonially
patriotically
patronisingly
patronizingly
peaceableness
peace dividend

peace-offering
pedestrianise
pedestrianism
pedestrianize
pendulousness
penetrability
penetratingly
penitentially
pennilessness
penny dreadful
pentadelphous
pentapetalous
pentaphyllous
pentastichous
penuriousness
perambulation
percussionist
peregrination
perfectionism
perfectionist
perfunctorily
perichondrium
periodic table
peripatetical
perishability
permanent wave
perpendicular
perscrutation
perseveringly
personalities
perspectively
perspicacious
perspicuously
petrification
petrochemical
phanerogamous
phantasmagory
pharisaically
pharmaceutics
pharmaceutist

pharmacopoeia
pharyngoscope
phelloplastic
phenobarbital
phenomenalism
philanthropic
Philhellenism
philomathical
philosophical
philosophiser
philosophizer
phonautograph
phonographist
phosphuretted
photochemical
photometrical
phraseologist
phrenological
phyllophagous
physiognomist
physiological
physiotherapy
pick and choose
picturesquely
pinking shears
piscicultural
place in the sun
plaintiveness
plastic bullet
platinum blond
platitudinise
platitudinize
platitudinous
platycephalic
platyhelminth
plausibleness
play hard to get
play havoc with
plectognathic
plenteousness

plethorically
pluralisation
pluralization
pneumatically
pneumatometer
pneumatophore
pneumogastric
pococurantism
poetic justice
poetic licence
poisonousness
police officer
poliomyelitis
polliniferous
polychromatic
polycotyledon
polydactylism
polysynthetic
polythalamous
ponderability
ponderousness
pooper-scooper
porcellaneous
possessionary
poste restante
powerlessness
power steering
power-striding
practical joke
practicalness
pragmatically
prayerfulness
precautionary
precentorship
precious metal
precious stone
precipitantly
precipitately
precipitation
precipitously

preconception
predestinator
predicability
predicamental
predicatively
predominantly
prefiguration
prefigurement
prehistorical
prejudication
prejudicially
preliminarily
prematureness
premeditation
premeditative
preoccupation
preordination
preparatively
preponderance
prepositional
prepossessing
prepossession
Pre-Raphaelite
presbytership
prescientific
prescriptible
presidentship
pressirostral
pressure group
pressure point
presumptively
pretentiously
pretermission
preternatural
preterperfect
prevarication
primary colour
primary school
prime minister
primitiveness

primogeniture
princess royal
prismatically
prisoner of war
privateersman
private sector
privatisation
privatization
probabilities
problematical
proconsulship
procrastinate
professoriate
profit and loss
profit-sharing
prognosticate
progressional
progressively
projectionist
proleptically
promiscuously
pronounceable
pronouncement
pronunciation
prophetically
proportionate
propositional
proprietorial
prospectively
prostaglandin
protectionism
protectionist
protectorship
proterandrous
Protestantise
Protestantism
Protestantize
proverbialist
provincialism
provincialist

provisionally
psychoanalyse
psychoanalyst
psychoanalyze
psychological
psychometrics
psychosomatic
psychotherapy
psychrophilic
public servant
public service
pull the plug on
pulverization
punctiliously
puritanically
purple passage
pusillanimity
pusillanimous
put in the shade
put new heart in
put one's back up
put out to grass
pyrheliometer
pyrotechnical

**Q**

quadragesimal
quadrifoliate
quadriliteral
quadrilocular
quadripartite
quadruplicate
quadruplicity
qualification
qualificative
qualitatively
quartermaster
querulousness
questionnaire
quick-tempered

quincentenary
quinquagesima
quinquangular
quinquevalent
quintuplicate
quotation mark

**R**

race relations
rack-and-pinion
radiant energy
radio spectrum
radium therapy
rag-and-bone man
rapaciousness
rapprochement
ratiocination
ratiocinative
ratiocinatory
rationalistic
readjournment
read like a book
read-write head
realistically
reappointment
rearrangement
receivability
reciprocation
recombination
recommendable
reconcilement
recrimination
recriminative
recriminatory
recrudescence
recrudescency
rectangularly
rectification
rectilineally
reduplication

reference book
reflexibility
rcflcxologist
refrigeration
refrigerative
refrigeratory
regimentation
registrarship
regurgitation
reimbursement
reimportation
reincarnation
reinforcement
reinstatement
reinterrogate
reinvestigate
rejuvenescent
religiousness
remissibility
remonstrative
remonstratory
remorselessly
remote control
replenishment
reprehensible
reprehensibly
representable
reproachfully
reprobateness
republication
repulsiveness
resistibility
resolvability
respirability
respirational
resplendently
restrictively
restructuring
resuscitation
retaining wall

retentiveness
retrogression
retrogressive
retrospection
retrospective
reverberation
reverberatory
reverentially
reversibility
revolutionary
revolutionise
revolutionist
revolutionize
revolving door
rhapsodically
rhizomorphous
rhythm section
rich as Croesus
rift in the lute
righteousness
right-thinking
riotous living
rise to the bait
rite of passage
rogues' gallery
roller-coaster
roll-on roll-off
Roman Catholic
Roman numerals
root and branch
rough-and-ready
round-the-clock
round the twist
rowing-machine
rule of the road
run a tight ship
run out of steam

**S**
sabre-rattling

saccharometer
sacerdotalism
sacramentally
sacrosanctify
sadomasochism
safety curtain
safety deposit
sagaciousness
salaciousness
salad-dressing
salade nicoise
Salvation Army
sanctimonious
sandwich-board
sanitary towel
sarcastically
satellite dish
save one's bacon
scalar product
scaly ant-eater
scandal-monger
scarification
scarlet runner
scenic railway
scepticalness
Schizomycetes
schizophrenia
schizophrenic
scholasticism
school-teacher
scintillating
scintillation
Scotch terrier
scripturalism
scripturalist
sculpturesque
search-warrant
secondariness
secondary cell
second chamber

second thought
secretary-bird
secretaryship
secretiveness
secret service
security guard
sedentariness
sedimentation
seditiousness
seismographic
self-addressed
self-assertion
self-confessed
self-confident
self-conscious
self-contained
self-deception
self-governing
self-induction
self-inflicted
self-possessed
self-propelled
self-righteous
self-sacrifice
self-satisfied
semiautomatic
semiconductor
semiconscious
semper fidelis
seneschalship
senior citizen
senselessness
sensitiveness
sententiously
sentimentally
separableness
septisyllable
septuagesimal
sequestration
Serbo-Croatian

sergeant-major
serve a purpose
serve one right
service charge
sesquialteral
seventh heaven
Seville orange
sewing-machine
sex chromosome
Shakespearean
Shakespearian
shamelessness
shammy leather
shapelessness
sharp as a razor
sharp practice
ship of the line
shock-absorber
shooting-stick
shoot one's bolt
shop assistant
short and sweet
short-tempered
shot in the dark
shoulder-blade
shoulder-strap
show one's paces
show one's teeth
Shrove Tuesday
sick as a parrot
sick to death of
side-splitting
sightlessness
sigillography
signature tune
significantly
signification
significative
significatory
sign the pledge

silver service
silver-tongued
silver wedding
simple-hearted
single figures
singularities
sitting pretty
sitting target
sitting tenant
sixteenth note
skirting-board
slap and tickle
slap in the face
sleep like a log
sleep like a top
sleight of hand
sling one's hook
slippery slope
small potatoes
smear campaign
smelling-salts
smoke detector
smooth-tongued
social climber
social compact
social contact
social disease
social science
social service
socioeconomic
Socratic irony
sodium nitrate
soft in the head
solar constant
soldering-iron
solemnisation
solemnization
sol-fa syllable
solicitorship
solid geometry

something else
something like
somnambulator
somniloquence
sophistically
sophisticated
sophisticator
sop to Cerberus
sorrowfulness
soul-searching
sounding board
source program
south-easterly
south-westerly
space-platform
Spanish guitar
sparks will fly
spasmodically
speaking clock
Special Branch
specification
spectroscopic
speculatively
speed merchant
spending power
spending spree
spermatophyte
spermatorrhea
spike one's guns
spill one's guts
spill the beans
spine-chilling
spinning-wheel
spiny ant-eater
spit and polish
spitting image
splanchnology
splendiferous
splenetically
splinter group

spontaneously
sportsmanship
sprightliness
spring balance
spring chicken
square bracket
square measure
squealishness
squeezability
stab in the back
stalactitical
stalagmitical
stalking-horse
stalworthness
staminiferous
standing order
starting block
starting price
state-of-the-art
statesmanlike
statesmanship
station-master
statistically
stay the course
steadfastness
steady as a rock
steering wheel
steganography
stenographist
step out of line
stepping-stone
stercoraceous
stereographic
stethoscopist
stick-in-the-mud
stick out a mile
stiff upper lip
stoloniferous
stone the crows
stop at nothing

storage device
storage heater
St Patrick's Day
straight angle
straight fight
straight flush
straight-laced
strangulation
strategetical
strategically
stratigraphic
stratocumulus
street-fighter
strengthening
streptococcus
stretch a point
strikebreaker
strike it lucky
string quartet
strip lighting
structuralism
structureless
subcontractor
subdeaconship
submachine gun
subordinately
subordination
subordinative
subpiritoneal
substantially
substantively
subterraneous
subtilisation
subtilization
successionist
suffraganship
suffumigation
sulphonic acid
sulphureously
sulphuric acid

superabundant
superaddition
superannuated
superdelegate
superdominant
supereminence
superfetation
superficially
superfluities
superfluously
superfortress
superlatively
supernumerary
superposition
supersaturate
supersensible
superstitious
supplantation
supplementary
suppositional
supranational
supra-orbitary
suprascapular
surreptitious
suspender belt
swallow a camel
swash-buckling
sweep the board
sweet nothings
swing both ways
syllogistical
symmetrically
symptomatical
synchronously
synecdochical
synecphonesis
syntactically
synthetically
syphilisation
syphilization

**T**
tabes dorsalis
*tableau vivant*
tablespoonful
tachistoscope
take a back seat
take a hard line
take liberties
take lying down
take some doing
take the mickey
take the plunge
talkativeness
talk of the town
tantalisation
tantalization
tape recording
tastelessness
tax deductible
teachableness
tear a strip off
telegraphical
telencephalon
telephone book
telephoto lens
televangelism
televangelist
temperamental
temperateness
tempestuously
temporalities
temporisation
temporization
tenaciousness
tenderhearted
tenosynovitus
tenpin bowling
tergiversator
terminational
**Terpsichorean**

terrestrially
territorially
tetrasyllable
thalamifloral
thaumaturgics
thaumaturgist
theanthropism
theatricality
the devil to pay
thenceforward
theologically
theoretically
the cat's mother
the party's over
the penny drops
therapeutical
theriomorphic
thermonuclear
thermoplastic
the whole shoot
think better of
thoroughgoing
thoughtlessly
threateningly
thunderstruck
time-consuming
time out of mind
time signature
tintinnabular
tip the balance
to coin a phrase
to good purpose
to kingdom come
tolerableness
tongue in cheek
tongue-twister
tonsillectomy
topographical
tortoiseshell
to say the least

touch on the raw
toxicological
toxoplasmosis
track and field
tracklessness
tractive force
traditionally
traffic circle
traffic island
traffic lights
traffic signal
trainspotting
tranquilliser
tranquillizer
transatlantic
transcendence
transcendency
transcription
transcriptive
transgression
transientness
transitionary
transliterate
translucently
transmigrator
transmissible
transmittable
transmittance
transmutation
transnational
transparently
transpiration
transportable
transport café
transposition
transpositive
transversally
treasure trove
treat like dirt
tremulousness

trial and error
triangularity
triangulation
tricentennial
tripinnatifid
troublesomely
trumpeter swan
tumbler switch
turkey-buzzard
Turkish coffee
turn of the year
turn on the heat
turn the corner
turn the tables
typographical
tyrannosaurus

**U**

umbelliferous
umbilical cord
unaccompanied
unaccountable
unaccountably
unadulterated
unapostolical
unappreciated
unassimilated
unceremonious
uncertainties
uncomfortable
uncomfortably
uncomplaining
unconditional
unconquerable
undercarriage
underclothing
underemployed
underestimate
undergraduate
under one's belt

under one's nose
understanding
undiscernible
undisciplined
undissolvable
unembarrassed
unenlightened
unexceptional
unfamiliarity
unfashionable
unfashionably
unforgettable
unforgettably
unfortunately
ungrammatical
unguardedness
unimpassioned
unimpeachable
unimpressible
uninhabitable
uninstructive
uninteresting
uninterrupted
unjustifiable
unjustifiably
unmentionable
unmindfulness
unmistakeable
unmistakeably
unnecessarily
unneighbourly
unobtrusively
unperceivable
unphilosophic
unprecedented
unpresentable
unpretentious
unputdownable
unrecompensed
unrepresented

unrighteously
unsavouriness
unserviceable
unsightliness
unskilfulness
unsubstantial
unsurpassable
unsusceptible
unsymmetrical
unthriftiness
untrustworthy
unwarrantable
unwarrantably
unwillingness
unworkmanlike
unworldliness
up to the minute
urban guerilla

**V**
vacuum-cleaner
valedictorian
value-added tax
value for money
value judgment
Vandyke collar
vegetarianism
venerableness
Venetian blind
ventriloquial
ventriloquise
ventriloquism
ventriloquist
ventriloquize
ventriloquous
vermiculation
vernacularism
versicoloured
versification
vexatiousness

vexed question
vice-president
vicious circle
video cassette
video recorder
violoncellist
visible speech
visionariness
vitreous humor
vitrification
vivaciousness
volatilizable
volumenometer
voluntariness
voraciousness
vraisemblance
vulcanisation
vulcanization
vulnerability

**W**
walking-papers
walls have ears
washing-powder
water-chestnut
water-hyacinth
watering-place
water-softener
wave mechanics
way of all flesh
weak as a kitten
weak of friends
wearisomeness
weather-beaten
weeping-willow
wee small hours
weight-lifting
weight-watcher
well-appointed
well-connected

well-preserved
well-thought-of
wheeler-dealer
whirlpool bath
white as a sheet
white elephant
whithersoever
wholesomeness
whooping-cough
wide of the mark
willow-pattern
winkle-pickers
with a bad grace
with a capital A
within an ace of
with kid gloves
with one accord
wonderfulness
wood-engraving
wool-gathering
word-blindness
word processor
work like magic
work the oracle
worn to a shadow
worthlessness
worth one's salt

**X**
xerophthalmia
xylographical

**Y**
yachtsmanship
yellowishness
yeoman service

**Z**
zebra crossing
zodiacal light
zygodactylous

# Fourteen-letter words

## A

abominableness
above suspicion
absorbefacient
abstemiousness
abstractedness
abstractionism
abstractionist
acceptableness
accomplishable
accomplishment
accountability
accountantship
Achilles' tendon
acknowledgment
across-the-board
action painting
action stations
adductor muscle
administration
administrative
adscititiously
advantageously
adventitiously
*affaire de coeur*
affectionately
aforementioned
against the odds
aggrandisement
aggrandizement
aggressiveness
ahead of the game
alcoholisation
alcoholization

all in a day's work
all over the shop
alphabetically
alphanumerical
amphibological
anagrammatical
ancient history
and all that jazz
angina pectoris
annus mirabilis
antaphrodisiac
anthropography
anthroposophic
antidepressant
antipathetical
antiperspirant
antiphlogistic
antiquarianism
anti-scriptural
antisyphilitic
antithetically
apheliotropism
aphoristically
apologetically
apophthegmatic
appendicectomy
apple of discord
apple of one's eye
apprehensively
apprenticeship
arboricultural
archaeological
archdeaconship
archidiaconate

archiepiscopal
architectonics
aristocratical
arithmetically
armed to the hilt
aromatherapist
arrondissement
Asiatic cholera
asset-stripping
associationism
as the crow flies
astronomically
at a rate of knots
at daggers drawn
at one's last gasp
at one's wits' ends
attainableness
at the expense of
attractiveness
audio-frequency
*auf Wiedersehen*
augmentatively
aurora borealis
auspiciousness
authentication
autobiographer
autobiographic
automatic pilot
autosuggestion

# B
babes in the wood
back-scratching
back-seat driver
backs to the wall
bacteriologist
banana republic
barnacle-goose
barometrically
barrage balloon

bathing-machine
be-all and end-all
beautification
bed-sitting-room
beetle-crushers
before the flood
beg the question
behind the times
believableness
belle of the ball
benefit society
beside the point
be the very devil
billiard-marker
bioengineering
biographically
bird of paradise
bituminiferous
blank-cartridge
blithesomeness
blood poisoning
blow hot and cold
boa-constrictor
boarding-school
boisterousness
Boolean algebra
borough English
bougainvillaea
*bouleversement*
brachycephalic
branchiostegal
bread-and-butter
bread-fruit tree
breakdown truck
break one's heart
break the back of
break the news to
break the record
breathing space
breathlessness

breech delivery
breeder reactor
Bright's disease
Bristol diamond
Bristol fashion
Britannia metal
broad in the beam
Brobdingnagian
Brussels carpet
brussels sprout
Buckley's chance
bulimia nervosa
bureau de change
burst the bubble
bury the hatchet
busman's holiday
buy a pig in a poke
by the same token

## C
cabinet council
calamander wood
calcium carbide
calico-printing
Canterbury bell
capitalisation
capitalization
capriciousness
captain-general
carbon monoxide
cardinal-flower
cardinal points
cardiovascular
carline thistle
carpet-slippers
carrot and stick
carry a torch for
cartridge-paper
cash on delivery
cast a cloud over

castle-building
castles in Spain
castrametation
catadioptrical
catch one's death
catch red-handed
catechetically
Catherine wheel
cathode ray tube
cauliflower ear
censoriousness
censurableness
central heating
centralisation
centralization
ceteris paribus
chalcographist
chalk and cheese
chamber concert
chamber council
chamber-counsel
chamois-leather
chancellorship
changeableness
change one's mind
change one's tune
characteristic
chargeableness
charitableness
charlotte russe
chase the dragon
Cheshire cheese
chest of drawers
chicken-hearted
chicken-livered
chimney-swallow
Chinese lantern
chinless wonder
chloral hydrate
chorographical

chromatic scale
chromatography
chronometrical
cinematography
circuit-breaker
circuitousness
circumambiency
circumambulate
circumferentor
circumgyration
circumlittoral
circumlocution
circumlocutory
circumnavigate
circumnutation
circumspection
circumstantial
circumvolution
class conscious
classification
claustrophobia
clear as crystal
clerical collar
clitoridectomy
cloak-and-dagger
close to the wind
clutch at straws
coconut matting
coessentiality
cognoscibility
collective farm
collective noun
Colorado beetle
colourableness
colour-sergeant
come full circle
come on the scene
commensurately
commensuration
commentatorial

commissionaire
commissaryship
commodiousness
common or garden
communion table
composing-stick
comprehensible
comprehensibly
concavo-concave
conceivability
concentrically
concessionaire
conclusiveness
condensability
conditionality
confidentially
conglobulation
conglomeration
conglutination
conglutinative
congratulation
congratulatory
congregational
conjunctivitis
consanguineous
conscriptional
constitutional
constitutively
constructional
constructively
constructivism
constructivist
consubstantial
consuetudinary
contagiousness
contemptuously
contiguousness
continentalism
continentalist
continuity girl

continuousness
contract bridge
contractedness
contradictable
contradictious
contraindicate
contraposition
controllership
controvertible
controvertibly
contumaciously
contumeliously
convalescently
conventionally
conversational
convertibility
convexo-concave
coordinateness
copper-bottomed
copper-fastened
cornet à pistons
corolliflorous
correspondence
correspondency
corrugated iron
corruptibility
cosmographical
cosmopolitical
counsellorship
counterbalance
countermeasure
county palatine
courageousness
covering letter
cramp one's style
credibility gap
creditableness
*crème de la crème*
crocodile tears
cross-fertilise

cross-fertilize
cross one's heart
cross-reference
cryoextraction
cry one's eyes out
cryptaesthesia
crystal-healing
crystallisable
crystallizable
crystallomancy
cucurbitaceous
culture vulture
current account
curtain-lecture
cut one's teeth on
cystic fibrosis

# D

dactylioglyphy
darken one's door
data-processing
data protection
de-accessioning
dead to the world
death's-head moth
deceivableness
dechristianise
dechristianize
decolorisation
decolorization
deconsecration
decorativeness
definitiveness
degenerateness
deliberateness
delightfulness
demi-semiquaver
demobilisation
demobilization
democratically

demonetisation
demonetization
demoralisation
demoralization
denominational
denominatively
deplorableness
depolarisation
depolarization
derogatoriness
descendibility
despicableness
despitefulness
destructionist
detestableness
devil's advocate
dextrorotation
diabolicalness
diagrammatical
diaheliotropic
dicotyledonous
diffusibleness
digestibleness
dig one's heels in
diminutiveness
diphthongation
diplomatically
disaggregation
disappointedly
disappointment
disapprobation
disappropriate
disapprovingly
disarrangement
disciplinarian
disconsolately
discontentedly
discontentment
discontinuance
discountenance

discouragement
discouragingly
discourteously
discretionally
discriminately
discriminating
discrimination
discriminative
discriminatory
discursiveness
disdainfulness
disembarkation
disemboguement
disembowelment
disenchantment
disenchantress
disencumbrance
disenfranchise
disengagedness
disenthralment
disgustfulness
disillusionise
disillusionize
disinclination
disincorporate
disinformation
disingenuously
disinheritance
disintegration
disinvestiture
disjointedness
disorderliness
disquisitional
disrespectable
dissertational
distemperature
distensibility
distinguishing
distractedness
distributively

diverticulitis
divertissement
dodecasyllable
dog in the manger
do one's homework
do one's own thing
do the spadework
do things by half
double-breasted
double entendre
double standard
doubting Thomas
down in the dumps
down in the mouth
down on one's luck
draw the long bow
draw the teeth of
dress rehearsal
drink like a fish
dynamoelectric

# E

ears are burning
ecclesiastical
ecclesiologist
editio princeps
educationalist
effeminateness
electioneering
electric guitar
electrobiology
electrodynamic
electrokinetic
electrolytical
electronic mail
electrostatics
electrotherapy
elementariness
eleutheromania
emblematically

emperor penguin
empyreumatical
encyclopaedist
endocrine gland
*enfant terrible*
enharmonically
enterprise zone
enterprisingly
enthronisation
enthronization
enthusiastical
entoperipheral
epigrammatical
equiponderance
escape velocity
eschatological
ethnographical
etymologically
eulogistically
Eustachian tube
evangelicalism
evangelisation
evangelization
evaporated milk
excommunicable
excrementitial
excruciatingly
existentialism
existentialist
expense account
experimentally
expressionless
expressiveness
extemporaneous
extended family
extinguishable
extinguishment
extortionately
extra-parochial
extrinsicality

# F
faint-heartedly
fair to middling
fallaciousness
fall on deaf ears
family likeness
family planning
fantasticality
farsightedness
fastidiousness
favourableness
feather-bedding
feather-brained
feel the draught
fellow-commoner
fellow-creature
ferromagnetism
ferromanganese
fibro-cartilage
fighting chance
figurativeness
figure of speech
filling station
finders keepers
flagitiousness
flat on one's back
flight recorder
flog a dead horse
floriculturist
flying buttress
Flying Dutchman
flying-squirrel
follow one's nose
for all the world
foraminiferous
foreordination
for good measure
forisfamiliate
formidableness
for the high jump

for the life of me
fortuitousness
four-letter word
fraternisation
fraternization
freedom fighter
free enterprise
free-spokenness
French dressing
friction-clutch
friendlessness
fringillaceous
frolicsomeness
from the year dot
fructification
fundamentalism
fundamentalist

# G
gamma radiation
garboard-strake
gastrovascular
genealogically
generalisation
generalization
general-purpose
geocentrically
geographically
German shepherd
get away with you!
get it in the neck
get off one's back
get off one's mark
get one's own back
get the better of
get the brush-off
get to first base
get to grips with
girlie magazine
give a wide berth

give free rein to
give the glad-eye
give the heave-ho
give up the ghost
Gnomes of Zurich
go like hot cakes
gone for a Burton
good-for-nothing
good-humouredly
go out of one's way
go out on the town
go to the country
grandiloquence
grasp the nettle
grease one's palm
great white hope
gregariousness
groundlessness
guillotinement
gyrencephalate
gyrostabiliser
gyrostabilizer

# H
hagiographical
hallucinogenic
handicraftsman
handicraftsmen
hard nut to crack
harmoniousness
have at one's back
have been around
have feet of clay
have had one's day
have it both ways
have one's number
have the hots for
heart-searching
helminthagogue
hemispheroidal

heresiographer
hermaphroditic
herpetological
heteroclitical
heteromorphism
heteromorphous
heterophyllous
hieroglyphical
hippopotamuses
historiography
histrionically
hit the bull's-eye
hold all the aces
hold no brief for
hold one's breath
hold one's head up
hold one's horses
hold one's tongue
holier-than-thou
honourableness
horticulturism
horticulturist
house decorator
human resources
hunt high and low
hydrographical
hydromechanics
hyperaesthesia
hyperbolically
hypercriticism
hypersensitive
hypocritically
hypostatically
hypothetically
hypothyroidism

# I
ichnolithology
ichthyological
ichthyophagist

ichthyophagous
icing on the cake
identical twins
identification
identity crisis
idiopathically
illegitimately
ill-gotten gains
illustratively
I'm all right, Jack
imparidigitate
impassableness
imperviousness
implacableness
impoverishment
impressibility
impressionable
impressionably
impressiveness
improvableness
improvisatrice
inalienability
inappreciative
inapprehension
inapproachable
inarticulately
inartificially
in a tight corner
in at the deep end
inauspiciously
incapacitation
incautiousness
incommensurate
incommunicable
incompressible
inconclusively
inconsequently
inconsiderable
inconsiderably
inconsistently

inconveniently
incoordination
incorporeality
indecipherable
indecipherably
indecomposable
indecorousness
indefiniteness
indemonstrable
indestructible
indestructibly
indeterminable
indeterminably
index arbitrage
indifferentism
indirect object
indirect speech
indiscreetness
indiscriminate
indisposedness
indistinctness
indivisibility
indoctrination
inexpressibles
inexpressively
infectiousness
infelicitously
inflexibleness
infrastructure
inharmoniously
*in loco parentis*
in one fell swoop
in one's bad books
in one's own right
inordinateness
in penny numbers
inquisitionary
in round figures
insatiableness
inseparability

insider dealing
insignificance
insignificancy
institutionary
instrumentally
insufficiently
insuperability
insuppressible
insuppressibly
insurmountable
insurmountably
insurrectional
intangibleness
intellectively
intellectually
intelligentsia
intercessional
intercommunion
intercommunity
interdependent
interferometer
interior angle
interjectional
interlineation
intermaxillary
intermediately
intermediation
intermigration
interpellation
interpenetrate
interplanetary
interpretation
interpretative
in the good books
in the limelight
into the bargain
intoxicatingly
intractability
intransitively
intransmutable

intuitionalism
invariableness
invincibleness
inviolableness
irrationalness
irrecognisable
irrecognizable
irreconcilable
irreconcilably
irremovability
irreparability
irreproachable
irreproachably
irresoluteness
irrespectively
it's a small world

## J
jobs for the boys
Johannisberger
John Barleycorn
Julian calendar
jurisdictional

## K
keep an open mind
keep a tight rein
keep one's chin up
keep one's hair on
keep one's hand in
keep on trucking
keyhole surgery
kick in the teeth
King James Bible
knickerbockers
knight-errantry
knitting-needle
knock into shape
knock on the head
know one's onions

# L

labyrinthodont
lamellirostral
lapidification
large intestine
larger than life
latitudinarian
law of the jungle
law unto oneself
lay it on the line
lay oneself open
leading article
letter of the law
let them eat cake
let the side down
leucocythaemia
libertarianism
libidinousness
library science
licentiousness
lie in one's teeth
lieutenantship
line one's pocket
liquid paraffin
listed building
lithographical
live and let live
live by one's wits
loaded question
long in the tooth
longitudinally
lords spiritual
Lutheran Church

# M

macadamisation
macadamization
macrocephalous
macroeconomics
magnetic needle

magniloquently
maidenhair fern
make a pig's ear of
make the running
mandarin collar
man in the street
man of the moment
marching orders
market gardener
market research
mass production
mathematically
Maundy Thursday
meat and drink to
mend one's fences
men in grey suits
mensurableness
merchant banker
merchant marine
meretriciously
mesdemoiselles
metaphysically
metempsychosis
metensomatosis
meteorological
metropolitical
mettlesomeness
microcephalous
microeconomics
microprocessor
millenarianism
mineralisation
mineralization
mineral kingdom
ministerialist
miraculousness
misanthropical
misapplication
misappropriate
miscalculation

misinformation
mismeasurement
mission control
monkey-business
month of Sundays
mountaineering
mucous membrane
multifariously
multiplacative
multiplication
multiplicative
multiple-choice
myrmecophagous
mysteriousness
mythologically

# N
national anthem
natural history
naturalisation
naturalization
natural science
Neanderthal man
neurohypnology
neurohypnotism
neuropathology
neutralisation
neutralization
never-never land
new lease of life
*Nibelungenlied*
night-blindness
nine days' wonder
nineteenth hole
nitroglycerine
noblesse oblige
no-fault divorce
noloepiscopari
non-cooperation
non-judgemental

northern lights
nothing daunted
not to turn a hair
nuclear fission
nuclear reactor
number-cruncher

# O
obligatoriness
obsequiousness
obstreperously
obstructionism
obstructionist
occult sciences
Oedipus complex
off one's trolley
offset printing
of the old school
omnium gatherum
one-armed bandit
one degree under
one in the eye for
one of these days
one of those days
one that got away
on one's beam-ends
on one's doorstep
on one's last legs
on the breadline
on the grapevine
on the off chance
open-cast mining
open one's eyes to
ophthalmodynia
ophthalmoscope
ophthalmoscopy
opinionatively
opisthocoelous
opisthographic
opposite number

oppressiveness
order of the boot
ordinary seaman
Ornithodelphia
ornithodelphic
ornithological
orthocephalous
orthochromatic
orthographical
ostentatiously
osteoarthritis
out for the count
out of one's depth
out of this world
outrageousness
overcapitalise
overcapitalize
over my dead body
overpoweringly
overproduction
over the counter
Oxford movement
oxyhaemoglobin

**P**

pachydactylous
pachydermatous
package holiday
palaeographist
papilionaceous
paragrammatist
parallelepiped
parallelopiped
paraphrastical
parenchymatous
parish registry
paronomastical
parsimoniously
passionateness
passive smoking

pâté de foie gras
patent medicine
pathologically
pentadactylous
perfectibility
perfidiousness
peripateticism
periphrastical
perishableness
perissodactyle
permissibility
perniciousness
perspirability
persuasiveness
pertinaciously
pestilentially
Peter principle
phantasmagoria
phantasmagoric
pharmaceutical
pharmacologist
pharmacopolist
philanthropist
phonographical
photochemistry
photo-engraving
photosynthesis
phraseological
phylogenetical
physiognomical
phytogeography
phytopathology
pick one's brains
pinch and scrape
pin one's hopes on
pins and needles
pisciculturist
pituitary gland
plaster of Paris
plastic surgery

platinum blonde
play gooseberry
pleased as Punch
plectognathous
pleonastically
pleurapophysis
pluck up courage
pneumatologist
polysyllabical
polytheistical
pop the question
popularisation
popularization
practicability
prebendaryship
precariousness
precociousness
preconcertedly
predestinarian
predestination
predeterminate
preferentially
preponderation
preposterously
presence of mind
president-elect
press secretary
pressure-cooker
presumptuously
prima ballerina
printed circuit
procrastinator
procuratorship
productiveness
professionally
professorially
prognosticator
prohibitionism
prohibitionist
proletarianism

propaedeutical
propagandistic
propitiatorily
propitiousness
proportionable
proportionably
proprietorship
prosperousness
protoplasmatic
providentially
pseudepigrapha
psychoanalysis
psychodynamics
psychoneurosis
public-spirited
pull one's weight
put in a good word
put on a pedestal
put one across on
put one in mind of
put one's shirt on
put the kibosh on
put the screws on
Pyrrhic victory

## Q

quadragenarian
quadridigitate
quadrisyllabic
quadrisyllable
quantification
quantitatively
quermioniously
quinquepartite
quintessential
quite something

## R

rack one's brains
radial symmetry

radio-astronomy
radio frequency
radiotelephone
radio telescope
raise one's voice
ranunculaceous
rational number
rattle one's cage
read only memory
read the riot act
rear-view mirror
reasonableness
recalcitration
recapitulation
recapitulatory
receivableness
recombinant DNA
recommendation
recommendatory
reconciliation
reconnaissance
reconstruction
record-breaking
Recording Angel
recreation room
rectilinearity
recurvirostral
redintegration
redistribution
reflectiveness
refractoriness
regardlessness
regenerateness
registered post
registry office
rehabilitation
reimprisonment
reindeer-lichen
reintroduction
rejuvenescence

relentlessness
religious house
relinquishment
Remembrance Day
reminiscential
remonetisation
remonetization
remorsefulness
remunerability
reorganisation
reorganization
reprehensively
representation
representative
requisitionist
resistibleness
resolvableness
resolving power
respectability
respirableness
responsibility
responsiveness
rest on one's oars
retrogradation
revengefulness
revivification
rhesus negative
rhesus positive
rheumatic fever
rheumatologist
Rhode Island Red
rhubarb, rhubarb
rhythm and blues
riding for a fall
ring the changes
rocket-launcher
root mean square
Rosicrucianism
Rosicrucianist
Rosicrucianity

rough and tumble
rule out of court
run the gauntlet

# S
Sabbatarianism
Sabbatarianist
sacchariferous
sacramentarian
sacrilegiously
Saint Elmo's fire
salt of the earth
salubriousness
sanctification
sanguinivorous
sanitary cordon
sanitary napkin
satisfactorily
saved by the bell
save one's breath
savings account
scandalousness
scatter-brained
scholastically
schoolmistress
science fiction
scientifically
screw-propeller
screw up courage
scrupulousness
scurrilousness
seasonableness
second thoughts
secularisation
secularization
security police
self-abnegation
self-absorption
self-effacement
self-expression

self-importance
self-indulgence
self-interested
self-regulation
self-sufficient
self-supporting
semi-lunar valve
send to Coventry
sensationalism
sensationalist
sensitive plant
sentimentalise
sentimentalism
sentimentalist
sentimentality
sentimentalize
septuagenarian
Sergeant-at-Arms
serous membrane
serum hepatitis
service station
servomechanism
sesquialterate
sesquipedalian
set one's heart on
shaggy dog story
share of the cake
sheet-lightning
shepherd's purse
ship's carpenter
shock treatment
shopping centre
shotgun wedding
shove-halfpenny
sign of the cross
silent majority
simple fraction
simple interest
simplification
simultaneously

single-breasted
skate on thin ice
slap on the wrist
slatternliness
slaughterhouse
slice of the cake
small intestine
smell of the lamp
snapping-turtle
social contract
social security
Society of Jesus
sociopolitical
Socratic method
sodium chloride
solicitousness
solidification
somnambulation
somnambulistic
sophistication
soul-destroying
southern lights
sparkling water
spatiotemporal
speak for itself
special effects
specialisation
specialization
special licence
spectroscopist
speechlessness
spermatogonium
sphaeristerium
sporting chance
sports medicine
stage direction
stainless steel
stamping-ground
standard-bearer
stand corrected

starting stalls
stationariness
stenographical
stick one's oar in
stigmatisation
stigmatization
stir one's stumps
stocking filler
storage battery
storm in a teacup
straightjacket
stratification
strawberry-mark
strawberry-tree
straw in the wind
streets ahead of
strike a balance
strike a bargain
strobe lighting
stumbling-block
stupendousness
*Sturmabteilung*
subarborescent
subconsciously
subinfeudation
submissiveness
substantialise
substantiality
substantialize
substantiation
sufferableness
superabundance
superannuation
supercelestial
superciliously
supereminently
supererogatory
superficiality
superincumbent
superintendent

supernaturally
superphosphate
superscription
supersensitive
superstructure
supposititious
supramaxillary
surgical spirit
susceptibility
suspiciousness
swallow the bait
synchronically
systematically
systems analyst

# T

tabularisation
tabularization
tachygraphical
tactical voting
take a dim view of
take a raincheck
take a rise out of
take in good part
take one's chance
take the biscuit
take the edge off
talking picture
Tasmanian devil
tatterdemalion
tautologically
teleconference
teleologically
telephone-booth
telephone-kiosk
telescopically
teletypewriter
terminological
*terra incognita*
tetradactylous

the cat's pyjamas
thenceforwards
the old Adam in us
thermodynamics
thermoelectric
thick as thieves
think nothing of
thoughtfulness
three point turn
thriftlessness
thrilled to bits
throw the book at
throw to the dogs
time immemorial
tintinnabulary
tired to death of
to feel the pinch
to gasp one's last
toing and froing
top of the ladder
to tell the truth
to the bitter end
to the nth degree
traditionalism
traditionalist
traffic pattern
training-school
train of thought
traitorousness
transcendental
transitoriness
transmigratory
transverberate
tridimensional
tripersonalist
troubleshooter
tumultuousness
turbojet engine
Turkish delight
turn a deaf ear to

turn upside-down
turpentine-tree
two-dimensional

**U**

ubiquitousness
ultimogeniture
ultramontanism
ultramontanist
unacknowledged
unapproachable
unappropriated
uncompromising
unconscionable
unconscionably
uncontrollable
uncontrollably
unconventional
undecomposable
underdeveloped
undermentioned
undernourished
under one's thumb
undersecretary
understatement
undiscoverable
unfaithfulness
unfruitfulness
ungracefulness
ungratefulness
unidirectional
unincorporated
unintelligible
unintelligibly
unintermitting
unipersonalist
universal joint
unmentionables
unmercifulness
unostentatious

unpremeditated
unpresumptuous
unprofessional
unprosperously
unquestionablc
unquestionably
unrecognizable
unrecognizably
unreliableness
unrestrainedly
unsatisfactory
unscripturally
unscrupulously
unsociableness
unsuccessfully
unsuitableness
untranslatable
up to one's elbows
up to one's tricks
upwardly mobile

**V**

valetudinarian
vanishing cream
vending machine
vent one's spleen
venture capital
verisimilitude
vested interest
vice-chancellor
villainousness
vindictiveness
virtual reality
virgin olive oil
vitreous humour
vituperatively
viviparousness
vivisectionism
vivisectionist
volatilisation

volatilization
vulnerableness

# W
walrus mustache
warrant-officer
washing-machine
Wassermann test
watch like a hawk
watch your speed
watercolourist
water-repellent
water-resistant
wave a magic wand
weather-station
weightlessness
weight-training
wellington boot
wet one's whistle
what's eating you?
what's it in aid of?
what's the damage?
whipper-snapper
white blood cell
whole bang shoot
whoopee cushion

wild-goose chase
wind-instrument
window-dressing
window shopping
with a good grace
with a vengeance
within an inch of
Women's Movement
wonder-stricken
word processing
working capital
working drawing
work like a charm
worth one's while

# X
xiphoid process

# Y
you're telling me!

# Z
zincographical
zingiberaceous
zinziberaceous
Zoroastrianism

# Fifteen-letter words

## A

absorbent cotton
absorption lines
acclimatisation
acclimatization
accountableness
acknowledgement
acquisitiveness
Addison's disease
adjutant-general
adventurousness
affranchisement
against the clock
against the grain
ahead of one's time
air-conditioning
aircraft carrier
alimentary canal
alive and kicking
all along the line
along the lines of
alternate angles
ambulance-chaser
ambush-marketing
*amende honorable*
amphitheatrical
amusement arcade
anabolic steroid
animal magnetism
animated cartoon
annihilationist
anomalistic year
anorexia nervosa
antepenultimate

antero-posterior
anthropocentric
anthropological
anthropomorphic
anthropophagous
anthroposophist
anti-clericalism
anti-evangelical
anti-monarchical
anti-sabbatarian
anti-trinitarian
any day of the week
any port in a storm
Apostolic Church
appropriateness
arboriculturist
archiepiscopacy
archiepiscopate
argumentatively
armed to the teeth
armillary sphere
as cold as charity
at close quarters
at cross purposes
Athanasian creed
atherosclerosis
at the drop of a hat
Attorney-General
aurora australis
authoritatively

## B

back to square one
Baltimore oriole

barbette-cruiser
be beside oneself
because it's there
bed and breakfast
behind the scenes
below one's breath
benefit of clergy
Bertillon system
bibliographical
binomial theorem
bite one's head off
bleaching-powder
blood and thunder
blood-guiltiness
blow one's trumpet
boat-billed heron
bolt from the blue
boots and saddles
brachycephalous
brake horsepower
branchiostegous
breach of promise
breathe one's last
breast screening
Brother Jonathan
brussels sprouts
bubble and squeak
building society
burn one's bridges
burn one's fingers
by hook or by crook

# C

cable television
calm as a millpond
campylospermous
cardinal numbers
cardinal virtues
cardiopulmonary
carnal knowledge

cash in one's chips
castles in the air
catch one's breath
catechistically
centre of gravity
ceremoniousness
Cesarian section
chamberlainship
chamber-practice
chapter and verse
chargé d'affaires
chemical warfare
chemico-electric
Chinese chequers
chloride of lime
Christadelphian
chronogrammatic
chronologically
circumforaneous
circumnavigable
circumnavigator
circumscribable
circumscription
circumscriptive
circumspectness
circumstantiate
circumvallation
Citizen's charter
clean as a whistle
close one's eyes to
cloud-cuckoo-land
coffee-table book
collision course
colour-blindness
combination lock
combustibleness
come into one's own
come to grips with
commonplace-book
communicability

communicatively
community centre
compassionately
complex fraction
complex sentence
comprehensively
compressibility
comptrollership
conceivableness
condescendingly
confessionalist
confidence trick
congratulations
conjunctionally
connoisseurship
conscience money
conscientiously
consentaneously
consequentially
considerateness
conspicuousness
consubstantiate
contemplatively
contemporaneity
contemporaneous
contemptibility
contentiousness
contraband of war
contractibility
contradictorily
controversially
convenience food
conventionalise
conventionalism
conventionalist
conventionality
conventionalize
conversableness
conversationist
convolvulaceous

cool as a cucumber
cordon sanitaire
Corinthian order
corporate raider
correlativeness
correspondently
correspondingly
corrugated paper
corruptibleness
cosmetic surgery
cosmopolitanism
costing the earth
cottage industry
counterapproach
counterevidence
counterirritant
countermovement
counterpressure
cover one's tracks
crook-shouldered
cross swords with
cross the Rubicon
crossword puzzle
cryptographical
crystalline lens
crystallisation
crystallization
crystallography
curriculum vitae
curry favour with

**D**

daylight robbery
decalcification
decarburisation
decarburization
decimal currency
decimal fraction
decommunisation
decommunization

defencelessness
delightsomeness
delirium tremens
deliver the goods
demagnetisation
demagnetization
demonstrability
demonstratively
dental hygienist
departmentalise
departmentalism
departmentalize
dephlogisticate
descriptiveness
desertification
destructibility
destructiveness
determinability
determinateness
devitrification
diacritical mark
diaheliotropism
dialogistically
diaphoretically
diaphragmatitis
differentiation
digital computer
dig one's own grave
diplomatic corps
direction finder
disadvantageous
discontinuation
discountenancer
discretionarily
disentanglement
disgracefulness
disinterestedly
disinthrallment
disorganisation
disorganization

dispassionately
displaced person
disproportional
disrespectfully
dissatisfaction
dissatisfactory
distastefulness
distinguishable
distinguishably
distrustfulness
diversification
do a roaring trade
dolichocephalic
domestic science
domestic servant
do one's dirty work
do one's heart good
do one's level best
double-barrelled
draughtsmanship
draw in one's horns
dredging-machine
drop into one's lap
dual carriageway
Dutch elm disease

## E

eat one's heart out
ecclesiasticism
echinodermatous
éclaircissement
efficaciousness
electrification
electrodynamics
electrokinetics
electromagnetic
electronegative
electropositive
eleutheromaniac
emancipationist

encomiastically
enfranchisement
Entente Cordiale
entomologically
environmentally
epidemiological
episcopalianism
eternal triangle
etherealisation
etherealization
evening primrose
exchangeability
excommunication
excrementitious
exemplification
experientialism
experimentalise
experimentalist
experimentalize
experimentation
externalisation
externalization
extra-curricular
extrajudicially
extraordinarily

**F**

falling-sickness
fantasticalness
feather one's nest
feel in one's bones
ferrocyanic acid
fine-toothed comb
finishing school
first-degree burn
fit of the sullens
flibbertigibbet
fluorescent lamp
fly off the handle
formularisation

formularization
foundation stone
fourth dimension
fragmentariness
funeral director

**G**

gastroenteritis
gate-legged table
general delivery
general election
gentleman-at-arms
gentleman farmer
gentlemanliness
get into the swing
get into the way of
get off one's chest
get off the ground
get on an even keel
get one's dander up
get one's head down
get one's skates on
get on one's nerves
gird up one's loins
give one a bad name
give one's back eye
give the game away
give the once-over
gold-beater's skin
golden handcuffs
golden handshake
go like clockwork
go off at a tangent
go off at half-cock
go one better than
go to rack and ruin
governor-general

**H**

hang on one's words

hang up one's boots
Hanseatic League
Harvest Festival
have a thing about
have designs upon
have made one's bed
have no truck with
have one's knife in
have one's measure
have one's moments
have over a barrel
have the last word
have two left feet
health insurance
heart specialist
hendecasyllable
hermaphroditism
hermeneutically
heterochromatic
heterodactylous
higher education
Hippocratic oath
historiographer
historiographic
hit the headlines
home electronics
homogeneousness
hope against hope
humanitarianism
humidifier fever
hydrostatically
hypercritically
hyperthyroidism
hypochondriacal

I

ideographically
impenetrability
imprescriptible
inaccessibility

inalienableness
in all conscience
in apple-pie order
inapplicability
inappropriately
inattentiveness
inauthoritative
in black and white
in broad daylight
incidental music
incommensurable
incommunicative
incompatibility
incomprehension
incomprehensive
inconsequential
inconsiderately
inconspicuously
incorrigibility
indecent assault
indemnification
Independence Day
indeterminately
indetermination
indisciplinable
individualistic
indomitableness
inefficaciously
inexcusableness
inexplicability
infantilisation
infantilization
infant mortality
inflammableness
infundibuliform
infusorial earth
injudiciousness
in mint condition
inoffensiveness
in one's right mind

inquisitiveness
inquisitorially
inscrutableness
inseparableness
in seventh heaven
insignificantly
instrumentalist
instrumentality
instrumentation
instrument panel
insubordination
insurrectionary
insurrectionist
intellectualise
intellectualism
intellectualist
intellectuality
intellectualize
intelligibility
intemperateness
interchangeable
interchangeably
intercollegiate
intercolonially
intercomparison
interconnection
interdependence
interdependency
interdigitation
interfoliaceous
interjectionary
internationally
interrogatively
interventionism
interventionist
in the altogether
in the first place
in the last resort
in the melting pot
in the nick of time

intolerableness
intractableness
intransmissible
introsusception
intussusception
invulnerability
irreligiousness
irreprehensible
irresistibility
it takes all sorts

## J
jack of all trades
jewel in the crown
jumping-off point

## K
kaleidoscopical
keep a low profile
keep one's counsel
keep one's shirt on
know a thing or two
know one's own mind
knuckle sandwich

## L
ladder-back chair
lares and penates
lateral thinking
laugh like a drain
laugh out of court
lay down one's arms
lead a double life
lead a merry dance
leading question
learn the hard way
leave high and dry
leave in the lurch
leg before wicket
let it all hang out

let one's hair down
lexicographical
lick and a promise
light of one's life
like a drowned rat
like the clappers
lily of the valley
little Englander
long arm of the law
look the other way
lophobranchiate
lose one's marbles
luncheon voucher

## M
machine language
machine-readable
mad as a March hare
magnetic equator
make a beeline for
make a break for it
make a clean sweep
make mincemeat of
make short work of
manic-depressive
manna from heaven
marginalisation
marginalization
Mephistophelean
Mephistophelian
merchant service
metropolitanate
microphotograph
microscopically
middle-of-the-road
mind one's ps and qs
mischievousness
misconstruction
molecular weight
money is no object

monochlamydeous
moral philosophy
Moral Rearmament
morning sickness
morphologically
mousseline sauce
much of a muchness
mutatis mutandis

## N
nationalisation
nationalization
national service
natural resource
New Scotland Yard
night on the tiles
non compos mentis
nonintervention
non-profit-making
not by a long chalk
not the done thing
not to get a look in
notwithstanding
nouvelle cuisine

## O
odour of sanctity
of one's own accord
Old Contemptible
once in a blue moon
on one's high horse
on one's own ground
on speaking terms
on the never-never
on the right track
on the strength of
on the wrong track
on top of the world
on with the motley
open and shut case

operating system
ophthalmoplegia
ornithorhynchus
over and done with

# P

paint the town red
palaeographical
palaeontologist
palaeophytology
par for the course
parliamentarian
parthenogenesis
parthenogenetic
pass the hat round
pathetic fallacy
pay lip service to
pergamentaceous
perpendicularly
personal trainer
*persona non grata*
personification
perspicaciously
perspicuousness
phenakistoscope
phosphorescence
photojournalism
photolithograph
photomechanical
photomicrograph
photosynthesise
photosynthesize
phototelegraphy
phrenologically
physical therapy
physiographical
physiologically
picturesqueness
pin back one's ears
pipped at the post

plenipotentiary
pleuropneumonia
poison-pen letter
polar coordinate
polyunsaturated
portmanteau word
positive vetting
poverty-stricken
practicableness
prepositionally
preservationist
press conference
prestidigitator
pretentiousness
prick up one's ears
Privy Councillor
procrastination
professionalism
prognostication
promiscuousness
proportionately
protemporaneous
psychopathology
public relations
pull one's punches
pulmobranchiate
punctuation mark
put back the clock
put in the picture
put one's back into
put the mockers on

# Q

quarter-sessions
quater-centenary
quick off the mark
quinquagenarian

# R

radiotelegraphy

rain cats and dogs
rattle one's sabre
rear its ugly head
refresher course
regius professor
relative pronoun
reproachfulness
retrogressively
return to the fold
ribonucleic acid
right-mindedness
rise with the lark
risk life and limb
rooted to the spot
round-shouldered
round-trip ticket
rub one's nose in it
Russian roulette

S
Sabbath-breaking
safety in numbers
schistosomiasis
sclerodermatous
Scottish terrier
scrape the barrel
scratch one's head
Sealyham terrier
sebaceous glands
secondary colour
secondary school
second childhood
Security Council
see eye to eye with
select committee
self-approbation
self-examination
self-explanatory
self-opinionated
self-pollination

self-rising flour
self-realisation
self-realization
self-reproachful
sententiousness
set great store by
set one's sights on
settle old scores
shift one's ground
shooting-gallery
shorthand typist
shoulder to cry on
show to advantage
shrinking violet
silence is golden
since the year dot
singing telegram
situation comedy
sleeping partner
slip of the tongue
snake in the grass
sodium hydroxide
soft-furnishings
sow one's wild oats
Spanish-American
Spanish omelette
sparring-partner
speak of the devil
special pleading
specific gravity
spermatogenesis
spitting image of
split infinitive
stage-door Johnny
stand on ceremony
stand one's ground
Stars and Stripes
State Department
stereochemistry
stew in one's juice

sticking-plaster
stick to one's guns
stick to one's last
storage capacity
straightforward
straight talking
strait-waistcoat
strategetically
stratigraphical
stretch one's legs
stubborn as a mule
studio apartment
sunrise industry
superexcellence
superficialness
supernaturalism
supernaturalist
supernumeraries
surf the Internet
surrogate mother
sweat of one's brow
swimming costume
swim with the tide
sword of Damocles
sympathetically
symptomatically
systems analysis

# T
take advantage of
take exception to
take it on the chin
take one's chances
take one's cue from
take to one's heels
talk one's head off
telephotography
tensile strength
tetrasyllabical
Thanksgiving Day

the bird has flown
the cat's whiskers
the coast is clear
the plot thickens
the sky's the limit
think the world of
thin on the ground
third-degree burn
throw in one's hand
throw in the towel
throw off balance
throw to the lions
thumb one's nose at
tighten one's belt
tightrope walker
till kingdom come
tilt at windmills
time is getting on
time on one's hands
tip of the iceberg
titanium dioxide
Tom, Dick and Harry
topographically
to the manner born
tower of strength
tracking station
transfiguration
transfigurative
transliteration
transliterative
transmutability
transparentness
transplantation
transpositional
treacherousness
tread on one's toes
treasonableness
trigeminal nerve
trigonometrical
trinitrotoluene

troublesomeness
trustworthiness
turn a blind eye to
turn one's stomach

## U

ultramicroscope
unceremoniously
uncommunicative
unconditionally
unconsciousness
unconstrainedly
undemonstrative
under lock and key
under one's breath
underprivileged
under the aegis of
under the counter
under the weather
unexceptionable
unexceptionably
ungentlemanlike
ungrammatically
unknown quantity
unparliamentary
unphilosophical
unprepossessing
unpronounceable
unrighteousness
unsophisticated

## V

valency electron
vasoconstrictor
venereal disease
vicissitudinary
vicissitudinous

vital statistics

## W

walrus moustache
wash one's hands of
waste one's breath
weak interaction
wear the trousers
weather the storm
well-intentioned
well-woman clinic
wet the baby's head
wheel-animalcule
whited sepulchre
windscreen wiper
wishful thinking
with a heavy heart
with bated breath
wither on the vine
without so much as
Women's Institute
woody nightshade
work like a beaver
writing chambers

## Y

yellow-blossomed
you never can tell
youth hostelling
yellow underwing
yellow archangel

## Z

zenith telescope
Ziegler catalyst
zoogeographical
zygophyllaceous